D0919338

Global Warming Gridlock

Global warming is one of today's greatest challenges. The science and economics of climate change leave few doubts that policies to cut emissions are overdue. Yet, after twenty years of international talks and treaties, the world is now in gridlock about how best to do this.

David Victor argues that such gridlock has arisen because international talks have drifted away from the reality of what countries are willing and able to implement at home. Most of the lessons that policy makers have drawn from the history of other international environmental problems to guide climate talks won't work on the problem of global warming. He argues that a radical rethinking is needed. This book provides a roadmap to a lower carbon future based on encouraging bottom-up initiatives at national, regional, and global levels, leveraging national self-interest rather than wishful thinking.

DAVID G. VICTOR is a professor at the School of International Relations and Pacific Studies at the University of California, San Diego, where he also leads the Laboratory on International Law and Regulation. His research has covered a wide array of topics related to international environmental regulation, energy markets, and international law. He is author or editor of eight books, including *Natural Gas and Geopolitics* (Cambridge University Press, 2006), *The Collapse of the Kyoto Protocol and the Struggle to Slow Global Warming* (second edition, 2004) and *Technological Innovation and Economic Performance* (2002).

Global Warming Gridlock

Creating More Effective Strategies for Protecting the Planet

DAVID G. VICTOR

CAMBRIDGE
UNIVERSITY PRESS

CAMBRIDGE UNIVERSITY PRESS
Cambridge, New York, Melbourne, Madrid, Cape Town,
Singapore, São Paulo, Delhi, Tokyo, Mexico City

Cambridge University Press
The Edinburgh Building, Cambridge CB2 8RU, UK

Published in the United States of America by Cambridge University Press, New York

www.cambridge.org
Information on this title: www.cambridge.org/9780521865012

© David G. Victor 2011

This publication is in copyright. Subject to statutory exception
and to the provisions of relevant collective licensing agreements,
no reproduction of any part may take place without the written
permission of Cambridge University Press.

First published 2011

Printed in the United Kingdom at the University Press, Cambridge

A catalogue record for this publication is available from the British Library

Library of Congress Cataloguing in Publication data
Victor, David G., 1965–
    Global Warming Gridlock : Creating More Effective Strategies for Protecting
    the Planet / David G. Victor.
        p.   cm
    Includes bibliographical references and index.
    ISBN 978-0-521-86501-2
    1. Greenhouse gas mitigation.   2. Global warming–Prevention.
    3. Environmental policy.   I. Title.
    TD885.5.G73V53 2011
    363.738′74–dc22
    2010045748

ISBN 978-0-521-86501-2 Hardback

Cambridge University Press has no responsibility for the persistence or
accuracy of URLs for external or third-party Internet websites referred to in
this publication, and does not guarantee that any content on such websites is,
or will remain, accurate or appropriate.

Contents

Figures

Tables

Preface and acknowledgements: a journey studying international environmental regulation

Most of my professional life has focused, in one way or another, on the ways that humans affect the global environment. Greenhouse warming is the most complex and sprawling of those global problems; politically it is the toughest to solve. It has taken a career to understand the problem, and along the way I have accumulated many intellectual debts.

Before enrolling in graduate school at MIT in the late 1980s I worked with a research group at Harvard that studied atmospheric chemistry and physics. That group, led by Mike McElroy and Steve Wofsy, taught me more about basic science of the atmosphere and oceans than I ever learned as a student. At the time, the ozone layer was the big planetary worry, and through their eyes I learned how to read and interpret the cutting-edge science. I soon shifted my academic discipline to political science, but most of my career has been an attempt at serious interdisciplinary research on atmospheric and oceanic issues. That style of research only works when the scholar can read and interpret the frontier of research across often disparate disciplines. I trace my enthusiasm for interdisciplinary research to the orbit of interesting things I learned from Mike and Steve and the many other people in Cambridge, Massachusetts working on similar atmospheric problems. They included Jim Anderson's research group (which flew a converted spy plane into the ozone hole in the late 1980s and found the smoking gun showing that humans were to blame), Dick Holland, Ron Prinn, and Mario Molina. Today I spend very little time in that community, but read their journals and do my best to stay abreast. I worry that the community of political and legal experts – especially those who study environmental issues where the technical details matter – don't spend enough time immersed in the natural science. As will be evident in this book, most of the attributes of the global warming problem that make it politically such a hard problem to solve trace back to the physical and biological characteristics of the chief pollutants.

When I arrived on campus to start my PhD, MIT assigned Professor Eugene Skolnikoff to be my advisor and fortuitously he had a similar interdisciplinary bent. I was part of the last cohort of MIT political science graduate students who studied science, technology, and international affairs. All of us were named David and we all had Gene as an adviser. As a graduate student I was an embarrassment to my department because I spent most of my time not with other political scientists but with chemists, physicists, oceanographers and especially engineers. Gene let me do that – he even encouraged such deviant behavior – and I am forever grateful. Jack Ruina, George Rathjens, and Carl Kaysen all encouraged such deviance. By luck, the few years centered on 1990 was the right time to be in Cambridge, Massachusetts. A dozen or so graduate students from all manner of disciplines – drawn mainly from MIT, Harvard, and Tufts – had a similar set of environmental interests. We set up a reading group, engaged faculty members, and did things. That orbit of folks included Thomas Bernauer, Beth DeSombre, David Festa, Tad Homer-Dixon, Tammi Gutner, David Keith, Marc Levy, Vicki Norberg-Bohm, Nancy Dickson, Ted Parson, Michael Molitor, and Peter Poole. We worked with faculty members such as Mike and Gene as well as Abram Chayes, Joe Nye, Bob Keohane, Bill Clark, Richard Cooper, Bob Frosch, Jay Fay, Lew Branscomb, Harvey Brooks, and Tom Schelling. When a field of research is taking shape geography really matters because most thinking and debating is done in person, and the early 1990s Cambridge was prime intellectual real estate.

I was unaware, at the time, just how much we all learned about politics from Bob Keohane. Bob, Peter Haas, and Marc Levy organized a series of studies on the "effectiveness" of environmental regimes. That is, do international regulatory systems, such as treaties, actually work? Their efforts shaped that field of study, and I soon found that most of my time as a political scientist focused on the question of effectiveness. That effort roped in Oran Young, then a professor at Dartmouth (now at Santa Barbara); Oran and Bob have blessed the study of environmental regimes with their insights. One of the things I have learned from them – perhaps to their horror – is that environmental research suffers because scholars care too much about their subject. An appreciation for the hard-nosed power politics needed, for example, to protect the ozone layer or slow global warming is often lost in the evangelism around the need to halt planetary destruction. A high ratio of green evangelism to hard-nosed politics was on full display in 1992 during the Rio Earth Summit, an event that was pivotal for me because it helped me see the value in skepticism about international institutions. The world is full of promises that are not kept, and the study of international institutions is about understanding when those promises are credible and have an impact on behavior and when they are smoke. As we shall see in this book, many of the promises around global warming are still smoke twenty years later.

Other than meeting Gene and another very helpful MIT adviser, Ken Oye, I can't say I learned very much from graduate school that was useful. Geography was the chief asset. By luck, MIT was gearing up what, today, is the premier university research program on global climate change. Jake Jacoby, Ron Prinn, and Richard Eckaus led the effort, and I arrived on their radar screen by complaining that the Intergovernmental Panel on Climate Change (IPCC) scheme for converting greenhouse gases into common units was all wrong and should be scrapped. (Young students often supply indignancy in large quantities.) It turns out that was also one of the first problems that Jake and his colleagues studied, and we worked together. They have built an extraordinary research team – the Joint Program on Global Change Science and Policy – that stands as an example of what can be done with interdisciplinary research if you invest a decade or more in the effort. It is also a reminder that truly interdisciplinary research needs a common task – in their case, building and running an integrated model – so that people from different disciplines can all lend their skills in a focused way. Interdisciplinary research requires disciplinary gains lest scholars not find much reward for their academic careers. One of the reasons political science has had a hard time with interdisciplinary research is that our research does not easily lend itself to integrated tasks such as model-building and integrated models produce few disciplinary benefits for political scientists.

Three things happened in graduate school that changed my life. First, Gene and Abe Chayes created a research project on international diplomacy on global warming. We got funding from someone (in Cambridge, Massachusetts money is always pouring in for something) and had no idea what we were doing. But we knew it was important. So I started attending the climate talks, which had just gotten under way, with the aim of keeping our endeavor informed of the latest events. (Young students usually have lots of time to do things that seem worthless but occasionally prove to be gold mines.) At the time – the very earliest days of what became the UN Framework Convention on Climate Change – climate diplomacy was such a backwater that NGOs were small in number and all of us were free to roam the negotiations. (That rule was quickly changed when one NGO – led by an American lawyer hired by OPEC – used free access to help block negotiations and became the de facto voice of the Kuwaiti government.) Milling around and watching the painstaking process in six languages taught me a lot about diplomacy and made me very skeptical that big UN talks would ever make much headway. John Maddox, editor of *Nature*, gave me six pages (a huge space, something I did not appreciate at the time) to explain my skepticism. I suggested that instead of big formal talks something different – smaller, more like the early years of the GATT, and focused on building complex package deals – should be tried. I still think that is right, and over the years I have learned a lot about why that approach to institutional design is better than many others. At the time, however, a dissenting view from a graduate student didn't have much impact. (Today that view still may have no impact.) The mania around global, legally binding global warming treaties was in full swing and hard to sway. Around the same time Gene wrote a piece in *Foreign Policy* explaining why the US policy process was prone to gridlock on global warming; that piece reads well still today, and hopefully he will see this book as a useful complement of insights on international gridlocks. I met a lot of people who were also present at the creation of the climate law, such as James Cameron and Philippe Sands (who had organized a coalition of low-lying island states and helped them become a truly effective voice), Dan Bodansky (who wrote an extraordinary diplomatic history of the talks), and Tony Brenton (who held the chair for the British government and came to Cambridge in 1992 for a sabbatical year, writing a wonderful book about environmental diplomacy called *The Greening of Machiavelli*). Richard Benedick, who had been the chief US negotiator on the ozone accords, helped all of us think about the right lessons from the history of environmental diplomacy. Jean Ripert was the senior French diplomat who led the climate talks and was always helpful; Michael Zammit Cutajar soon led the climate secretariat and was a fountain of insight and discretion.

Abe, Gene, and I hosted meetings with the diplomats – culminating in sessions in Bermuda and Bellagio – that led to the idea of "prompt start." Once the talks leading to a climate treaty in 1992 were done, technically nothing more could happen on the diplomatic front until the treaty entered into force. "Prompt start" offered a way to keep the momentum so that useful efforts, such as building the procedures for reporting data, could get under way immediately. Abe, Gene, and I developed the idea; Ken Prewitt, head of the Rockefeller Foundation, helped us strip away the ideas that were distractions and focus on prompt start in particular; and the climate diplomats who participated in our meetings helped make it practically relevant. That idea turned out to be quite influential, and from the effort I learned a lot about how to organize meetings and get things done diplomatically. Lesson 1 was that offering locales like Bermuda and Bellagio would help. Lesson 2 was to keep it small. Lesson 3 was to treat the participants well. Academics forget that much of life is about getting the right people in the room and treating them with grace and respect; I was honored to learn that lesson at an early age from masters at the art.

Second, with help from Gene and Bill Clark, I spent my first summer of graduate school in Austria at the International Institute for Applied Systems Analysis (IIASA). Originally I was assigned the task of working with a group that studied acid rain to find ways to use computer models to make the negotiations on acid rain in Europe more effective. That was a good idea, but there wasn't much a graduate student could do on that front because the key questions hinged on politics rather than geeks doing research. So I wandered to a different part of IIASA's castle and met Nebojša Nakićenović and Arnulf Grübler. By the end of my first day I moved my office and started working with them on the question of why and how technology diffuses. They had put me on the task of modeling the diffusion of liquid hydrogen-powered aircraft and natural gas vehicles – two darling technologies of the day that might, one day, take a large share of the market. (Today, hydrogen aircraft are dead but natural gas vehicles have once again become the darlings of technologists who want to solve problems like dependence on oil and high emissions of warming gases.) The question was how large a share? And if those technologies diffused, what would be the impact on things that people care about, such as emissions of warming gases or consumption of oil? I built some models that could answer those questions, wrote some scientific papers on the questions, and started a career with a foot firmly in the study of technological change. It is hard to over-estimate the importance of what I have learned working with Naki and Arnulf and the people in their orbit – among them, Hans Holger Rogner, Robert Pry, and the dean of their world view, Cesare Marchetti. Through that community I met Jesse Ausubel and worked with him for a summer as part of the Carnegie Commission on Science, Technology and Government. From Jesse I learned how to write, and since writing is about thinking and logic in reality I learned a whole way of thinking from him. For most students, graduate school is a time to get narrow and to lose useful communication skills. With Jesse's helping hand my experience was pretty much the opposite, and for that I am eternally grateful. Jesse also sent me to the National Center for Atmospheric Research (NCAR) for a summer to work on my thesis; there I met Mickey Glantz, Will Kellogg, and Steve Schneider. NCAR's Mesa lab is a great place to visit since it is the epicenter of so much research on climate change and it is physically stunning. I spent the summer reading about verification of international agreements; Jesse and I wrote a big review essay on the topic and that area has since become a large part of my research. Over the years he has included me on interesting projects – among them a meeting at the Scripps Institute of Oceanography at UC San Diego where I met Roger Revelle, Bill Nierenberg, Wally Broecker, Gordon MacDonald, Ram Ramanathan, and Dave Keeling for one of the early discussions of geoengineering and whatever else Roger and Bill had on their minds. The importance of that meeting didn't fully settle into my brain until I moved back to UCSD as a faculty member almost two decades later. I think it was through that meeting that I met Bill Nordhaus who is the dean of climate change economics; much of what the world thinks about climate economics goes back to his pioneering efforts and I have learned a lot from him over the years. Notably, from Bill and Dick Cooper I have more fully appreciated the use of emission taxes as a way to address global warming; they are among the few who have kept a focus on that instrument when the rest of the world became obsessed with emission trading. I am a huge fan of market-based policies, but I don't think the enthusiasts for emission trading appreciated how hard it is to make a system of property rights work at the international level when the institutions for assigning and enforcing rights are so weak. I ended up spending a lot of time on that problem because it helps explain why emission trading systems in the real world function so differently from the ideal theory – a topic I will take up in this book.

Third, early in 1993 IIASA held a contest for research groups to bid for three years of funding to study international environmental cooperation. I put together a team with many of the academics who were in Cambridge studying environmental issues at the time. We sent off our application and promptly forgot about it. To my shock, we won, and that meant moving to Austria to run the enterprise. I withdrew from graduate school (returning later in the decade for a few months to file my thesis), hired Gene as a co-director, and we set out to study why some international environmental agreements are effective and others not. From the effort I learned a lot about the scholarship and even more about management. I'm proud that our effort funded the international regimes database – led by Oran Young, Marc Levy, Michael Zürn (who had been in Cambridge for a sabbatical and now leads the Hertie School in Berlin), and a young political scientist, Helmut Breitmeier, who carried the regimes database to fruition. We sponsored some of Ted Parson's research on negotiation games and also wrote a big book on the effectiveness of international environmental commitments (Victor, Raustiala, and Skolnikoff 1998). Among the many people involved in the effort were Owen Greene, Chris Stone, Julian Salt, Steiner Andresen, Olav Schram Stokke, Jon Birger Skjaerseth, Jørgen Wettestad, Juan Carlos di Primio, Alexei Roginko, and Elena Nikitina. In addition, Peter Sand, Arild Underdal, Abe Chayes, Georgi Golitsyn, Alexander Kiss, Peter Sand, Tom Schelling, and Oran Young all played helpful roles on our advisory board. Winfried Lang, the senior Austrian diplomat who worked on the ozone layer, came to know of our work and helped us immensely as we tried to apply our findings in practical ways. Inside the climate and ozone talks Jo Butler and Hugo Schally were instrumental, and I thank them. Among our many students, Kal Raustiala and Cesare Romano played especially central roles and it has been a pleasure to collaborate with them in the years since our time at IIASA. Much of what I know as a political scientist about the design and effectiveness of international environmental regimes comes from that time. Along the way, Gordon MacDonald became IIASA's director, and I much enjoyed working with him on some scientific issues. Gordon was a big figure in geophysics, and from him I learned still more skepticism about political institutions and also something about the value of time. Rather than spend two weeks at the Kyoto conference on global warming we stayed home in Austria and built a model that let us predict future emissions of some nasty greenhouse gases – sulfur hexafluoride (SF_6) and perfluorocarbons (PFCs). Building that model – for which Eddie Löser in IIASA's library was invaluable, as on so many issues – was much more fruitful than watching diplomacy grind along in Kyoto. It also convinced me that the approach in vogue – then and now – to treat all warming gases together in a single basket was bad for the environment and also bad politics. SF_6 and PFCs were so nasty and yet so easy to regulate that a much smarter strategy would have seen the world focus on them separately. But the diplomats weren't much interested in such advice since including all the gases in a single basket gave them the illusion that they were creating more flexibility in the climate treaty. Flexibility is often helpful, but for most of the history of climate talks it has been a ruse to avoid facing hard truths, and by lumping all the gases into a single basket the diplomats missed a big opportunity to tailor regulations around the distinct interest groups that would shape any serious program to regulate each gas. While at IIASA I found some time to build a model of the world transportation system with a young German PhD student, Andreas Schafer, and focused on the practical challenge of introducing new technologies into transportation. Andreas later went to MIT and helped Jake and Ron's team add those kinds of important details to the models that the Joint Program was building. While I am a political scientist, perhaps my sobriety about how quickly the global warming problem can be solved comes from having studied technology so closely with so many wise collaborators.

When I left IIASA I moved (with Gene's help) to the Council on Foreign Relations (CFR). The Council's President, Les Gelb, wanted to create a larger think tank because he rightly believed that applied foreign policy was becoming an orphan in universities. My recollection is that there were three of us young scholars on the payroll at the time – Gideon Rose (now editor of *Foreign Affairs*), Liz Economy (one of the nation's leading scholars on China's environmental policies), and myself. That contingent grew quickly, and I very much enjoyed my time at CFR. My bosses – Gary Hufbauer at first and then Larry

Korb and Jim Lindsay – were tremendously supportive. CFR is a place of constant turnover, and I had a serial army of young research assistants coming and going and always keen to lend a hand. Among them were Lesley Coben (who came with me when I left CFR for Stanford University), Valerie Karplus, and Rebecca Weiner. While at CFR Jesse Ausubel and Brian Lessenberry, Derek Loyd I played squash regularly and starting talking about the plight of the world's forests. With help from the Lounsbery foundation we enlisted some of the world's experts to help us look at the real threats to forests (they are mainly agriculture and ranching, but timbering plays a role) and laid out a detailed vision for how quickly the world's forests could be protected and expanded. That effort taught me a lot about how to tame deforestation as a source of CO_2 (deforestation accounts for perhaps one-seventh the world's emissions of this warming gas, maybe more) and also a lot about how technologies can protect the environment. Our view was that higher yielding agriculture and timber plantations would allow more food and fiber to be supplied from much smaller footprints of land, leaving the rest for nature. Doing more with fewer natural inputs is the essence of sustainable development, and the vision for protecting forests (which Jesse and I published in *Foreign Affairs*) applies to a lot more than just trees. (Jesse has worked extensively with Paul Waggoner to outline such visions in other areas, such as agriculture and industrial ecology.) As in most environmental problems, policies that prescribe hardships – eating less or using fewer wood products – were unlikely to work. Technology, not castor oil, is how most environmental problems get solved. If technological change allows people to lighten their footprint at a cost – in money and effort to change behavior – that they don't much notice then the political prospects for environmental are brighter.

While at CFR I also had the pleasure to work on a few other large projects that came from fruitful collaborations – one on technological innovation and economic growth (with Benn Steil, Richard Nelson, and Dick Foster) and one on genetically engineered foods (with C. Ford Runge). Richard Garwin and I ran a little group at CFR that studied areas where technology had a big impact on foreign policy. Most foreign policy was organized by topic (e.g., arms control) or area (e.g., China); we were geeks who worked on technology and pretty much ran the gamut. He worked mainly on weapons and I on the environment. Both of us were inspired by the view that technological change drives many political outcomes. Rod Nichols, who at the time was head of the New York Academy of Sciences, chaired a study group that I ran on how technology might influence the problem of global warming. Rod has been a big supporter over the years; from him I learned a lot about technology policy and also how to chair a meeting. (He is a master chairman, and the data flow in meetings with him at the helm is so much higher that everyone has a much better time and learns a lot more from the event. Chairmanship is an under-appreciated skill.) That study group convinced me that one of the many things wrong with international diplomacy on global warming, such as the Kyoto Protocol, was its nearly complete failure to focus on encouraging policies that would accelerate the innovation and diffusion of new technologies. That was not a popular message those days – Kyoto was a darling of most people who called them-selves environmentalists – and I touched off a debate that started on the op-ed page of the *Washington Post* with the US government offi-cials who were Kyoto's biggest supporters. Op-eds are short, but my beef with Kyoto was a lot more detailed. Soon I was circulating a full length defense of my position and discovered that I had written a book, *The Collapse of the Kyoto Protocol and the Struggle to Slow Global Warming*. I published that book in 2001 a few weeks before the Bush administration withdrew from Kyoto. The timing was good for sales but it made me uneasy since my vision was an alternative, more effective regime. The Bush administration proved better at bashing the existing regime than building a new one, and when the terror attacks on September 11th 2001 arrived they could ignore this problem (and many others) for a long time. In many ways, the present book picks up where *Collapse* left off.

I left CFR for Stanford University in the fall of 2001 but stayed on as an adjunct fellow. CFR's new president, Richard Haass, gave me a warm welcome and for a few years I worked on foreign policy issues from afar. I had a special pleasure writing, for CFR, a series of presidential speeches that offered three radically different ways of thinking about the climate problem. Margaret Winterkorn provided invaluable research assistance on that effort, which reads well even today. I also ran, with John Deutch and Jim Schlesinger, a task force on energy security – my first experience crafting consensus language with a group of two dozen well-informed and highly opinionated experts on energy from across the US political spectrum. That and related research benefitted from Divya Reddy, Arathi Rao, Lindsay Workman, Mark Bucknam (who was on leave at CFR from the Air Force for a year), and Sarah Eskreis-Winkler. Lee Feinstein guided the effort admirably, and it was a pleasure to work with him. Later, I chipped in as George Pataki, Tom Vilsack, and Mark Warner, aided by Michael Levi, ran a task force on climate change policy. My academic colleagues are horrified that I spend time on such activities that generate no academic output and occasionally become black holes that inhale time and energy. But they offer some insight into how real-world policy must be crafted and offer some tactile insights into the areas where political disagreements run deep as well as the speed with which political problems can be managed. In later years I have spent similarly huge amounts of time on productive task forces of various types for the World Economic Forum – notably with Armen Sarkissian, Pawel Konzal and Linda Yueh.

Stanford hired me to create and run a new research group – what became the Program on Energy and Sustainable Development (PESD). We were funded by the Electric Power Research Institute (EPRI) and BP, plc. For me, the shift west was an opportunity to make two big changes in my intellectual orientation. One was to focus on Asia, and I spent a huge amount of time on the road in China and India especially, getting a feel for how those economies were evolving. The other was to focus on energy markets more centrally. One of the reasons that climate change is a hard problem to tackle is that analysts think about it as an environmental problem. In reality, its root causes and solutions lie in the functioning of energy markets and in the incentives for technological change within those markets. I needed to know a lot more about those markets. And that's what I did at Stanford, with major studies on the globalizing markets for gas and coal, the experience with power sector reform around the world, and an in depth look at some of the most vexing energy problems such as electrifying poor, rural populations. I believe in fieldwork because what is really happening at the level of plant managers and field operations is often quite different from what's reported in textbooks and academic articles, and thus I dragged my students around the world visiting oil and gas fields, refineries, power plants (lots of power plants), coal mines and such. I regularly crossed swords with bureaucratic administrators over the expense and logistical nightmares surrounding all that, and that was an unpleasant shadow that loomed over much of my time at

Stanford. Administrators play essential roles in every organization, but remote and at times dangerous field research is alien to people who spend their days among palm trees and in air conditioned offices. In a decade I bet our students will look at those experiences as among their most formative. I certainly did.

I had many colleagues at Stanford from whom I learned a lot – among them, Tom Heller, Steve Schneider (who had moved to Stanford from NCAR years earlier), Scott Sagan, Nick Hope, Ken Arrow, Larry Goulder, Mike May, Burt Richter, Lynn Orr, Sally Benson, Mark Thurber, Frank Wolak, Jim Sweeney, Mike Wara, John Weyant, and Hill Huntington. Much of what Stanford did on energy policy revolved around Alan Manne and his network of students and ideas who carried the mantle after Alan passed away. PESD was particularly well run because of the efforts of Kathy Lung, Tonya McPherrin, Michelle Klippel, Bob Sherman, Cassaundra Edwards and many others. During the period I started working on this book Aranzazu Lascurian got me started with very helpful research assistance. I have had the great pleasure to work closely with an array of students and post-doctoral students through PESD. Chi Zhang was there at the beginning and from him I started to learn about China. Mark Hayes, Varun Rai, Jeremy Carl, Richard Morse, Mike Jackson, Sam Shrank, Megan Hansen, Ale Nunez, Sarah Joy, Joshua House, Lesley Coben, Becca Elias, Rose Kontak, Bob Sherman, Ngai-Chi Chung, Henry Tjiong, Ify Emelife, Paasha Mahdavi, Megan Hansen, David Hults, Erik Woodhouse, BinBin Jiang, Narasimha Rao, Gang He, Danny Cullenward, Ognen Stojanovski, Jeff Rector, Peter Lamb, Pei Yee Woo, Xander Slaski, Chris Warshaw, Kassia Yanosek, and Hisham Zerriffi all worked, many as my students, on things that have influenced my thinking in this book. PESD also built a network of overseas collaborators from whom I learned a lot about the real world – James Ball, Rob Shepherd, Barry Carin, Gordon Smith, Kirit and Jyoti Parikh, Adilson de Oliveira, Jose Goldemberg, Felipe Araujo, Gary Dirks, Rob James, Trevor Gaunt, Mark Howells, Alison Hughes, Gary Goldstein, Lindsey Jeftha, Tom Alfstad, Anton Eberhard, Katherine Gratwick, Victor Carreon, Armando Jiminez San Vicente, Juan Rosellón, Li Zheng, Lan Xue, Leming Zeng, Pan Jiahua, Yu Yufeng, Wenying Chen, Christian von Hirschausen, Franziska Holz, Christine Jojarth, Frank Jotzo, John Pezzey, Zheng Lemin, Huaichuan Rui, Peng Wuyuan, Rahul Tongia, Lars Schernikau, Mike Toman,

Bart Lucarelli, Francisco Monaldi, Debashis Biswas, Tirthankar Nag, Amee Yajnik, P. R. Shukla, and Subash Dhar. For a large study on the global gas market we built a constructive partnership with the Baker Institute at Rice University; Amy Jaffe and Jillene Connors helped put that together. PESD's research benefitted from a lot of helpful advice from Pete Nolan, Howard Harris, Chris Hobson, Katrina Landis, Chris Mottershead, Atul Arya, and Bryan Hannegan who sat on a PESD advisory board and often visited our team. Stanford's campus is so beautiful that it was not hard to apply the lessons that Abe Chayes and Gene Skolnikoff taught me long ago: invite thoughtful people, choose a good locale, and treat everyone well.

While at Stanford George Shultz involved me in the North American Forum – a three way venture with senior leaders from Canada, Mexico, and the United States. (It's a talk shop of the type that academics usually abhor but I loved because it gave access to people who did things in these countries – especially Mexico, which is in the midst of so many important political changes.) He and Jim Goodby also welcomed me at the Hoover Institution's task force on energy security. It has been a pleasure to work with them on the practical problems of today. Early in the process of scoping out this book Tom Heller and I had very helpful discussions with Nick Stern (who was in the early days of assembling the team that delivered what became known as the "Stern Report" on climate change, a particularly thoughtful and important assessment of climate economics). Nick asked us about the problem of engaging developing countries, which is one of the most difficult challenges in global warming and an area where existing policies (notably the Kyoto Protocol's "Clean Development Mechanism") were not working well. We suggested that a better approach would focus on big "deals" with large developing countries – that is, packages of policy reforms that those countries would undertake, some with external support that aligned with what those countries already saw as their interests. That discussion got me thinking about how to make those deals work – especially how to use competition to encourage countries to provide reliable information about possible deals and then to honor their commitments once the deal was crafted. Over a couple years working with several colleagues at Stanford we fleshed out what those deals might entail, their practical impact on emissions, and how they might be codified. There aren't many relevant experiences in environmental law, but I found that trade law has handled a similar problem with accession to the WTO. The idea of "climate accession deals," which plays a large role in this book, emerged from that line of thinking.

Hopefully built into the DNA of this book is a deep understanding of energy and technology markets and an appreciation for where policy can really make a difference. When society confronts really hard problems there are strong pressures on policy makers to avoid costly decisions. The result is symbolic policies – that is, policy ventures that look serious but have no real impact. Figuring out which policies matter and which are smoke and mirrors is crucial. On that front, I am especially grateful to our funders not just because they have supported my research but even more because they have given me windows into understanding when firms actually believe that policy will be relevant. At EPRI, Kurt Yeager and Steve Specker were unfailing in their support; also at EPRI I am thankful to Hank Courtright, Bryan Hannegan, Mike Howard, Revis James, Chris Larsen, Arshad Mansoor, Rosa Yang, Norma Formanek, Rich Richels, Tom Wilson, and Geoff Blanford. EPRI put me on their advisory committee – chaired by Granger Morgan and Ellen Lapson and orchestrated by Barbara Tyran – which was a special pleasure because one-third of the members are regulators. (Jeanne Fox, David Ziegler, David Garman, Ron Binz, Michael Dworkin, Bob Fri, and Ernie Moniz were among the many advisory board members from whom I learned so much.) Academics often forget that most of the energy industry is highly regulated and understanding how regulators think is invaluable. About the same time that I started working on this book EPRI also started its "prism" analysis that looks at the real potential for emission reductions from the power sector; I benefitted from sifting through the assumptions in that analysis in detail, for that is a helpful reminder of what people who are closest to the industry think is practical and how practical policies may affect the deployment of capital. They aren't always right (who is?) but it's a very good place to start. At BP, our relationship was created by Chris Mottershead who linked PESD's work to Peter Hughes (who later went to BG and helped us understand the global gas industry), Tony Meggs, and BP's CEO at the time, John Browne. Chris is a fount of knowledge; he and Atul Arya were immensely helpful in teaching me about the firm. Working with BP has been a reminder of the fickleness of public opinion on environmental matters, which is understandable yet disturbing. It probably makes it hard for our society to manage truly long-term problems. Those days BP was the environmental darling of the oil industry. (Shell had lost its green shine in the wake of a disastrous protest over its Brent Spar platform in the North Sea.) Today, at this time of writing, it is in the midst of an environmental catastrophe in the Gulf of Mexico that led politicians to paint the company as a villain in America. BP along with EPRI's members – who span nearly all of the largest electric utilities in the US and many overseas – are invaluable for scholars because they deploy massive amounts of capital. If you want to understand technological change at large scale in the energy industry the place to start is by studying the decisions around capital expenditure. Academic scribblers often have lots of ideas of cool technologies that might be deployed and overly clever policies that might be enacted into law, but there is no substitute for looking at deployment through the lens of companies that are on the hook for the billions of dollars if the deal goes sour. The hardest thing for policy makers to do is establish credibility; for investors who make massive fixed capital investments credibility is essential. I learned that lesson through hours of interviews with people responsible for strategy inside companies and plant managers responsible for keeping the lights on. In addition to the severely practical business people already mentioned, I am grateful to Manpreet Anand, Bruce Braine, Andrew Brandler, Roberta Bowman, John Bryson, Xavier chen, Ted Craver, Peter Davies, Gary Dirks, Brent Dorsey, David Eyton, Brian Flannery, Sylvia Garrigo, George Gilboy, Charles Goodman, Edgard Habib, Lew Hay, Dick Hayslip, Chris Hobson, Rick Karp, Gail Kendall, Steve Koonin, Steve Lennon, Wayne Leonard, Rogerió Manso, Drew Marsh, Tony Meggs, Ed Morse, Dave O'Reilly, Maria Pica, Bill Reilly, Cameron Rennie, Jim Rogers, Christof Rühl, Mark Savoff, Dale Simbeck, Greg Tosen, Jim Turner, Phil Verleger, Steve Westwell, Ellen Williams, Jeff Williams, Eileen Robinson, and Dan Yergin for many conversations over the last few years that have shaped how I think about the deployment of capital. Thanks also to Sheryl Carter, Ralph Cavanagh, Reid Detchon, David Hawkins, Fred Krupp, Jonathan Lash, Michael Oppenheimer, Jonathan Pershing, Annie Petsonk, Mark Tercek, and Tim Wirth among many others who spend much time in the environmental community for helpful discussions on the interaction between policy and environmental regulatory strategy. There is no way that all these people in different communities will agree with what I write here, but hopefully they will find my views well informed by the realities of the energy industry.

Having spent a long time building a research institute that works across disciplines I have come to appreciate others who have done that well. At the top of my list is the Engineering and Public Policy Program at Carnegie Mellon, and it has been a pleasure to work over the years with Granger Morgan, Jay Apt, David Keith, Alex Farrell, Lester Lave, Ed Rubin, Elizabeth Wilson, Hisham Zerriffi, Hadi Dowlatabadi, and others who are part of the CMU orbit. Granger, Jay and I – along with John Steinbruner and Kate Ricke – have spent some time over the last few years looking closely at the challenge of governing geoengineering, and their thoughts have helped inform Chapter 6 of this book. Geoengineering, which is the direct intervention in nature to offset (crudely) the effects of global warming, matters because it may be the best way to buy some time if climate change turns ugly. Dieter Helm and Cameron Hepburn invited me to develop these ideas in more detail in an essay they published in the *Oxford Review of Economic Policy*; along the way, Scott Barrett, David Keith, Ken Caldeira, Steve Rayner and especially Tom Schelling have also influenced my thinking about how to manage geoengineering.

While at Stanford I joined the faculty at Stanford Law School. Dean Larry Kramer was the key person behind that appointment, and I am forever grateful for his support. I had terrific colleagues, among them Josh Cohen, Deborah Hensler, Michael Wara, Buzz Thompson, Mitch Polinsky, Al Sykes, Richard Morningstar, Tino Cuellar, and Mark Kelman. Josh Cohen, who was also editor of *Boston Review* (a literary magazine), commissioned a huge essay on the global coal market for his magazine – a brave move in a publication more accustomed to fine literature than strip mining. It is one of the publications in the last decade of which I am most proud. No plan for slowing global warming can work without an answer for coal.

I left Stanford for the University of California San Diego in summer 2009 and here in San Diego I am making still another big shift. With my partner and colleague, Emilie Hafner-Burton, I am building a laboratory that studies the effectiveness of international law. Some of our thoughts are reflected throughout this book, which is really a full length examination of how to make international law more effective in the area of climate change. I am grateful to Peter Cowhey who worked with Miles Kahler, David Lake, Barb Walter, Paul Drake and others to bring us to UCSD. I am also delighted to work with them and other new colleagues – among them James Fowler, Peter Gourevitch, Josh Graff-Zivin, Steph Haggard, Tony Haymet, Charlie Kennell, Yon Lupu, Walter Munk, Ram Ramanathan, Fang Rong, Susan Shirk and Linda Wong. For help getting our lab up and running efficiently, many thanks also to Amanda Brainerd, Derek Brendel, Jill Coste, Teresa Olcomendy, Elizabeth Rich, Amy Robinson, and Brent Wakefield. The UCSD move has allowed me to spend more time closer to my professional roots, which are in political science. And a special thanks to EPRI and BP who, as earlier, have been unfailing supporters of my research.

This book is the third I have published with Cambridge University Press, and for that I thank the wonderful Chris Harrison, my editor, and Philip Good who assists him so ably. A special thanks to Chris and two anonymous reviewers who gave me a good steer on the penultimate draft of the manuscript – leading, I hope, to a more coherent and better written story. Hank Courtright, Frank Jotzo, Charlie Kennell, Bob Keohane and Steve Specker all read parts (or all of) that draft and for their detailed comments I am most grateful – notably to Bob who sifted through the full argument in detail. And thanks to Linda Wong at UCSD who signed on to help me with references and ended up doing much more, from editing and advising on writing strategy. At various stages in the preparation of this manuscript I gave talks at Stanford, Yale, UCSD, Northwestern, Entergy Duke (the university and the energy company), Columbia, the Salt River Project, EPRI, BP, Chevron, and Harvard; thanks to those seminar participants for feedback. Rob Stavins and Joe Aldy edited two books on global warming policy and invited me to publish a chapter in each – those chapters help develop some of the core ideas in this book. A special thanks to everyone who has disagreed with me over the years – a long list – for their objections have helped me sharpen my message.

In the midst of our move, Emilie and I had a wonderful son, Eero. Surely the vagaries of life will lead him to do things other than worry about global warming, but given the slow pace of serious efforts to tame this problem my guess is that his generation (and the next one too) will still be struggling with the issues I discuss in this book.

Hard truths about global warming: a roadmap to reading this book

After two grueling weeks of negotiations, late in 2009 the Copenhagen conference on global warming ended with a whimper. On nearly every major agenda item, including the need for a new treaty to replace the aging Kyoto Protocol, the meeting failed to produce a useful agreement. Diplomats did the easy things, such as making bold proclamations that global warming should be stopped at 2 degrees and promising huge new sums of money to help developing countries control their emissions and adapt to the changing climate. They also invited countries to make pledges for how they would contribute to these planetary goals.[1] In the months since Copenhagen, analysts have shown that those national pledges won't come close to stopping global warming at 2 degrees.[2] Many of the pledges are missing serious plans for how they will be fulfilled. And the new financial promises for developing countries are also slipping away. Even worse, while everyone agrees that more formal global talks are needed, there is little consensus on the best strategy.

As global talks have become stuck in gridlock, the picture inside the countries whose policies will matter most in determining the future of global warming isn't any more encouraging. Of the industrialized countries, for many years the members of European Union (EU) and Japan have made the biggest policy efforts. But these countries account for just 18 percent of world emissions and their share is shrinking.[3] The other big industrial emitters, notably the US but also Canada and Australia, are doing very little. The most encouraging news in the run-up to Copenhagen came from developing countries. These countries, which account for nearly half of world emissions, have historically refused even to discuss emission controls because they had other priorities such as economic development. But through the Copenhagen process all the largest developing countries pledged to slow the growth in their emissions. However, behind that encouraging story is deep skepticism and wariness about policies that could impinge on their economic prosperity. In the months since Copenhagen, China, India and most other large developing countries have underscored that their pledges are not binding and will be abandoned if they become inconvenient.

Putting numbers on the picture reveals just how little progress has been made. Compared with 1990, by 2008 the annual emissions from the core group of European countries that have devoted the most attention to regulating warming gases were less than 300 million metric tons lower.[4] The flagship of Europe's regulatory effort is an Emission Trading Scheme (ETS). While the ETS is an important model and the world's largest emission trading system, by some estimates the ETS has not yet had any significant impact on Europe's emissions.[5] By contrast, over the same period US emissions were 1 billion metric tons higher, and Chinese emissions were 3.6 billion tons higher.[6] Diligent Europe has been squeezing water from a stone while the rest of the world's warming pollution keeps rising. (Japan, too, has been making diligent efforts but is also squeezing from an economy that is already very efficient.) And most of what Europe has squeezed from its emissions has nothing to do with climate policy. The single largest influence on its emissions trend from 1990 to 2007 was the collapse of the East German economy, whose severe impact on emissions is included in these statistics.

The failure of the Copenhagen meeting is hardly the first diplomatic setback in the worldwide effort to slow global warming. But it is a reminder, two decades since formal UN talks on this subject began in the late 1980s, that the current approach isn't working. The troubles with Copenhagen were easy to predict long before the meeting began.[7] The sheer length and complexity of the diplomatic agenda made it impossible for countries to focus on practical actions that would make a difference. (Indeed, the one bright spot in Copenhagen came from one of the narrower agenda items: the need for new rules to help protect the world's forests.) Keen to show progress on the urgent problem of global warming, diplomats set an aggressive two-year timetable for negotiations during the run-up to Copenhagen.[8] That schedule was impossible to meet and it encouraged diplomats to focus on bold-sounding, abstract promises rather than a hard-nosed look at what their governments could actually deliver. Not surprisingly, when the diplomats took stock of their progress by attempting to draft an agreement seven months before the Copenhagen conference opened, the best they could do was cobble together a text that had 1,142 pairs of brackets signaling areas of disagreement.[9]

Gridlock exists not simply because global warming will require costly policies. In fact, with reasonable efforts to design sensible policies, the cost is not far outside the scale of what societies already spend on other pressing social problems such as the alleviation of poverty and the provision of basic health care. Stopping global warming won't be free, but the costs are not unfathomable. Nor is gridlock just an accident of poor timing since the Copenhagen event arrived in the midst of a global economic recession that has focused most policy makers on immediate issues rather than distant goals. Gridlock was present long before the financial system imploded and was evident even in boom times such as the 1990s when the Kyoto Accord was crafted. Nor is the failure of the United States to lead by example the root cause for global inaction on warming. While the US plays the leader role much less often these days than it did in the 1970s through the 1990s – a topic to which I return in Chapter 9 at the very end of this book – even the brief periods of US leadership on global warming have not lessened the grip of gridlock. None of these factors has helped, but none (even in concert) can explain decades of dithering.

Fundamentally, diplomacy is failing because the architects of the diplomatic process adopted a strategy that could never succeed. This book offers a diagnosis for why that strategy, doomed from the start, was so appealing. It also offers a roadmap for how to do much better in the coming years.

The UN process has not worked because it involves too many countries and issues; it aims for progress too quickly. The result is a style of diplomacy that concentrates on getting agreement where agreement is possible rather than on crafting deals that actually make a difference. Diplomats concentrate their energies on symbolic goals, such as limiting warming to 2 degrees, while largely ignoring the more important practical need to set goals that governments can actually honor.

This approach reflects the conventional wisdom on managing international environmental challenges, and in the early years of global warming talks it seemed to work. The 1992 United Nations Framework Convention on Climate Change (UNFCCC), for example, was negotiated in less than two years and has earned nearly universal support. But those early successes were an illusion because the UNFCCC actually did very little beyond setting a framework for future diplomacy.

It had almost no impact on the actual emissions of gases that cause global warming. As nations tried to tighten the screws on emissions of warming gases – first with the 1997 Kyoto Protocol and most recently in the Copenhagen talks that were intended to find a successor to the Kyoto treaty – all the failings of this strategy were laid bare. Where the Kyoto targets proved convenient, mainly in the EU and Japan, governments have complied. But other industrialized countries, notably the US, easily abandoned the Kyoto strictures when they proved inconvenient. The Kyoto Protocol imposed no limits on emissions for developing countries but did offer indirect payments through a Clean Development Mechanism (CDM) that allows industrialized nations to earn credits for investing in emission control projects in the developing world. The CDM has proved to be an administrative nightmare since it has been impossible to distinguish new investments that have a genuine reduction in emissions from the investments that would have happened anyway in the course of normal economic development. Those administrative nightmares have encouraged developing countries and CDM traders to focus on projects where they can easily claim credit for trivial and uncontroversial changes in technology and behavior. And it has encouraged a lot of fraud. Yet serious solutions to global warming require the opposite approach: focus on complicated policies that transform the way energy is used in modernizing economies. Perversely, by paying developing countries to tinker at the margins – or at least pretend to tinker since a large fraction of the CDM credits are actually awarded for investments that would have happened anyway – this approach has encouraged countries to avoid more meaningful policy reforms.

Warts and all, the Kyoto talks nonetheless produced a treaty because diplomats are skilled at finding agreement where agreement is feasible and pushing other issues into the future. In the run-up to Copenhagen, as governments tried to tighten the screws even further and close the loopholes that made the Kyoto Protocol and other earlier agreements possible, gridlock set in. Just when the strategy of global talks focused on binding treaties was supposed to deliver its biggest accomplishment it reached a dead end instead.

The global strategy has been successful in earlier environmental problems that have proved relatively easy to solve. But it is poorly suited for problems, such as global warming, that are caused by economic activities that are more costly and complicated to regulate.

Truly stopping warming will require cutting global emissions by half over the coming few decades, which will require a lot more than just tinkering at the margins. It will require massive investment in wholly new and probably expensive energy systems. When confronting such large challenges, the central task for effective international cooperation is to ease governments' worries about the impact of regulations on their economic competitiveness. Few countries will adopt costly national policies aimed at solving global problems unless they are confident that their biggest economic competitors are enduring similar obligations. Thus what one country is willing to do is contingent upon confidence that others are also making an effort. The diplomatic challenges in crafting contingent deals are compounded by the fact that most governments do not know exactly what they can implement. The more demanding and complex the change in policy the harder it is for governments to make credible promises to the rest of the world. This problem of credibility is particularly acute for modern democracies because their political processes are, by design, buffeted by many interest groups. Yet it is the richest democracies that must be the engines of global cooperation in this area because they are most worried about global warming and most willing to spend their own resources on the problem.

While the experience with environmental diplomacy offers few models for solving such problems, other areas of international cooperation have a more germane history. Among the many important precedents is the generally successful cooperation on international trade through the General Agreement on Tariffs and Trade (GATT) and the World Trade Organization (WTO). One goal of this book is to introduce such alternative models – along with lesser known examples of successful coordination over costly and complicated policies – to the diplomats and scholars who have mostly focused on environmental cooperation and not looked to other issue-areas. A central lesson from that history is that progress is usually first made in smaller groups – "clubs" – and then expanded.[10] The more complicated the regulatory challenge, the more important it is to start with small, practical efforts by the few countries that matter most. Small approaches matter not just because they are more tractable but also because they make it easier for club members to concentrate the benefits of cooperation – such as access to new markets for low-emission technologies – on other club members. Those benefits reinforce cooperation; they make governments more willing to offer more ambitious promises and they make it easier to observe what other countries actually implement. In recent years there has been no shortage of small groups – such as the G8, the G20, the Major Economies Forum (MEF) – trying to make headway on global warming. But all those efforts have failed because none has focused on generating practical benefits that would keep club members focused on cooperation. Governments have been good at sending invitations to club meetings but have not focused enough on the hard-nosed, practical strategy that would encourage real coordination of policies to regulate warming emissions.

The central argument in this book is that a better strategy for global warming begins by slowing down and refocusing on fundamentals. Better diplomacy requires models for international cooperation that are well suited to the problem at hand.

The starting point for my analysis is recognition that global warming poses three distinct challenges for policy. One, the toughest, is cutting emissions. Getting serious about controlling emissions requires an international legal framework that is flexible enough to accommodate many different national approaches. To date, most diplomacy has focused on setting targets for emissions. That choice is odd since the level of emissions reflects many forces, such as the immediate state of the economy and the relative prices of fuels, that are largely beyond direct government control. As coordination focuses on increasingly costly efforts it will become even more difficult for governments to make useful promises about their exact future level of emissions. I will show that a better approach would focus on policies, instead of just emissions, because that's what governments can adjust more reliably. Serious policy coordination is complicated, and that requires initially working in small groups – clubs – rather than a global UN framework. Within these clubs governments should focus on contingent commitments. What each government offers other club members toward the global good of less warming will be contingent on what others promise and implement as well. Creating incentives for each country to make bigger contingent promises – rather than having every nation sitting on its hands waiting for others to go first – is the central diplomatic challenge in global warming. The club approach will make it easier to meet that challenge because it is easier to negotiate complicated contingent deals in small groups. And with experience the clubs can deepen in what they demand from their members and also broaden in the countries that are involved.

The second distinct challenge is technological innovation, for no serious solutions to global warming are possible without radically new technologies. Oddly, today's global warming talks create few incentives for governments to make massive investments in innovation. No government gets "credit" in today's global warming diplomatic talks for a big investment in innovation, and useful mechanisms for coordinating a global approach to innovation are practically nonexistent. Here, too, the best place to start is with clubs focused on practical policies rather than overly ambitious global goals. Only about ten countries matter most in innovation. They account for four-fifths of all world spending on research and development (R&D) and 95 percent of the world's patents. An active technology strategy will also require patience. History suggests that the world's energy systems are unable to change much faster than at a 50–70 year pace.

Slowing down and shifting focus will be deeply unsettling to people who understandably believe that the perils of climate change loom so large that the world's energy and agricultural systems must be reorganized quickly to make deep cuts in emissions. It is hard to follow climate science closely and avoid the conclusion that severe dangers lurk in unchecked global warming. It is also hard to follow the regulation of warming gases closely and escape the hard truth that the deck is stacked against quick solutions.

Even with diligent efforts, greenhouse gases will accumulate; the planet will warm and climate will change. Thus the third challenge in global warming is bracing for change. On the ground, a changing climate means different patterns in rainfall; higher sea levels; altered growing seasons; and many other effects. Societies must become more adaptive so they can, where possible, adjust to these changes in their stride. While adaptation is rising on the international agenda, I suggest there is very little that the international community can do on this front. Adaptation is mainly a function of each nation's internal wiring. Large, well-intentioned international programs will have an impact only in very special circumstances. And if they are badly managed such programs have as much chance of making things worse as improving the state of affairs. This hypothesis will raise deeply unsettling moral challenges in a world where a certain amount of climate change is unstoppable.

Along with adaptation, societies must prepare for the possibility that changes could be swift and ugly. That means investing in emergency response systems, also known as "geoengineering." The longer governments wait to develop effective schemes for controlling emissions the higher the odds climate change will take an ugly turn.

The core of this book focuses on these three distinct challenges – regulating emissions, investing in technology, and bracing for change.

For the reader with little time, I suggest reading this preface (you are almost finished) and Chapter 1. For scientists, engineers and diplomats who are mystified about why the world doesn't sit up and follow your advice, read Chapter 2. There is no shortage of advice in the climate debate, but most of it is far removed from the realities of what governments can put into practice. Chapter 2 explains why most of the key players in the climate debate are deluded by myths about their own importance. Those myths make it hard to focus on how the policy process really works. Chapter 2 slays them. It also includes a basic history of the science of global warming, which is important because the technical attributes of warming gases largely determine the major policy challenges.

The detailed analysis of the three distinct challenges is found in Chapters 3–6. Climate experts will be interested in that analysis; other readers can peruse just the opening paragraphs of each chapter and get the main messages.

Part of this book is a withering attack on the current strategy for managing global climate change, and Chapter 7 explains why such a wrongheaded strategy was chosen and why there have been so few efforts to find better strategies. That chapter will be useful for readers who want a history of climate diplomacy – albeit a history that most of the key diplomatic architects will find offensive. Chapter 8 picks up the wreckage and offers a different strategy. Written for the nonexpert but challenging for the experts whose conventional wisdoms I think are off base, Chapters 7 and 8 explain why diplomacy is stuck in gridlock and how governments can do a much better job in the future. Finally, instead of a conventional conclusion, I close with Chapter 9 by exploring what all this means for the future of UN diplomacy, the organization of firms, and the roles for the United States and China. Getting serious about global warming implies the largest and most comprehensive planned reorganization of the economy, and Chapter 9 examines some of the likely side effects.

So far, the world has done a terrible job of building institutions to slow global warming. The result is two decades of dithering. A serious program will require ejecting nearly all of the conventional wisdoms that have guided diplomacy so far. Even with a serious program, making a big dent on emissions and truly stopping global warming will be expensive (but affordable) and time-consuming. Those attributes of the warming problem are unavoidable, and successful diplomacy must take them head on.

PART I

Setting the scene

1 | *Introduction and overview*

In the late 1980s the United Nations began the first round of formal talks on global warming. Over the subsequent two decades the scientific understanding of climate change has improved and public awareness of the problem has spread widely. These are encouraging trends. But the diplomacy seems to be headed in the opposite direction. Early diplomatic efforts easily produced new treaties, such as the 1992 UN Framework Convention on Climate Change (UNFCCC) and the 1997 Kyoto Protocol. Those treaties were easy to agree upon yet had almost no impact on the emissions that cause global warming. As governments have tried to tighten the screws and get more serious, disagreements have proliferated and diplomacy has stuck in gridlock.

This book aims to explain the gridlock and offer a new strategy. My argument is that the lack of progress on global warming stems not just from the complexity and difficulty of the problem, which are fundamental attributes that are hard to change, but also from the failure to adopt a workable policy strategy, which is something that governments can change. Making that change will require governments, firms, and NGOs that are most keen to make a dent in global warming to rethink almost every chestnut of conventional wisdom. In this opening chapter, I will summarize my argument in six steps.

Step 1: why the science of global warming matters

Any serious effort to slow global warming must start with one geophysical fact. The main human cause of warming is carbon dioxide (CO_2). Other gases also change the climate, but compared with CO_2 they are small players.[1] Making a big dent in global warming requires making a big dent in CO_2. Most of the economic and political challenges in slowing global warming stem from the fact that CO_2 lingers in the atmosphere for a century or longer, which is why

3

climate policy experts call it a "stock pollutant." The stock of CO_2 builds up from emissions that accumulate in the atmosphere over many years. As the stock rises global warming follows in tandem. Because the processes that remove CO_2 from the atmosphere work very slowly, big changes in the stock require massive changes in emissions. Just stopping the build-up of CO_2, for example, requires cutting worldwide emissions by about half. Lowering the stock, which is what's ultimately needed to reverse global warming, demands even deeper cuts. Exactly how much of a cut will be needed is hard to pin down because the natural processes that remove CO_2 are not fully understood. There's a chance they will become a lot less effective as the stock of CO_2 rises, which would imply the need for even deeper cuts.

Because CO_2 is a stock pollutant the problem of warming is global. Emissions waft throughout the atmosphere worldwide in about a year, which is much faster than the hundreds of years needed for natural processes to remove most of that pollution. Politically, this means that every nation will evaluate the decision to cut emissions with an eye on what other big emitters will do since no nation, acting alone, can have much impact on the planetary problem. Even the biggest polluters, such as China and the US, are mostly harmed by pollution from other countries that has wafted worldwide.

Because our chief pollutant is CO_2, we know that serious regulation will mainly focus on energy policies. CO_2 is an intrinsic by-product of how society burns fossil fuels today, and the vast majority of useful energy that powers modern economies comes from fossil fuels. Tinkering at the margins of the energy system won't make much of a difference. Deep cuts in CO_2 will probably require a massive re-engineering of modern energy systems. Such an effort will alter how utilities generate electricity and the fuels used for transportation, among many other implications. Such a transformation is not impossible; in fact, over history it has happened several times.[2] But no country – let alone the world community – has ever planned such a transformation in energy infrastructure. At this stage nobody knows what it will cost, but most likely it will be expensive. Because energy systems are based on complicated infrastructures it is likely to unfold slowly. And because this transformation will require new technologies and business models that do not yet exist the political interest groups that can keep the process on track do not yet exist. The pace of this transformation will be impossible to plan and predict to exacting timetables.

That's the first step in this book. CO_2 is a stock pollutant, and from that simple geophysical fact comes two important political insights. One is that regulation will require international coordination. The other is that governments will have a hard time making credible promises about exactly how quickly they can make deep cuts in CO_2. Because CO_2 is interwoven with energy systems that are costly and sluggish to change, when governments tighten the screws on emissions – something that has not yet happened except in a very small number of countries – they will find it increasingly difficult to plan and adopt the policies needed to make a difference. As the cost of this transformation rises, what every country does will depend on confidence that other countries are making comparable efforts. Yet even governments working in good faith will be in the dark about what they can really deliver.

Step 2: myths about the policy process

Second, I will argue that international coordination on global warming has become stuck in gridlock in part because policy debates are steeped in a series of myths. These myths allow policy makers to pretend that the CO_2 problem is easier to solve than it really is. They perpetuate the belief that if only societies had "political will" or "ambition" they could tighten their belt straps and get on with the task. The problem isn't just political will. It's the imaginary visions that people have about how policy works. Chapter 2 devotes some space to puncturing these myths.

One is the "scientist's myth," which is the view that scientific research can determine the safe level of global warming. Once scientists have drawn red lines of safety then everyone else in society optimizes to meet that global goal. The reality is that nobody knows how much warming is safe, and what society expects from science is far beyond what reasonable scientists can actually deliver. Policy makers often ask for a "scientific consensus," but nothing that is really interesting to scientists lends itself to consensus. The climate system is intrinsically complex with few useful simple red lines; "safety" is a product of circumstances and interests not just geophysics. The result is an obsession by policy advocates with setting false and unachievable goals.

Over the last decade many scientists and governments have set the goal of limiting warming to 2 degrees, which has now become the benchmark for progress on global warming talks. Two degrees is attractive because it is a simple number, but it bears no relationship to emission controls that most governments will actually adopt. And it isn't based on much science either.

Serious policies to control emissions will emerge "bottom-up" with each nation learning what it can and will implement at home. Just as countries learn how to control emissions they will also look at the science, along with their own national vulnerabilities to climate change, and determine the level of warming they can stomach. It is highly unlikely that countries will arrive at the same answers.

I puncture the "scientist's myth" because it creates a false vision for the policy process – one that starts with global goals and works backwards to national efforts. When pollutants such as CO_2 are the concern, real policy works in the opposite direction. It starts with what nations are willing and able to implement.

A similar myth explains much of diplomacy. Environmental diplomats imagine that progress toward solving problems of international cooperation hinges on the negotiation of universal, legally binding agreements that national governments then implement back at home. The scientist's myth starts with scientific goals and works backwards to national policy. Diplomats make the same kind of error and start with binding international law and draw the same backward conclusion. Events like the Copenhagen conference are the pinnacle of this mythical legal kingdom. They are heroic events organized to produce global treaties. When these events fail to produce consensus the diplomatic community doesn't shift course but merely redoubles its efforts to find universal, binding law.

The reality is that universal treaties are a very bad way to get started on serious emission controls. Global agreements make it easier for governments to hide behind the lowest common denominator. Binding treaties work well only when governments know what they are willing and able to implement. Most of this book is devoted to creating an alternative vision for international law. But getting starting on that alternative requires setting aside the conventional wisdom – widely held in the diplomatic and environmental communities – that has made it hard to focus on better approaches. I will offer my skepticism about this view first in Chapter 2, and when I look at the history of the climate change diplomacy in Chapter 7 I will fully skewer that point of view. Universal binding law has played a useful role in some areas of international environmental cooperation, but the attributes of the climate change problem require a different approach.

Finally, I will take aim at fictions about technology. The "engineer's myth" holds that once inventors have created cheaper new technologies, these new devices can quickly enter into service. This belief is appealing because it offers hope for quick and cheap solutions. It is also appealing because many engineers believe that the needed technologies already exist. Energy efficiency, for example, is widely believed to be a readily available option for making deep cuts in emissions at no cost. The reality is that much of the exciting potential for using energy more efficiently is not presently practical because the needed technologies are not yet married to how real firms and households make energy decisions. Technological transformation is a slow process because it depends on a lot more than engineering. New business models and industrial practices are needed. The more radical (and useful in cutting the use of fossil energy and CO_2) the innovation, usually the greater the technological and financial risks. Putting those innovations into practice hinges on creating the policies and business practices to manage the risks – especially financial risks – that accompany new technologies. Even when those policies are written in treaty registers and in national laws and regulations, firms that invest in new technology and practices must believe they are credible.

Pretending that engineering innovation is the key step leads to policy goals that are overly ambitious and divorced from the realities of what determines whether these new technologies will actually enter into service quickly. The engineer's myth also allows governments to avoid grappling with the kinds of technology policies that will be needed to make a difference. Innovation is relatively easy; creating the policy environment to encourage the testing and adoption of innovations is almost always the weak link.

That's the second step in my book. It clears away false models of the policy process and lets us focus on what really works. The first step laid bare the essence of the warming problem; the second step helps clear the landscape of confusing ideas. The rest of the book builds a new vision.

Step 3: regulating emissions

The third step in the logic is the most important. Slowing global warming requires a big reduction in emissions of CO_2. Achieving that goal will require international coordination. Before I focus on how to make effective international coordination, I must look closely at what individual national governments are willing and able to implement. That is the task of Chapters 3 and 4.

Oddly, most studies of international coordination on global warming ignore national policy and treat governments as "black boxes." Few analysts of international policy peer inside the box to discover how it works; most just imagine that the national policy process will behave as needed once people have political will and international commitments have been adopted. Black boxing national policy is convenient because it makes it easier to focus just on the simpler and sexier topic of international diplomacy. Such studies start by imagining various ideal mechanisms for international coordination and then expect that the black boxes will follow along with implementation.

The reality is that the black boxes are prone to produce certain kinds of policies. Ignoring those tendencies raises the danger that international coordination will become divorced from what real governments can implement at home. These dangers were not much apparent in the early years of global warming diplomacy because international agreements weren't very demanding. The black boxes could comply without doing much beyond what they would have done anyway. But as governments have tried to tighten the screws on emissions of warming gases, a huge gap has opened between the agreements that diplomats are trying to craft at the international level and what their own governments can credibly implement at home. That gap produces gridlock. It lowers confidence that international law is relevant, and as confidence declines governments become less willing to make risky, costly moves to regulate emissions. In the extreme, the result are agreements such as the Copenhagen Accord – legal zombies that have no relationship to what governments will actually implement yet are hard to kill or ignore. Crafting a more effective system of international coordination requires a vision for how to avoid such international outcomes.

The third step builds a simple theory of national policy. Politically viable policies to control emissions must avoid imposing high costs on politically well-organized large groups and also avoid making high costs evident to poorly organized but potentially dominant groups, such as voters. Policies that are politically viable will therefore not be identical with policies that are economically optimal, and in some cases the dispersion between the viable and the optimal will be huge. Armed with that theory, later in this book I will outline a new vision for international cooperation that is more likely to mesh with policies that real governments can adopt at home.

My starting point is power, interests, and capabilities. Power tells us which countries really matter and must be engaged in coordination. Interests reveal what those countries will be willing to do. And capabilities are what they are actually able to do.

In global warming, state power is first and foremost a function of current and future emissions. China and the United States are the most powerful countries on global warming because they have the largest emissions and thus the greatest ability to inflict global harm and avoid harm through their actions. Although the United Nations (UN) officially registers 192 countries on the planet, when it comes to emissions only a dozen or so really matter. I show those big emitters in Figure 1.1. Eventually, all governments will need to play a role in controlling emissions because even the big emitters will be wary about adopting costly policies if small countries become pollution havens. China, for example, will not be keen to control its emissions if the outcome is much higher costs of doing business in China and investments (along with jobs and incomes) "leak" to Vietnam, Thailand, Malaysia or other countries that would become more formidable economic competitors without the burden of costly emission controls. But getting started on controlling emissions requires a vision that is connected to the reality of how the most powerful countries – the biggest emitters – might actually control emissions at home.

Whether big emitters actually control emissions is a function of their interests and capabilities. The full list of factors that determine interests is long, and scholars should spend more time trying to explain and predict the variation in national interests. Some countries are highly vulnerable to global warming, such as the low-lying island states; others, such as frigid Russia, are less worried or might even welcome a thaw. Rich countries are usually more worried than poor ones because wealth brings the luxury of focusing on more than just immediate survival. Democracies seem to be more concerned

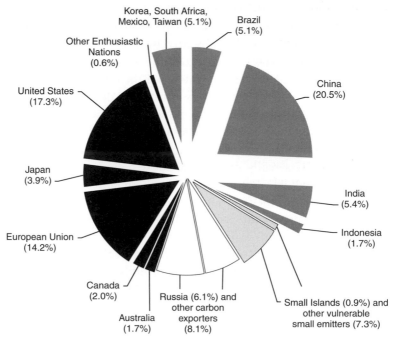

Figure 1.1 National interests and emissions
The figure shows the most recent complete inventory for emissions of CO_2 from burning fossil fuels and changes in land use. "Enthusiastic" countries are shown in black. "Reluctant" nations are shown in dark grey. Together, those twelve countries (treating the EU as one) account for 77 percent of emissions. Excluded from that group is the very large number of small countries (mainly low-income, developing countries) and countries that are large carbon exporters and under little public pressure to regulate emissions, such as Russia and the largest OPEC members. This data set includes full data for CO_2 emissions from fossil fuels drawn from the Carbon Dioxide Information and Analysis Center at Oak Ridge National Laboratory (Boden, Marland, and Andres 2010) augmented with nationally reported data on emissions (and sinks) from land use (including forestry and agriculture) as reported in official emission inventories (see www.unfccc.int and also UNFCCC 2010b). The land use data are 2006 for UNFCCC Annex I countries (i.e., industrialized nations); for non-Annex I countries land use data are 1994 except Mexico (2002) Korea (2001), and Kazakhstan (2005); failures to report data by Angola, Iraq, Kuwait, Libya, and Qatar led me to exclude those countries from the analysis.

than nondemocracies because the ability to organize interest groups and a free press are empowering to NGOs that carry the messages about warming dangers to people and governments around the world. Parliamentary systems are often more energized about warming than presidential governments when green parties become members of ruling coalitions. A nation's interests also depend on what it thinks other countries will do. If one country thinks that emission controls at home will inspire other nations to follow suit it will be more keen to make the move. My home state of California is on the cusp of adopting costly state controls on CO_2 with that theory in mind. A full-blown theory of national interests would need to look at all such factors.

In this book I get started by dividing the world into two categories: *enthusiastic* and *reluctant* countries. Enthusiastic countries are willing to spend their own resources to control emissions. These countries are the engine of international cooperation. The bigger that group and the more resources they are willing to spend on controlling emissions, the deeper the cuts in global emissions. Some of the troubles with global warming diplomacy during the last two decades simply reflected that the group of enthusiastic countries was pretty small and consisted of little more than a few EU members and Japan. But that group is getting bigger and now includes the US and essentially all members of the OECD. Not all these countries have the same interests, of course. What the US is willing to do is a lot more modest these days than the French, German or British effort. And what countries actually do is often not formally labelled climate policy. The US has struggled with national political gridlock on a federal global warming policy, but through direct regulation and many state policies it is making an effort – albeit one that falls short of what it should pursue.

The reluctant nations, such as China and India, also matter. They are already big emitters, and most studies suggest that such countries will account for essentially all growth in future emissions.[3] Because these countries don't put global warming high on the list of national concerns, they won't do much to control emissions except where those efforts coincide with other national goals. Outsiders can change how these countries calculate their national interests by threatening penalties such as trade sanctions or offering carrots such as funding for investments that lower emissions. Outsiders can also provide information on global warming dangers, which will (in time) help reluctant

countries see their interests differently. A country whose government
and NGOs are better informed about the perils of unchecked climate
change will be more likely to mobilize for change – especially if there
is an international framework that would allow their national efforts
to be magnified through efforts by other big emitters.

The capabilities of governments to regulate emissions is highly
correlated with interests. In general, the enthusiastic countries have
well-functioning systems of administrative law and regulation and
can control all manner of economic activities within their borders.
In reluctant nations those systems are generally much less well developed. Typically in the reluctant countries some sectors are under tight
administrative control and others beat to their own drummer.

Chapter 3 develops a theory to predict how enthusiastic countries
will regulate emissions. They could use market-based strategies, such
as emission taxes or "cap and trade" schemes. Or they could use traditional regulation that, for example, forces companies, farmers, and
consumers to utilize particular technologies and practices that reduce
emissions. I will show in Chapter 3 that the most likely outcome is a
hybrid of emission trading and regulation. Emission trading systems
are attractive because they create extremely valuable assets (emission
permits) that can be awarded to politically well-connected interest
groups. Once the initial awards are made, those same groups become
a powerful lobby to keep the system in place. Where these lobbies
are well organized to manage a market that channels resources to
themselves and prevent new entrants, emission trading is the policy
instrument of choice. Where regulated firms have close ties to their
regulators, then direct regulation better suits their political interests. Many environmental NGOs also like regulation because that
approach makes it easier to hide and shift the cost of policy. The political viability of policies rises when the cost can be imposed on groups
that are highly diffused and often unaware of what they are paying.

Within this broad range of hybrid outcomes, every nation will make
a different choice because each government faces differently arrayed
interest groups and different relationships between organized group
and government. I will call these hybrid outcomes "Potemkin markets" because on the surface they often look like emission trading markets solutions yet are designed, exactly contrary to the principle of
markets, to hide the costs of action and to channel resources only to
well-organized groups. This is a prediction of what governments will
actually do and one that I will test with evidence. It is not an argument

that Potemkin markets are good economic policy. In fact, as a policy analyst, I find that outcome deeply unsettling.[4] A simple economy-wide cap and trade program would be more cost-effective than a big dose of regulation. Even better would be a simple economy-wide emission tax. But ideal visions for policy often clash with political realities. Chapter 3 predicts that clash. It also suggests that international accords must be designed with flexibility for governments to adopt different kinds of Potemkin markets since that untidy outcome is unavoidable.

Chapter 4 develops a theory to predict how the reluctant nations will approach emissions controls. My argument is that reluctant nations, so far, haven't done much to control emissions for two reasons. One is that the enthusiastic nations have dithered in creating carrots and sticks that will convince these countries to see the world differently. The biggest existing carrot is the Kyoto Protocol's Clean Development Mechanism (CDM), which is badly administered and creates perverse incentives for reluctant nations to avoid serious emission controls. Sticks, such as border adjustments and trade sanctions, are barely used at all. Better sticks and smarter carrots are needed. The second argument is that much more can be done to encourage these countries to implement policies that satisfy local goals, such as energy security and lower local pollution, while also fortuitously reducing emissions of warming gases. In Chapter 4 I look at a sample of such opportunities, such as the deployment of more efficient technologies in coal-fired power plants, fuller use of natural gas (which has much lower emissions than coal), and better management of endangered forests.

The idea that there are huge "win-win" opportunities is hardly new. Like other studies, I put numbers on the emission reductions to show just how much warming can be avoided by getting serious about this opportunity. (The numbers are huge.) Oddly, the existing literature is largely silent on the question that matters most for policy: which "win-win" opportunities that exist in theory will actually be feasible in the real world?[5] There are lots of things that governments can do in an imaginary world of perfect information, foresight, and ability. But the real world is different. In this book I offer a framework for determining which "win-win" policies the reluctant nations will be willing and able to implement and a vision for how outsiders can help them do more.

Often, "win-win" policies aren't pure winners on their own merits; they require outsiders to help with financing, technology, diplomatic support or other assets. The problem is that the existing sticks and carrots are nearly always irrelevant to encouraging countries to implement these kinds of policies. Notably, the CDM encourages governments and investors to find marginal projects whose exact impact on emissions is easy to measure. Yet the biggest opportunities for "win-win" policies are those where the emissions impact is hardest to predict and where no rational CDM investor will tread. (Nor does it help that many CDM projects have no impact on emissions, which floods the market with cheap CDM credits and discourages more costly investments that could actually make a difference.) A different system is needed. Rather than thousands of small CDM projects, efforts to engage the reluctant countries should focus on a small number of huge opportunities where there is large leverage on emissions and where the opportunity aligns with the administrative abilities of the host government. A reformed CDM can play a subsidiary role, but the real diplomatic effort should focus where leverage is greatest. Reluctant countries should compile their opportunities, declare the external resources they will need for each, and let enthusiastic countries compete for the privilege of playing a role.

Eventually the reluctant nations will have to do more and spend their own resources on emission controls, but a big effort to seize "win-win" opportunities is the right way to start. Not only will it make a dent in emissions, but it will also establish a track record of credible engagement that will be needed for the future when global warming politics will get a lot tougher to manage and stiffer incentives will be needed – including bigger sticks to punish recalcitrant nations. In global warming, like most areas of international diplomacy, it is better to lead with positive engagement before bringing out the big sticks.

Chapters 3 and 4 lead to one simple conclusion about emission controls. The tighter the screws on emissions the harder it will be to plan regulation according to exact targets and timetables. And the tighter the screws the more that efforts by one government will depend on what others do as well. This helps explain some of the gridlock from Kyoto to Copenhagen. International negotiations have been organized mainly to encourage governments to coordinate around emission targets and timetables. But no government that is serious about making credible promises actually knows the emission levels that will emanate from its economy.[6] The insights from Chapters 3 and 4 suggest that international cooperation should be designed differently. It should revolve around what governments can credibly promise to implement. Moreover, cooperation should elicit contingent promises – that is, governments should outline what they will do on their own merits as well as the schedule of additional efforts they will adopt if other governments make comparable efforts. The theories about national policy in Chapters 3 and 4 can guide serious efforts to design international cooperation that meshes with what governments will be willing and able to implement at home. That's step 3.

Step 4: investing in innovation

Steps 4 and 5 are detours. I include them in this book because ignoring them leads to a global warming plan that doesn't work over the long term and leaves the planet highly vulnerable.

Step 4 deals with technology. As the cost of emitting CO_2 rises and as regulations tighten, companies and governments will know that they should find technologies that can lower the cost of compliance. Those built-in incentives for innovation go a long way, but not far enough. Really deep cuts in emissions will require radically new technologies but few companies can justify spending the resources on that kind of innovation because the benefits are so uncertain and difficult to internalize. So an active "technology policy" is needed.

Getting started on technology policy requires focusing on the countries that matter most. Luckily, that list is short: about 95 percent of the world's innovative activity occurs in only ten countries. A big push is needed not only within these countries but also through collaboration between those governments. Increasingly, the market for technology is global. Good ideas in one country diffuse quickly, which means that individual countries will under-invest in new technology unless they are confident they can create new markets for innovation around the world. In the past there has been almost no serious international collaboration on technology policy. Chapter 5 offers some models for doing that and also looks inside the national systems of innovation in a few of the most important countries. As with emission controls, I show that how every country tackles the innovation challenge is likely to vary with its own national circumstances. Even more than with emission controls, the innovative process does not lend itself to strict targets and timetables; outputs are unpredictable.

Technology policy has become a poor cousin of serious efforts to slow global warming. Nearly everyone agrees that massive innovation is needed.[7] Oddly, very few studies actually examine the question that matters most for policy: how to design a big push on innovation. A growing number of advocates call for a "Manhattan project" on global warming but that model is exactly wrong for global warming. In the Manhattan project, the US crash program to develop nuclear weapons, there was just one customer (the US military); commercial competition was irrelevant and costs were no object. "Putting a man on the Moon," another common refrain, followed the same model and is equally poorly suited for global warming. These are inspiring goals that signal the scale of the needed effort, but they are terrible metaphors for policy. Almost as dangerous are wild ideas for quickly and radically increasing R&D spending without any serious plan for how new money can be spent well. Ramping up spending too quickly will just raise the price of R&D without much affecting what really matters, which is innovative output.

Getting serious about technology policy starts with realizing just how dreadful governments have been over the last generation. From the early 1980s through 2008 world spending on energy technology innovation appears to have plummeted. There's been an uptick since 2008, notably in the US, but most of that mainly reflects a huge pulse of "stimulus" money that will soon disappear as governments grapple with their fiscal poverty and struggle to provide funding to other national projects that are politically more popular. As this blip in funding fades, what should be done? I argue that good answers to that question have been hidden by a series of fallacies about technology policy. One fallacy is that government is unable to do the job because it will squander resources on white elephants rather than the viable technologies. A second fallacy is that carbon markets will encourage and pay for technology innovation. In Potemkin markets, well-organized interest groups make sure there isn't much money left over for other purposes; they channel most of the resources to themselves and vest it mainly with incumbent technologies. And carbon prices are so volatile the special grants of emission credits don't have a value that is reliable enough over the long term to finance the slow commercial gestation of new technology.[8] The only serious way to fund technology innovation is with reliable funding, mainly from government, and credible guarantees that new technologies will find viable markets if they perform well. In the US, especially, there has been a historical wariness about technology strategies because it is often assumed the nation's record with government-led energy innovation is a string of unmitigated disasters. The real record is actually a lot better than commonly assumed, and looking outside energy there are many other useful models where the track record is even better. Government is essential and its track record with technology policy is encouraging. Dangers loom, of course, because an active technology policy can also become industrial policy. The right models – with clear sunrises and sunsets – can help avoid those well-known pitfalls.

Economists argue that technology policy is needed to overcome a market failure. That is true, but an equally important role for technology policy is to help manage a political failure. Governments underinvest in innovation because innovators are usually political orphans. Nearly always, the invention of a radically new way of doing things arrives on the scene with no natural political constituency. And the innovation creates many incumbents who are politically well organized and unfriendly to change. Technology policy helps fix these problems; it also helps build confidence that emission controls won't be impossibly costly to implement. All that reinforces the central task for policy, which is the adoption of credible emission controls that will pull new technologies into the market.

I suggest in Chapter 5 that the problem of political orphans is getting slightly easier to solve for two reasons. One is the growing interest in green jobs – an area where politicians are making reckless claims about the prospects for job creation, but those claims help build a political coalition that so far has been supportive of spending on low-carbon innovation. The other is the possible merging of information technology (IT) with energy. The innovation model in iT and a few other areas such as biotechnology is based on "blockbuster" inventions – that is, new ideas that spread rapidly and generate massive returns to innovators. The belief that energy is shifting to that mode of innovation makes it somewhat easier for private firms and governments to mobilize the resources needed for energy innovation. These are political arguments; whether a new dawn of green jobs or the integration of IT with energy are actually real remains to be seen. (I think most green jobs claims are largely baseless, and I doubt it will be easy to measure "green" versus "brown" job creation.) Politically, though, such arguments are changing the landscape and making it easier to muster the political support for innovation policy.

That's step 4. A technology policy is essential to overcoming market and political failures. But it won't happen without good models for how government can be most effective.

Step 5: bracing for change

Step 5 is my other detour. Even a serious effort to control emissions is unlikely to stop global warming. The climate system and the energy system that emits CO_2 are big, complicated systems that are laden with inertia. They are pointed in the wrong direction, and they won't change course easily. Worse, so far the most important emitters haven't created a viable international scheme to coordinate policies to cut warming gases. Once such a system is in place the benefits of slower warming will be felt only after perhaps twenty years of sustained effort and another few decades will be needed actually to stop warming. Even more time will pass before the stock of CO_2 declines decisively from its peak and warming abates.[9] (However, technology wildcards, such as devices that can remove CO_2 and other warming gases directly from the air, might indeed accelerate the ability to stop and reverse warming.) These timetables will be seen by experts, who have invested heavily in efforts to set "safe" goals for warming such as limiting warming to 2 degrees, as too pessimistic. My sense is they are about as fast as serious regulatory and technology deployment efforts will run. And this optimistic scenario assumes that governments actually launch serious, prompt efforts to control emissions and invest in new technologies.

Even under the best scenarios the world is in for probably large changes in climate. Chapter 6 looks at how societies can brace for the changes. For many years, this subject was taboo in most circles because many of the most ardent advocates for global warming policy feared that talking about the need to prepare for a warmer world would signal defeat. Worse, it might signal that warming was tolerable, and that might lead governments to lose focus on the central task of regulating emissions. It is much sexier to imagine bold schemes that stop global warming rather than the millions of initiatives that will be needed to cope with new climates. Yet the unsexy need to brace for change is unavoidable.[10]

Humans are intelligent and forward-looking, and those qualities make them adaptive to a point, so long as they can anticipate the needed changes and have the resources required to adjust. Farmers, for example, can plant different seeds and switch to new crops. Real estate markets can adjust to the likely effects of rising sea levels and stronger storms that could inundate ocean-front properties. Water planners can anticipate rainfalls of different levels and variability.

The central role for policy is to lubricate these natural human skills in adaptation. More timely information about climate impacts can help; more efficient markets for scarce resources such as water can be created; funding for infrastructures that are less sensitive to changing climates can be mobilized. For rich, capable societies, success in adaptation is hardly guaranteed but at least it is a familiar task.

Much tougher issues arise in less wealthy countries where climate-sensitive agriculture dominates the economy and people are already living on the edge. Small changes in climate can have a big human toll.

When I began this book project I expected to conclude that rich countries, which are most responsible for climate change, should create huge funds to help poor countries adapt. Instead, I have arrived at a much darker place. Such efforts are well meaning, but they are unlikely to make much difference. Adaptation does not arise as a discrete policy. It comes from within a society and its governing institutions, and there is very little that outsiders can do to help. Most so-called "adaptation projects" – for example, building sea walls or creating a national weather service to provide farmers with more useful climatic information to help them adapt – make no sense unless implemented within institutions that can actually deploy and utilize these resources efficiently. I'll call these adaptation-friendly contexts. One of the hard truths about global warming is that these contexts are self-reinforcing. When they exist, the list of discrete adaptation projects where outsiders can be helpful is short because societies invest in adaptation on their own. When these contexts don't exist adaptation spending isn't very useful. Readers will recognize this problem as analogous to the problem of economic development. Foreign assistance for development can be extraordinarily important when applied under the right circumstances, but only a subset – perhaps a small subset – of countries actually enjoy those circumstances. The same is true for adaptation.

The Copenhagen Accord includes promises of massive new funding for adaptation, and it appears that most of those promises will be broken. More money can assuage guilty feelings that rich polluters feel, having imposed climate harms on poor societies that already have enough troubles. But more money, alone, probably won't do much to make those countries less vulnerable and to boost their welfare. I devote a large space in Chapter 6 to checking whether this insight is correct, and I think it is robust. It raises troubling questions of international justice. So far, most of the theories of international justice that have been applied to the climate problem have focused on how to divide the burden of controlling emissions; they have not much grappled with the more practical and immediate challenge of how the rich industrialized societies that are most responsible for the build-up of warming gases can help the most vulnerable societies cope with these inevitable changes in climate. My answer is that the rich countries need to be more diligent in controlling their emissions while, in tandem, working harder to facilitate adaptation-friendly contexts across the developing world. In practice, creating those contexts means investing more in economic development rather than focusing solely on adaption. All of that is hard to do and in many developing countries, if not most, won't work perfectly.

If the news about adaption for humans is dark, the news for nature is even more troubling. Unlike humans, nature responds to changing circumstances mainly through natural selection. That means that a changing climate is likely to bring a lot of extinction to species that are already living on the edge while promoting hardier plants and critters such as weeds and cockroaches.[11] The impacts will be felt not just in individual species but whole ecosystems. Avoiding these unwanted outcomes will require a more active human hand. Because humans can look ahead and behave strategically they can implement projects such as installing corridors between ecosystems so that plants and animals can more readily march to more favorable climates. Through such efforts, humans might help steer nature away from unwanted nasty outcomes. If climate changes in extreme ways this will turn humans into zookeepers. Huge areas of wild landscapes will be put under environmental receivership, and managing them will require human handling on a scale never imagined. Doing all this across nature will probably cost a lot more than people are wiling to pay, and in many ecosystems human management may be worse than letting nature sort itself through the Darwinian method. The need for triage will appear. So far, barely any such discussion is under way.[12] The last century has seen a sharp rise in international funding for nature, much of it managed by NGOs and focused on preserving gems of nature. In a world of changing climates, these NGOs will be on the front lines of nature's triage. They will probably have a difficult time accepting this mission because zookeeping and triage run counter to their core historical missions, which center on protecting nature in its original state. The most successful international nature

NGOs are steeped in a culture of protection – they buy lands, create parks, erect fences where possible, and do their best to keep humans away and to lighten the human footprint. Triage will require more or less the opposite strategy.

If all that isn't dark enough, I also look at some worst case scenarios. Barely a month goes by without a publication of new research suggesting that climate could change more rapidly than previously expected. Once such changes are under way the effects on things that matter could be more horrendous than earlier thought. The unknown unknowns of global climate change might hold pleasant surprises or horrors. The evidence at the horror end of the spectrum is mounting.

Thus I also argue that bracing for change also requires readying some emergency plans. Those will include intervening directly in the climate to offset some of the effects of climate change, which is also known as "geoengineering." Volcanoes offer a model, for their periodic eruptions spew particles into the upper atmosphere that cool the planet for a time. Man-made efforts along the same lines might include flying airplanes in the upper atmosphere and sprinkling reflective particles that might crudely cool the climate.[13] So far, most of the public discussion about geoengineering treats the option as a freak show of reckless Dr Strangeloves tinkering with the planet. Yet it is hard to digest the most alarming scenarios from climate science without concluding that serious preparations are needed on the geoengineering front. I argue for a research program in this area so that some of the most viable options can be tested. I also argue that such a program needs to follow special rules such as transparency, publication of results, pre-announcement of tests, and careful risk assessments that focus on the possible side effects. That approach is needed so that if governments ever get to the stage where they might actually deploy geoengineering systems, a set of norms and practices are in place about how to treat these technologies. There are two big dangers with geoengineering. One is that the technology will be so controversial that the countries with the best scientists don't invest in testing the options responsible and readying them in case of need. The other is that a desperate country will launch geoengineering without preparing for the side effects. A dozen or so nations probably already have the ability to deploy geoengineering and the list is growing. A race is on between building a responsible research program that can lay the foundation for good governance of geoengineering technologies and the desperate "hail Mary" pass of a country that can't stomach the extreme effects of warming and is disillusioned with the lack of serious efforts to stop global warming through regulation of emissions.

Step 6: a new international strategy

The sixth and final step in the logic of this book is a redesign of the international diplomatic strategy. It will seem odd in a book that is about overcoming the gridlock in international diplomacy to wait so long before a new diplomatic vision arrives fully on the scene. But I have started this book with a detailed look at national policy because international agreements that don't align with national interests and capabilities are unlikely to be effective.

I take on this task in two stages. First, I explain why diplomatic efforts so far have led to gridlock. My argument is that the diplomatic toolbox used over the last two decades is the wrong one for the job. That toolbox comes from experience in managing earlier international environmental problems, which have little in common with the costly, complicated regulatory challenges that arise with warming gases. I show in Chapter 7 that all of the canonical elements in that toolbox are wrong for global warming. Those elements include global agreements, which diplomats cherish because they believe they are more legitimate than smaller more exclusive accords. They include binding treaties, which most analysts wrongly think are more effective because governments always take binding law more seriously. And they include emission targets and timetables, which are a mainstay of environmental diplomacy because most diplomats and NGOs think targets and timetables are the best way to guarantee that governments actually deliver the environmental protection they promise. These conventional wisdoms are so ingrained in environmental diplomacy that Chapter 7 offers a new history of international environmental protection and shows why nearly all the canon of conventional wisdom in this area is wrong for the problem of global warming.

Chapter 8 offers an alternative. It starts with one central insight: effective international agreements on climate change will need to offer governments the flexibility to adopt highly diverse policy strategies. Instead of universal treaties, I suggest that cooperation should begin with much smaller groups – what international relations experts often call "clubs."[14] It should begin with nonbinding agreements that are more flexible. And it should focus on policies that governments control rather than trying to set emission targets and timetables since emission levels are fickle and beyond government control. Cooperation challenges of this type are rare in international environmental diplomacy, but they are much more common in economic diplomacy where governments often try to coordinate their policies in a context where no government really knows exactly what it will be willing and able to implement. The closest analogies are with international trade and the model I offer draws heavily from the experience with the GATT and WTO. Chapter 8 explains how a system for global warming based on that model would work.

The backbone of this new approach would be a series of contingent offers. Governments would outline what they are willing and able to implement as well as extra efforts that are contingent on what other nations offer and implement. Negotiations within the club would concentrate on the package of offers that are acceptable to participating nations. By working in a small group – initially about a dozen nations or fewer, as suggested in Figure 1.1 – it would be easier to concentrate on which offers were genuine and to piece together a larger deal that takes advantage of the contingencies. As individual countries gain confidence that others will honor their commitments then they, too, will be willing to adopt more costly and demanding policies at home. As part of this process, enthusiastic nations would also scrutinize the many opportunities for "win-win" emission policies in reluctant nations and offer resources to those that were most promising. A system of bids by those countries would make the range of opportunities more transparent and would encourage enthusiastic countries to compete for the best opportunities.

Deals created in this small group would concentrate benefits on other club members – for example, a climate change deal might include preferential market access for low-carbon technologies and lucrative special linkages between emission trading systems in exchange for tighter caps on emissions. Concentrating benefits on other club members will create stronger incentives for participating governments to deepen their cooperation. Focusing cooperation on contingent offers will help each club member see its efforts multiplied, which will help ensure that the offers are not too modest. In time, this approach of offering benefits that are exclusive and contingent will make club membership more attractive to potential new members. Such club approaches often fare better than larger negotiations when dealing with problems, such as global warming, that are plagued by the tendency of governments to offer only the lowest common denominator. Clubs make it easier to craft contingent deals and channel more benefits to other members of the club, which creates stronger incentives for the deals to hold.

This system of bidding, negotiation and crafting of contingent deals has an analogy in the process of accession that governs how countries join the WTO, that makes is useful for global warming diplomacy. I call the agreements that could result from this system "Climate Accession Deals," or CADs.

The logic of diplomacy in small clubs underpins many efforts and proposals in recent years to focus on warming policy in forums that are smaller and more nimble than the UN. Those include the G20, the "Environmental 8," the Major Economies Forum on Energy and climate (MEF), and similar ideas.[15] These are all good ideas; what is missing is a strategy that will make such smaller forums relevant. Governments that care most about slowing global warming need to invest in these small forums and focus their efforts on creating benefits that will entice other governments to do more. I am cautiously optimistic that such club approaches will regain favor in the wake of the troubles at Copenhagen, but I am not blind to the power of conventional wisdom. The conventional wisdoms that have created gridlock on global warming remain firmly in place and are hard to shake. Creating a club that works will require leaders who will make the first contingent offers that create incentives for other countries to act. The EU has not been a leader on this front because it is overly invested in the UN approach. Japan has not because it is too timid to swim against the current of conventional wisdom. And the US has not played the leader role because what America says these days on most matters is so volatile that it is not seen as credible. A smarter EU, a more credible US or a big move by China or India could be very helpful. And this book suggests what those leaders could do to make their efforts relevant.

Clubs are a way to get started, but they aren't the final word. Eventually the clubs must expand. Indeed, the global UNFCCC will remain as an umbrella under which many global efforts unfold. The advantage of starting with a club is that the smaller setting makes it easier to set the right norms and general rules to govern that expansion. In practice, this will be a lot easier than it seems because international emission trading can be a powerful force working in the same direction. With the right policies, the international trade in emission credits creates a mechanism for assigning prices to efforts. It rewards countries with strict policies by giving higher prices to their emission credits. Over the history of the GATT/WTO, the most powerful mechanism for compliance was the knowledge that if one country reneged on its promises, others could easily retaliate by targeting trade sanctions and removing privileges to punish the deviant. With the right pricing policies, emission trading could provide similar kinds of incentives. Making CADs contingent on similar behavior will create additional incentives for compliance.

There is no shortage of institutions already working on climate change. What's missing is a strategy focused on getting countries to make reliable promises about what they can and will implement. The central diplomatic task in the coming years will be to couple those national promises to the efforts that other nations will undertake so that, over time, each major country sees growing incentives to implement more effective policies to control emissions. In this book I draw on models from international economic cooperation where such diplomatic challenges are much more familiar. Indeed, the challenges that climate diplomats face today are analogous to those that have defined much of the history of international efforts to create a rule-based system for advancing international trade. Those same models are the best guides for getting serious about global warming.

The future

This chapter has summarized the main logic and central arguments of this book, and thus I do not include a conventional conclusion that rehashes the argument once again at the end of this book. The global warming problem is a complex one and the solutions offered here are complex as well. It is more useful to have the conclusion at the beginning so that it is easier to see how the pieces fit together as the book proceeds.

Instead of a conclusion, the final chapter of the book speculates on the future. As governments get serious about controlling emissions their efforts will have far-reaching implications for diplomacy, commerce, and the organization of government. The emergence of a serious regulation to regulate warming gases may also affect how international relations theorists think about the international order. Chapter 9 explores several of the implications that are likely to be more important.

First, I speculate on the implications of my argument for the UN. The UN has had some hard knocks in recent decades – many of them at the hands of American politicians. This book won't be helpful on that front, for it suggests that the UN is ill-suited to take the starring role on the flagship issue of our era.

Ever since UN talks began on the global warming issue analysts have debated whether UN-sponsored deals – the UNFCCC, the Kyoto Protocol, and the process that limped through the Copenhagen Summit – have been good or bad. My view is that those deals have been largely irrelevant. The UN style of diplomacy is not structured in a way that will deliver much leverage on emissions of greenhouse gases in either the enthusiastic or the reluctant nations.[16] It is steeped in conventional wisdoms about how to manage problems that are not aligned with the fundamental attributes of the pollutants that cause global warming. These are not criticisms of the UN, however. The institution is struggling to address a problem that an open, global forum is unable to tackle. The fault lies not with the UN but with the governments that are keen to address the warming problem and have failed to work seriously on alternative approaches that would be more effective.

For too long, governments that care the most about global warming policy have also worked the hardest to protect a UN monopoly on climate diplomacy. Monopolies are especially dangerous when the best strategy is unknown. In every area of the international process on global warming – from crafting commitments by the enthusiastic nations to engaging the reluctant nations to investment in technology to adaptation – there is no consensus on what will work best. In commerce, the solution to such problems is diversity and competition, and the same lesson holds for diplomacy. This suggests that the best role for the UN is as an umbrella under which many different experimental efforts flourish and compete. The ones that succeed will attract diplomatic and industrial resources; the others will wither. And it suggests that the UN itself will become much more effective as an institution if it faces competition. One of the areas where more market competition is especially needed is in international trading of emission permits, for more competition and experimentation in that setting could shift power away from the UN-based system (the Kyoto Protocol's CDM) and back to nations that have much more reliable control over their markets and a stronger incentive to ensure that markets are actually performing as expected. The result will be markets that are more fragmented yet much better at sending signals about which regulatory strategies are actually working. Chapter 9 explores not just what that means for the UN but also how this market-oriented way of enforcing international obligations will determine which countries have the greatest power and influence over climate negotiations.

Second is the organization of industry and its relationship to government. Deep cuts in emissions – on the scale outlined earlier in this chapter as a best case scenario for emission controls – imply the need for a massive reorientation of energy systems. The pattern of investments needed to obtain that outcome is likely to involve massive financial risks, for most of the technologies needed are not proven at scale, are not yet competitive with incumbent technologies, and will not automatically achieve widespread deployment at carbon prices that are likely to be tolerable. Investors will seek special incentives to make these risks tolerable, and the role of government in the industrial economy could rise sharply. So far, every country that has made serious efforts to control emissions has done so with extensive intervention by government in the industrial economy. Most other tasks that will be needed for climate protection also imply bigger roles for government. For example, the creation of emission trading schemes will require systems for monitoring and enforcing trading, which will require strong national legal and administrative systems.

Serious efforts to address warming gases will require much more capable governments. And those nations with a tradition of capable, intrusive governments may thrive especially well in this world. China, for example, may do well in these circumstances. India, by contrast, is less well poised to intervene in its economy in nimble ways, although a broad array of reforms under way will improve in time the Indian government's administrative abilities. Most of Africa is poised to do poorly.

A much larger role for government in the economy will reopen a long-standing debate over the merits of different systems of economic organization. State-led systems such as in Japan may find the world of government and industry working together closely a familiar one. For the United States this role for government is much less familiar and politically more toxic. In the early 1970s, at the onset of the last big rise in social regulation, economists warned that regulation does not only serve social purposes but it can also be used by firms to frustrate competition.[17] Those same worries deserve airing today.

In an ideal world government would set clear and credible emission policies and leave industry to invest in many different rival approaches. But governments often find it very difficult to set credible, long-term rules. One of the chief functions for international institutions in this area will be to help national governments become more credible, such as by making policies more transparent and enforceable and by helping governments craft interdependent deals that will be harder for any particular nation to abandon even when those deals prove inconvenient. (Success in the GATT and WTO is rooted, in part, on the ability of these institutions to help governments tie their hands so their promises are more credible.) However, the credibility-enhancing roles for international institutions will take a long time to create. In the short term, my worry is that governments will use direct intervention in industry – with huge subsidy programs and direct control – as a substitute for credible long-term policies. The political logic for that approach is easy to understand, but as a student of regulation who has spent a career worrying about regulatory costs this political expedient outcome carries large dangers for the economy. Looking to the future this tension – between transforming the carbon economy through private market forces or through state-led programs – looms large.

As the long-term viability of state-led programs comes under question then much of the conventional wisdom about the best ways to control emissions will be open for fresh debate. In Chapter 9 I suggest that one area of hopeful questioning will be on the role of carbon taxes. The theory I will offer in this book suggests that carbon taxes would be the best way to control emissions but the worst way to mobilize political support. Emission trading and direct regulation are politically more popular because they allow well-organized groups to create and channel benefits to themselves. But that political logic only helps explain the initial choices of governments. Emission trading – especially international emission trading – is extremely difficult to administer. It creates large incentives for fraud, and if poorly managed it will encourage countries to monetize emission credits and then exit the system after pocketing the proceeds. Tackling those problems will require a new kind of international financial regulation, and it will also create incentives for governments to shift away from emission credits and toward taxes where it will be easier to manage economic and fiscal outcomes. In Chapter 9 I will outline how that shift may occur and why it is a good idea. (In practice, that shift will probably occur through the inclusion of price floors and ceilings in emission trading schemes, which in theory will combine the political and economic advantages of trading-based and tax-based systems into a single instrument.)

Third, and finally, I note that in many respects, the climate system is already evolving in the direction I advocate – not by design but through default. The UN efforts are stuck in gridlock, and that has left smaller clubs as one of the few places where progress is emerging. While that shift is encouraging, climate strategy by default won't solve the problem of global warming. Making the club strategy work will require active efforts to build institutions and focus on practical policies. So far, there isn't yet much evidence of that kind of heavy lifting. Hopefully this book will offer a roadmap for the countries that care most about slowing global warming to lead the world in doing a better job of actually protecting the planet.

2 | Why global warming is such a hard problem to solve

Most books on global warming policy start with a chapter on the science. Because that's been done so many times before, I will do something different. I start with a brief *history* of the science.

Scientifically, much of what was needed to start worrying about global warming was known in the late 1950s. Yet no society really became concerned until much later in the 1980s. The shift reflects a change in mindset about whether human activities could have adverse global consequences.

Although this book is about global warming, serious efforts to solve that problem really began with a different atmospheric problem: the ozone layer. From the early 1970s industrial societies worried – at first about supersonic airplanes and then spray cans – that they were thinning the life-protecting ozone layer. Ozone concerns changed the mindset and made it easier to spot and manage other global problems, including global warming. Unfortunately, the ozone experience also created a model for how to regulate global problems that worked well for ozone but is a terrible way to handle more complex and expensive problems like global warming. The wrongheadedness of that model is a topic for later in Chapter 7.

In reviewing the basic science of climate warming I boil it down to three central facts that matter for policy. At the top of that list is the fact that carbon dioxide (CO_2), the chief human cause of warming, has a very long atmospheric lifetime. Because it lasts so long in the atmosphere, CO_2 easily mingles around the world, which means that any serious plan for regulating the pollutant must include a large role for international coordination. The scientific properties of CO_2 largely explain why global warming is such a hard problem to solve and they offer a starting point for building a theory that will explain how governments will attempt to regulate warming gases and how they can coordinate their efforts internationally. The rest of this book after Chapter 2 is mainly focused

on building that political theory and exploring its implications
for policy.

While reviewing the history of climate science, this chapter punctures some myths that are hindering political efforts to solve the global warming problem. A surprisingly large number of the people most
active in global warming policy have visions of a policy process that
aren't accurate. First on that list are scientists. Scientists have given
inordinate attention to drawing lines in the sand on the theory that
once policy makers know the level of warming that is dangerous that
policy will follow. Most of these line drawing efforts have very little
real impact on policy. The most famous line in the sand is the goal
of limiting warming to 2 degrees – a goal that nearly every major
international organization has now adopted and that real emissions
policies routinely ignore. Such false goals obscure the fact that different societies will view their interests (and thus goals) in quite different
ways, and the hard-nosed politics of global warming start with those
differences in interests.

Another myth is that global warming is an environmental problem. A large number of people, including most policy makers, look
at warming through the lens of environmental regulation. While this
problem worries environmentalists for good reasons, most of the
underlying causes and nearly all of the policies that will fix warming
are rooted in economics. Too much greenery is making it hard to focus
on the economic causes and consequences of global warming. The
environmental lens on global warming has also inspired diplomats
to use models from the history of environmental diplomacy, such as
the treaties that are protecting the ozone layer, that don't work well
for coordinating complicated economic policies. Better models come
from international economic cooperation.

Lastly, the engineer's myth, as I call it, puts too much emphasis on
invention of new technologies and not enough on the practical factors
that will actually determine whether new, low-emission technologies
are actually used. Engineers are optimistic by nature and prone to
conclude that if people just knew about all the cool technologies that
existed they would instantly use them. Energy efficiency, for example,
could be a lot higher if firms and households adopted a host of technologies that are already available and also save money. This myth
obscures the wide array of factors that determine the rate at which
new technologies actually enter into service and leads to an obsession

about inventing new technologies. It obscures the important policy challenges that surround field testing and the slow, patient process of deploying those technologies. The engineer's myth allows societies to pretend that radical technological change will be a lot easier to manage than is likely.

How scientists and society decided that climate change was dangerous

The basic physics that leads to climate warming has been known since the nineteenth century when scientists first explained how tiny quantities of "greenhouse gases" could alter the climate across the entire planet. Those gases allow visible sunlight to pass readily through the atmosphere to heat Earth's surface. The warmer planet then radiates a different kind of energy back to space, known as "infrared radiation." All greenhouse gases are largely transparent to visible solar energy but trap, to different degrees, the outgoing infrared radiation. By trapping more infrared radiation and altering the planet's balance of energy, greenhouse gases warm the climate.

The warming these gases cause is often called the "greenhouse effect." Greenhouses don't actually work this way, but once a common sense term gets used widely, it is hard to shake. (Greenhouses are warm mainly because the glass keeps the toasty air inside from blowing away.) While "global warming" is a general description of the outcome, the biggest dangers from this phenomenon aren't just warming. They are changes in rainfall, ocean currents, growing seasons, and pretty much everything else that depends on climate. Most experts have thus settled on the more vague term "climate change" to describe the process. I use that term and "global warming" interchangeably and prefer the latter because, while incomplete, it is descriptive. In the public debate about global warming it is very hard to get the terminology both compact and accurate, and many of the disagreements that political groups have about climate change are reflected in the language they use.[1]

Carbon dioxide is the most ubiquitous of the warming gases that humans emit. Molecule for molecule, it is actually one of the weakest greenhouse gases – in part because there is so much of the stuff already in the atmosphere that each new molecule has a small effect.[2] All the other greenhouse gases that humans emit cause barely half the warming of carbon dioxide, although the warming impact of a few is still hard to pin down. A few gases, such as sulfur hexafluoride and other "industrial gases," are particularly nasty warming agents, but thankfully these are emitted in such tiny quantities that they are bit players.

It wasn't until the 1950s, about a century after the basic physics of greenhouse gases was first worked out, that scientists reliably connected human emissions of greenhouse gases with possible changes in the global climate. That long delay reflects not just the lengthy gestation of new science but also a change in mindset. Until a few decades ago, nobody dreamed that the human impacts on natural systems could spread to such a large scale. When the first calculations of human emissions of carbon dioxide were done in the 1930s, the numbers were small enough that the human fingerprint was hard to discern.[3] At the time, nobody had actually measured those gases in the atmosphere over time, and when scientists projected industrial activity into the future, they never imagined that compound growth would multiply the human emission many times. (The 1930s, in general, were not a time for optimism about industrial growth.) And when scientists started to trace where all the carbon dioxide that came from burning fossil fuels actually went, they just assumed it found its way safely into the oceans. The interesting scientific puzzles did not swirl around whether humans were changing the planet. Rather, most of these scientists were interested in a different question: what caused the ice ages? One contending theory held that cycles in the activities of volcanoes, which spew large amounts of carbon dioxide, might drive ice ages. That theory sank when a rival hypothesis, which pinned the ice ages on variations in the sun and the planet's orbit, worked much better.[4]

A human link to global warming was first proffered systematically in the 1950s. Making the link required looking at many different facets of the problem – the source of emissions, their possible build-up in the atmosphere, and then the climatic impacts that might follow. Answers required not just new thinking but eventually large amounts of data from ships and sensors that were costly to build and operate. Only one entity, the US government and the scientific apparatus that it supported, could supply the needed resources.

The Second World War had marked a big change in the role of government in science – huge government-sponsored research programs worked on radar, atomic weapons, aviation, and a handful of other topics including weather and climate, all of which helped win the war. When the war ended, well-organized scientists made sure the research did not.[5] Among the points to investigate was to unravel how the global cycles of water, heat, and chemistry actually functioned – questions that were impossible to answer without access to the fleet of ships and airplanes that big government-sponsored science could supply. The leading sponsors of this work included the nations with the biggest stakes in exploring and preserving access to the open oceans and the arctic (e.g., Norway and Sweden) and, paramount among them, the new superpowers of Russia and especially the United States. They teamed together in the 1950s for the first global collaboration on science – the International Geophysical Year (IGY). Over eighteen months, ships and planes from the science powerhouses of the day scanned the oceans and atmospheres. The exact timing of the event – 1957–1958 – coincided with the peak in activity in the solar cycle, which reflected that the central mentality of the scientific community was to understand how nature, itself, made things work.[6] For scientists, the models for the IGY were the two previous "polar years," which marked sustained international efforts to investigate the workings of the polar regions, but the IGY was much bigger and a lot more expensive. IGY was the first scientific program that intended to utilize Earth-orbiting satellites; governments were keen to invest in that technology not just for the benefit of pure science but also because flying satellites helped set the rules that would govern which nations controlled outer space.[7]

One of the IGY's most lasting results was the first systematic measurement of greenhouse gases, in particular CO_2. Today, CO_2 is interesting because, as the main by-product of burning fossil fuels, it is the central actor in the growing worries about global warming. But in the 1950s, CO_2 was interesting because the gas is mixed throughout the biosphere and oceans; tracing it would help unlock the major geophysical cycles that governed the planet. The IGY offered the first data point in the longest continuous direct measurement of CO_2 in the atmosphere – started by David Keeling who perched CO_2 sniffers on the 4,200 meter high Mauna Loa volcano in Hawaii where they could smell the real global atmosphere free from any local pollution. Roger Revelle, who organized the funding for Keeling's sniffers, had just published a paper showing that most of the CO_2 would stay in the atmosphere rather than being sucked up in the oceans.[8] The belief that CO_2 would be absorbed mainly in the oceans had been so strong that the draft of Revelle's paper carried that assumption until recalculating the equations led to a last-minute change taped to the manuscript before publication.[9] The US Navy and Air Force – which were keenly interested in how materials such as nuclear waste and fallout moved in the atmosphere and oceans – funded most of the work that led to these insights and the sniffing that proved them valid. Combining the "Revelle factor," which governed how much CO_2 would actually go into the oceans and the "Keeling curve," which confirmed that more CO_2 was lingering in the atmosphere, it was hard to avoid the conclusion that the burning of fossil fuels was a chief cause of the mounting atmospheric CO_2.

The 1950s, though, were not a time of worry about polluting human footprints on the planet. In fact, Revelle's 1957 paper ended with the speculation that burning fossil fuels offered the world a "great geophysical experiment" that might help to unravel the carbon cycle. Today, if a scientist published a new theory that forecast much higher concentration of a human emission, the conclusion would muse about the prospects for global regulation. In the 1950s the musing was on the benefits for science if the great geophysical experiment was properly observed as it unfolded. Nobody spent much time, then, thinking about global regulation.

What caused a shift in perspective from CO_2 as an oddly welcome curiosity to a dangerous global pollutant? One answer, to be sure, was all the science done since the 1950s to nail down the theory of global warming and begin to identify some of the possible dangers lurking in a warming world. But another answer is the change in human mind-set about environmental risks. The tail end of the 1950s saw a shift to worrying about a host of invisible yet pernicious drains on environmental quality. Most people date this shift to the 1960s, especially the protest-laden late 1960s, but the seeds were planted much earlier. During the 1950s there was a rapid rise in atmospheric testing of nuclear weapons and, in time, growing attention on the effects such as the build-up of radiation in human milk. Unexpected high yields and winds that differed from the forecast on the day of the 1954 "Castle Bravo" test, for example, sprayed radiation on nearby Pacific islanders (who were soon evacuated) and a Japanese fishing boat. Such events spawned a movement, with policy-minded scientists in the lead, to ban atmospheric testing of nuclear weapons. (That ban finally went into effect in 1963.)[10] The build-up of DDT in the atmosphere was another concern,[11] which soon inspired some countries to ban the chemical that had been wiping out bird populations. The late 1960s and early 1970s also saw publication of new reports that explored whether burning of fossil fuels and forests might be sucking the oxygen from the atmosphere.[12] As scientists starting thinking about the human footprint on the environment differently they found many things to worry about. Some analysts worried about how large dams and river projects, such as massive diversions that the Soviet Union was planning, might alter the world flow of water. Some worried about whether sulfur pollution might cause too much reflection of incoming sunlight, which could cool the planet. (The 1970s, it was generally thought, was a period of unusually cool weather; some analysts feared that a planet already prone to cooling might tip into an ice age.) Scientists who had worked on unraveling the cause of past extinctions, famously the dinosaurs, explored many hypotheses and finally pointed the finger at climate changes caused by asteroids and comets. Some of the same team that answered that question also proffered the hypothesis that global nuclear war could also trigger an ice age – so-called "nuclear winter." Climatologists who built models that made it possible to simulate the effects of wars (as well as carbon dioxide) suggested that perhaps "nuclear fall" would be more apt. (Whether "winter" or "fall", it did not require climatologists to arrive at the conclusion that nuclear war was generally bad for the planet.)

What really cemented research on global climate to environmental worries was a dispute over supersonic airplanes. In the early 1970s the leading aircraft manufacturers in Europe and the United States were exploring the option of building large fleets of high-altitude long-distance aircraft. European firms, backed by European governments, were in the lead with the Concorde program. When Congress debated whether to let Concorde land at American airports it probed a host of environmental objections from local noise to global climate and found it difficult to sift through the competing evidence. (Those objections were also laced with commercial interest since US airplane manufacturers were lagging in supersonic innovation for commercial aircraft and were not keen to allow the European advantage of landing their aircraft on US soil. Often when companies lag in competition they have a strong incentive to point a spotlight at the environmental ills of their rivals.)[13] One result of the controversy over supersonic aircraft was a massive study, the Climate Impact Assessment Program (CIAP), aimed at providing independent analysis for a debate that had been operating mainly on hunches and superstition. CIAP looked at possible cooling as well as warming.[14] By the time CIAP appeared in 1975, the supersonic debate was already over. The global economic meltdown as well as difficult engineering killed the supersonic aircraft programs; the European program survived but only at a small scale with lavish public subsidy. Congress allowed landing rights so long as the planes didn't cause sonic booms, which was the only environmental effect that had gained much political traction. The niche fleet of Concordes was too small to have much impact on the climate. But CIAP lefts its mark as the first "integrated assessment" study of climate – that is, a study that assessed the whole chain of cause and effect, from the demand for supersonic transport, the technologies involved, and ultimately the level of emissions and their environmental impacts. Today, "integrated assessment" is the mainstay of global climate research. (Interestingly, in CIAP's day most climatic fears centered on cooling from the high-altitude contrails; CIAP concentrated its efforts there and found that cooling would be worse news than warming.)

The change in mindset helped put more spotlights on an array of other possible global dangers. What all of them had in common was a long lifetime for their chief pollutants – usually decades, sometimes centuries. Long lifetimes meant that emissions anywhere were a problem everywhere. Moreover, once emissions occurred the effects would be slow to reverse. Such problems forced societies to think differently about how they managed risk. It is no surprise that the "precautionary principle" – the idea that extra caution is needed in allowing pollution that has unknown and irreversible effects – emerged as one of the organizing ideas around modern environmental law at the time. In practice, the precautionary principle is nearly useless because it doesn't advise just how much caution is needed or what society is willing to pay. But its emergence reflected the new challenge in environmental policy, which was managing complex problems with unknown and possibly irreversible consequences.

Long-lived pollutants also focused attention on the need for global approaches to environmental protection. From the early 1970s governments had adopted a wide range of international regulations focused on environmental problems – for example, trade in endangered species – and a few issues that animated the publics of many countries appeared on the global agenda, such as protection of the whales. But no serious efforts had been made to stop a global pollutant.

The first big test for global atmospheric policy was the accidental discovery that chlorofluorocarbons (CFCs), at the time used mainly in spray cans, could deplete the ozone layer. (When the environmental effects of the supersonic airplane debate first appeared, the initial concern was the ozone layer as well. The fear was that the airplanes injected large volumes of nitrogen oxides into the stratosphere and would cause local depletions of ozone. Using similar chemistry, CFCs proved to be a bigger worry.) For industrial chemists CFCs were beautiful chemicals because they were so stable and thus safe when used near humans. But their stability also meant that they could linger long in the atmosphere and drift into the upper atmosphere above the ozone layer where, finally, strong ultraviolet radiation from the sun would zap them apart. So zapped, the CFC fragments then caused a nasty chain reaction that would destroy ozone. A 1974 paper outlined that chemistry and earned its co-authors, Sherry Rowland and Mario Molina, a Nobel prize later in life. The third person to share the prize that year, Paul Crutzen, was the key player in earlier efforts to explain the chemistry of nitrogen oxides in the stratosphere.[15]

Rewinding the tape of history to the 1960s, it would have been hard to predict that the ozone layer would be the first test for global atmospheric policy. But other global atmospheric dangers proffered at the time – for example, the fear that deforestation was removing the planet's lungs and would cause the atmosphere to run low on oxygen – did not survive much scientific scrutiny. And in the early 1970s scientists could not agree which way the climate would change. The build-up of CO_2 and other greenhouse gases pointed to global warming. But local pollution pointed the opposite direction since emissions of sulfur caused the formation of particles that, in turn, caused more numerous and brighter clouds that would reflect away more sunlight – a pattern that the supersonic aircraft might exacerbate. Even as there was growing concern about a changing climate it was a throw of the dice which way – hotter or cooler – the human hand would push temperatures. The regulation of local sulfur pollutants (which were linked to respiratory diseases and acid rain and thus unwelcome) along with the continued build-up of warming gases shifted the odds to warming.

It is hard to date precisely when scientists stopped worrying about global cooling, but a paper in 1981 by James Hansen and several colleagues is probably the inflection point.[16] Hansen, like most of the community that built the first climate models, had been trying to understand the climate of other planets – in his case, Venus. The Venetian atmosphere is filled with clouds and warming gases that make it much warmer than if the planet had no atmosphere. The models that were useful for predicting the temperature of a planet were generic; Hansen and his team built one for Earth and concluded that we were poised for major warming from the build-up of CO_2. In 1987 he and his colleagues also published one of the first data sets on global temperature which showed that temperatures were actually rising and probably consistent with the theory of human-caused warming. Outside scientific circles, Hansen is most famous for his 1988 Congressional testimony on the dangers of global warming (requested by then Senator Al Gore) that had been clumsily edited by White House officials skeptical of the science of climate change and wary about exposing the economy to the extra costs of regulating CO_2 pollution.[17]

Why global warming is such a hard problem to solve

From the late 1980s the regulation of global warming gathered steam, and in time I shall fill in those details. But ever since the original work by Roger Revelle and David Keeling little has changed about the key facts. CO_2 is an unusual pollutant because the processes that clean it from the atmosphere run very slowly. The average lifetime of CO_2 emissions is about a hundred years, and some of the processes that finally remove CO_2 run over many thousands of years.[18] The stock of CO_2 builds up in the atmosphere slowly; once it is there the pattern is very hard to reverse.[19]

The torrent of CO_2 emissions from humans has been far larger than the natural chemical and biological processes that permanently remove the excess gas from the atmosphere. That fact defines the central political challenges in slowing global warming in three ways.[20]

First, because the natural processes that clean the atmosphere only work at a trickle, stopping global warming will require very deep cuts in emissions. Even if governments were able to hold emissions constant – itself a heroic act since CO_2 emissions have risen on average 3 percent per year for the last century – atmospheric concentrations of CO_2 would continue to build.[21] Actually stopping and eventually reversing the build-up of CO_2 and other long-lived gases would require reductions of about 50 percent below current levels by 2050 and even deeper cuts in the decades beyond. Put differently, roughly the same rate of *growth* in emissions that has held steady for the last century would be needed in *decline*.[22]

For the foreseeable future – the next couple decades – such deep cuts in emissions are hard to fathom. CO_2 is unlike conventional pollutants because it is intrinsic to an economy powered with fossil fuels. About 85 percent of CO_2 emissions come from (in order) burning coal, oil, and natural gas.[23] Most other CO_2 emissions stem from land clearing, mainly deforestation in the tropics. Burning is a chemical reaction that releases energy by breaking carbon bonds; oxidized carbon is thus an unavoidable by-product of an economy that depends on burning fossil fuels. Very deep cuts in emissions imply the need for totally new methods of burning that sequester the CO_2 safely away from the atmosphere or for an economy that makes only sparing use of fossil fuels.[24] Any scheme that achieves very deep cuts in emissions is likely to involve high costs and will require changing energy infrastructures that are very slow to evolve.

Second, because CO_2 is a long-lived gas its regulation will be plagued by inconsistent time horizons. The cost of efforts to control the pollutants is immediate, but the benefits are uncertain and mainly accrue in the distant future after many years of effort. If the processes that removed CO_2 ran at a swifter pace then it would be easier to line up the incentives for action because expensive efforts would yield more visible returns. The people who paid the costs of regulation would be the same who benefit. Political scientists and economists call this problem "time inconsistency." Policy makers call it big trouble. Normally, political systems favor policies that are exactly opposite to what will be needed for global warming: policies that deliver immediate benefits while pushing costs into the future. That logic explains why governments are usually tempted to under-fund their pension systems and other social benefits that rest on distant promises, and why private companies might do the same if regulators allowed such behavior.

The politics of time inconsistency are ugly. Global warming makes them uglier because the future benefits of avoiding warming are hard to visualize and pin down. There is a long chain of causes and effects starting with emissions of warming gases and ending with harmful effects on humans and ecosystems. Each link in the chain is steeped in uncertainty; the further along the chain the more the uncertainties grow. Indeed, it is hard to know just how bad climate changes could become since global warming involves stressing the complex climate system faster than humans have ever observed. There is a chance – small, but not zero and growing as societies dither – that severe, catastrophic effects could be lurking in global warming. The risk of catastrophe may focus human minds a bit more because the human psyche is tuned to avoid losses, but the sheer abstractness, diffusion, and uncertainty in the benefits that might arise from less warming in the future are powerful inspiration for political inaction.

Third, the slow processes for removing CO_2 explain why warming is a global problem. Any air pollutant that lingers more than 1–2 years mixes throughout the atmosphere. Emissions anywhere cause global warming everywhere, a fact that creates tremendous political opportunities and difficulties. The opportunity is that regulation can take place anywhere, which offers the prospect of searching the planet for the cheapest place to control emissions. By lowering the cost, the politics of slowing global warming could become easier to manage. The difficulty is that regulatory efforts in one country are also easily erased by laxity anywhere. The opportunities and difficulties, alike, create a strong incentive for international coordination in regulating CO_2.

These three political conclusions are anchored in the geophysical facts of global warming. They are unavoidable. They explain why global warming is perhaps the hardest international problem that societies have tried to solve. Unlike regulation of nuclear weapons, the consequences of failure are not so obvious and immediate. And compared to conventional air pollution, the costs are likely to be a lot higher. Unlike most conventional air pollutants, success will require coordination between countries with wildly different interests and abilities to work in tandem. The geophysical basis for this political theory has been known since the 1950s when Roger Revelle and Dave Keeling worked on the CO_2 cycle. But the political energy for doing something about the problem is a lot younger.

Warming is hardly the only global environmental problem. Before we turn to crafting a viable policy strategy for managing this particular problem, it is worth looking closely at the lessons that scientists and other important experts have learned about how to solve problems like this one. I'll call those lessons myths because they are based on visions of how the policy process works that are not rooted in reality. They focus political energy in the wrong places. These myths are so pervasive that I must clear them away before turning to the messier task of building a strategy that will actually work, which begins in Chapter 3.

Myth 1: the scientist's myth

The first myth is that policy will follow a scientific consensus. Belief in this myth leads policy advocates (and their opponents) to invest heavily in finding a scientific consensus (or undermining it). They believe that once the science is "in," regulation must follow. They believe that scientific uncertainty impedes regulation. To be sure, the science is crucially important since it focuses minds on the need to regulate pollutants and it is one guide for setting priorities. But it is easy to overstate the importance of scientific consensus, and a false idea that science sets the tune leads policy makers to make major investments in science-based regulatory systems that don't necessarily lead to successful regulation. This mythical view of science leads to policy processes that easily become disconnected from the reality about how societies manage risks.

The mythical role of science is evident in a case of global regulation where science supposedly played the biggest role: protection of the ozone layer. The conventional story about the ozone layer is that scientists, having identified the problem, also set the agenda for regulation. Once the basic science of ozone depletion was worked out – which took some time and, like the debate over warming, was steeped in controversy about whether the central hypothesis was correct – it was simply a matter of determining the "safe" level of ozone-eating pollutants.

This myth played out in the ozone experience in two ways – both of which are unfolding now in the case of climate change. First was the question of whether there was a scientific "consensus" around the theory that humans could deplete the ozone layer. In reality, most of the regulation on ozone-depleting gases was created prior to any scientific consensus and was heavily influenced by other nonscientific factors. The United States and a few others banned CFCs in aerosol cans in the late 1970s even as the newest science suggested that CFC-caused ozone depletion would not be as bad as previously thought.[25] Yet other countries looked at exactly the same science, reached the opposite conclusion for policy, and refused to regulate any ozone depleting substances. While a ban on CFCs in spray cans wasn't very expensive, it made a major dent in emissions and helped start the policy process that led to global regulation. Meanwhile, the science of ozone depletion was all over the map and there was no consensus view of the severity of the problem. Careful assessments of the scientific research by the US National Academy of Sciences yielded estimates that varied substantially each time the leading experts updated their understanding of the key chemical reactions. In the midst of all that unsettled science, in 1985 a "hole" in the ozone layer was detected over Antarctica, which was a huge surprise since the conventional scientific view was that Antarctica should have the highest concentrations of stratospheric ozone on the planet, not the lowest. All of the key reactions that were thought to drive ozone depletion depended on sunlight, and thus it was assumed that ozone would build up over the Antarctic winter aloft and be highest with the onset of spring. Instead, the ozone hole appeared at spring. Nobody expected such low ozone readings in the Antarctic spring and thus nobody was looking for that early warning. Indeed, the satellites that measured stratospheric ozone were originally programmed to reject low readings in the Antarctic spring.

In retrospect, the ozone hole is seen as a signal that galvanized governments to action. At the time, however, it marked the low point in scientific consensus about ozone depletion. By the fall of 1987 the field was marked by a wider (and wilder) set of theories to explain ozone trends than at any point since scientists first theorized a link between CFCs and ozone depletion more than a decade earlier. Right in the midst of all that uncertainty, in September 1987, governments penned the Montreal Protocol – the first treaty to require reductions in ozone-depleting substances. Only months *later* did the first high-altitude airplane flights into the ozone hole start to unravel the mystery. One data series, in particular, created by a team led by Jim Anderson at Harvard, found the smoking gun that linked human emissions of CFCs and other pollutants to the ozone hole. New science helped keep momentum for regulation. But what is most striking is that the biggest regulatory steps were taken when the science was the most uncertain. This occurred mainly because the decisions to regulate were function of underlying interests and abilities. By the fall of 1987 some of the leading manufacturers of ozone-depleting substances endorsed the need for regulation, and the political support for that move – including the negotiations on a new treaty – hinged on industrial support not just the science. (For more on the ozone treaty see chapter 7.)

The myth about scientific consensus survives in part because nonscientists do not appreciate how science makes progress. Science advances through skepticism; the giants of the field, for the most part, earn their status by showing the weaknesses of their ancestors. The most revolutionary science – the kind that wins Nobel prizes – generally pokes the biggest holes in established truths. That means that true "consensus" in science is rare in a field that changes quickly. Where consensus is feasible it centers on the more mundane centrist assessments. This helps explain why the most respected icons in science are often pitted against a "consensus" view – especially when the consensus is politically popular. The incentives in science strongly favor the curmudgeon who questions, probes, and punctures. Nobody wins a Nobel prize for riding with the herd.

The myth also survives because even where a meaningful consensus is available, scientists don't play much of a role in setting the goals for safety. In the ozone-layer experience, scientists were asked to calculate the level of ozone-eating emissions that would avoid depletion of the ozone layer – by implication, the "safe" level that should be the goal for regulatory efforts. The answer was approximately zero.[26] But that assessment had very little impact on the real regulatory strategy to manage emissions because zero was an inconvenient number – when regulatory efforts began nobody knew how to get to zero in a politically feasible manner. When the United States imposed its first rules on CFCs, it banned the uses that were essentially costless to control – that is, mainly spray cans. (Some of the initial spray can substitutes for CFCs were flammable, which inspired young children of the pyrotechnic persuasion – including me – to create blow torches from spray cans. Why more of us did not explode is a mystery. Luckily safer replacements were invented in time.)

When the Montreal Protocol was signed in 1987 it required only a 50 percent cut in the use of these chemicals by industrialized countries – a goal that was easy for most countries to meet because they had not yet imposed limits on spray cans and other uses that were cheap to regulate. (The US, which had already banned the least costly uses, was expected to make an additional effort – which it did, in part because the environmental community in the US was well organized and pressed for policy change that proved, in practice, to be quite inexpensive.) And just to be sure that these modest first efforts did not accidentally force governments to regulate uses of ozone-depleting chemicals that would be particularly costly or inconvenient, the architects of the Montreal Protocol included an exemption for "essential uses."

Over the years since 1987, nearly all governments have agreed to tighten limits on ozone-depleting substances, including nearly all developing nations that originally were especially skittish about new regulatory burdens. They tightened the screws not simply in response to scientific findings but also because they discovered it would be relatively easy to switch to new chemicals and practices. Governments in the developing countries accepted these rules because the industrialized countries created a fund that paid essentially all the extra cost of all policies to control ozone-depleting substances. From the perspective of every major country, international coordination to regulate ozone-depleting substances worked because it stayed aligned with their interests. For the industrialized nations, it was relatively inexpensive to avoid the many risks they saw in ozone-depleting substances. And for the developing countries, the effort was a no-lose proposition because they were paid to comply. By the early 1990s a scientific consensus had emerged that these chemicals were to blame for the ozone hole (as well as ozone depletion around the rest of the planet). Even then, it was mainly national interests rather than just science that defined policy. What got the world to agree that zero should be the goal was a shift in how the leading countries understood the real costs of regulation and the size of piggy bank they would provide to developing countries for fully regulating the substances. As governments learned more about their interests they adjusted and amended the Montreal Protocol to reflect their new interests.[27]

The lesson that it is interests rather than just science that largely determines regulation has been lost in the debate over global warming. Much of the public debate, especially in the US, focuses on whether scientists agree that warming is happening and humans are to blame. In reality, those scientific questions are largely resolved in the affirmative and have been for a long time. But a simple "yes" isn't very useful. Most of what is really important in climate science will never get nailed down fully. Whether the science is "in" or "out" isn't what will determine how society manages the risks of global warming. Pretending otherwise – believing in a mythical view of science as the starting point for regulation – leads to policy efforts that are organized to influence a regulatory process that does not exist in the real world.

One of my jobs as a graduate student at MIT in the early 1990s was to assist my thesis advisers, Eugene Skolnikoff (MIT) and the late Abram Chayes (Harvard Law School), with a project on the design of more effective institutions to manage the problem of global warming.[28] Part of that job included visiting the UN in New York in 1991 to watch the negotiations on the UN Framework Convention on Climate Change (UNFCCC), which was just taking shape, and distribute our papers to the diplomats. One of the first times I arrived in the giant hall and installed the plastic earphone that delivered diplomacy real time in six languages, the agenda item was a question that became Article 2 of the UNFCCC: what is safe? Master atmospheric scientist Dan Albritton from NASA was in the chair for the United States and offering a tutorial on climate science. Other diplomats were disagreeing and adding square brackets. In the end, their handiwork in Article 2 was intended to provide a compass for the climate treaty:

The ultimate objective of this Convention and any related legal instruments that the Conference of the Parties may adopt is to achieve, in accordance with the relevant provisions of the Convention, stabilization of greenhouse gas concentrations in the atmosphere at a level that would prevent dangerous anthropogenic interference with the climate system. Such a level should be achieved within a time-frame sufficient to allow ecosystems to adapt naturally to climate change, to ensure that food production is not threatened and to enable economic development to proceed in a sustainable manner.[29]

The original idea behind Article 2 was that scientists could identify some "safe" level of global warming. Policy would work backwards from this red line to calculate the emissions cuts needed to avoid those dangerous thresholds. This basic approach was endorsed not only in the UNFCCC but was also echoed in the Kyoto Protocol. A cottage industry of scientific research has sprung up with the goal of finding the red lines. What that industry has learned over two decades is that safety isn't simply a scientific question. And the red lines they draw are irrelevant unless they are connected to a political process that can couple "safety" with real policies that control pollution. So far, a lot more energy has focused on the red lines than on the messier political processes that would actually honor them.

Initially it was thought that limiting atmospheric concentrations of carbon dioxide at 550 parts per million (ppm) would be "safe" – a number that emerged because it was about twice the pre-industrial level and most of the models used to assess the economics of climate change had been run with these scenarios. Then it was thought that safety should be set in terms that were more closely linked to the real change in climate, not least because most nonscientists didn't understand what 550 ppm meant. Thus the goal of limiting warming to 2 degrees above pre-industrial levels emerged. That number was also largely invented. At a time when actual measured warming in the atmosphere was not yet one degree, two sounded manageable and not too dangerous. Two degrees translated into roughly 450 ppm. Today, some scientists think even that number is too dangerous, and nobody can be sure if 450 ppm would really stop warming at two degrees since the exact sensitivity of climate to greenhouse gases is uncertain. Thus today 350 ppm is coming into vogue. Since actual concentrations are already way above that limit – today atmospheric CO_2 stands at about 390 ppm and when other warming gases are included the equivalent is in the low 400s – the implication is that the safety threshold has already been passed.

The setting of long-term goals has occupied a huge amount of attention in climate change diplomacy. For example, starting in about 2005 the global warming issue was regularly a prominent part of the agenda for meetings of the G8 group of industrialized countries. The G8 members have had a hard time agreeing on what each of them should do to regulate warming gases, but they did agree that the long-term goal of such efforts should be about 2 degrees of warming.[30] The

EU has also adopted that number as the central goal for European efforts.[31] A group of environmentalists, meanwhile, are pouring resources into setting the 350° ppm goal, or roughly 1.5 degrees. At best, these goals help frame an agenda for action. But that agenda remains far removed from what most countries are actually doing to control emissions. Serious policy in areas that require complicated costly regulatory reforms does not start only with scientific goals and work backwards to tolerable human behaviors. Instead, it is rooted in a clear vision for the risks that society wants to tame and a practical plan for how it will adjust its behavior. In the Montreal Protocol, the goal-setting efforts were tightly coupled to serious regulatory planning. In global warming, the two are divorced. Thus, oddly, the scientists who work on drawing red lines have been declaring the need for evermore ambitious goals even as actual emissions trends are running ever faster in the opposite direction.

This myth leads to a false policy debate because it frames the climate problem in ways that don't reflect how governments are most likely to manage climate change. Real management will reflect trade-offs – such as between controlling emissions and investing in adaptation – that each government will evaluate differently.

This mythical view that once the science is "in" the scientists should set the goals also ignores the weakest and most complex part of the science in most environmental problems: the assessment of impacts. Indeed, ozone studies that attempted to link lower ozone concentrations with measurable impacts on humans and ecosystems were shrouded in uncertainty until long after the regulatory effort began. But because it proved so inexpensive to regulate ozone-thinning emissions, the difficult trade-offs needed – between tolerating some (unknown) effects of thinner ozone versus the cost of a more serious regulatory effort – never required much public debate. The climate change issue is poised to be different because each country's perceptions of climate dangers are likely to vary much more than in the ozone case, and it is highly unlikely that these questions will conveniently disappear because it proves unexpectedly inexpensive to solve the problem at hand.

The science of climate change is also shifting into a realm that will make useful consensus increasingly difficult to obtain. Two decades ago the Intergovernmental Panel on Climate Change (IPCC), the international mechanism for evaluating climate science, performed its first assessment. That study looked almost entirely at the most likely global effects of climate warming, such as rising sea levels. With each new assessment the IPCC has accurately conveyed a centrist view on those effects that have been studied sufficiently that scientists could agree on a consensus view. Along the way, however, climate science started focusing more on extreme impacts, or what is sometimes called catastrophic climate change. These impacts are a lot more consequential and thus probably more important for policy, but they are also much harder to pin down. Wally Broecker at Columbia, who published one of the first of the major papers on these nasty extremes, called them "unpleasant surprises" in global warming.[32] (Broecker was on the leading edge in many other ways. In a 1975 paper he probably coined the term "global warming.") Broecker was particularly concerned about a sudden shift in the ocean currents. Since then, others have looked at rapid warming of the Arctic region – an unpleasant scenario that is not so surprising any more since it is actually unfolding right now – as well as the possibility of mass extinctions and other impacts.[33] A consensus view on these kinds of impacts is particularly hard because these kinds of risks are intrinsically steeped in uncertainty and elude consensus.

The scientist's myth matters because it has allowed policy makers to imagine that the real process of crafting policy will rely on independent, expert calculation. The reality is totally different. The policy processes that matter most are those that elicit what governments are willing and able to do. And the role of international institutions – which is the topic of this book – is to help governments deliver as much as they are willing and able to implement so that the collective effort better reflects the collective good.

Myth 2: the environmentalist's myth

The second myth is that global warming is a typical environmental problem. Certainly it is true that some of the most worrying effects of climate change concern the impacts on nature. Global pollution might even redefine the meaning of "nature" since CO_2 is so pervasive in the atmosphere that there is no longer any place on the planet's surface where the impact of humans can't be detected.[34] The effects of climate change could be so severe that whole ecosystems disappear. Humans may face god-like questions such as the need to decide which species and ecosystems to protect and which to abandon. The environmental stakes in global warming are huge.

But thinking about climate change as an environmental problem has led policy makers to focus on solutions that don't work. That's because the environmental policy toolkit is poorly matched to the central regulatory task in slowing global warming. Most environmental problems are solved through relatively simple technological shifts and regulatory policies. Most of the politics of environmental policy are handled by ministries that in most governments are peripheral to the real policy challenges of global warming, which are the design and management of a slow, costly, and difficult transformation in how society obtains and uses energy.

One area where the branding of warming as an environmental problem has been particularly unhelpful is in the use of universal policy instruments – that is, international treaties open to every country on the planet. Universalism runs rampant in environmental diplomacy, and the standard arguments for universalism come in three varieties. One is fairness. Agreements that include all players, it is thought, are seen as more representative and thus fair, which might also make them more effective. This view is held widely although evidence for its veracity is uneven. A long time ago, I looked at this question of whether fairness mattered in international environmental agreements and found little evidence for the proposition. The legitimacy that comes from giving all nations a voice can be important, but it comes at a cost of much more complicated negotiations that are more prone to gridlock. That's one reason why most of the world's most effective international institutions began with large doses of discrimination and inequality – including the GATT, the IMF, the UN Security Council, and the G8.[35] I will return to the issue of fairness in Chapter 4 when I look closely at strategies for engaging developing countries that are reluctant to spend their own resources on global problems such as climate change.

The second argument for universalism is that it helps spread norms of good behavior more widely. Universal agreements, it is thought, engage more players and thus are more effective over the long term. The serious evidence for this proposition is relatively scarce in environmental agreements although some scholars have detailed such processes at work in human rights accords. This argument merits attention, but like the claims for fairness, it comes at a huge cost because it puts leaders and laggards under the same tent. In the case of global warming diplomacy it even gives countries that are dead-set against cutting emissions a voice in how those rules are set. I will return to this problem in Chapter 7 when I look at whether inter-national agreements have helped spread useful norms about global warming policy.

Third, universal participation, it is thought, helps avoid "leak-age" – the phenomenon that tight regulations on some countries will cause industrial activities to migrate ("leak") elsewhere in the world where regulations are lax. Environmentalists have rightly worried about leakage – not just because it could undermine the effectiveness of environmental controls but also because if governments are overly skittish about leakage then they will be a lot less willing to adopt costly environmental controls.

For any aggressive climate control regime, leakage is clearly a prob-lem that demands attention. The bedfellow of "leakage" is the hypoth-esis that regulatory efforts will trigger a "race to the bottom" – each country, keen to attract industry, will outbid its competitors by offer-ing the lowest cost, least regulated and dirtiest environment. Although the hypothesis is alive and well, actual research done on races to the bottom long ago showed that the fear of industrial flight due to differ-ences in environmental regulation is largely overblown.[36] The rarity of these debilitating races reflects that many different factors affect industrial location – such as the pool of talented labor, the variation in infrastructure and energy prices – and analysts who focus just on environmental policy tend to forget that those rules are just one of many pressures that will affect where firms decide to invest. In fact, already today there is a substantial ($20–30 per ton CO_2) difference in carbon costs between the US and EU with no evidence that this is affecting industrial decisions.

The interest in universal agreements, which are commonplace among international environmental diplomats, is making it harder to get serious about slowing global warming. Opening the doors to all emitters encourages inaction. The more demanding the agree-ment, the greater the need to tailor the agreement to each country's particular interests, regulatory capabilities, and such. Especially when those countries are already wary about costly regulation – which is true for most countries, including all developing countries that, together, already account for about half the world's warming emissions – negotiations that involve large numbers quickly mire in gridlock. Each new country brings a new wariness and special demands; tailoring the agreement to meet those needs becomes more complicated. And each tailoring affects the needs and interests of other members, which adds to the complication and gridlock. Few environmental diplomats have had to address these kinds of negotiating challenges because most environmental agreements have not been particularly demanding. But other policy areas, such as international coordination of economic policies, offer much more relevant experiences. Focusing on those better models requires setting aside the idea that global warming is, first and foremost, an environmental problem.

Myth 3: the engineer's myth

The third myth imagines that technological innovation leads directly to implementation. Serious solutions to the climate problem will require profound changes in the industrial economy. Engineering will be pivotal to this process. Indeed, a sign that governments are getting serious about global climate change is that the people at the center of policy making are no longer just the scientists who rang the alarm bells but also the engineers who will invent and deploy new technologies, the economists who will assess the costs, and the political experts who will craft schemes that are politically sustainable.

Yet the engineering perspective, which is so essential to technical innovation, is deeply naïve about the factors that govern when new technologies actually survive in the commercial marketplace and the rate at which they can diffuse into service. The engineer's myth is that technological change hinges on imagination and innovation. It leads to unfounded optimism on how quickly the CO_2 problem can be solved because it focuses on the existence of new technologies rather than the long, hard process of actually testing and installing new technologies in the real world.

The engineer's myth reflects both history and temperament. Most of the early history of environmental regulation involved relatively straightforward changes in industrial technology. England's efforts to clean its cities of coal soot in the 1950s inspired government to adopt relatively simple bans on old technology (coal fireplaces) and mandates that required switching to cleaner sources of urban energy – notably oil synthetic gas, and later natural gas where it was available. In the 1970s when governments in the industrialized world started regulating other air pollutants they relied mainly on technology mandates. Where the pollution sources were easy to identify and the technological fixes did not much alter the underlying industrial processes this technology-forcing approach yielded prompt results. In the US, for example, catalytic converters on automobiles helped clear smog from cities and also forced governments to remove lead from gasoline, which poisoned the catalysts and also caused health effects of its own. Catalytic converters and unleaded gasoline diffused into service over about a decade – the same period over which the automobile fleet turns over. As more of these technologies were purchased their performance improved.

So-called "learning curves" describe the relationship between experience using a new technology and its performance. They also lead policy makers to the conclusion that once a technology has been imagined and tested a self-reinforcing process unfolds. As the technology spreads into ever larger markets the result is better performance; in turn, better performance encourages even more widespread diffusion. Most environmental law is based on the theory that regulators should require new pollution sources to install the best available pollution technology, often with cost playing a subsidiary role in that decision; once technologies are in place it is assumed that performance will improve through experience.

Looking back across this history leads to the conclusion that invention and forced use set the pace for technological change. And it allows analysts to conclude that the early estimates of compliance costs are always wrong because once companies start deploying new technologies costs will fall.

That view of history resonates with the generally optimistic temperament of engineers. During most of the period I was writing this book, I lived in Silicon Valley, which is ground zero for successful engineering. Whenever the issue of climate change arose so did a host of clever ideas for making useful energy without all the emissions. Google, which became kingpin of the Valley in those days, poured money into an initiative, "RE<C," that was rooted in the sunny idea that if innovations in renewable energy (RE) were bold enough the problem of global warming would disappear because it would be cheaper than generating electricity from polluting coal (C). Pour

in enough money and market experience and new technologies will become viable. The most enthusiastic advocates for this perspective even calculate the amount of money needed, which is simply the sum of all the areas under all the learning curves.

This perspective helps explain why policy makers focus on ambitious but unachievable goals for transformations in technology needed to solve problems like climate change. They focus too much on the existence of new technology and assume that deployment will take care of itself through technological learning.

Truly solving a problem like global warming doesn't just require a massive infusion of inventive engineering. It also requires careful attention to managing business and regulatory risks that will arise as real firms try to deploy new technologies. It isn't so much a Manhattan project – a crash effort focused on a specific goal without regard to cost. It is more like economic development – a slow, subtle process of profound social change. That change will come not just from inventing new widgets but also the deployment of new systems of widgets and business models that allow the most viable clusters of technologies to become commercially competitive.

History offers a guide for how rapidly this process might unfold. Figure 2.1 shows three large-scale systems of energy technologies that began diffusing into service at about the same time. One is commercial nuclear power in the US; another is desulfurization technologies on power plants; a third is liquefied natural gas (LNG) technologies supplying Japan. Each of these technologies displays the kind of complexity that might be involved with technologies to cut CO_2 – for example, the deployment of coal-fired power plants that include carbon capture and storage (CCS), which is a widely discussed option. The pattern on Figure 2.1 isn't a knife edge where the technology quickly enters into service once the new technology is less expensive than its rivals. Even in these three cases where policy makers gave a strong push to the favored technology, diffusion was slow.

The lesson from the experiences shown in Figure 2.1 is that invention is a tiny part of the history of a technology. The success of a technology hinges on a process of demonstration and then the creation of viable business models for deployment. The examples in Figure 2.1 are for individual clusters of technologies. The full challenge of removing CO_2 from the energy system requires changing clusters

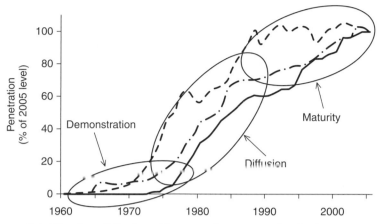

Figure 2.1 The slow diffusion of large-scale energy technologies

The process of early demonstration can take a decade or longer even once an innovation is initially proven. After that is a long period of diffusion (about two decades) and then maturity. Shown are diffusions of three large-scale technologies that entered their "pioneer" market at about the same time – nuclear power in the US (long dash lines), flue-gas desulfurization in the US (solid lines) and LNG in Japan (alternating solid-dash line). The vertical access is the penetration of their eventual market, thus allowing all three technologies to be presented on the same normalized scale. (For example, the nuclear share is the percent penetration into the ultimate US market of 104 reactors.) The result is the characteristic S-shaped diffusion curves that explain the spread of technologies, ideas, viruses and much else that diffuses through contact and experience.

Source: from Rai, Victor, and Thurber (2009).

of clusters – an even slower process because when there are tight interconnections between technologies the whole system is more sluggish and resistant. Conventional automobiles reinforce conventional liquid fuel supply systems; switching to electric vehicles, for example, would require changes in both the vehicles and fueling systems. Success requires unprecedented cooperation between firms and policy makers across multiple industries. That helps explain why there are many dreams for massive technological transformation – such as the Chevrolet "Corphibian" aquatic car launched in 1961 with the aim of erasing the barrier between land and sea, the electric car of the late 1980s, the hydrogen car of the 1990s, and once again the electric car today – and most fail, even in the face of compelling benefits such as ridding dependence on liquid petroleum or taming local pollution. I may be overly sensitive to this problem since the first scientific paper I ever wrote was a close look at the diffusion of liquid hydrogen-powered aircraft.[37] My hypothetical scenarios began with the first commercial flights in 2000. So far, in the real world, nobody has flown a single mile on a commercial hydrogen-powered plane.

Indeed, a sober look at history reveals that *ex ante* estimates of just how rapidly a technology will improve and diffuse are usually wrong. The engineer's myth depends, in part, on learning curves – the idea that pouring in money and experience yields a reliable improvement in performance. The learning curve theory is attractive because it offers a simple guide for policy, which is to spend enough money and guarantee a large enough market for a novel technology that the device will become competitive. But learning curves are nearly always compiled by looking historically with perfect hindsight, and that process leads to severely biased results. History is written by the winners who are most keen to celebrate their success; the losing technologies don't have much to show.

What matters for policy isn't the rate at which winners have improved in the past; it is the rate at which a technology – which might be a winner or a loser – can reliably improve in the future. Such a forward-looking approach is hard to implement because the many fizzles and wrong turns in a technology are hard to anticipate, and the backers of any new technology are usually keen to look only at the winners from history to guide the learning curve policies that will award the largesse of subsidies and guaranteed markets.[38] Even historical examples often don't tell the real story about learning. Arnulf Grübler, an energy expert based in Austria, has obtained data on the history of performance of nuclear reactors in France. Conventional wisdom usually points to the French nuclear as the ideal model for scaling up a technology because the reactors have standard design and were built and purchased by centralized institutions dominated by a culture of engineering performance. Instead, Grübler found that the recent generation of reactors are actually more expensive than their predecessors. There is no learning – in fact, the opposite.[39]

These real-world experiences are inconvenient for the engineer's myth. Steeped in the engineer's myth, policy focuses on invention and on getting technologies to a "breakeven" point where they automatically become viable. But the real tasks for technology policy are much more challenging. Serious technology policy requires choosing among technologies with highly imperfect information about which will really succeed; attention to the commercial risks and regulations that will determine which technologies will actually diffuse widely; and patience, because these processes play out slowly. Crafting policies to deliver such changes is a lot harder than the engineers would have us believe. In Chapter 5 I look in more detail at the approach, including policies, that will be needed.

Conclusions

This chapter has shown two things. First, the main pollutant in global warming is CO_2. The properties of that gas assure that climate change policies will require international coordination and will focus mainly on the energy sector Because CO_2 is intrinsic to fossil energy systems it is highly likely that wholly new energy systems will be needed; inventing and deploying them will be complicated, time-consuming, and involve substantial risks that will take effort to manage. And because CO_2 is a long-lived pollutant the benefits from costly regulations will not appear quickly, which means that much of policy making will need to focus on channeling benefits to the countries that make the biggest efforts so they have a stronger incentive to act.

Second, the policy process responds to many forces, and in the rest of this book I will outline a political theory that can explain how that process is likely to unfold and how it can be most effective. Before I begin, however, in this chapter I have cleared away some simple myths that get in the way. Among those is the view that scientific consensus is achievable or even important. In fact, on the matters most relevant for policy, such as the risks of extreme climate change, a useful consensus is highly unlikely to appear. I have also suggested that it is unhelpful to view climate change as an environmental problem – while many of the effects will be environmental, the most useful models for policy come from other areas of international cooperation and regulation. Yet another unhelpful myth is the view that invention is the key step to solving climate woes. This "engineer's myth" has focused too much effort on the supply of cool new technologies and not enough on the practical strategies for managing business and regulatory risk that will determine which technologies are actually deployed. It has also led to overly optimistic views of how quickly new technological systems can diffuse into service.

With the fundamental properties of CO_2 in mind and these myths cleared from the landscape, in the next chapter I start with the task of building a theory that can predict (and hopefully alter) the real course of policy in this area.

PART II

The three dimensions of climate policy strategy

3 | Regulating emissions part 1: the enthusiastic countries

The problem of global warming requires policy efforts in three distinct areas. One is regulating emissions that are building up in the atmosphere and causing changes in the climate. A second is boosting investment in new knowledge – so that future efforts to control emissions are better informed and so that cheaper technologies for controlling emissions are closer at hand and easier to deploy. A third is bracing for the large (possibly catastrophic) changes in climate that may occur. Each of these problems is related, but each requires its own distinct policy strategy. In this part of the book – Chapters 3 to 6 I look at each of these three policy challenges.

This chapter and the next are about the first and most central area for policy: regulating emissions. Experts also call this "mitigation." The best place to start building a theory to predict how individual countries will mitigate is to look at two main groups of countries. This chapter is about the "enthusiastic countries," and Chapter 4 is about "reluctant countries."

If a reliable world government existed then it might not be so important to look at these two groups of countries separately. The world government would set policy and then firms and people across the planet would comply. But in the real world, international policy is trickier to craft because it hinges on what every nation, individually, is willing and able to implement. Every country will make its own assessment of the resources it is willing to devote to mitigation. Enthusiastic countries are willing and able to spend their own resources on mitigation. Reluctant nations are more skittish because they have other priorities and often don't have the administrative systems in place that would let them regulate polluting activities.

I start with enthusiastic countries because the whole global effort depends on their level of ambition and how they organize their national mitigation policies. Their willingness to spend resources on warming will affect not just what they do at home but also the resources they might channel to reluctant countries to help convince them to make a dent in emissions as well.

This chapter builds a theory to explain and predict what I will call the *structure* of national regulation. Having such a theory is important because it will determine the kinds of international agreements that are likely to be feasible and effective. International agreements that are well matched to the structure of what nations will implement at home are likely to be a lot more effective than those that are blind to the form and content of national policy.

By *structure* I mean two aspects of national policy. First is the level of ambition in the mitigation policies countries are willing to adopt. Ambition depends especially on a country's assessment of the dangers lurking in global warming as well as the costs and opportunities in regulating warming emissions. Some countries are dominated by policy makers who think that regulation will plunge the economy into darkness; others hope to find new green industries in the regulation of carbon and seem less paralyzed by costs. And because regulation affects economic competitiveness, ambition will be a function of what policy makers think economic competitors are likely to implement as well. In this first aspect, the theory I develop claims nothing new beyond what is already widely known. All the best theories of international cooperation begin with national goals, and nobody who has observed the climate debate unfold can avoid the conclusion that those goals vary quite a bit across countries. Indeed, that's how the real world is already unfolding. The level of effort in the EU, for example, is perhaps ten times higher than what the US has been willing to adopt when measured by the economic cost EU and US policy makers have been willing to impose on their economies for the purpose of mitigation.

Second, the structure of national policy includes what I will call *regulatory strategy*. Will governments adopt conventional regulations that instruct firms and individuals to adopt certain technologies? Or will they use market signals? If they use markets, which kinds of market signals will they favor? International relations scholars rarely pay close attention to such questions because they usually treat national regulatory systems as a black box whose outcomes are unpredictable and largely irrelevant to the work of international institutions. And the diplomats who craft international environmental agreements have been particularly prone to make this error. In this chapter I will develop a theory to predict national regulatory strategies. And I will show that the regulatory strategies that governments are most likely to adopt within countries are particularly ill-matched for the system of international emission targets and timetables that climate change diplomats have been struggling to negotiate for the last twenty years. By treating national regulation as a black box – rather than crafting international agreements around how national governments are likely to implement them – diplomats have put climate change policy on a track that is doomed to make international treaties a lot less effective than they could be.

This second point – that the regulatory strategy countries adopt will influence the kinds of international agreements that will be most effective – is a lot less obvious. In this chapter I focus on that question.

A theory of regulation

The problem of warming gases is not unlike many other pollution externalities. Without regulation, it is costless for firms and individuals to emit warming gases. Yet those emissions cause harm to others – in this case, the harm extends to the whole planet.

Policy analysts have well-rehearsed answers for the best ways to fix such problems. Government can create market signals, such as pollution taxes, to encourage emitters to change their ways. Or it can impose conventional regulations such as requirements for polluters to install particular technologies. Because the latter approaches are usually a lot less flexible than using markets, analysts who abhor traditional regulation usually call it "command-and-control" to evoke the specter of a Soviet-style *Gosplan* that aims for central state control over industrial choices. The debate between markets and "command and control" is an old one in the study of regulation.

Nearly always, market-based strategies are a less costly drag on the economy when compared with technology mandates. Indeed, since the 1970s, a host of market-oriented pollution policies have allowed huge savings in the cost of pollution control compared with more prescriptive regulatory approaches, and yielded large environmental benefits.[1] It is not surprising that economists and a growing number of environmentalists have wisely concluded that markets are usually best.

Once in the realm of markets, an important question arises: what kind of market incentive is best? Governments could set the *price* of environmental damage, such as through the imposition of pollution taxes. Or governments could limit the total *quantity* of allowable pollutants, imposing a cap on total emissions and allowing firms to trade emission credits under that cap. By either route, the market is left to sort out the best adjustments in behavior and technology, but the design of the market for each route and its outcomes are quite different. By the first route – known in shorthand as "prices" – government regulators assure that firms reflect a certain cost of pollution in their production decisions. The market itself determines the quantity of emissions. By the second route – "quantities," also known as "cap and trade" – regulators set a bombproof limit on the total quantity of emissions while the market determines the cost that firms (and society) must pay to meet that limit. By setting prices, a government focuses on the *effort* required to control pollution; by setting quantities, it focuses on the *output* from that effort. In the ideal world, the choice between regulating effort or output is a choice that requires looking at which instrument is best aligned with the problem at hand.

Ever since a seminal 1974 paper by Martin Weitzman, economists have elaborated on a robust theory to explain when "prices" or "quantities" are best.[2] The answer hinges, in part, on uncertainty. If government regulators and firms are perfectly informed about the environmental consequences of emissions and the cost of controls then the two strategies – prices versus quantities – are identical. Government sets a price and a certain quantity of pollution arises; or government caps the quantity and the market delivers a certain price. But if the exact relationship between efforts and outputs is unknown then the best choice of policy instrument depends on which errors are most harmful. If the environmental effect of an extra ton of pollution is possibly catastrophic then caps on quantities are the best policy because a cap can help assure that catastrophe is avoided. But if the cost of regulating emissions is highly uncertain and possibly astronomical then the best policy is a price instrument. The uncertainties in these two worlds play out in different ways. When a cap on emissions is imposed, government is sure of the environmental goals that will be achieved but has little idea what it will cost. And when a price instrument is chosen, government can be confident about costs yet have little clue about the level of pollution and environmental harm that will result.

Global warming has uncertainties of both variety, so which dominates? Purely on economic grounds, the evidence strongly favors a price instrument such as a pollution tax. Global warming, to be sure, will create many dangerous thresholds, perhaps even tipping the planet into a wholly new climate or some catastrophe. If we knew where those thresholds were located then some guard rails, such as emission caps, could be helpful in keeping the accumulated emissions from plunging the planet into a nasty canyon. But nobody knows where those thresholds actually exist and thus it is impractical to design a policy around guard rails.

Difficulty in finding those thresholds arises not just because climate science is uncertain but also because the cause of global warming is a very slow accumulation of carbon dioxide in the atmosphere. That's what Roger Revelle demonstrated back in the 1950s, as I showed back in Chapter 2. Tinkering with particular limits on emissions over a few years – which is the main time horizon for most policy because most political systems are not geared to make credible long-term commitments – won't have much impact on the overall stock of CO_2 in the atmosphere. Guard rails on emissions aren't much use because nobody has reliably mapped the dangerous canyons and no particular twist or turn is likely to be harmful.

By contrast, the actual cost of strict emission limits could be astronomical if governments tighten the caps on emissions much more rapidly than companies are able to adjust. Nobody is sure just how quickly firms will be able to adjust in the real world, but much of the evidence suggests that after easy emission reductions are made, further adjustments will be difficult to plan precisely because they will require complicated technological and behavioral changes. In such settings it is much easier for firms to plan around known compliance costs (an emission tax). And when such adjustments are more predictable for individual firms then the overall cost to society is also probably lower. By contrast, the cost of compliance with strict emission limits is harder to fathom and could be intolerably high.

This is the logic that points to emission taxes as the best policy instrument.[3] Indeed, for most problems that stem from infrastructures that are hard to alter quickly according to precise time schedules and require stable long-term planning, the logic outlined here may generally favor a policy rooted in effort (prices) rather than pollution outcomes (quantities).

The theory, then, leads to very clear advice. Governments should favor markets over mandates. And when choosing between types of market instruments, they should favor taxes over cap and trade.

The real world is producing nearly the opposite outcome. Most governments are relying heavily on regulatory mandates rather than markets. And where markets are used, they are based on emission caps rather than taxes. Nearly every government that has tried to create market-based systems for managing climate change has chosen cap and trade. The few exceptions, such as Norway and Sweden that have adopted emission taxes, are in the midst of changing their policies to cap and trade.

Politics explains why the regulatory strategy usually observed in practice violates the best theory. The task of government isn't simply to find the most cost-effective way to regulate emissions. Politicians run governments, and the first task of any politician is electoral survival.

Except in a very few countries, politicians are unable to survive politically solely with the accolades of environmentalists. Deep green interest groups are a tiny fraction of the electorate in most countries. Environmentalism that commands broader public support is fickle because so many other issues like the economy and unemployment drive attention cycles and the interests of voters. Al Gore the Nobel laureate gives rousing advice to protect greenery, but Al Gore the politician facing re-election did much less because the two jobs – Nobel laureate and politician – have completely different rewards. Politicians who want to pass environmental policies need to build a supporting coalition that includes larger swaths of the population. Those efforts will be frustrated if the policy imposes highly visible, painful costs on well-organized groups. This simple political theory of regulation helps explain the kinds of policy instruments that politicians, keen on survival, are likely to favor. Those policies are exactly the opposite of what sage economists advise would be best. I look at two large deviations.

In the real political world, command-and-control regulation, despite its often high costs compared with market-based systems, is highly attractive. Unlike market-based strategies, direct regulation gives government much more control over the visibility and allocation of costs and benefits. Indeed, the political logic that favors regulation by command is nearly as old as government itself. Government channels benefits to well-organized groups and away from the pockets of the unsuspecting. This helps explain why policy makers often favor technologies by setting the market shares (e.g., for wind power) or adopting favorable rules on depreciation and cost recovery (e.g., for nuclear power) – such arrangements are tuned to benefit only well-organized interest groups while diffusing the cost of such choices to the unknowing and poorly organized citizens such as electric rate payers.

The problem with direct regulation is that it can be a lot more costly than more efficient market-based approaches. Whether governments actually choose direct regulation depends on who bears those extra costs.[4] If the costs are concentrated on groups that are well organized and powerful then they may prefer more efficient market-based strategies over command and control. If they know their pollution must be controlled then almost always they will favor a flexible market system over a scheme that gives authority to make decisions about which technologies to install to government bureaucrats.[5]

When market strategies are preferred, which approach is most likely?

The politics of trading and taxation are radically different. Politically, new emission trading systems offer the opportunity to create new assets – emission credits – that are usually not included in government financial accounts. In most countries, the rules of public finance don't impose much discipline on new assets, and that makes it easy for policy makers to give them away for free to well-organized groups. By contrast, reallocation of existing assets is one of the hardest tasks in politics because it requires, by necessity, taking something away from one group and giving it to another – a process that usually leaves losers unhappy and motivated to block their defeat. Well managed, the politics of creating emission trading systems initially involves no taking. It is all giving. Once the emission credits have been allocated the owners of these new assets will organize to protect them and avoid future reallocations. Under some circumstances, those owners may even organize to tighten regulation – stricter caps mean higher compliance costs but also more valuable emission credits.[6]

In theory, tax systems also create opportunities to channel new resources (tax revenues) to well-organized groups. But new tax revenues must come from somewhere. And in most governments money raised through taxes is fungible and thus hard to appropriate reliably. That is probably why the only jurisdictions to create emission tax systems of any consequence have been in governments of small countries where key policy decisions are taken by government bureaucracies that are strong, durable, and trusted. It is not surprising then that Norway and Sweden have adopted carbon taxes. By contrast, for most well-organized political groups in the United States, the mention of carbon taxes is immediately met with the suspicion that politicians will use the tax money for other purposes and will not be given back.

Thus far, I have developed a simple theory that will be useful in predicting the policy instruments that governments will choose. The theory suggests that direct regulation will play a large role and will dominate especially when the groups that pay the cost of action are not well organized. By contrast, market-based strategies will dominate when well-organized interest groups are sensitive to the extra cost that regulation imposes. And the market-based strategy of choice will usually be emission trading because when trading systems begin well-organized groups can seize the valuable emission credits for themselves. The theory also suggests two outcomes that should not be observed: emission taxes and emission trading systems in which all of the permits are auctioned.

In a nutshell, political forces strongly favor policy choices that are exactly reverse the advice of expert economists who favor markets over regulation and prices over quantities.

This simple theory helps explain much of what has happened on global warming policy in the real world. I start in Europe which has done more than anywhere else to develop emission control policies. It is a leading indicator of how those policies might unfold in other jurisdictions. Policy analysts have focused on the novel and important Emission Trading Scheme (ETS), which is the world's largest pollution market. In fact, only emissions from industrial sources are part of the ETS. The rest – more than half of the EU's emissions – are controlled with direct regulatory policies such as standards on buildings, fuel economy regulations, and such. In part, this division reflects practicality – it is easier to run a trading scheme that involves a few thousand large industrial sources than one that spans millions of small emitters such as buildings and automobiles. But the reality is that good market design could easily allow inclusion of these many small sources. The real explanation for this fragmented approach – the use of markets for emissions from large industrial sources and direct regulation for dispersed sources – is political.

Direct regulation prevails in Europe where sources are costly to control (making it beneficial to hide the real costs) and where the firms and individuals who must pay the cost have been poorly organized or actually prefer direct regulation. The owners of buildings are highly decentralized and generally poorly organized; the providers of building retrofit services are well organized and poised to benefit handsomely from direct regulations that require large numbers of retrofits. Automakers, who in theory might lose from more costly regulations, actually prefer direct regulation because that corresponds with the long-standing approach in the auto industry of negotiating fuel standards (and other rules) directly with European governments. Historically, this negotiated rulemaking has helped stabilize the market and may also have raised barriers to entry by new suppliers – all to the benefit of most of the incumbent auto manufacturers. Consumers who will ultimately pay the cost of these rules are highly diffused, poorly organized, and generally unaware of what regulation costs. Most consumers are immobile – their buildings, for example, are literally fixed to the ground – and thus they have few choices but to comply. The best organized of the public groups are environmentalists, and for them the top priority is a policy that guarantees reductions in emissions rather than lower compliance costs. Direct regulation probably imposes a much higher cost on the European economy than a market-oriented approach, but the political benefits that arise from hiding and channeling those costs more than outweighs the extra cost.

Market strategies have been favored in Europe when the emitters are well organized and sensitive to cost. Nearly all large emitters within the ETS are part of well-established lobbies and have a long history of regulation that makes them aware of new costs they might be asked to bear. Industries exposed to international trade, a growing fraction of the total industrial base, are especially sensitive. (In some countries, politically well-organized exporters even obtained special relief from global warming regulations that allows them to avoid some costs that might harm competitiveness.) And most of these large industrial emitters favored emission trading over taxation because a trading scheme that awarded most of the emission credits for free to existing emitters would let the firms keep more of the surplus for themselves. Indeed, when the EU first created the ETS it also barred any European government from auctioning more than 10 percent of the emission credits. In practice nearly all the non-auctioned credits went to existing emitters.

This experience doesn't prove that emitters will always favor trading over taxation, but looking to the earlier history of European efforts to regulate emissions adds more support to the theory. In the early 1990s the EU worked hard to adopt fiscal reforms that would impose taxes on carbon emitters. But the tax failed because its costs were transparent and would have fallen mainly on existing, well-organized emitters such as the coal industry. Politicians knew about this opposition, so they designed a tax scheme that would blend carbon content and energy – a so-called carbon/energy tax – to assure that clean carbon-free power sources (notably nuclear power) would also pay hefty taxes and big emitters (notably coal-fired utilities) would not bear as much burden. But as the tax was broadened an even larger coalition of energy firms mobilized to block it for fear that the revenues would disappear inside governments. Mindful of the bruising experience with the carbon/energy tax, the architects of the ETS required a largely free allocation of emission credits to make the scheme politically much more attractive. Industry quickly aligned around that option in the late 1990s when carbon policy was back on the agenda and Europe struggled to find a politically viable way of meeting its Kyoto obligations.[7]

The few instances where well-organized groups favor price instruments are in the realm of subsidies: policies designed to channel large benefits to political support. For example, one of the main ways that European power generators are reducing emissions is by shifting to wind, solar, and other renewable power supplies. These technologies are darlings of powerful groups such as green parties, but the carbon market, alone, does not offer much incentive for that shift because carbon prices are too low and volatile. Large direct subsidies – so-called feed-in tariffs (FITs) – have made it much easier for investors to back these technologies. To help keep the politics in line, FITs are designed to reward particular technologies and strategies – in most countries there are separate tariff and regulatory systems for onshore wind, offshore wind (where relevant), solar, and energy efficiency. These schemes survive politically because they concentrate benefits on particular niches. For example, one recent estimate puts the value of Germany's solar photoelectric feed-in tariff at more than 700 euros per ton of CO_2 avoided, or more than twenty times the price of CO_2 in the ETS.[8] Smart analysts call for general clean energy policies so that all comers can compete for the same benefits such as subsidies; smart politicians fragment those systems so they align with the organized political forces.[9] Even with a fragmented, niche approach the politics of subsidy are probably harder to sustain than those that favor emission trading. As the total subsidy for renewable power in Europe has risen and become more visible so have calls to scale back the programs.

Other regions also support this theory that direct regulation will dominate when the less well-organized groups pay the costs. In Japan, essentially all of the national effort to control emissions takes the form of direct regulation administered sector-by-sector from a highly powerful government and through established government–industry relationships. In every sector, internal markets are abhorrent because they make costs transparent and by allowing competition they could destabilize existing well-organized firms and their political relationships. The only role for markets in Japan's emission reductions is in markets that the government controls fully – notably, Japan is the largest single buyer of emission credits under the Kyoto Protocol's Clean Development Mechanism (CDM). The government buys CDM credits to assure that if its efforts at home fall short of the 6 percent reduction in emissions required by the Kyoto Protocol that extra credits from overseas projects can offset the difference.

At this writing the US is struggling to craft a federal climate policy, and thus it is not possible to comment on how the politics finally shapes that scheme. However, several states are devising their own policies, the largest in California. The California strategy also follows this same hybrid logic. Most of the California effort takes the form of direct regulation, such as mandates to improve energy efficiency, lower the carbon content of automotive fuels, or utilize renewable power. These regulations survive politically because their costs are hard to observe. (And when those costs have become apparent they inspire backlash. I finalized this book in October 2010 on the eve of a ballot initiative to roll back California's climate policy due to concerns about costs. And in Massachusetts the nation's first large offshore wind project inspired a political backlash when people learned that the guaranteed tariff for this new electric source would be radically higher than existing supplies.) For large emission sources, as in Europe, the emitters that must pay the cost are much better organized and thus prefer a market-based strategy. That strategy, as in Europe, is one that uses emission trading to allocate emission credits mainly to well-organized incumbents.

In Australia and New Zealand the policy strategies are perhaps the most "pure" of any country on the planet. Both countries are adopting economy-wide market signals to reduce emissions. In both cases emission trading is the preferred policy over taxes for the same political logic outlined above: emission credits are valuable assets that can be given to powerful groups to obtain their support. Nonetheless, both countries plan to use market trading across all sectors – in sharp contrast with the fragmented approach in Europe and the United States or the all-regulation approach in Japan. These two cases are admirable for their purity in design – and various Australian plans have even envisioned auctioning the emission credits – but both have found it very difficult to get their schemes into operation because politicians have found it difficult to hold together the needed political support. While there are many factors at work – Australian politics, for example, is plagued by the need to navigate around a clique of powerful politicians who doubt the dangers of global warming – perhaps their troubles reflect that policies have been too cleverly designed by policy analysts and not well enough engineered politically.

Implications for international coordination

So far, I can predict that most governments that limit emissions will use a blend of direct regulation and emission trading. The exact blend will vary by country because the organization of interest groups will vary and the relationship between government regulators and industry will vary. In countries where emitters have a close relationship with government and can use regulation as a way to advance their interests, such as Japan, direct regulation will prevail. For firms in a regulated industry there is little better than a cozy relationship with the regulator. In countries and sectors where the cost of regulation will be politically toxic and can be diffused across poorly organized firms and individuals, the policy outcome will also rely on direct regulation – as in the transportation and buildings sectors in Europe and California. And where costs are concentrated on well-organized groups those groups will either block attempts at regulation (as in Europe with the failure of the carbon/energy tax in the early 1990s, or in the United States and Australia today) or will favor less costly market-oriented alternatives. And when policy turns to markets, the political forces favor emission trading over taxes.

In addition to these variations in regulatory strategy, the level of ambition will vary by country because countries view the dangers of climate change and the consequences of regulating emissions differently. Their "interests" vary.

With this simple theory in hand I can now suggest why the international regulatory strategy built into the Kyoto Protocol has been prone to gridlock. The architects of the Kyoto treaty began their negotiations in 1995 with two goals. One was to set emission targets and timetables for industrialized countries. The other was to impose no obligations on developing countries unless the full cost of complying with those obligations was paid by the industrialized countries.[10] That two-goal approach was the same strategy used in the Montreal Protocol on the ozone layer and is the standard approach in international pollution law. A similar pair of goals inspired the negotiations that had intended to craft a treaty to replace the Kyoto Protocol in time for the Copenhagen conference.

On the surface, these two goals seem to make sense. The goal of setting targets and timetables would seem to align with the need to control emissions. And expecting developing countries to get paid if they undertook costly obligations would seem to align with their interests. In global warming, the size of those payments is likely to be huge. Thus, in Kyoto, the problem of international funding was tackled through the creation of an international emission trading system – the so-called Clean Development Mechanism (CDM). In theory, the CDM offered economic and especially political advantages. If countries were likely to adopt trading systems at home then an international system would offer an even larger opportunity for market-based emission controls. And politically, an international trading would solve the problem of how to pay developing countries for the extra cost of controlling emissions in a way that wouldn't be highly visible as an official government-to-government transfer.

In reality, neither of these goals – targets and timetables nor international funding through emission trading – meshes well with the regulatory strategies that the theory in this chapter suggests countries will actually implement. I look at each in turn, and when we finish eliminating these goals we will know more about the kinds of approaches that might be more feasible.

Implications for emission targets and timetables

When diplomats focus on emission targets and timetables they guarantee that international negotiations won't mesh with how governments will actually implement commitments at home. If most countries relied mainly on national cap and trade systems then international coordination of caps could be sensible. Once each country agreed to its international emission cap then it would be a simple matter to translate that cap into national law. But if national regulatory strategies vary wildly and include a large role for policies such as direct regulation whose impact on actual emission levels is hard to predict then diplomats will find it extremely difficult to negotiate emission caps with any confidence that those limits will be honored. As it is, the job of a diplomat in this area is extremely difficult because it is hard to know with confidence what policies the home government can implement and sustain. Codifying commitments as targets and timetables compounds those difficulties.

During the negotiations and operation of the Kyoto Protocol this mismatch between international commitments and national regulatory strategies was not debilitating because the level of ambition was not particularly high. In Kyoto, most countries agreed to emission targets that mirrored the policies they were already planning to implement. It was easy to manage the national political forces that would arise in response to the extra costs of emission limits. Where compliance costs could be diffused across poorly organized groups, it was done – such as building owners in Europe. Where the firms that would pay extra costs were well organized then a system of emission trading with free allocations of credits was adopted. And if a country's actual emission surpassed the Kyoto target the government could simply arrange the purchase of CDM credits to make up the difference.[11] The divergence between what governments thought they could achieve through national policies and their actual Kyoto targets was not so large that committed governments could not find a way to make the books balance. Japan's total purchase of international credits has been only $10 billion, which is a relatively small amount of money for guaranteeing compliance with the highly visible and popular treaty. The EU governments and firms within the EU have followed a similar logic and purchased international credits to make the books balance.[12]

But this approach will not work when a nation's policies don't for-tuitously stay in line. In those cases, the result is international law that either lacks ambition, is brittle, or both.

The dangers are evident by looking at three countries – Australia, Canada, and the United States – whose diplomats made commitments to cap emissions that were far more stringent than what their governments could actually implement at home. Some of these troubles arose because diplomats promised a lot more than they knew their publics would be willing to deliver and hoped the people would eventually come along – notably in the US. Some of the errors arose because governments were a lot less willing to spend money on global warming policy when their lar-gest trading partners refused to adopt policies – notably Canada, which has been reluctant to join costly treaties that the US does not also honor. But most of the troubles arose because events far beyond the control of national governments caused emissions to rise unexpectedly, which made it particularly difficult for these governments to align international com-mitments (a binding cap on emissions) with real national policies that would be a hodgepodge of market and regulatory systems whose exact impact on emissions would be hard to predict. When domestic realities drifted away from international commitments all three of these govern-ments found it easiest just to ignore the international obligation. None of these three initially ratified the Kyoto treaty. (Australia and Canada later ratified, in 2007, but without viable plans to comply.) And in all three cases the political forces arrayed against regulation of warming gases have been emboldened by the experience of successfully opposing an impractical international commitment.

This implies that the choice of international emission targets and timetables will not determine national policy. Instead, if diplomats want more effective agreements they should consider turning the equation around. The likely structure of national policies should drive the design of international commitments. Creating better alignment between national implementation and international commitments will require a system of commitments that is more flexible and which governments can tailor to their own mix of national policies, and in Chapter 8 I look at how this could be done.

Implications for international emission trading

My simple theory of national policy also helps explain behavior in the international trade of emission credits. That behavior matters because international emission trading has become one of the most salient features of international diplomacy on global warming. It is the linchpin to the second goal of the Kyoto talks, which was to engage reluctant countries in emission controls in a way that didn't burden them with the extra cost. Trading through the CDM was supposed to mobilize the investment needed to meet that goal. International trading was also the linchpin for the talks in Copenhagen and beyond, which were based on visions for even larger financial transfers through private markets.

How realistic are these goals? Answering this question requires looking at how linkages between national emission trading systems create value for the CDM. The CDM is a viable solution to the problem of compensating developing countries only insofar as the credits earned through such projects have reliable value. And the scheme is sustainable only insofar as enthusiastic countries, which are the source of that value, allow large amounts of money to flow through international trading systems.

International trading is the logical extension of an international regulatory system that relies on strict international emission caps and national regulatory systems that are based on national caps. Within each nation firms would trade emission credits to find the lowest cost way of controlling their emissions. Internationally the same logic applies. The logic is impeccable – indeed, one of the most important results from economic modeling in the 1990s when the Kyoto Protocol was taking shape underscored that there would be huge economic advantages from so-called "where" flexibility. That is, give firms the choice of where – anywhere on the planet – to pay for emission controls. (The logic for "where" flexibility extended to "when" and "what" – that is, allow firms the flexibility to borrow and bank over time and to choose the gases and activities that were cheapest to control.) That logic inspires international emission trading.

Indeed, in the late 1990s after the Kyoto treaty was negotiated, many analysts imagined that a large, global emission trading system would emerge as each nation adopted its own trading system to assure compliance with its international Kyoto cap. A vision for global trading assumed that national regulations would converge and harmonize. I'll call this the convergence hypothesis. Most analysts treated convergence as a technical question. With good technical design, interconnected markets converge, which is why buying this book on

Amazon is likely to cost about the same as the purchase on rival web-sites. Politically, convergence is a pretty radical idea because most international law, including the Kyoto Protocol, is carefully crafted to underscore that every nation has its own sovereign right to choose its own policies. If global emission trading is actually the goal then that implies that every nation will be severely constrained in how it implements international commitments at home. And every nation will face the same price for emissions, which means that the marginal effort everywhere will be identical. It wasn't just analysts who believed this. Many of the diplomats in Kyoto also thought they were laying the foundation for global emission trading, which was attractive in part because it helped solve the problem of how to compensate the developing countries for the extra cost of compliance. Most developing countries were more skeptical at first, but many of them changed views once Kyoto entered into force and money started flowing through the CDM.

The experience in the real world has left the convergence hypothesis in tatters. There is no single global price for emission credits. In fact, as countries have tightened the screws at home while others impose less ambitious caps the price of emission credits has diverged. Moreover, rather than welcoming unfettered international trade in emission credits, which was the original vision for international trading in Kyoto, every country that has actually created an internal trading system has led to further fragmentation. Figure 3.1 shows the actual experience with emission trading – both the volumes and prices for emission credits in all the major trading systems that have existed since countries first started tightening the screws on warming emissions.

My theory of regulatory structure explains why divergence is the norm. The fundamental reason for this variation is that the level of ambition varies and thus prices must vary as well. Governments that are deeply worried about global warming and also skilled at managing the visibility and allocation of costs will deliver high prices. Those that are more lax will see lower prices. Figure 3.1 reveals this by comparing the strict emission trading system in Europe with the less robust voluntary US market; the markets of intermediate stringency taking shape in Australia and New Zealand are likely to price between these extremes. Economists rightly criticize this dispersion in prices as highly inefficient, but it survives for the same reasons that

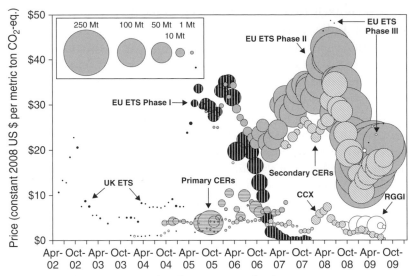

Figure 3.1 The dispersion of carbon prices and volumes

Despite the original Kyoto vision of a single global market, in practice many carbon markets have emerged. The largest is where political interest in controlling emissions is most acute and the institutions best organized – the European Union's Emission Trading Scheme (ETS). The ETS rules have changed slightly over its three phases. As Clean Development Mechanism (CDM) credits – known as Certified Emission Reductions (CERs) – have grown those prices have begun to converge with the ETS, the main market where CERs are sold. The chart shows primary CERs (which are the CERs earned by project originators through the CDM) and secondary CERs (which are converted into legal currency in the ETS and thus less risky and higher priced). The transition from primary CERs (which were the best measure of CDM activity as the market was just getting started) to secondary CERs (reflecting the maturity of the CDM market) is somewhat arbitrary but reflects an important trend: as the CDM matured it encouraged specialization, with project originators focusing on their functions and ETS traders taking over the function of final trading. Also shown are early markets in the UK (now supplanted by the ETS), one semi-voluntary trading scheme in the US (the Chicago Climate Exchange, CCX) and a binding market for the north-eastern US states (the Regional Greenhouse Gas Initiative, RGGI). At the time of writing new markets were emerging in Australia and New Zealand although determining the real price levels in those markets is difficult; a market in the US state of California is also taking shape along with numerous other voluntary markets. Data on the ETS are from ECX, the largest central European carbon market but hardly the only place where such credits are traded. Data governments select regulatory strategies that deviate from the most efficient outcome – they want to control the level and allocation of costs and benefits from regulation.

The need to control national costs and benefits from trading also explains why governments are actively managing the connections between their national emission markets and those in other countries – usually by restricting trade and encouraging a more fragmented market – rather than allowing unfettered trade. The EU has restricted the availability of emission credits from Russia to the ETS on the belief that the Russian credits are mostly "hot air" – that is, they are credits on paper that don't reflect real reductions in emissions – and Russia does not deserve to earn a windfall from emission trading. But it has allowed largely unfettered access to CDM credits despite evidence that many of those are also "hot air" because the CDM creates the extra advantage of channeling resources to more worthy developing countries. Evidence that the CDM has created many "hot air" credits has inspired the EU to explore creating its own system of rules, tighter than the Kyoto CDM scheme, to govern those credits. As that happens international markets will fragment further. Meanwhile, every serious proposal for a federal US emission trading system has envisioned an alternative to the CDM, which means that rather than a single integrated international market the US and EU are likely to have different mechanisms for international trading that overlap only partially. California is designing still another international offsets scheme with a similar logic – lower compliance costs but skepticism about how other countries administer their markets – and other jurisdictions are facing similar pressures. The fragmented outcome is unavoidable in a world where the most consequential market decisions are taken at the national level.

Caption for Figure 3.1 (*Cont.*)

for CCX are reported by CCX; RGGI data come from RGGI auctions but do not include secondary trading of those same credits. CDM data are obtained from an industry group, PointCarbon. (The secondary CER data are from ECX.) ECX and PointCarbon data do not reflect the full market prices and thus volumes shown are representative but not 100 percent of trades. All prices and volumes are monthly unless otherwise indicated. A special thanks to Danny Cullenward for compiling and analyzing the data and helping me understand the markets. This chart is based on earlier versions in Victor *et al.* (2005) and Victor and Cullenward (2007).

The theory of regulatory strategy outlined in this chapter also suggests that fragmentation is likely to rise and a truly integrated international emission trading scheme is unlikely to appear any time soon. Countries will vary in the regulatory strategies they adopt. When the emission trading system is the dominant force then the prices will reflect the real cost of emission control efforts. If two countries with a similar level of ambition connect their emission trading systems through international trade then the unified system will expand the opportunities for real emission reductions. This is the canonical case that makes economic experts enthusiastic about international trade. Yet the canonical case will be rare because the political forces at work within countries will usually lead to large, varied roles for direct regulation. For example, suppose that a country adopts a cap and trade system that covers the electric power sector and also a regulatory mandate that electric utilities invest in large quantities of wind, solar, and other forms of renewable energy. If the renewable energy mandate is a potent force then it will dominate the investment and operation decisions of utilities; emissions will be lower and the cost of those emission controls will be diffused and hidden in the electricity tariff (which is why direct regulation is so attractive to politicians). And the demand for emission credits will be low because, in effect, the emission price does not drive investment decisions. This example is not far-fetched. In fact, every major industrialized country has in place, or is considering seriously, a regulatory approach in the electric power sector that blends direct regulation with market forces. (Even developing countries, notably China and India, are considering these kinds of hybrids.) This contagion is also spreading to petroleum fuels with the rising popularity of low-carbon fuel standards.

In other writing I have called these outcomes "Potemkin markets." They are emission trading systems that look like real markets on the surface but, in fact, are designed to hide the real costs of compliance and to channel resources to well-organized groups. They are markets where prices are artificially low because the real binding constraint comes from regulation rather than market signals. By political design, those low prices help hide the real marginal cost of emissions controls.

National Potemkin markets make a genuine, integrated international trading system unlikely. When Potemkin markets interconnect the result is just a larger volume of trading around prices that falsely understate what the society is actually paying for emission controls. When Potemkin markets interconnect with genuine markets the result is the global warming equivalent of Gresham's Law. The bad credits drive the good ones from circulation. Overall price levels drop to the lowest common denominator. Countries that want to adopt national policies that reflect a greater ambition to tackle global warming find their efforts undermined. Governments know all this because they face the same troubles when they allow international trade in money. It's why true monetary unions, such as the Euro, don't happen unless all countries adopt strict common standards about how they will implement national policies and subscribe to common goals. And it's why governments are so wary about allowing unfettered trade in international emission credits.

The insight that fragmented, Potemkin markets are likely to emerge matters for two reasons. First is that it focuses policy makers on outcomes that are politically feasible. For advocates of a single, global emission trading system the fragmented outcomes observed in the real world are understandably a disappointment; these trading systems are riven with barriers that make truly efficient outcomes hard to fathom. My view is that the appearance of highly fragmented markets was always predictable and an unavoidable outcome in a world where national governments adopt the most powerful rules and few of those governments will choose economically pure policies.

Pretending that integrated global trading is feasible will lead not only to wasted efforts but it will actually undermine international cooperation. Forcing truly unfettered trade will make every nation's national efforts highly sensitive to the least ambitious, least well-administered, and most corrupt efforts of other nations. It will guarantee that emission credits will trade at the zero price and no nation will have much incentive to control emissions. Fragmentation can fix that problem. If governments with the largest and most lucrative emission trading markets set rules that allow linkages only with other well-administered markets then the price mechanism will reward investments that flow into the highest quality projects. In Chapter 8 I will suggest in detail how those market rules could work. Getting serious about this opportunity requires embracing fragmentation and using it strategically. The good news is that most of the power in this strategy will lie in the countries with the most lucrative markets, and those countries also have the strongest incentives to make the biggest investment in slowing global warming.

Second, the Potemkin markets insight explains why the standard strategy for engaging developing countries – to pay them for the cost of compliance – won't work. The hope has been that international emission trading will generate the huge piles of cash – at Copenhagen diplomats focused on $100 billion per year by 2020, mainly from private emission trading markets, as a goal with even larger sums in later years. In a world of Potemkin markets, though, international flows will be a lot smaller, under tighter government control, and a lot less reliable. Markets, by themselves, won't fix the problem of engaging developing countries. They aren't useless, of course. A well-managed, fragmented system offers the ability to channel higher valued incentives to the reluctant nations that make the biggest efforts to control their emissions.

If markets, on their own, can't deliver on the goal of compensating developing countries for the full cost of complying with limits on warming emissions then what's the best way to engage those countries? I take up that question in the next chapter.

4 | *Regulating emissions part 2: engaging reluctant developing countries*

The reluctant countries are different from the rich, enthusiastic nations examined in Chapter 3 for two reasons. One is to do with interests. Reluctant countries have other priorities than spending their own resources to slow global warming. The other reason is low and variable administrative capacity. These countries are "developing" in part because their administrative systems are weak, fragmented, and often erratic in their functioning. In some sectors of the economy, the government has mercurial control – for example, most energy systems in the largest developing countries are directly owned by governments and staffed with government employees. Yet in other parts of the economy, the government is barely able to monitor behavior and implement policy.[1] In such settings, even with strong inducements it is hard for governments to make credible commitments about policies they will reliably implement at home.

Such problems are hardly new in international affairs. Diplomats fix them in two ways. One is by creating incentives that lead reluctant nations to rethink their interests. Those incentives include sticks (e.g., trade sanctions) and carrots (e.g., subsidies for projects that reduce emissions and for administrative capacity-building). I start this chapter by looking at the sticks and carrots that have been deployed so far and showing how they can be made more effective. Sticks are difficult to use because they create many risks. Trade sanctions against countries that don't mitigate emissions can easily touch off broader trade wars that leave people much worse off. Politically, carrots are easier to offer. But if the carrots are offered for too long and get too large they create perverse incentives. Smarter sticks and carrots must play a role in a new strategy to engage reluctant countries.

Part of that new strategy must be reforms for the Clean Development Mechanism (CDM), the biggest carrot that has been offered to reluctant countries. Eventually a credible sunset for the CDM and other carrot mechanisms will be needed so that developing countries don't expect a subsidy whenever they adopt policies that control emissions. A world of permanent subsidy is one that will be plagued by perverse incentives for reluctant countries to avoid even policies that align with their national interests. And dreams of permanent subsidy will make countries especially wary of taking their own initiative to adopt the really big policy reforms that could allow deep cuts in emissions.

I also focus on a second way to make progress with reluctant countries. Many of the policies that will limit the growth in emissions – and in some cases even allow for deep reductions in emissions, such as by slowing deforestation – aren't costly. In fact, many align with these countries' other goals, such as taming local pollution or promoting energy security. I put some numbers on the large reductions possible by focusing on these kinds of policies. I also offer a framework for examining which of these policies will emerge on their own, as governments get smarter about their own national interests, and which will require foreign assistance.

My focus is on interests and administrative capacity because those largely determine what happens in international relations. They largely define why and how the enthusiastic countries must engage with reluctant nations. But I note that fairness points in the same direction. Nobody really disputes the fact that industrialized nations must, in the words of the United Nations Framework Convention on Climate Change (UNFCCC), "take the lead" in controlling emissions. The industrialized nations, on average, have nearly five times the per-capita emissions of the less wealthy developing world. They worry more about global warming and have the resources at hand to make a dent in their emissions. Meanwhile, governments of nearly all developing countries point to the deep unfairness in expecting poor countries to adopt possibly costly policies while other more basic human priorities are unmet. Developing nations account for only a small fraction of the warming gases that have already built up in the atmosphere. However, I am not relying on fairness as a driving force for international behavior because fairness usually leads to vague prescriptions and is a lot less powerful than interests in explaining international diplomacy. For analysts and politicians who are keen to ensure that global warming policy reflects a broader vision of what is just in world politics it is important to start with a clear picture of the emission controls that governments in the developing world are already willing and able to achieve on their own. This chapter suggests that the reluctant countries can do a lot already to help control warming emissions. And the historical strategy of separating the world into two tidy boxes – industrialized countries in one and developing countries in the other, with the former paying the latter for the full cost of compliance – is poorly suited to how these countries can interact and the leverage they have available to control their global pollution.

Better sticks and carrots

So far, the sticks and carrots that have been mobilized in the area of climate change have not had much impact on investment and behavior in the reluctant countries. Could governments design better sticks and carrots?

I will start with sticks, such as trade sanctions and border tariffs. These ideas have been discussed widely, but so far they have never been used. In 2007 the French government suggested using trade sanctions against the United States, for the latter had long been reluctant to undertake any serious federal controls on emissions. If France had actually deployed trade sanctions the result probably would have been a crisis for the WTO, which is largely silent (but generally unsupportive) on the use of trade sanctions to force other countries to adopt international environmental standards. Among the most widely discussed sanctions are various border tariff adjustments (BTAs). Most serious plans for US legislation on climate change have included BTA schemes to penalize countries that did not implement substantial controls on emissions.[2] While France had been worried about a laggard America, the US Congress is worried about developing countries – China in particular.

When I began writing this book my strong assumption was that border tariffs were a bad idea, and absent border tariffs there were no other major sticks that countries might practically use. That meant that efforts to engage developing countries should concentrate on carrots. Indeed, policy in the real world has concentrated on carrots, and I will turn to that in a moment. My bias against tariffs came from earlier research I had done in a very different area of the WTO: disciplines on food safety standards. It was clear that countries were accustomed to using food safety standards as hidden barriers to trade, and with heroic efforts the WTO could smoke out legitimate food safety standards from those that were just hidden protectionism. But the process of smoking out was difficult and unreliable even though food safety was one of the areas where protectionism was easiest to detect. Countries have lots of food safety standards, and it was a fairly simple matter to compare food safety from one area with that of another. If there were wild differences in protection then that was cause for suspicion. But more subtle differences were very hard to spot and that's the situation most analogous to global warming. Especially if governments made heavy use of regulatory mandates rather than just market forces – a likely outcome, as I explained in Chapter 3 – then the potential for protectionist mischief was huge. Indeed, most national governments would face strong pressure to protect and advance national industries, and complex regulations offer a myriad of ways to do that. Worse, most governments would suspect other nations of using regulation in the same way. If trade sanctions were allowed to punish such behavior not only would it be hard to decide which countries were violating the rules but sanctioning could easily get out of control. Protectionism – real and imagined – could trigger trade wars and harm to the WTO, which is an institution that is already in a fragile state. There is nothing that western countries have done more to improve the global welfare – especially in the poorest nations – than to actively liberalize trade in goods and services, notably through the WTO.

I've changed my views. The danger of carbon protectionism still looms, and careful studies of the economics of border tariffs show they could be very costly.[3] Politically, however, they are essential. It is hard to see how reluctant countries will face the right long-term incentives to control emissions unless there is a cost – one that will appear reliably, starting perhaps in a decade or two – for countries that drag their feet. (That cost applies to countries of all types that drag their feet – including the US.) A recent major report from the US National Academy of Sciences as well as a bipartisan consensus on climate change from the Council on Foreign Relations draw similar conclusions that cautiously support the use of BTAs.[4] It is inevitable that as the issue of climate change rises in salience that trade measures will play a larger role; it is also inevitable that the WTO will require reforms to accommodate these new demands. Other trade institutions, such as bilateral trade deals and free trade areas, will also require reform in time. Serious planning for those reforms, including a vision for how those sanctions could be kept in check to help avoid protectionist trade wars, is overdue.[5]

Nonetheless, it will be hard to design a smart scheme of sticks, and great care will be needed in threatening and using them. So that leaves carrots.

Carrots have come in two varieties. The first is the well-worn system of international carrots: government-to-government transfers, such as official development assistance (ODA). Although it is known as "development assistance," in fact there are many purposes for ODA funding beyond just development. Perhaps half of the US government's aid budget, for example, is targeted for countries where there are special US interests at work in addition to the pure task of economic development – for example, Afghanistan, Iraq, Israel, and Egypt. In most countries as well as most international institutions that manage development assistance, such as the World Bank, concerns about global warming have been added to the long list of other goals that aid is supposed to help deliver.

While the practice of foreign aid is complicated, for my purposes one simple, central insight is crucial: ODA is largely irrelevant. Much of the drama at UN conferences on global warming focuses on the size of official new funding promises, but there are two reasons why those dramas have almost no impact on the central political challenge of engaging the developing countries in controlling emissions. First, ODA budgets are largely fixed and roughly flat ODA budgets are largely fixed and roughly flat over the last two decades (net of one-time debt relief payments). Adding new missions, such as global warming, requires that governments relax their focus on other missions, such as pure economic development. One of the results from research that has looked at the effectiveness of foreign aid is that aid programs don't work well when they are crowded with many missions that make it harder to measure performance and hold governments accountable. Most aid experts and suppliers of development assistance, such as the World Bank that operates a large program of foreign grants in addition to its even larger traditional government lending program, know this. That's why they resist creeping new missions. They don't think global warming is an unworthy cause, but they think economic development is even more important. Delivering on development is hard enough without focusing on many other goals at the same time. And the recipients know this, which is why international agreements that call for more ODA to help developing countries with new missions such as controlling warming gases usually include the phrase "new and additional." The recipients want a bigger pie and they rightly suspect that the pie won't enlarge as quickly as the growing list of new missions. Looking to the future, my guess is that foreign aid budgets will remain largely fixed because in these hard economic times and with aging populations on the edge of retirement, western donor governments face an extraordinary set of national demands on public budgets and severe constraints on new tax revenues. Except in a few heroic countries, aid isn't very popular, and even the heroic providers of foreign aid such as the Nordic countries, Germany, Canada, and Japan face tight constraints on what their governments will deliver.

Second, development assistance isn't that relevant for emission controls in the largest and most rapidly growing reluctant nations. Many of these countries are already sufficiently wealthy that donors don't provide them with much foreign assistance – for example, Brazil and China, which have historically been large recipients of foreign aid but are now rapidly exiting the aid rolls. (Both are still prominent users of World Bank and other development loans, but that's partly because most lending of that type must be repaid and development banks that have commercial lending as one of their goals need reliable borrowers to stay fiscally afloat.) Most of these countries are growing rapidly because economic reforms have empowered the private sector to invest in new factories, cement plants, electric power generators, and other hardware of industrial development that yield large new emissions. Gaining leverage over those new emission sources is mainly a function of creating new incentives that influence private investors, rather than government-to-government mechanisms. Even in the poorest of these large reluctant countries most of the growth in emissions comes from the private sector – for example, in India where a rising fraction of new coal-fired power plants are being built by private companies or by the largest state-owned power supplier that is managed much like a private company. These are credit-worthy borrowers that have many options for financing new investment. If western donors impose too many constraints on the kinds of projects they will finance then these borrowers can turn elsewhere. Development assistance – that is, direct foreign aid rather than commercial-like lending – plays a much bigger role in countries and sectors that have fewer options.

Nobody has done the careful analysis needed to know exactly what fraction of world emissions might be leveraged by traditional development assistance, but I would be surprised if it were more than one-tenth. Quite simply, poor countries with weak industrial sectors don't emit much, with a few exceptions such as deforestation. And even in these exceptional cases the real leverage available through official government assistance is probably small. For example, deforestation in the Congo is worrying, but that country's forests are so lawless that it is hard for anyone – especially outside funders who are already struggling to make development assistance work for development – to make much of a difference.[6]

Although official development funding probably doesn't much matter for the warming problem overall, the small resources that have been targeted to specific climate change projects in developing countries appear to have been used well. Developing countries have been worried that new climate change priorities would supplant traditional funding for other purposes. Donor nations have worried that traditional systems aren't well suited for new missions such as climate change. Thus governments have crafted special new funding mechanisms. The model for these efforts is the highly effective Multilateral Fund (MLF) of the Montreal Protocol. Following that model, the UNFCCC created a dedicated "financial mechanism" to transfer resources to help countries build their capacity and control emissions. That financial mechanism has transferred a total of about $2.34 billion over its entire nineteen-year lifetime.[7] That program has many important accomplishments, to be sure: it helped jump-start developing country assessments of climate impacts and also reporting of data. It has helped build government capacity in other ways, and it has paid for diplomats to attend meetings that help spread useful information about climate politics and policy. As befits government-to-government funding, these programs have worked best when they are focused on particular missions that governments readily control – such as the training of government officials and the creation of government-managed data reporting systems. All of these are worthy goals and should continue, but they don't have much direct influence on emissions from the largest reluctant nations. And the scale of effort is small in perspective. The entire investment cost for a modern multi-unit coal-fired power station is about $3 billion (with wide variations depending on local circumstances such as labor, material, and land costs), or more than the entire sum of official UNFCCC money spent on climate change in developing countries over the last two decades. The world builds the equivalent of 10–30 such stations every year and they are the single largest source of likely new emissions of warming gases over the coming few decades.[8]

Because official government-to-government funding is unlikely to grow much, a second variety of carrot is proving to be more important: international trade in emission credits. As I have already shown in Chapter 3, most of the enthusiastic countries are creating national emission trading systems, and all of those national systems envision links to developing countries where it is less costly to control emissions. Since developing countries don't have caps on their total emissions, these links all take the form of credits that can be earned for particular actions, such as investment projects in low emission energy technologies. The largest of these international credit schemes is the Kyoto Protocol's Clean Development Mechanism (CDM). Nobody is sure just how much financing the CDM has mobilized because there isn't a single market in which all CDM transactions are tracked and priced, but some of the most bullish estimates put the international transfer at perhaps $50 billion over the lifetime of the Kyoto Protocol.[9] That would make the CDM ten to perhaps twenty times more important as a flow of funds than the official UNFCCC financial mechanism. Equally, the CDM dwarfs government-to-government ODA spending that has been targeted to climate change, not least because much of the ODA spending is appropriately devoted to the poorest countries where emissions tend to be small. Increasingly it concentrates on ways to help those countries adapt to climate change. (I will deal with the problem of adaptation later – in Chapter 6.)

The same kinds of relationships are likely to hold in the future – government-to-government funding will remain dramatically smaller than the private sector flows. The Copenhagen Accord, for example, was barely able to commit industrialized countries to about ten billion dollars per year in new government-to-government funding while envisioning that total funding by 2020 would be on the scale of $100 billion per year.

Not only is the CDM much bigger than official government-to-government climate change programs, such as the UNFCCC's financial mechanism, but it is designed to influence investments in the private sector that offer potentially large leverage on emissions. Private investors are likely to face the strongest incentive to make a scheme that offers low-cost emission controls actually work, and often private firms have the best information on how to control emissions at the least cost. Crucially, a private sector scheme offers a huge political advantage because it doesn't rely on official government funding. In a world of flat and constrained ODA, budgets schemes such as the CDM offer, in theory, much greater potential for scaling and remaining politically viable.[10]

Thus thinking about better carrots requires starting with the CDM. It isn't the only system for international climate change transfers that is linked to the private sector. But it is the biggest; it has many supporters; and any future scheme for transfers is likely to be modelled in part on the CDM. Getting started in the search for better carrots requires looking at whether the CDM actually works.

Not surprisingly, firms and governments in the EU and Japan are the biggest suppliers of funding for CDM projects for they have the most stringent Kyoto obligations. (If the US had joined the Kyoto Protocol most economic models predicted that it would have been the largest player in the CDM. Today, without US demand, prices for CDM credits are probably a lot lower than they would have been.) In 2008 EU governments and firms cashed in 80 million tons of CDM credits toward complying with the Kyoto Protocol, and while nobody is sure exactly what those credits are worth, the scale of transfer that year alone was to the order of $1 billion.[11] The total market, however, is much larger because most CDM projects are still at an earlier stage – their credits have not yet been cashed in and retired – and many backers are banking credits for future use when they are likely to be even more valuable.

A few years ago just as the CDM was taking shape, a colleague at Stanford, Michael Wara, and I tried to figure out if the CDM was actually having its intended impact on emissions. Michael had already written a paper showing that as the CDM got started, private investors flocked to an odd set of industrial gases that were thousands of times more potent than CO_2 and thus possibly thousands of times more attractive for earning offset credits under the CDM.[12] Michael found that it was easy under CDM rules for firms to pretend that they would not install the latest pollution control technologies – which would largely eliminate these industrial gases – and then request large numbers of CDM credits when they actually installed those same technologies. Because these projects were easy to monitor they were prized by governments and firms, especially in the EU where the credits could be used within the EU's emission trading scheme and where governments and firms were particularly nervous about finding ways to comply with emission caps in a cost-effective manner. For many EU governments the Kyoto commitments (and the legal instruments that were used to implement Kyoto into European law) were highly visible politically. Compliance was essential. If local policies could not guarantee emissions would be below the cap then obtaining a bank of CDM credits was the only way to assure compliance.

That these powerful gases would distort the CDM was easy to predict because for a long time it was obvious that a much better way to handle these gases was to target them directly using a program just like the one that had been so successful under the Montreal Protocol. Nearly all these emissions came from a small and well-known set of sources; in fact, some of those sources were already regulated under the Montreal Protocol. The total cost for eliminating them would be small – perhaps to the order of $100 million, or perhaps even less since the technologies for destroying the gases were widely available.[13] Back in 1997 when the Kyoto Protocol was taking shape, geophysicist Gordon MacDonald and I built one of the first models that made it possible to project emissions of these industrial gases, and from that exercise we readily concluded that the Kyoto treaty would be much better off by tackling these gases separately – because they were so cheap and easy to regulate – rather than commingling them with the much harder, longer-term and costlier effort to control CO_2.[14] But that argument fell on deaf ears in part because commingling all the gases in the Kyoto treaty made it easier for governments to pretend they were doing more to slow global warming through the Kyoto treaty. Putting all warming gases in a single basket made the industrial gases fungible with short-lived gases such as methane and with the most important warming gas (CO_2) even though these gases had distinctly different properties and politics. Many economists loved this approach because it produced more flexibility. And the diplomats loved it even more because it allowed them to set bold targets for emission controls that would be easier to honor on paper. MacDonald and I warned that the flexibility came at a huge cost because nobody really knew how to set the exchange rates that converted the gases into common units and the gases were so easy to regulate that commingling would distract from the central mission of managing CO_2.

As we feared, when the Kyoto treaty lumped all the gases into a single basket practically no major player in the new CDM had an incentive to reveal that the system was providing massive numbers of credits for emission reductions that were nearly costless to implement and would have happened anyway.

When Michael's work first came out, it caused a firestorm of criticism for the CDM. The CDM's most ardent supporters were extremely defensive, and the reactions revealed the central problem with the CDM. The fundamental political logic behind the CDM was to move the cost of resource transfers off government budgets. That meant that the system, by design, ran with an administration that was under-funded and had strong built-in incentives to encourage off-budget transfers without much scrutiny of whether the transfers were actually doing much to slow global warming. Independent oversight was weak and erratic. The Kyoto treaty created an Executive Board that would manage the CDM, but inside the UN system, the Executive Board was initially staffed with diplomats chosen with an eye mainly for regional diversity rather than skill. Administrative rules, such as on conflicts of interest, that were standard fare in well-run regulatory bodies were alien and thus never really settled. And the Executive Board never built the capacity to regulate individual CDM projects – instead, it empowered independent verification agencies and brokers to do most of that job. Since project sponsors paid the fees, the verifiers soon figured out where their toast was buttered and a huge surge in CDM projects pulsed into the system with no clear scheme in place to figure out which were real and which were bogus. Worse, since the CDM was based on the idea that credit should be awarded only for the difference between the level of emissions that would have occurred otherwise (the so-called "baseline") and actual level of emissions, host governments soon figured out that the best strategy was to manipulate local policies so that hypothetical baselines would be high. The higher the baseline and the more seemingly irrational the project, the more likely it was that CDM credit would be awarded because in those circumstances the Executive Board, the verifiers, and the project sponsors could most easily pretend that the project was delivering tangible results. Some firms emerged with the goal of investing only in high-quality CDM projects, but that business model was hard to sustain when so much of the rest of the industry sought the least common denominator.

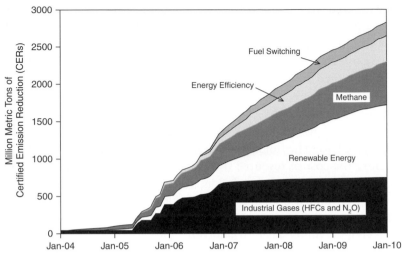

Figure 4.1 The Clean Development Mechanism (CDM) "pipeline"
The chart shows the emission reduction credits (known as "CERs") expected from projects either undergoing or having completed registration with CDM administrators. Actual issued credits are likely to be lower as some projects may be rejected, but the exact relationship between credits in the pipeline and final delivery depends on a number of regulatory decisions that are not always predictable. The figure is redrawn from UNEP Risoe data (http:// cdmpipeline.org/) with the assistance of Richard Morse and Gang He.

As shown in Figure 4.1, the early years of the CDM pipeline was dominated by industrial gas projects. Over time, other projects have accounted for a larger share. Today, projects around renewable energy – mainly hydro and wind power – are rising rapidly in importance.

When Michael and I looked at the whole pipeline of CDM projects we found it very hard to assess whether credits were being given for projects that were truly additional in their investment and reduction in emissions. What we did see was lots of evidence that host governments and project sponsors were getting very good at gaming the system, for example, by adopting policies that would inflate their baseline. And we were skeptical that an under-funded CDM Executive Board would ever know (or care) it was being hoodwinked. It would be too difficult, sitting in Bonn where the Executive Board had its secretariat, to know if governments in Beijing, Delhi, or Pretoria were twisting their local rules to make it look like projects that would have happened anyway should get CDM credit.

To test our suspicions we started looking at small clusters of projects in much more detail. We looked, for example, at all the projects for hydro electricity, natural gas, and wind in China. China was the single largest market for CDM credits. (It still is, by a wide margin. In 2009 it accounted for 72 percent of the CDM credits generated.[15]) And these kinds of energy projects were growing rapidly once the CDM moved beyond the industrial gases. We found that nearly every project in the whole country was applying for CDM credit. That was a warning flag because it suggested that China was claiming it would make no effort to deploy natural gas power plants and renewable electricity technologies without the CDM. From our other research on the Chinese energy system we knew that was wrong. There were similar warning flags around the world.[16] More recently, other colleagues in the research group I created at Stanford started looking even more closely at Chinese wind power projects and they found the same story – Chinese officials were setting the country's official wind tariffs to make these projects look unattractive on paper, which would boost their chances for getting CDM credit.[17] Yet China would have built most of those projects even in the absence of the CDM scheme.

When we published our findings another firestorm erupted, and this time it included investigative reporters – notably Jeff Ball at the *Wall Street Journal* – who started drilling into particular projects and earning a good name for free press. Everywhere they and we looked, it was hard to find real evidence that CDM credits were genuine.[18] In parallel, I ran my own unscientific study. As part of other research projects and teaching, I was dragging my students around the world visiting industrial sites to see how managers operated refineries, power plants, and other facilities. Fortuitously, those sites were also just the kinds of places where major CDM projects might occur. So we imposed a gag rule: whenever visiting a site where we knew the managers were thinking about claiming CDM credit, nobody on our team was allowed to mention the CDM. We would meet with managers and strategists and talk with them about their investment plans and wait to see when CDM arose as a driving factor. So far, that's never happened. It's not a very scientific approach because the information is only good if our sample of industrial visits isn't biased, and we didn't know whether that was true. But having looked at the CDM from many angles it's hard to escape the conclusion that the system is severely broken. My guess is that about one-third to two-thirds of CDM credits don't represent real reductions, but I could be wrong. Although it is unlikely to be less than one-third, it could be a lot more than two-thirds.[19]

The CDM experience reveals something important about incentives. Carrots can be helpful – especially when there are no sticks – but administration is essential. When governments were paying for carrots, such as in the Montreal Protocol's Multilateral fund, they knew how to administer the system and had a strong incentive to do a good job. When they delegated such functions to other agents the incentives for performance weakened. Only once the system was up and running did academics, journalists, and NGOs discover that the CDM was generating large numbers of bogus credits, but even then the vested interests in the system were so strong that it has been extremely difficult to adopt the needed radical reforms. Success with an international scheme like CDM requires a carefully designed international administrative system and, ultimately, hinges on the interests and ability of national governments to make it work.

I draw four conclusions about how to make carrots work better. First, official government-funded programs are probably already at their maximum in size and they work best when focused on things that governments control directly. Much of the drama at UN conferences is about how to make these official programs a lot bigger, but all the signs of reality suggest that goal is neither practical nor desirable.

Second, most of the resources for emission controls in reluctant nations will flow through offsets mechanisms such as the CDM. Those mechanisms are not ideal – they are intrinsically difficult to administer, laden with transaction costs, and purveyors of perverse incentives. I am particularly worried that such schemes encourage countries to inflate their baselines and might even lead some governments to avoid national policies that would be sensible because by holding out they think schemes like the CDM will pay them the cost of adjusting to a new policy. These problems put big warts on any international offsets scheme – whether the CDM or future schemes that governments are contemplating. But for now such offsets schemes, warts and all, are the only practical carrot available at a large scale. Because they are deeply flawed and they create perverse incentives the longer they exist, these mechanisms should be used only on a transition basis. A credible sunset period is needed – with early sunsets for the wealthiest of these countries such as Brazil and China (2020–2025) and later sunsets for the others. Oddly, there has been no serious diplomatic attention to sunsets because there isn't a political constituency that favors that outcome. Industrial emitters like offsets because they lower the cost of compliance even if badly administered offsets don't do much to slow global warming. Governments of enthusiastic nations like them because they make it easier to guarantee compliance with emission targets, and governments in the reluctant countries like the investment. The NGOs along with the governments in the most enthusiastic countries need to rethink their strategy on offsets and demand much higher quality and also sunsets. With their support, an industry that backs good offsets will have an easier time establishing itself in the market and pushing for the kinds of reforms that will make offsets more effective.

A full-blown theory of the sunset is beyond the space I have here in this book, but most likely the best sunsets will include both a date and a volume of credits so that investors are encouraged to act early and so that the arrival of sunset is more credible and easier to predict. Credibility is one of the hardest things to establish in international law, and thus the largest buyers of emission credits should write these sunsets into national law as well – to make it extra clear to investors when the sunset will arrive and to embolden interest groups that will defend the sunset if there are efforts to change the terms. The ultimate presence of sticks on the same time horizon as the sunset will also help keep the incentives in line.

Third, at the time of writing, it isn't clear which offsets rules will perform best. The CDM has revealed deep flaws that are hard to fix because the intergovernmental system of administration is not flexible and has built-in incentives to resist reform. Some alternatives to the CDM are emerging as well, and these will no doubt have their own flaws. The lack of a clearly superior solution suggests that a monopoly is a terrible idea. Multiple offsets systems should be encouraged – each operating with a basic set of floor standards – so that various ideas can be tested. And the countries that care the most about global warming should set strict national rules for offsets. If those strict markets are also large ones – for example, the US, which will develop its own offset rules distinct from the CDM – then national rules will encourage a "race to the top" in offset quality because only the highest quality offsets will be legal tender in all markets, including the most lucrative markets. (The present gridlock in Washington on climate change suggests that California and other states will need to play this role in the offsets market).

Similarly, instead of seller liability rules (which dominate the CDM and other Kyoto trading mechanisms) a system of buyer liability would create stronger incentives for buyers to check the quality of emission credits and for ratings agencies and the other quality-focused institutions that are abundant in the debt markets to emerge around offsets as well.[20] Most analysts and most of the major players in the offsets market abhor this kind of thinking because they want the largest market possible with the fewest restrictions and the least fragmentation. (That same logic leads most analysts to abhor fragmented national carbon markets, as I discussed in Chapter 3.) My conclusion is exactly the opposite: fragmentation, buyer liability, and a multiplicity of markets is the only way to experiment in a novel setting where the best answers are unknown. Moreover, fragmentation can help avoid the race to the bottom that looms over the offsets markets and which the checkered history of the CDM reveals is a big threat.

Fourth, making better carrots will require stricter rules – starting with the CDM and extending to all offsets mechanisms. That will necessarily laden the mechanism with higher operational cost and will narrow the niche in which the CDM and other offsets systems can operate. This idea of much stricter rules and tighter administration, which I favor, has come under heavy criticism by governments and firms that fear a tighter system of administration will radically shrink the offsets market. Their fears are understandable, for a smaller offsets market will expose the enthusiastic nations to higher compliance costs and will shrink the investment that flows into reluctant countries through offsets mechanisms. But these fears are easily overstated. Economists who have modeled how offsets markets might function in a world of high transaction costs show that the opportunities in international offsets are so large that a better system of administration won't fundamentally alter the economic advantages.[21] The best policy solution to fears about compliance costs isn't to undermine the integrity of international offsets but to change the design of national emission trading systems to make compliance costs easier to predict and manage. Countries that have binding caps on emissions have used offsets as a "safety valve" to keep costs from spiraling out of control – that is especially evident in the EU today where governments and firms are buying large numbers of

CDM offsets to hedge against future compliance costs. This error in market design has created perverse incentives. Buyers of these credits have the best information on whether or not credits are bona fide, yet they also have the strongest incentive not to reveal that information because offsets are their only means of managing compliance costs. A better safety valve – notably, a price cap on emissions – would remove this perverse incentive.

Beyond sticks and carrots

Better carrots and sticks can help change what reluctant countries are willing to do, but even highly successful efforts on the carrots and sticks fronts will have only a modest impact. In the best of circumstances, sticks are hard to use. Better carrots will require massive reforms of the CDM and would benefit from the creation of alternative, competitive offsets schemes. Even in the best of worlds, however, international off-sets schemes will be difficult to design and administer because baselines are hard to evaluate and the problem of perverse incentives is unavoidable. Mindful of those troubles, the best-designed offsets systems should include a credible sunset arrangement. If investors and host countries know that offsets are truly a transition measure they will focus on transition projects only; perverse incentives will be fewer.

Today, the CDM appears to encourage on average less than $10 billion per year of new investment. As the US and other jurisdictions create their own offsets markets and reforms tighten up the administration of offsets it is hard to see total new investment in offsets exceeding perhaps $50 billion per year.[22] (That does raise the question of how western governments will honor the promise in the Copenhagen Accord of supplying $100 billion per year of new finance to developing countries. Broken promises are commonplace in international diplomacy, and I will revisit that problem in chapters 8 and 9 when I look at what the world's most powerful nations might do to increase the credibility of climate commitments.) I am skeptical that even that level of finance can be sustained – especially if the idea of sunsets is adopted – because more people are asking the kinds of questions that Michael Wara and I have asked of the CDM. There are small islands of serious investment activities – some connected to the CDM and others following their own stricter rules. Hopefully those will grow, but that growth requires patience and is easily derailed by other factors, such as the turmoil in the world financial markets and the collapse in carbon prices that followed the world economic meltdown in 2008.

Fifty billion dollars per year of carrots sounds like a lot of money, but it isn't in the energy industries that account for most warming emissions. The International Energy Agency (IEA) projects that the total energy sector worldwide will require $26 trillion in investment over the next two decades (through 2030) just to sustain a business-as-usual trajectory. Another $11 trillion in investment would be needed if the energy sector were transformed on a path consistent with stabilizing global concentrations of CO_2 at 450 ppm (roughly equal to about 2 degrees of warming). That extra spending for the 450 Scenario, as IEA calls it, is based on models that assume governments and firms behave optimally; one thing that is clear from this book is that politics makes it hard to be economically optimal, so the real investment needs may be even greater. These cumulative numbers are huge; they dwarf the flows that can reasonably be expected under the CDM and other offset markets. In the IEA scenario the extra investment needed to reform the energy system on the 450 Scenario is $400 billion per year in 2020 (mostly in developing countries) and three times that in 2030.[23] Today, China's electric sector alone spends about $100 billion per year on power plants and transmission lines.[24]

Finding more leverage

At best, a well-designed and vigorous system of offsets will have influence only at the margins, and the overall influence is likely to be small. Indeed, by design well-administered offsets schemes are tuned to work only at the margins on discrete projects that represent only truly additional investments. Big dents in emissions won't come one project at a time. Instead, they will require transforming whole energy systems, which is unlikely within an offsets scheme because transformation makes it particularly difficult to establish the baseline against which offset credits are measured. (Big dents will be hard to come by in the CDM, as well, since many of the most attractive large-scale options – such as nuclear power, large hydro, and carbon capture and storage – are unpopular with governments that designed the CDM and thus essentially barred from earning CDM credit.)[25]

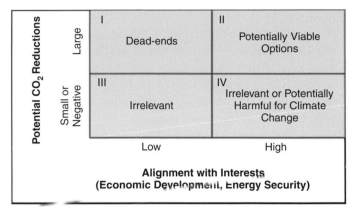

Figure 4.2 Framework for evaluating the viability of a reluctant country's global warming policy options. The potentially viable options are in the upper right corner (box II). The structure of box II is further unpacked in Figure 4.3.

Making a larger dent in emissions will require going back to fundamentals: the interests and capabilities of the reluctant developing countries. Over the long term those interests and capabilities will change in ways that probably will lead them to undertake more vigorous efforts to control emissions. Awareness of climate dangers will grow, economic development will create extra resources that can be devoted to goals beyond just reducing poverty, and better systems of public administration will improve these countries' abilities to control emissions. But those processes will unfold slowly. What more can be done on a faster schedule?

The interests of a country stem from many factors. A core goal is prosperity and security. Most governments are also under pressure to provide jobs to certain groups, protect the environment, and deliver other outcomes. Imagine an array of policies that may or may not align with national goals – as shown on the horizontal axis on Figure 4.2. Some policies align with national goals and countries should be willing to implement them without an external nudge. But policies that run against national goals will be infeasible or will require external pressures (sticks and carrots) before they are adopted.

The vertical axis in Figure 4.2 shows the potential for reducing emissions – a concept I will call "leverage." At the bottom of the chart, boxes III and IV are options with minimal impact on emissions or even the potential to make emissions worse. In many countries these include, for example, renewable energy technologies that are costly and hard to scale – attributes that are unattractive to countries with scarce resources. Examples in box III include widespread deployment of solar photovoltaics. China, for example, is in the news as the largest manufacturer of solar cells, but the vast majority of those products are made for export since costly solar does not fit well with China's own energy priorities. Wind, by contrast, is expanding rapidly in China. Others align with the host country's interest but are unhelpful to the goal of slowing warming (box IV). Current examples include large coal-to-liquids projects that China is pursuing with the goal of promoting energy security. These projects help China reduce imports of insecure oil but they make emissions of warming gases a lot worse.

The interesting box is the upper right (box II) – also known in global-warming policy parlance as "co-benefits." The search for a viable strategy that can engage reluctant countries without large sticks and carrots and perverse incentives starts here.

Not all options in box II are equal. Efforts in this box can vary by whether the host country will have the financial and technical ability to alter industrial practices in ways that affect emissions – what I will call "practical ability." And efforts can vary in their administrative feasibility, for some policies are very difficult for governments to craft and administer while others are relatively straightforward. Figure 4.3 unpacks box II along these two dimensions. The options along the bottom row in Figure 4.3 (boxes IIc and IId) are marked by administrative difficulties. In India, for example, there are many options in agricultural and forestry policy that could have large leverage on the country's emissions, but the government finds it difficult to exert much influence on outcomes because the activities are widely dispersed and far from the administrative eyes and ears of Delhi administrators. In China, policies and projects that influence buildings are of this variety. With a concerted effort to build administrative capacity – which itself might merit external funding – some options in this row may become viable. Similarly, with effort – perhaps funded with outside help – a country can boost its practical abilities. Again, using India as an example, there are large potentials for reducing emissions from coal-fired power plants using the latest, ultra-efficient coal boilers. None of that technology

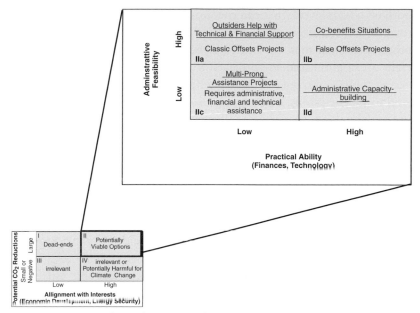

Figure 4.3 Unpacking box II: administrative feasibility and practical abilities

is presently used or even tested at scale in India. Outsiders will be needed – at minimum to license the technology (as has happened on commercial terms in China) or perhaps to offer it on concessionary terms. By contrast, with technology already available to Indian firms it would be possible and cost-effective to make fuller use of natural gas (which has lower CO_2 emissions) or deploy slightly less new-fangled ("supercritical") coal boilers that Indian firms are already building.

Box II defines the space of activities that the enthusiastic countries should be keen for the reluctant countries to expand. But making that happen requires a strategy that differentiates between the initiatives that reluctant countries would be likely to pursue on their own – perhaps with a small nudge – and those that will require external help in building technical capacity (box IIa) or administrative capacity (box IId) or both (box IIc). This framework offers a simple way to discuss what each reluctant country can offer the world – what it can deliver on its own and, where necessary, the kind of external assistance that will be needed. The rest of this chapter offers some examples and then outlines a framework that can encourage reluctant countries to search for and implement a wide array of box II options. The CDM and other offset schemes have helped encourage some initiatives, especially in box IIa and for projects where the extra effort needed is easiest to measure, but a much bigger push in all the boxes is possible. And using the wrong external instrument – such as CDM incentives in box IIb – leads to wasted or illusory effort.

Box II in action: some examples

The idea that there are large emission reductions feasible within many countries' self-interest has been around for a long time, but the literature is surprisingly thin on practical examples. How would these policy efforts be organized? Which kind of efforts would reluctant countries launch on their own and which would require an external nudge?

A few years ago, working with a range of colleagues, especially Varun Rai at Stanford, I started looking closely at such questions. I looked at more than a dozen countries.[26] Varun and I looked in depth at one country in particular – India.[27] This research taught us two things. First, there is massive potential leverage. Just the examples we explored over a dozen countries suggest leverage of about 2 billion tons of CO_2 per year within the next decade or so.[28] To put that into perspective, it is about five to ten times the emission reductions actually achieved under the Kyoto Protocol.[29] Those savings were just for the policy initiatives and investment projects that we scrutinized in detail; a full-blown investigation of box II would probably yield even larger emission reductions.

Second, very few of these projects are classic "co-benefits" situations, which policy analysts also often call "win-win" because the host country "wins" by adopting a policy that aligns with its interests and the global environment wins due to fewer emissions of warming gases. Such policies are very attractive to analysts because they suggest that a lot can be achieved without any net effort. Varun and I discovered that most of these policies actually weren't like $20 bills sitting on the sidewalk just waiting to be picked up. And few were eligible for classic offset financing such as through the CDM. Calling these policies "co-benefits" or "win-win" obscured the fact that nearly all of them would require substantial changes in public administration, technology and finance. All would require that governments take on politically powerful groups that favor the status quo. Some of these changes the reluctant countries might pursue on their own, but most would require external assistance, which might be offered by enthusiastic countries. The packages of external assistance would need tailoring to each circumstance, and most often the key resource wasn't just money.

As Varun and I started working on this issue it became clear that huge leverage on emissions was possible at very little cost, but realizing this potential would require a radically new way of engaging developing countries. That new approach would need to elicit accurate information from reluctant countries about the real policy reforms they might implement and also credible promises from others, such as the governments in enthusiastic countries, about the kinds of assistance they could reliably offer. Getting that information, rather than just bromides, wouldn't be easy. So we imagined that deals could be crafted through competition. Reluctant and enthusiastic countries, alike, would compete over which policies would be reformed, the types of external resources that would be provided, and the credit that each country would earn for participation. Because each of the policy reforms in box 2 would have its own character, such a competition would not have the character of market competition to supply or purchase a commodity such as pork bellies or credit default swaps or CDM projects that compete on price and delivery terms. The competition would, instead, focus on complex packages of efforts. How that scheme could be organized will be one subject of Chapter 8, and a partial model for that kind of negotiation is in the deal-making that frames how countries accede to the WTO. But before I offer a vision for how that complicated competition might be organized, I close this chapter with some brief illustrations of four kinds of policy initiatives that might be crafted: a natural gas scheme in China, a clean coal program in India, a forest protection initiative in Indonesia, and a subsidy reform initiative in the oil-rich Gulf states.

China

I start with China because that country's emissions are the largest and its growth the highest, which offers the greatest potential for leverage. Those high emissions stem from the country's heavy dependence on coal, which accounts for 69 percent of its energy system.[30] Throughout the 1990s, structural reforms in China caused a decoupling of energy demand from economic growth, with the former growing at about two-thirds the rate of the latter. All that changed around

2000 as Chinese economic growth turned more aggressively to heavy industry and thus hinged, to a greater degree, on energy.[31] Since then the country's stellar economic growth has driven a similar rise in energy demand that has in turn caused shortages in energy supply and upward pressure on energy prices that has been felt worldwide. Chinese officials know that this rapid growth poses a danger for their economic health and thus have initiated a broad program with the aim of, once again, decoupling economic growth from energy consumption. Those efforts include pressuring power generators to install more efficient coal-fired power plants (and close older units), improving standards on energy-using appliances from refrigerators to automobiles, and promoting an aggressive economy-wide goal to reduce energy intensity.[32] Measured in sheer level of effort and importance for world energy demand and emissions, no country on the planet is doing more today to manage its energy problems than China.

In addition to what China is already doing, what more could they do on their own and also with external assistance? I concentrate here on the power sector because it is still under strong direction from the central government and the governments of the major provinces. The administrative feasibility of changes in Chinese power policies is relatively high because most of the sector is under strong state control. Within the sector there are many opportunities to slow the growth of emissions, notably in improving the efficiency of power plants and the grid. Already, for example, Chinese state-owned power companies are building more ultra-supercritical highly efficient coal-fired power plants than the rest of the world combined. It is hard to see what outsiders can do to help China do what it already sees as its strong national interest in burning coal a lot more efficiently, although there are interesting opportunities for collaboration on coal technologies with carbon storage and perhaps more exotic and more efficient coal technologies such as gasification. Some such collaborations are already taking shape.

Here I focus on natural gas where China won't reach its potential without foreign assistance. The country's central planners have already indicated that they want to shift to a greater share of gas to help balance China's power generation portfolio away from its excessive reliance on coal and to help clear the air. So far it has fallen short on its own goals for gas due to the difficulties in building gas infrastructure quickly, fears of insecure supplies and relatively higher cost for the fuel. (The rising price of coal has helped advantage gas a bit, but coal still remains much more familiar and less expensive in nearly all Chinese electric power applications.)

China can speed its shift to gas by tightening local air pollution rules – a move it already favors to clear the skies in polluted cities – since tighter rules also tilt the balance away from coal (which requires costly pollution clean-up equipment) toward cleaner fuels. Elsewhere, colleagues and I have calculated that just one province in China (Guangdong) could cut its annual CO_2 emissions 100 million tons by 2025 if it tightened local air pollution regulations and encouraged a switch to gas.[33] The leverage on CO_2 emissions from using a fuel that the government already wants to use would be huge.

The central obstacle is supply. China has little gas of its own, although the country's planners have great hopes for potentially large fields in the far west. A sign of the priority the country places on security that comes from all-Chinese supplies is that the country has favored building long, uneconomic pipelines from the far west (and from even further away, such as from landlocked Turkmenistan and Kazakhstan) because it thinks it can secure those supplies more reliably. But a big push on gas will require much bigger and more economic supplies, which probably means imports. The country is already building a network of terminals to receive imported liquefied natural gas (LNG) via ship with a diversity of suppliers. It could build a larger network. And it could invest, along with other countries that have a vested interest in secure sea lanes, joint exercises, confidence-building, and anti-piracy squads in crucial straits such as Malacca – all of which would give China more confidence to rely on LNG and speed its shift to gas.

For the long term of Chinese gas, however, the key relationship is with Russia. China's most cost-effective bulk gas supplies probably come from the huge untapped fields in eastern Russia that could be linked with a large pipeline network to supply northern and central China. To date, Chinese-Russian wariness, along with Russian Gazprom's vision that it should send its gas to Western Europe for the best price, has made China unwilling to depend on Russia. Outsiders can't fix this problem, but they can make it easier to strike deals that will be self-enforcing once new pipelines are in operation, just as the big Soviet pipelines built in the 1970s and 1980s to Western Europe

have been remarkably reliable suppliers of gas once put into operation.[34] A compact with Russia, China, and Europe might be needed
to give Russia and China, alike, the confidence they need to develop a
bilateral gas supply arrangement.

So long as China sees its energy supplies as a purely national affair
it will be hard to avoid coal. Cooperation on gas – in LNG and with
Russian pipeline supplies – can help tilt the balance.[35]

India

India's energy system also hinges on coal. Thus, like China, achieving
leverage on India's energy system requires finding ways to use coal
more efficiently while also shifting to cleaner fuels. Beyond those similarities, however, the details of a viable engagement strategy must be
completely different because the organization of India's energy system
is distinct from China's and thus so are the challenges and opportunities for engagement.

The greatest opportunity for leverage on India's emissions lies
in boosting the efficiency of converting coal to electricity. (As with
China, there is great theoretical opportunity in boosting the efficiency of processes that burn coal directly, such as its use in brick
kilns. But it is hard to see how anyone, especially outsiders, could
have much impact since the Indian government itself is barely able
to administer such uses.) Electricity is interesting not only because
it is the largest single user of coal but also because the country is in
the midst of radically improving management of its electric infrastructure. The single largest operator of coal-fired power plants is
the National Thermal Power Corporation (NTPC) owned by the
central government; for illustration, I will focus there since it offers
the greatest single potential for leverage. However, similar opportunities may also exist in some of the so-called State Electricity
Boards (SEBs), the regional state-owned companies that also build
and operate power plants. The SEBs are a more challenging source
of leverage, though, as all are technically bankrupt, pulled in many
directions by local political priorities, and most are badly managed.
NTPC, by contrast, is remarkably well managed for a government-
owned corporation; it is in touch with technological opportunity,
attentive to cost, and steeped in competence. While there are many
players in the Indian coal-fired electric system none is as important
as NTPC.

NTPC, while the most efficient of India's government-owned power generators, is notable for sitting far back from the world technological frontier. It built the nation's first "supercritical" coal-fired plant – a less efficient version of the "ultra-supercritical" plants that are the world's most efficient conventional coal-fired power units – decades after the technology was available in the west. NTPC has realized that it has a strong incentive to find even more efficient ways to burn coal because Indian coal supplies are running short. The country, in fact, is poised to become a large coal importer, and imported coal will be more expensive than cheap local coal that historically has dominated the Indian power system. The era of cheap coal is over, which means that outsiders interested in cutting CO_2 emissions from coal will find their interests align with the Indian goal of cutting growth in coal consumption along with local pollution from coal.[36]

For NTPC, these patterns put a premium on efficiency; NPTC is already seeking arrangements that offer the prospect of more efficient combustion. A program to rebuild old coal-fired power plants with advanced supercritical units and to test deployment of ultra-supercritical plants could help the country lift its average coal combustion efficiency from 29 percent to perhaps 35 percent over two decades. Looking to 2025, such a program could avoid about 600 million metric tons of CO_2 annually. The Indian government has already removed the most serious obstacle to this approach in the 1990s by dismantling the requirement that coal combustion technologies be supplied only by Indian vendors. A viable plan to work with NTPC (and perhaps some of the better managed SEBs) in applying new technologies could work on two tracks – one with outside vendors (perhaps using ExIm financing from countries keen to export the technology) and the other in consortium with India's main equipment manufacturer (Bharat Heavy Electrical, Ltd) so that the two ventures compete. NTPC would be a welcome partner not only because this aligns with its severe problems in assuring adequate coal supply, but also because it is suffering, somewhat, the reputational harm that comes from being the world's third largest source of CO_2.

Such a program would operate under the useful shadow of competition from private investors in power plants, as India has just embarked on a program to build up to fourteen "ultra mega power projects" – all based on private investment for power parks that would rely partly on captive coal mines and mainly on imported coal. All of the ultra mega power parks are expected to use super-critical technology. It would be useful to explore whether some might even use ultra-supercritical technology, already available in commercial markets and increasingly used in China, or even other technologies such as coal gasification. So far, nearly all the policy attention around the business models that are being used for the ultra-mega projects has focused on the price of the electricity they would generate. From the Indian government's perspective, a central focus on prices is understandable because power prices are politically salient and important to the national economy. A direct incentive for the companies that propose projects that would also compete on plant efficiency would provide a stronger incentive for firms to experiment with and introduce new technologies to the country that move far beyond the supercritical boilers. The Indian government, on its own, could justify some of that effort. But outsiders, especially from countries that have a stake in licensing more efficient technologies, could help accelerate this shift with extra incentives.

Outsiders who want to help big coal-fired countries get leverage on their emissions will need to do a better job managing their own political troubles. Foreign funding institutions have found it increasingly toxic to finance big coal-fired power plants, such as in India and South Africa, even though these projects speed the introduction of more efficient combustion technologies. It has been expedient to pretend that coal can be ignored. Yet the reality is that one of the largest sources of practical leverage that outsiders have is in helping the coal-inclined nations burn their fuel more efficiently.

Indonesia

After Brazil, Indonesia is the world's biggest deforester by area.[37] As with Brazil, the country has become keenly interested in slowing and reversing deforestation. And outsiders, such as the Norwegian government in a recent deal, are lining up to help.[38]

Making a difference requires focusing not just on the forests but on the underlying governance troubles that contribute to deforestation. In most forest-rich countries deforestation is most rampant in the most lawless locales where government is most corrupt. Deforestation is a symptom (and often also a cause) of government failure. In Indonesia, as in Brazil and other forest-rich countries, uncomfortable choices will need to be made to help arm the police; to build new systems for governance; and to make resources contingent upon performance.

Indonesia's main source of CO_2 emissions is deforestation by fire on peat soils. Such soils are a particular concern because they are especially rich in carbon; when they burn they yield not just CO_2 but also noxious regional haze. The clearing season during the dry years of 1997/1998, for example, was particularly bad; it animated regional efforts in southeast Asia to ban all land clearing by fire. So far, however, they have not had much impact because pivotal players – notably Indonesia, which hosts most of the fires – have not seen fire control as an essential national interest. Many fires are used to clear land for agriculture (e.g., palm plantations) and those powerful interest groups have seen fire controls generally as a threat to their industry. (With the incentives that have been available so far, they are probably right.) On its own, Indonesia probably would not do much to make a big dent in deforestation.

Coupling fire control to global pollution concerns helps to fix that problem by providing funds that can inspire the Indonesian government see its interests differently. Focusing a fire control program first on peat fires would target the largest source of CO_2 and be most attractive for funding by outsiders who are concerned about global warming. And such an approach would start with kinds of fire control that pose relatively less threat to the agricultural and palm plantation activities that are lucrative to the nation and whose political opposition is most essential to manage. With success, a peat-focused effort could expand to other soils.[39]

In practice, focusing on peat probably would require two elements. First would be an effort to help build Indonesian capacity to map the country's soils and agricultural practices to understand the major burning areas. Monitoring and technical assistance, in the context of a broader engagement with international scientists, could be helpful since much of the needed data already exist. Second, a national program to police those areas, leading in time to a ban on fire clearing on peat lands, would be established. Already public concern is rising, and 2010 marks the start of a two year moratorium on conversion of natural forests or peat lands – a policy that stems from Indonesia's partnership with Norway. Some of the needed elements already exist to make such policies effective, but the problem within Indonesia has been the lack of administrative capacity and incentive to control burning in outlaw areas. Where the government did not have the muscle to impose a ban, a fund could be established to pay the extra cost of manual non-fire clearing. (Clearing by fire is preferred by land owners when there are no constraints on their actions because it costs about one-fourth the amount of manual clearing. But manual clearing yields much lower emissions.) Outsiders, with direct cash transfers as well as forestry credits under REDD+, could help fund the incentives along with the needed improvements in government administrative capacity – a model that Norway is proving. While the exact emissions are difficult to calculate, an analysis of the 1997 wildfires in Indonesia found that the emissions from that event were approximately equal to 13–40 percent of worldwide annual emissions from fossil fuels.[40]

Gulf states

Finally, I speculate whether the countries that have been most wary of climate policy – the oil-exporting Persian Gulf states such as Kuwait and Saudi Arabia – might be engaged in useful ways. These are not merely reluctant nations; in fact, many are hostile to the mission of cutting carbon. Engaging them, if feasible at all, will require measures that strictly align with their interests. Their largest sources of emissions come from consuming oil and, unlike most other countries – which are becoming more efficient in their oil consumption thanks to higher international prices – the Gulf states generally insulate their populations from the real world price of oil. Certainly the petrostates could raise internal prices for oil products and also build more effective natural gas supply systems (which would reduce the need for oil in power generation and also, fortuitously, allow deep cuts in CO_2 emissions) – indeed, some petrostates are doing exactly that already because they know that burning gas and exporting the oil that would have been used for power is strongly in their national interest. Such efforts should be encouraged, but outsiders will have little influence on this process except to jawbone on the need for such reforms and to provide advice such as on how to integrate gas-fired power plants into their electric systems.

Outsiders could have more leverage in the Gulf petro-states on deploying carbon storage systems, however. If successful, carbon storage could help lower that region's emissions, accelerate deployment of the technology worldwide, and squarely advance the interests of the Gulf states because the most interesting niche for testing carbon storage at scale is in enhanced oil recovery. BP is advancing in the region's first demonstration plant – an enhanced oil recovery and carbon storage venture in Abu Dhabi. The Gulf, by virtue of its large historical oil production, is well endowed with empty pore space suitable for storing carbon underground. Other Gulf states might follow suit after Abu Dhabi's demonstration, and the West should be willing to help clear roadblocks and share technology where needed, although most of these projects will probably proceed on their own commercial merits. It is hard to assess how much CO_2 could be stored through such ventures, but a Gulf-wide initiative in this area might scale up over the lifetime of large new investments in the power sector and new oil production fields (i.e., about 15–20 years) and the level of effort could be on the order of magnitude of 100 million metric tons CO_2/yr. An effort of that magnitude would involve 50–100 projects on the scale of the large CO_2 injection projects already being tested in Norway or Algeria and is roughly comparable with all planned CO_2 injection projects worldwide today.[41]

While I have focused on carbon storage, an equally important way to cut CO_2 is nuclear power. Abu Dhabi is also building the country's first commercial nuclear reactor – to be supplied by a Korean firm that has one of the best track records for economic performance in the worldwide nuclear industry. Scaling nuclear power in the region will require much better systems for managing the nuclear fuel cycle, and outsiders should accelerate efforts on that front so that better fuel management systems are available in tandem with opportunities to build commercial reactors.

Conclusions

For too long, analysts and practitioners in the field of international environmental cooperation have had a blind spot on how to solve the problem of developing country participation in a global climate regime.

Analysts have imagined two ideal worlds that do not exist. In one ideal world, all countries would apply carbon pricing such as through a global system of emission trading. That world does not exist because most countries have neither the interest nor the ability to regulate carbon emissions. A global carbon market, as I showed in Chapter 3, is not only unlikely but also undesirable since the weak efforts of some countries would flood the more diligently applied carbon limits in others.

In another ideal world, the industrialized countries would simply compensate developing countries for the full cost of compliance. That was done in all other major international environmental accords where rich, industrialized nations have tried to convince reluctant, poorer nations to make an effort. But that world does not exist because the industrialized nations are hardly ready to mobilize the hundreds of billions of dollars needed for such a compensation scheme.

Faced with these two untenable options, most governments have seized on the idea of carbon finance through international offsets, such as credits under the CDM. That scheme has allowed the mobilization of seemingly large sums of money. In practice, the CDM experience has revealed just how difficult it is to administer such a scheme effectively. And while the CDM has mobilized resources that are much larger than if governments relied just on traditional government-to-government funding, the actual level of new investment under the CDM is tiny when compared with the scale of the challenge in getting developing countries to control their emissions.

This chapter has suggested that the challenge of engaging developing countries should revolve around three lines of effort. First, better carrots are needed. That means tightening the administration of the CDM and allowing countries to adopt alternative schemes so that a competition between offsets markets can encourage a "race to the top." At the same time, the nations that are buying the largest quantities of offsets should establish sunsets on these schemes to dampen the perverse incentives that exist whenever a country knows it can demand payment for changing its policies – even when such policy reforms are in a country's self interest. Politically, such sunset clauses have been difficult to fathom because the large industrialized countries have been worried about assuring a supply of offsets credits so they can comply with emission targets and timetables. A new strategy for setting international commitments that is more flexible and relies less singularly on emission targets and timetables will ease that political challenge.

Second, sticks must be added to the mix of incentives. As offsets carrots sunset, sticks should rise. Governments must be cautious in how they threaten and use such penalties, but it is hard to see how a politically viable scheme for regulating emissions of warming gases will arise without the prospect of penalties for countries that fail to join and make serious efforts to control emissions. Sticks and carrots, in tandem, can help get the incentives right.

Third, and most importantly, engagement must look beyond sticks and carrots. The biggest leverage on emissions from these countries will initially come from encouraging them to rethink their development plans in ways that satisfy their interests, align with their capabilities and also make deep reductions in emissions. In this chapter I have offered some illustrations of the potential. None of these is the proverbial $20 bill lying in the street – just sitting there waiting to be picked up. Few will happen automatically. Most will require external resources, such as technology, money, administrative training, or security guarantees. The problem is that those resources don't match what the CDM and other offsets systems can deliver. In many cases, offsets systems actually create incentives for governments to avoid the kinds of policy reforms that would yield large leverage on emissions.

The reluctant developing countries are essential to the task of controlling global emissions. Their emissions are already about half the world total and rising rapidly. The challenge for international diplomacy is to change how they calculate their interests (with sticks and carrots) and to engage them more fully in finding the ways they can control emissions through policies that align with core national interests. This chapter has made the case for that new approach. Later, in Chapter 8, I will offer a blueprint for how to make it work.

5 | *Promoting technological change*

It is very hard to make much of a dent in the problem of global climate change without inventing and deploying new, radically different technologies. Most emissions of warming gases come from industrial energy systems that will be expensive and difficult to alter until new technologies appear. In the electric power sector, for example, deep cuts in emissions are feasible with massive deployment of new renewable energy supplies or thousands of new commercial-scale nuclear reactors, among many other options. Yet today's intermittent renewable energy supply options are impractical at a large scale without new systems for storing power and assuring stability of the power grid. Expanding today's worldwide fleet of 436 nuclear reactors to perhaps 1,500 or 2,000 reactors will probably require wholly new reactor designs as well as new systems for supplying fissile fuel that are more frugal and less prone to proliferate nuclear weapons.[1] Huge leverage on emissions probably will require rethinking the whole energy system.

This chapter is about policies that could spur invention and use of those technologies – what I will call "technology policy." The pace of serious efforts to control warming emissions will depend, in part, on success with technology policy. I will focus on energy, which accounts for most warming gases, although big innovations may also play a role in agriculture, forestry, and other activities that also cause substantial emissions.[2] About five-sixths of all CO_2 and a large portion of other warming cases originate in the energy system.

It has become fashionable to argue that the problem of energy emissions actually isn't so hard to solve because all the technologies needed to make a deep cut in emissions are already at hand.[3] If that view were correct then there wouldn't be much need for an active technology policy. The main task for policy would simply be to encourage firms, governments, and individuals to make fuller use of existing technologies. One of the reasons this viewpoint is fashionable is that it suggests the global warming problem can be solved quickly. The only thing standing between humanity and a cooling planet perhaps a couple decades of effort – using the market signals and direct regulation examined in Chapters 3 and 4 – to encourage the full deployment of technologies we already understand how to use.

I don't share that optimistic view. None of the technologies already at hand will scale quickly and widely to stop global warming. Over the next few decades world emissions would need to drop by half just to halt the growing stock of CO_2 in the atmosphere. Those cuts would be needed even as the world economy and population expand. More buildings must be heated and cooled; more miles driven and flown; more electricity supplied for more capable computers and appliances. The useful energy delivered to customers must roughly quintuple over the next half century. But to expand energy services fivefold while cutting emissions in half means that capabilities of the energy system – the useful energy delivered for every ton of emissions – must rise tenfold. With present policies, the world energy system is on track to improve by perhaps a factor of three.[4] Tinkering at the margins with existing technologies – bigger and many more wind turbines, more nuclear reactors, marginally more efficient power plants, a fuller shift from coal to gas, and such – won't close that gap. Even the countries that are doing the most to mitigate warming emissions, notably in Europe and Japan, are struggling just to keep emissions flat. A much more capable energy system will be needed and that requires invention as well as deployment of new technologies.

This chapter explains why technology policy is needed and how policy makers can design the most viable policies. The logic builds in five steps. First, the availability of technologies is essential to making the politics of global warming more manageable. So long as slowing global warming is seen as a costly and difficult venture then all the political problems that have occupied this book so far will loom large and probably prove impossible to solve in the real world where well-organized interest groups can block inconvenient policies. Thus I start by looking historically at the relationship between technology and other areas of environmental and social policy. Technology helps transform policy challenges that are divisive and not ripe for political action into topics that are politically much easier to manage. Improved technology and experience gives policy makers the room needed to make politically bolder moves.

Second, I make the standard argument that a technology policy is needed because markets left to themselves will lead to an under-investment in new ideas. The problem with that standard argument is that markets can fail in many ways and absent a clear theory that focuses on the most important failures technology policy can become a broad license to tinker in many mischievous ways. I offer a framework here that focuses on two goals for technology policy – fixing the problem of appropriability and reducing the barriers that "lock out" better new technologies from market. Then I examine each goal in turn.

Third, I look at how to overcome the problem that the benefits from most important new ideas are usually not appropriable. Society gains from these ideas, but investors don't have a strong enough personal incentive to invest in such public goods because they usually don't reap all the benefits. The solution to such problems isn't stronger intellectual property rights, which is a fashionable argument these days, but a bigger public investment in innovation. There is no shortage of calls for bigger public research and development (R&D) programs – and this book is one of them – but much less attention to how those programs can be designed to be politically viable.

Fourth, I suggest solutions to the problem of lock-out. Even superior new ideas often fail to find customers because the incumbents are so well organized and existing infrastructures favor familiar and compatible technologies and impose high barriers to novelty. Policy can help fix these problems by lowering the barriers to entry. The solution is not weaker intellectual property rights, which oddly is also fashionable these days, but a careful focus on the real factors that create market barriers. With a clearer path to lucrative markets investors will be more likely to support innovation.

Fifth and finally I look at what all this means for international coordination. A serious technology policy – one that will foster, over several decades, a complete transformation of the energy system – will require an international approach. Today, unlike even two decades ago, the systems for innovation and the markets where new technologies will be deployed are global.

Although essential, technology policy alone won't work.[5] Technology policy helps push new technologies into use, but the push must be married to a pull from the market and regulation.[6] Pushing without a pull raises the odds that technology policy will lead to wrongheaded priorities, waste, and distraction. Over history, the worst examples of technology policy in practice nearly always arose because policy makers tried to push new technologies into service in the absence of a market pull.[7] Chapters 3 and 4 were about how to pull more effectively. This chapter is about the push.

The politics of technology and policy

Nearly all of the great successes in environmental policy stem from the invention and use of simple, relatively inexpensive changes in technology and behavior. That's because when a simple technological change is available then the politics of policy focus on large and visible environmental benefits while the apparent costs are small and often invisible. That combination is the key to political success because many environmental problems, including global warming, are plagued by the problem of time inconsistency discussed in Chapter 2. The cost of action appears immediately and hits established industries while the benefits arrive later and accrue often to interest groups that don't yet exist or are poorly organized for political influence. The losers are well positioned to block costly changes; the winners aren't yet on the field, and the broader public won't see much benefit from a cleaner environment for some time. That combination is toxic for politicians – especially in democratic countries where policy choices come from the jostling of interest groups and where big policy decisions usually require a measure of public support.

In 1858 the British Parliament was forced into session by a "great stink" as sewage that had been freely dumped in the Thames mixed with warm weather to create a foul-smelling brew. It also generated a massive public health hazard as the water intakes for some of the city's supply were located downstream in the same foul river. The problem had magnified not just from London's growing population but also from the innovation of cost-effective flush toilets. The first toilet had been invented in 1596, but only two of that vintage were produced: one for the British queen and one for the inventor. The toilet took off as a prized device for urban living only when innovations of better and more cost-effective valves made the device commercially viable in the late eighteenth century and over a few decades toilets diffused widely. More toilets meant more black water. From 1850 to 1856 alone London's water usage doubled, mainly due to toilet flushing. More black water with no well-functioning sewerage meant the great stink.

The solution was a costly public infrastructure and a series of reforms that created much stronger public administration that, over history, nearly always accompanies big infrastructures. The new institutions created to manage this infrastructure – starting with London's Metropolitan Board of Works – took over much of London's urban planning and also became a prime mover in most of the innovation in sanitary technology and infrastructure.[8] The immediate pressure on Parliament to act came, as is often the case when democracies confront their environmental ills, from an acute crisis that focused minds and literally kept the politicians indoors focused on solutions. But the speed at which politicians could order the water to be cleaned and consider the choice of solutions to the stench was mainly a function of what was technologically and institutionally possible. As the Metropolitan Board of Works got started on the task of building a sewerage it found that many aspects of the new infrastructure were a lot easier to build and operate than originally expected. In turn, that fortuitous experience made a more effective sewerage not just technologically possible but also politically tractable. London opened its fat wallet and bought a better sewerage system, and what it learned helped other cities follow the same course. The London experience showed how the network of pipes could be constructed, what it would cost, and institutionally how such a large public works could be managed.

The regulation of air pollution has followed a similar path. The invention of automobiles and road networks made sprawling, peri-urban lifestyles possible. That meant much higher emissions of pollutants from the cars and from all the distributed industrial activities. Problems first came to a head in the late 1950s in Los Angeles where a brown smog soon regularly appeared over the city. Stopping the smog first required understanding its causes. It is no wonder that many of the best air pollution scientists tended to hail from universities that sat inside the LA basin with a ready pollution laboratory outside their windows, such as the California Institute of Technology in Pasadena and the University of California at Irvine. Much of the basic science about smog was worked out in the 1960s, and once the science was understood adequately it was possible to map out technological responses, costs, and eventual policies. As is often true with complex environmental problems – from cutting water pollution to protecting public health and now slowing global warming – it is hard to craft policy until the underlying physical causes are understood. But the policies that actually result are a function of both the science and especially the resources the society is willing to devote.[9]

Although California itself started regulation on its own in the early 1960s and cobbled together its various regulatory agencies into a single, coherent body in the late 1960s, a big hammer also came from federal legislation. In the early 1970s the US Congress – animated by widespread public concern about environmental degradation of all forms – passed amendments to the Clean Air Act that set extremely strict air pollution standards. Los Angeles and many other cities didn't come close to honoring those standards, and for the last three decades most US air pollution regulation has focused on cleaning the air as quickly as the technology would allow and the public would stomach. On paper, US air pollution regulation looks like the scientist's myth from Chapter 2 – environmental protection in which government experts set levels that are "safe" and then states and firms must work backwards to implement plans to comply. In practice, the "safe" pollution levels are not hard and fast standards when they prove inconvenient. The real pace of regulation is determined by what is feasible at acceptable cost.[10] Many forces help explain the cost that societies will stomach, but the arrival of new technologies and practical system for deploying them has been centrally important.

Technology has also been the determining factor in the most successful case of international air pollution regulation: protection of the ozone layer. When governments first set international regulations on ozone-depleting substances they agreed to cut emissions only in half. For most countries that meant adopting regulations that were nearly costless – for example, switching from ozone-destroying chlorofluorocarbons to more benign substitutes in spray cans.[11] As public concern about ozone depletion spread – in part because of new evidence that the ozone "hole" was man-made and dangerous and in part because the media covered ozone issues more heavily in the advanced industrialized countries – so did willingness to adopt more expensive regulations.[12] As new technologies appeared that made deeper cuts feasible governments almost immediately agreed to tighter limits. Indeed, the international regulations were written carefully to guarantee that regulatory limits never exceeded what was technologically feasible at costs that most countries were willing to bear. They included, for example, exemptions for "essential uses" as well as a regular review of treaty obligations to ensure that they navigated around political obstacles that would appear if the treaty obligations became more stringent than societies were willing to tolerate. As new technologies appeared those obstacles melted away.[13] (And for the countries that were most reluctant to spend their own resources on controlling emissions, the Protocol included a funding mechanism that was explicitly linked to the cost of purchasing and installing new technologies.[14])

These insights into the interaction between technology and policy suggest three lessons for how technological innovation will influence the politics of climate change. First, at best, governments initially will be willing to adopt limits on emissions that are cheap or costless and for which governments are largely confident the technologies will appear at acceptable cost in a timely way. Indeed, almost every country's effort to date reflects this proposition. (Some countries, such as the United States, have not even been able to adopt limits on warming gases of this inexpensive variety.) For many observers, the global warming problem is so pressing that swift action is required immediately. But even when the pace of global warming regulation is compared with other environmental problems where the costs for action were much smaller, what is striking is that regulatory efforts in cutting emissions are still in their early stages. It took about two decades for public concern to grow about local air pollution in America's cities and another nearly two decades before most of the main sources of pollution were under broad-based and effective regulation. In the case of the ozone layer it took about fifteen years from the middle 1970s to the late 1980s for the idea to spread widely that the problem was serious enough to warrant spending some resources on regulation. And when that idea spread it was relatively easy for governments to act because it soon became clear that the total cost of controlling ozone-depleting substances was probably measured in the tens of billions of dollars worldwide – a number so small that it was not material to any country's economic growth. Households that paid the extra cost of controlling ozone-depleting substances did not notice. In cases where the costs were more apparent – such as in the use of methyl bromide as an agricultural fumigant – regulation was delayed. (Methyl bromide rules are systematically more lax than those on the original ozone-depleting substances such as refrigerants. That's because methyl bromide regulation affects well-organized agricultural interest groups and low-cost substitutes have proved harder to find.) Firms that made the original substances were, for the most part, unaffected by the phase-out because these substances were mainly low-value commodities that accounted for a tiny share of total revenue, and intransigence about their regulation would create political risks for firms such as DuPont that were concerned about protecting brand reputation. In some cases, firms may actually have profited because the new regulations created demand for new substances and appliances that were more likely to be under patent protection.[15]

Second, it is important to keep perspective about costs. While there is a chance that the global warming problem will disappear with the sudden appearance of new technologies – just as the problem of mud and dung that plagued so many cities in the early twentieth century disappeared when automobiles replaced horses and cities paved more roads – that outcome is unlikely. Cutting emissions will probably cost something. Nobody is really sure of the price tag, but probably the numbers will be big. My read of the economic literature is that the cost for eliminating most emissions over the next five decades will be about 2 percent of GDP.[16] Worldwide that is about one trillion dollars per year, and obviously that number will swell or shrink depending on whether the policy is economically well designed. (Many of the factors that lead to politically savvy design, as I showed in Chapter 3, often lead to economically costly outcomes. The basic logic of good economic design is fungibility and transparency. The basic logic of politics encourages the hiding and channeling of costs and benefits. If governments adopt economically inferior policies maybe 2 percent would become 3 percent.) Health for the planet is expensive, but it is not different from other major national priorities. The British Parliament approved one of the country's largest public works projects after the great stink because public concern was high and a pathway to the needed technology was conceivable. In the US about 15.3 percent of economic output is devoted to health care. From 2000 to 2006 the total burden of health care on the US economy grew about 2 percent. Thus the entire cost of the global warming venture could be paid if the country found a way to offset just six years of growth in health care costs. And if the US could make its health care as efficient as it is in, say, Sweden – which delivers a healthier population but spends only 9.2 percent of economic output on health care – then the resources freed would far exceed the cost of warming policy. So while we are still in the early stages of public concern about climate warming, the size of the task is not out of line with other national priorities in social policy. And the cost is far less than acute priorities that periodically afflict nations, such as wars. The most expensive

American war, the Civil War, cost about one-fifth of economic output every year for about a decade.[17] Wars are unparalleled in their ability to mobilize sustained public expenditure, and it is no surprise that major efforts have gone into reframing the climate change problem as a matter of national security.[18]

Third, what matters most politically is the visibility of costs and who pays them. In the pure, idealistic world of public policy the best approach is to ensure that the costs of policies are minimized and the total cost should align with the benefits. But the benefits from many policies, including those concerned with global warming, will always be hard to pin down because they are complex, and the worst damages will usually be in the future rather than staring people in the face. Because damages are distant and abstract, the politics of climate change will probably be driven disproportionately by the apparent costs of regulation. All else equal, policies that create a visible and memorable increase in the cost of polluting activities – notably the cost of energy services – will face large political obstacles.

The importance of visible costs is evident when looking at how societies respond to changes in the price of energy. In most countries the cost of energy is politically salient. People notice when these costs change, and politicians are under strong pressure therefore to regulate energy prices and to manage prices within politically tolerable ranges.[19] By observing how the public and politicians react we can get a feel for just how much a variation in energy prices is politically tolerable. As an example I will look at power prices in the US, shown in Figure 5.1. Those prices are remarkably stable. The historical periods when regulators have allowed the greatest autonomy for electric power suppliers have generally coincided with low (or declining) retail prices. When prices rise there are strong regulatory pressures to push them back down.

I'll call this the "Specker Law" after Steven Specker, former head of the Electric Power Research Institute who has suggested that the historical stability of power prices will constrain the ability of politicians to limit warming emissions if those policies cause a substantial rise in retail power prices.[20] The Specker Law isn't an elaborate social science theory, but it is rooted in the well-grounded proposition that humans anchor their expectations around what is familiar and they are particularly averse to losses. Future scholars might elaborate the theory a bit. It probably prevails especially when regulators owe their jobs to

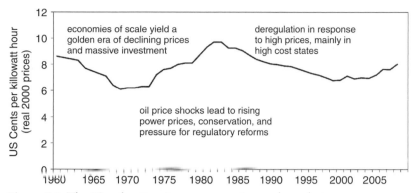

Figure 5.1 The "Specker Law" on power prices and regulation
Average retail power prices in the United States move within a narrow band.
Rising prices trigger political responses such as regulatory reforms aimed
at stopping and reversing the trend – evident in regulatory reforms such as
opening power supplies to the use of natural gas (1980s) and, after a lag,
efforts in many states to pursue deregulation. In recent years, rising prices
have led many states to question deregulation and seek alternative regulatory models. Data shown from 1960 in constant (2000) dollars. Based on
Energy Information Administration Annual Energy Review (2008 and 2009
editions).

local populations that actually pay electric bills – especially true in
the United States where most regulation is done at the state (and even
local) level rather than by more distant national regulators.

The Specker Law helps explain why countries that already have
high taxation of energy services – in much of Europe, for example,
retail energy taxes are major revenue-raising devices – are ironically
the jurisdictions least likely to oppose environmental regulations. The
extra cost of requiring new pollution controls has a relatively small
impact on the final retail price in countries where taxes are already a
large part of the total cost. In the US, ratepayers in California and the
northeast already pay high prices for power and thus are less sensitive
to the extra costs that might arise from limits on warming emissions.
Consumers in the southeast enjoy much less costly power and are
more likely to notice the impact of rules, such as limits on warming
emissions or requirements to purchase more costly renewable power
supplies, that would raise the cost of wholesale power. The Specker
Law suggests that perhaps the political geography of global warming

policy has more to do with original expectations for the cost of energy than with other factors such as awareness of global warming or political party affiliation.

The Specker Law is a useful benchmark for understanding the limits to politically viable policy. As public concern about global warming rises, the Specker Law might relax a bit as the public becomes more willing to pay extra costs. But it is sobering to look at history and see the fickleness of public opinion when policies mess with the cost of electricity.

Until the early 1970s prices declined and most utilities operated with only a light touch from their regulators. Utilities reliably earned cash and reliably avoided onerous and unexpected regulatory burdens, which is why utilities were dull investments that required little management. The stocks were prized by pension funds, widows and orphans, and other investors who were risk-averse and in stocks for the long haul. Rising prices from the late 1970s through the 1980s led to more aggressive regulation and a variety of experiments such as deregulation – all largely inspired by the political backlash against high prices.[21] The states that tried deregulation first were those that generally had the highest power prices, and most deregulation included special mandates known as "rate caps" that kept prices from rising quickly and thus kept political support intact. As those rate caps have expired consumers have once again seen higher prices and regulators have once again asserted much stricter controls. Some states, such as Maryland, have experienced such a public backlash with the expiration of rate caps that the legislature was forced into special session to search ways to keep prices in check. Regulatory reforms for electric utilities have happened mainly in places where deregulation coincided with a rise in prices. Over the last two decades Florida has created one of the United States' most investor-friendly legal and regulatory systems for electricity. For a while it worked, but when politicians and the regulators they appointed to office focused on high electricity costs they dismantled some of the investor protections in favor of keeping power prices low. Of course, many factors explain regulatory policies in the power sector, but one thing is clear: it will be hard to sustain political support for the policy if, at the same time, it visibly raises rates.

A few years ago the leaders of eight industrialized nations started spending a large part of their annual "G8" meeting talking about global warming. They were all politicians and thus they instinctively knew that the Specker Law would constrain what could get done. So they asked the International Energy Agency (IEA) in Paris to prepare roadmaps for the possible introduction of new energy technologies and to explore the costs. In one of IEA's costing scenarios, emissions would be held constant at today's levels, which would greatly slow (but not halt) global warming. In another, emissions would be halved by 2050, which would probably stop global warming in its tracks – a variant of the 450 scenario discussed in chapter 4.[22] What IEA found is that the impact on wholesale power prices varied radically – from 10 percent to perhaps 211 percent above the level otherwise expected – and assumptions about technology largely determined whether costs would stay in check or skyrocket. Stopping global warming would cause the biggest increases, especially when IEA added more realistic assumptions to their models – limiting, for example, the total number of nuclear plants that might be built and slowing the rate at which the world could embrace renewable energy. (The models that analysts use for such calculations are often naïve about the real world; making them savvy about how politics and engineering slow the likely real rate of technological change usually raises costs.) A doubling or tripling of wholesale power prices would cause a rise in retail prices of 50–100 percent in the US – a change never observed in modern US history and one that would run seriously afoul of the Specker Law.

The good news from IEA's models is that with radical improvements in technology the impact on power prices would be quite small. For example, the smallest increase in power prices came in scenarios that assumed technological improvements would make new nuclear plants particularly easy to build.[23] With radical innovation the impact of at least modest limits on emissions could remain in line with the normal variations that consumers already experience – something the Specker Law suggests is politically feasible. Even with highly optimistic technological assumptions, however, deep cuts in emissions imply that wholesale electricity prices will double on average worldwide, which probably means a rise of about half in retail prices, which is far outside the realm of what the Specker Law suggests will be feasible.

That is the nub of the political problem. Deep cuts in emissions will not be politically feasible without technologies that will keep costs low – ideally within the range that consumers already experience. Achieving those deep cuts with market forces that pull new technologies into service will require price signals so large that political support for the policy probably would evaporate. Some other way will be needed to entice these new technologies into service – a push from technology policy that can work in tandem with the weaker pull that will come from politically viable market forces. The case for a technology push rests not just on a market failure but on the political failure that the Specker Law reveals. Organizing that push requires a framework to explain which technologies are most likely to need and respond to an active technology policy. To that I turn next.

A logic for technology policy

Even if governments did everything outlined in the earlier chapters – if the enthusiastic nations adopted costly regulations to limit warming gases up to the limit of what they are willing to expend and if more reluctant nations also got started by finding ways to lower emissions at little extra cost – the needed technologies still will not spring into place on their own. Economists have long known that society, in total, is likely to under-invest in new technologies because the people and companies who come up with new ideas can't reap all the benefits themselves. New ideas leak easily, which is one reason that innovation is so valuable to society. The leakiness of technology, however, can be bad news for inventors and funders who will be wary about pouring time, money, and other resources into bold new ideas that yield only distant, uncertain, and incomplete benefits. Selfless, lone inventors (especially the independently wealthy or the irrational) can put resources into public goods, such as innovation. But most key players in the economy don't. None of the obvious fixes to this problem works without troubling side effects. Bombproof, long-lived patents or other forms of intellectual property, for example, might give inventors and their funders more incentive to search for new ideas. But an overly strong patent system would undercut leakiness that is essential to economic growth. Indeed, in industries where inventors have engaged in extensive patenting efforts – such as biotechnology and information technology – there is growing evidence that thickets of patents actually impede innovation.[24] Other obvious solutions are equally troubling. Getting the government to spend a pile of cash on research and development (R&D) is a standard recommendation, but such advice isn't very useful without a vision for how such funds can be used wisely.

A full-blown technology policy will have many elements. It will include R&D funding and possibly also tinkering with systems for protecting intellectual property. It might also look to anti-trust enforcement to ensure that better new rival technologies can gain a foothold in the market by competing fairly with incumbents. In countries where authorities are divided between central and local governments, a technology strategy might involve efforts by many different policy-making institutions to coordinate their efforts. One of the difficulties in devising a technology policy is that there are so many levers for policy makers to pull – and often a need for complex coordination across government (and even between governments) – that it is hard to stay focused on the central strategy. Here my goal is to outline how such a strategy could be crafted.

The design of technology strategy requires starting with the attributes of the technologies in question. Figure 5.2 suggests the two attributes that are most consequential. Along the vertical axis is "appropriability" – the extent to which investors in innovation can internalize the value that arises if a new idea proves useful. Where appropriability is high, market failures are generally few or easy to fix. Some analysts have also pointed to the sheer size of risky invest-ments in innovation that will be needed to fix problems like global warming as a cause for market failure. But size is much less of an obstacle than appropriability. The Suez canal and the Channel tun-nel were both massive innovative projects steeped in risk yet able to obtain most of their funding from private sources because the investment vehicles, in both cases, were designed to appropriate the most reliable sources of revenue (tolls) for the private investors who backed the ventures. Even extremely expensive and risky innovations can attract private capital on the belief that a return will follow. That belief is often wrong, as the backers of the Channel tunnel learned painfully, but it is right frequently enough to allow private investors to place big bets on innovation. Fifteen years have passed from the day that Amazon.com – the locus of many online retailing innova-tions – opened its doors for business and the company still (as of 2010) had not passed the point where its cumulative net earnings finally exceeded its total cumulative investment.[25] (In 2001, however, it turned its first annual profit.) The incentives to invest in innova-tion are less a function of risk or even scale and more a question of appropriability.

		Lock Out	
		High	**Low**
Appropriability	**High**	Medical Drugs	Internet Technologies
	Low	Energy	Traditional Agriculture

Figure 5.2 The attributes of innovation and their implications for technology strategy

On the other axis is "lock out." Even when superior innovations appear they may have a hard time gaining market share. Such lock-out problems are especially prevalent in networked systems such as electric grids and other infrastructures that play such a central role in determining which energy technologies can thrive. Networks require standards to function; once established, the very benefit of common standards becomes an obstacle to radical innovation.[26] Switching from one standard to another can require overt, complicated, and costly coordination – as Sweden knows well when at 5am on a Sunday morning in September 1967 the entire country, in unison, switched from driving on the left side of the road to the right. In addition to physical lock-outs, political and regulatory forces can impose barriers for new technologies. Incumbent technologies generate huge rents that can be channeled into political lobbying and propaganda to preserve market share. The US conventional ethanol industry has long understood this logic. Most US ethanol is produced from distilling corn, which is highly inefficient at converting sunlight and dollars into combustible fuel but extremely effective at generating jobs and votes in politically pivotal parts of the US such as the Midwest. Technically, much better ways to make ethanol start with sugar, but the US doesn't have much of a sugar industry and has little capacity to compete with sugar ethanol powerhouse Brazil.[27]

Essentially all major types of technology can be situated in Figure 5.2.[28] The easiest cases for policy are in the upper right corner. Markets in this quadrant are highly contestable because private investors can justify spending their own money on novel ideas that face few barriers to entry. Thus there is no real need for overt technology policy. Now that the Internet exists, much of the industry that focused on internet technologies takes this form. Although the original building blocks for the Internet came from government-supported R&D, today essentially all innovation in internet technologies arises in response to private market forces. There are few apparent market failures. Monopolies, which in many industries stifle innovation, are short-lived and thus probably don't much dampen innovation. The market for web browsers, for example, has seen serial monopolists – Netscape, Microsoft's Internet Explorer, and (to a lesser degree) the nonprofit Mozilla Firefox – and yet many firms, new and established, make continuous massive investment in new browsing technologies. Search engines have seen a similar experience with Excite, Altavista, Hotbot, Yahoo!, AOL, and now Google (among others) – each with their day in the lucrative sun, and each investing in making their product better for fear that they will soon be eclipsed. While there may be little role for overt technology strategy in this box, government has other levers that it must be ready to use. Competition authorities, in particular, play an essential role in ensuring that markets remain contestable so that new ideas are not locked out.[29]

Moving outside the easy box produces areas of innovation where policy must be more active. In medical drugs, the gains to innovation are huge and readily appropriated because most drugs are easy to patent. Indeed, while there is a lot of public investment in basic research related to health, private research is even larger because private firms know that the only way to identify the frontier ideas (which in turn can yield patentable products) is to work at the frontier.[30] Nonetheless, private investors will not back all forms of basic research, and there remains a large role for government funding of pre-commercial ideas as well as active efforts to ensure that government-backed ideas can spread easily from the laboratory to viable commercial products that actually improve public welfare.[31]

For advanced drugs, appropriability is not the main source of market failure because firms have strong private incentives to invest in basic research and because governments also fund basic research at such a high level. Instead, the chief difficulty is getting approval to sell useful products. Most health and drug safety regulation is inherently conservative and driven by fear of erroneously approving products that later kill or maim patients. There are good reasons why it is hard to get approval for new drugs; indeed, the modern drug approval process arose due to fears that medicines on the market were either ineffective or harmful. Among the policies that help lower these regulatory barriers for new products are, for example, fast-track drug approvals (usually requiring special payments, which inventors are happy to provide for high-value innovations) and special windows that make it easier to approve "off label" uses of drugs. Such efforts make it easier for new, better rival products and practices to gain market share. Much of the debate under way in the US over health care reform hinges on further reducing such market barriers – not just for drugs but especially for more cost-effective medical practices such as the provision of insurance and the management of hospitals.

An example in the lower right corner of Figure 5.2 is traditional agriculture. Existing practices – such as the choice of crops, seed varieties, and farm practices – are not firmly locked into place. Farmers would change practices if they knew about better alternatives and if those alternatives existed. But private investors have little ability to appropriate returns from innovation. Better seeds are not profitable if farmers can simply hold back extra seeds produced with last year's crop or borrow some from the neighbors. Many of the most important innovations in traditional agriculture, such as efficient irrigation systems, are similarly hard to contain because ideas leak easily. Improved traditional agriculture can produce huge social benefits since the poorest populations on the planet are usually farmers. But the poor are not a large reservoir of rents that can readily be tapped to repay investors in innovation, and the poorest farmers often are even unaware of innovations that could be of immediate benefit and free for the taking. (Similar forces explain why little private money goes into drugs for diseases such as malaria or schistosomiasis that don't much harm the wealthy.) Thus left to its own devices, traditional agriculture would see very little market-driven investment in innovation.

For traditional agriculture, the technology strategy has involved public funding of R&D and extensive efforts to make farmers aware of new innovations and to train them on their use. That insight has guided the creation of agriculture research stations and extension services in the US, other countries, and now globally through the Consultative Group on International Agricultural Research (CGIAR). The CGIAR network of fifteen research centers was created by the Ford and Rockefeller Foundations and the World Bank and invests in improving all the major food crops and also organizes (in tandem with national agricultural authorities) local extension services.[32] Nearly all research and extension on basic food crops is funded by governments because no other institution has historically had an incentive to create general public benefits; however, some of these functions are now shifting to private foundations, such as the Gates Foundation.[33]

Over the twentieth century a large part of agriculture has migrated up Figure 5.2 as private firms have found clusters of innovations that yield benefits that are much easier to appropriate. Some hybrid crops, such as corn, produce sterile or substandard offspring; it is easier to control intellectual property and appropriate the benefits when farmers are required to buy new seed each season. And, since about 1980, the ability to patent innovations in life forms – thanks to a series of technological innovations along with a legal innovation blessed by the US Supreme Court – has created even stronger controls on intellectual property.[34] At this writing, a segment of agricultural innovation is now shifting left in Figure 5.2 – into the upper left corner typical of the health and biomedical industries – since many of the most important innovations face large regulatory barriers to entry. Examples include genetically engineered crops that despite their large benefits have struggled to gain regulatory approval in many markets.[35]

Energy technology strategy: the basics

Technologies situated in the lower left corner of Figure 5.2 pose the greatest policy challenges. Large barriers on both fronts mean that market forces, alone, will fail to inspire innovation and technological change. Private investors lack confidence that they can appropriate adequate benefits from spending on innovation. And even if they concocted new technologies there are high barriers that lock the most radical ideas out of service.

Most of the energy industry is in this corner. Big new ideas come from far-flung fields of research; it is financially treacherous for profit-oriented companies to back them from conception all the way to final, profitable products. Indeed, the energy industry has historically been among the lowest investors in radical innovation. Electric utilities, in particular, are prone to invest less in R&D than any other major segment of industry. In a recent survey of twenty-nine US industries, electric utilities had the lowest intensity of R&D effort by far. The national average for R&D spending in industry was more than ten times the rate in the utility sector. The next lowest spender was petroleum, which was tied with the warehousing industry for the silver medal of low spending on R&D. Interpreting such data is

tricky because the structure of the electricity and petroleum industries makes them look less innovative than they really are – much
innovation in electricity comes from equipment suppliers who aren't
included in the power industry figures, for example – but the numbers
are striking and indicate the real barriers that a massive technology
strategy will face.[36] Most R&D concentrates on technologies that are
useful within existing networks, such as "drop-in" biofuels or more
efficient boilers for central power stations – innovations that can be
adopted readily if they are immediately superior to incumbent rivals.
But technologies that require new standards, a reorganization of the
energy infrastructure, or long gestation periods find it extremely difficult to gain market share and are unattractive for private investors
to support.

What makes an energy technology strategy hard to implement is
that policies are needed in parallel on both fronts – to overcome the
problem of appropriability and to lower the barriers that lock out
new technologies. The relevance and success of policies on each front
depend on the other. Inventors and investors must have confidence
that the promises of policy makers to work on both fronts are credible.
Each front poses its own daunting challenges, but devising a credible
strategy to solve both has proved taxing for most governments. That
helps explain why so many governments, based on what they actually
spend on energy technology policy, seem to have abandoned efforts to
alter the course of energy technology and why so many energy problems that new technology could fix remain stubbornly unsolved.

Figure 5.2 offers a framework for thinking about policy. And at
this point in building a logic for technology policy, most analysts then
focus on a toolbox of favorites – R&D tax credits, public funding
for energy research, demonstration projects for new technologies,
mandates to purchase "green energy," loan guarantees to help investors manage the financial risks from backing novel technologies and
such. That's because it is easier to focus on particular policies. But
the more fundamental questions of credibility and strategy are harder
to fathom.[37] Oddly, therefore, analysts rarely focus on such issues.
Here I will do the opposite – I will look at some particular policies as
examples but focus mainly on how all of the efforts sum to an effective, credible technology strategy. What really matters for a technology strategy is the overall credibility of the policy effort rather than
the particular nuts and bolts of individual elements.

Appropriability and the innovation trap

Many of the pivotal ideas for the coming revolution in energy supply are likely to arise from so-called "basic research." That is, research into ideas at their most fundamental, earliest stages in development – long before they are commercially viable. The main benefits of basic research are intrinsically hard to contain, which is what makes them so important and also creates the problem of appropriability. And strategies that would lead to better containment and thus perhaps fix the appropriability problem, such as secrecy or strict patenting, would undermine the huge social benefits that arise when the fruits of fundamental research are widely available. The great social value in basic research is inseparable from the fact that basic ideas are leaky. This is why basic research tends to be done in institutions, such as universities, that adhere to norms of transparency and openness. And it is why the primary funder of basic research is usually an institution charged with looking after the broader public good – in most of the world that means governments, but in some settings NGOs and foundations also play important roles.

It is very hard to measure the benefits that arise from basic research. Efforts to look at all forms of research – so-called research, development, and demonstration (RD&D), which includes research of the basic variety as well as more commercially oriented applied research and development and the nearly commercial demonstration of new technologies – find that typical social returns on investments are perhaps 30–50 percent. Government investment in research – basic research especially – is comparable in its social return to spending on education, infrastructure, and public health. There is very little else that government does that generates such a high social return. By contrast, normal capital investments by firms typically earn the firm and society about 10 percent.[38] The general logic that leads government to support basic research applies specifically to the particular issues surrounding the need for innovation in energy, and a large number of studies have worked through that logic in detail.[39]

One of the difficulties in mustering public support for basic research is that the benefits are hard to imagine. Most basic research probably produces little of value; a small fraction, hard to identify at the outset, yields blockbuster ideas. The importance of this point for policy can be gleaned by looking at recent revolutions in biotechnology or computers. In the late 1990s, worried that public support for basic research was eroding, the US National Science Foundation and one of the major computer industry associations asked the National Research Council (the research arm of the US National Academy of Science) to examine the history of the computer revolution and identify places where federally funded research made a difference. They found that essentially all of the most important innovations in computing – such as relational databases, the Internet, theoretical computer science, artificial intelligence, and virtual reality – trace back to government funding for ideas that were far from commercially viable at the time. Many of those ideas arose in universities, but some also came from industrial laboratories (e.g., at IBM's fabled laboratory in Armonk, New York, and Bell labs at Murray Hill, New Jersey). The NRC study found that government-funded research "has tended to complement, rather than preempt, industry investments in research." And they identified three areas where government-funded research has been particularly valuable: a) long-term basic research (also called "fundamental research" in some circles); b) large system-building efforts that require the talents of diverse communities of scientists and engineers; and c) work that might displace existing, entrenched technologies. In none of these areas does private industry have much incentive to invest its own resources.[40]

Only in rare circumstances does the general rule that government must take the lead in funding basic research not hold. In some special industries, private firms have proved willing to pour large funds into innovation. Industrial sponsors at the Bell System (the US telecommunications monopoly until the 1970s) and IBM have been major and productive backers of fundamental research. But that support existed only so long as the industrial parent was the dominant player in their industry. When the Bell System was broken up in the early 1980s its commitment to basic research soon evaporated. The commercially viable functions were separated from Bell labs, which was eventually spun off to a stand-alone entity (Lucent) and finally withered to a mere vestige of the original. Benevolent monopolies have done much good in the world, but the problem of monopoly is that it is hard to keep them vibrant and benevolent. Thus governments with an eye to the broader health of the economy wisely usually try to avoid monopolies, as the US government did when it broke up the Bell System. But government has been less skilled at spotting and fixing the market failures that arise when they shift to more competitive industrial structures. The lack of investment in fundamental research is at the top of that list. Parts of the energy industry have witnessed this failure during the eras of deregulation, which have caused the double harm for investment in innovation of both concentrating minds on near-term competition (at the expense of long-term innovation) and also sowing the industry with chaos and uncertainty. When electric power utilities and the gas industry in the US were exposed to competitive markets starting in the late 1980s funding for the two industry research associations – Electric Power Research Institute (EPRI) and the Gas Research Institute (GRI) – plummeted.[41]

Few profit-oriented, competitive firms find it worthwhile to keep smart (and costly) people on the payroll, following their whims, turning over whatever stones may appear. The exceptions are in industries in the upper right corner of Figure 5.2 for which basic ideas can lead directly to final profitable products, such as biotechnology (a big investor in basic biological science) and some elements of information technology (such as search engine companies, which are motivated by the prospect for commercial gains from some fundamental advances in mathematics).[42] It is possible that in the future the energy industry – steeped in smart grids, "plug and play" electric technologies, advanced biofuels and other innovations – will look a lot like today's biotechnology and information technology industries. For now, however, most of the energy industry is not structured in ways that create a strong incentive for firms to invest in basic research. Most new ideas that are relevant for cutting emissions from the energy industries are not practical until the inventor has erected a lot of steel and poured a lot of concrete to test whether the idea works at scale, tweaked the idea, and then built a few operational plants.

Thus the key to fixing the appropriability problem is public funding of research. But that answer is incomplete because it does not tell us what kind of research must be funded. Beyond pre-commercial basic research, when does the government's role in supporting innovation stop and when should the private sector take over? The answer to this question reveals why serious energy technology policy is so hard to design and implement.

For most energy technologies, a long gestation period – measured in time and money – is required between the relatively inexpensive process of cooking up ideas and the stage at which ideas are sufficiently

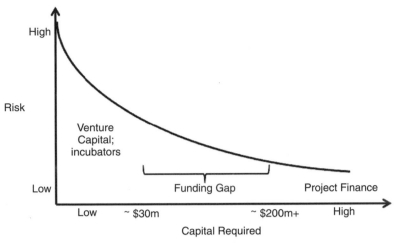

Figure 5.3 The commercialization gap for energy technologies
In the early stages of innovation risks are high but capital requirements are
low. Specialists such as venture capital firms or incubators back a large portfolio of such innovations knowing that a few will succeed spectacularly even
if most fail. At commercial scale the capital requirements are radically larger
but traditional financial mechanisms, such as balance sheet financing and
project finance, are available because risks are dramatically lower – notably
for regulated industries that buy such technologies with the credible blessing
of their regulators. In the middle is a no-man's-land where the risk/capital
relationship is unattractive, giving rise to the need for an active government
policy to help technologies cross this threshold – also known as the "valley
of death." The figure has been redrawn by the author after Kassia Yanosek
(Hudson Clean Energy Partners) and Dan Goldman (Highland Capital
Management).

close to commercial viability that the private sector will largely take
over financing. Time and money, together, mean risk. For private
investors to justify supporting an idea over the whole gestation period
the possible future earnings must be so monumental and reliable that
their present value can justify a massive deployment of initial capital
and other resources. This problem is also called the "valley of death,"
shown in Figure 5.3. Crossing the valley of death requires patient or
reckless investors (a rare breed, though a few exist and even fewer
produce truly viable ideas) or monopolists whose regulators will let
them place huge bets with the rate payer's money (less rare). Or it
requires institutions whose investment profiles are focused on public

benefits rather than private appropriation – that is, governments and public interest research groups such as foundations.

As investors look at technologies that are more radically different from the existing energy system the valley of death becomes wider, deeper, and more treacherous to cross. This is the key to understanding the problem of appropriability. When valleys of death are narrow or easy to navigate reliably then even private investors will find ways to invest in fundamental research because – as in biotechnology and information technology – they can plot a path from basic ideas to commercially viable products. When they are deep and treacherous then all the well-known failures of competitive markets to encourage private investment in fundamental research are amplified. The problem of appropriability can't be solved by just sprinkling money on institutions such as universities so they generate a bigger supply of interesting ideas. A whole strategy is needed that carries the best ideas across the valley.

I'll call this problem – the combination of low appropriability and deep treacherous valleys of death – the innovation trap. The problem isn't that innovators are absent from the scene but that the system for innovation produces a trap that yields technological stasis. The energy industry today, which faces radical, market-transforming challenges like global warming, is a prime example. The firms that are most closely connected to energy markets have the strongest incentive to focus on innovations that scale readily and earn reliable returns with few risks. Along the way they discover many other radical ideas that languish. Institutions that sit outside the energy industry, such as start-up companies, aren't so wedded to the status quo, which gives them a stronger incentive to pursue radical ideas yet also creates much higher barriers to putting those ideas into viable markets. The more disruptive the idea the more beneficial it is to be an outsider yet harder for profit-seeking firms to gain enough of the benefits from innovation to justify the expense and risk. Outsider status also makes it hard to use access to monopoly markets that incumbents can readily tap to help manage risk.

This innovation trap helps explain why the engineer's myth – that energy problems can be quickly solved if known ideas are just applied widely – is so hard to shake. There is no shortage of plausible ideas for what might be done and no shortage of dreams for how they might scale. What is in short supply are the real bankers and regulatory institutions that will allow these ideas to be carried across the valley of death.

Before looking at policy solutions that might unspring the innovation trap, first I explore some popular ideas that probably won't work. One is stronger intellectual property rights. Just making it easier to protect novel ideas – for example, stricter and longer patent protection, as now offered in much of the pharmaceutical industry – won't much alter the risk and capital equations that define the valley of death. Stronger intellectual property rights might make it a bit more practical for private investors to back new ideas, but an inevitable consequence of such an approach would be patent thickets and such troubles of excessive intellectual property rules that are already evident in other industries. Another popular proposal is to weaken intellectual property rights, which has become a favored idea for helping the spread of new energy technologies. That idea only works in theory once technologies have been tested and are ready for widespread commercial application. Even then, such a policy only works once. Weakening intellectual property rules would signal to investors that in the future the benefits from novel ideas might be stripped away if those ideas prove useful. Some analysts have imagined schemes that would compensate innovators for lost revenues and thus preserve the incentive to innovate – an idea gaining some traction by analysts who are trying to find ways to speed the spread of low-emission innovations to less developed countries – but such policies are extremely difficult to make functional in the real world.[43] They are exciting to academic analysts but terrifying to real innovators who matter a lot more. Still another idea is market competition. Perhaps if regulated parts of the energy market were deregulated then firms would have stronger incentives to back new ideas. This, too, is unlikely to unspring the innovation trap though is a good idea for most countries to explore for other reasons. The gestation periods are so long that deregulated firms would need to believe that deregulation would prevail long enough to earn super-normal profits from a risky valley-crossing venture. As we have seen with the US electricity and gas industries, deregulation had the opposite effect on innovation. Indeed, most efforts to deregulate the electric power industry worldwide have not actually produced much real competition.[44] And most firms in electric power markets know that if super-normal profits actually appear that governments will usually step in to strip them away. Deregulation in political visible industries survives so long as it produces politically convenient results such as low power prices that respect the Specker Law. Moreover, well-managed regulated firms in these kinds of industries often take much larger risks with new technologies that have no immediate commercial prospects than do firms in highly competitive markets. (Those risks often also end badly – a topic to which I will return later.)

Still another idea in vogue today is to spur private innovation with tax credits. By this logic, the private sector is more efficient at spending R&D money when compared with government because the private sector has better information about which technologies are most likely to be commercially viable and is better able to couple innovation with the financial support and business organization needed to put new ideas into commercial practice. The tax credit is attractive because it offers an extra incentive for private firms to invest but keeps the decisions about exactly where and how to invest inside the firms.[45] The R&D tax credit in the United States has, indeed, spurred more investment in R&D.[46] But getting private firms to invest more in R&D doesn't unspring the innovation trap because private investors use tax credits to subsidize R&D efforts that align with their own interests. With a tax credit they might invest more in R&D, but the basic direction of the effort appears to remain largely unchanged. The innovation trap exists because private firms, following their own interests, won't back risky and early-stage ideas.

A similar idea envisions creating public–private partnerships (PPP). Indeed, across many areas where governments seem to be falling short, PPP is often advocated as the solution. The logic for this approach is to vest – fully or partly – decisions about where to spend funds in the hands of private sector partners. In theory, this would help avoid the perennial trouble with government R&D programs, that the managers who choose the areas of research spending don't know much about the true commercial prospects for new technologies. In practice, such partnerships seem to run afoul of the same problem that afflicts R&D tax credits. They are good ways to get the private sector to do more of what they would have done. In 1993, early in the Clinton administration, the United States created a government–industry Partnership for a New Generation of Vehicles (PNGV) with public funds to spur innovation in the auto industry. Independent assessments of PNGV's progress could never pin down where its activities actually made a difference in auto sector innovation. By the time PNGV was phased down under the Bush administration (which had different priorities), some of the goals that already aligned with the industry's interests had been met. The tougher goals – such as building an 80 mile per gallon vehicle – that had been PNGV's original purpose were far from in sight.[47] Just as PNGV was starting to build stable working relationships between the government and the auto industry, the shift in government administrations and policies dumped the program for FreedomCAR, with a more sprawling research agenda – a reminder that government is often an unreliable partner for research activities that have a long gestation. In addition to the low credibility that comes from fickle policy priorities, one lesson from the PNGV and FreedomCAR programs is that it is hard to push the frontier of technology in a global industry while working just with one country's firms. Over the same period that these programs were in place, some of the most important innovations for auto efficiency – such as in hybrid drivetrains and turbo diesel engines – were made in firms that were largely excluded from US government innovation funding because they were headquartered overseas. Well-designed public–private partnerships, in short, have a role to play but they don't fix the fundamental problem.

Some analysts also advocate the much greater use of prizes to spur private investment into favored ideas. This idea has merit, and there is a large body of research on the idea of using prizes to encourage investment in areas where government has a goal but has imperfect information about how to reach it.[48] In practice, prizes aren't quite so novel as today's enthusiasts for this policy instrument seem to believe. Indeed, prizes of many different types are as old as modern government – such as patents and other kinds of monopoly awards, research grants and such. Recently, some NGOs have offered prizes such as for improvements in automobile efficiency. Prizes can help, but the enthusiasm for prizes is plagued by many naïve ideas. For really large, game-changing innovations, a prize intended to yield commercially viable concepts would need to be big enough that it could induce investors to cross the valley of death while also compensating for the high risk that the valley experience will prove fatal. For example, a prize of several billion dollars would be needed to encourage private investors acting alone to test billion-dollar-scale technologies typical of what might be needed to carry a novel kind of power plant across the valley of death.

To be effective, the prize must be well administered and highly credible – two goals that are hard to meet when prizes are so large that they are bound to be highly politicized. The most famous prize in the history of technology – the £20,000 offered in the eighteenth century for a solution to finding longitude accurately at sea – was never awarded to the innovator, John Harrison, who actually found a winning solution. The jury had a different solution in mind – based on lunar observations, rather than more accurate timepieces that were Harrison's preferred method – and kept moving the goalposts so that Harrison could not win. (The jury did award some lesser prizes along the way – to Harrison and others – that partially subsidized the costly innovation.) Only late in life did Harrison appeal to the British monarch for justice, and finally in 1773 (twenty years after he started work on the winning design and more than fifty years after he built his first clock in pursuit of the longitude prize) Parliament intervened and delivered a pile of cash.[49] Despite repeated abuse by the jury, Harrison kept working on his clocks – a reminder that inventors respond to many forces not just money. But backers of truly radical ideas know that better technical performance is just one factor that determines whether they will win prizes and gain market share. Administrative and regulatory risks often loom even larger.

The lesson for today is that prizes work better when the scale of the effort is smaller, when the missing link in innovation is an idea or a device rather than the nuts and bolts of commercialization, and when the particular function that must be performed can be tightly specified in advance so that every idea, no matter how nutty it seems to the jury, can compete on an equal footing. Prizes help push discrete ideas forward by focusing innovators on a particular goal. And they work especially well when the prize giver knows the goal that must be reached but has no clue how best to get there. But governments do not yet have a good enough sense of how to travel toward a low-carbon future to use prizes as a central mechanism for driving innovation.

Serious solutions to the innovation trap require brute force on two fronts. One front is increasing the supply of fundamental ideas. That means basic research, and the timeless method of prodding basic research is best: government funding concentrated in institutions where the norms of pre-commercial investigation prevail, such as universities and other noncommercial institutions. (I will not address here the question of whether government labs are a good way to do this kind of research. The US experience is mixed and generally not encouraging. Many other countries, such as China and Russia, have national lab networks that are more important sources of innovation.)

While the sheer quantity of money spent isn't the only measure of innovative effort, it is the best place to start. In constant dollars, US energy research funding fell from its peak in the late 1970s to nearly one-quarter that level by the late 1980s and had been little changed until energy research started rising steadily in the 2000s. Then, from late 2008, a wall of research money related to the economic stimulus packages has appeared. By some measures, stimulus funding could triple total energy R&D, but that boost will last only a few years.[50] An urgent concern is how to spend such quick sums wisely, and the next concern will be what to do when the stimulus money dries up. A long-term energy R&D strategy must look beyond today's blip at a level of spending that is viable and useful.

Nobody is quite sure how much new funding is needed for basic energy R&D. The correct scale of effort seems to be a rough doubling over a period of perhaps a decade.[51] The doubling of the budget for the leading biomedical research institution in the United States – the National Institutes of Health (NIH) – over just six years is a caution that ramping up funding too quickly can exceed the capacity to spend basic research dollars wisely. (One of the main effects of NIH's higher budget was to drive up the cost of research.[52])

In addition to sustaining adequate funding the strategy for spending resources is also important. Funds are needed not just for established researchers but also junior scholars contemplating careers. And framing the goal as "basic energy research" would be too narrow. In most areas of noncommercial basic research, including energy, nobody knows which fields will produce the best ideas. Already the fields of interesting "energy" innovations span the frontiers of genomics and biology (biofuels), mathematics (systems controls), materials (turbine blades and battery designs), chemical engineering (low emission combustion of coal), nanotechnology (solar cells and batteries), and sundry other areas that are more traditionally the province of energy research, such as electrical and mechanical engineering. Boosting basic research requires spreading resources across so many fields that it is not much different from the broader task of boosting overall spending on basic research. Organizationally, spending those new resources probably requires working across many government agencies rather than relying on a single agency that, like the longitude jury, could easily become a prisoner of its own preconceptions and stovepipes. In basic research, like any fundamentally undirected activity, too much coordination can prove catastrophic. When Craig Venter's Institute for Genomic Research first sought government support for its "shotgun" method of sequencing genomes its ideas fell on deaf ears at the NIH – the logical place to fund such research. (Venter at the time was trying to sequence an influenza bacterium.) NIH's masters had other genomic methods and thought influenza was too big a genome to tackle. The Department of Energy was more receptive. (Ironically, many energy researchers think DOE is beset with its own prejudices and often look elsewhere for patrons for their innovative ideas.) Nurtured outside its logical funding home, the success of shotgun sequencing spread to other organisms – including humans. Eventually it stood on its own with private funding, although the private investors in such work are still puzzling about how they will earn a return on their outlay.[53]

Put simply, a bigger supply of fundamental ideas probably requires a rough doubling of basic research spending and the resources should be spread widely across the basic research enterprise. Coordination matters a lot less than the total effort of high-quality research.

The second front of effort in unspringing the innovation trap involves crossing the valley of death. Here, too, big dollars and a diversity of efforts will be needed. Devising systems to help promising technologies cross the valley of death requires not pretending that tinkering with incentives at the margins will lead the private sector to solve these problems on its own. The challenge lies in the fundamental risks that keep the private sector from making more than just the short, reliable forays across the valleys of death. Getting serious about crossing the deepest and most treacherous valleys requires a focus on the sheer scale of the effort needed. A single project to demonstrate an advanced coal technology might cost $2 billion. Demonstrating a new design for a nuclear reactor (and, crucially, that such a design can be licensed and built in the US) will require a total investment of perhaps $10 billion.[54] Such single projects cost, today, more than all worldwide spending for basic energy research. Errors in the optimal allocation of basic research funds don't much matter because such projects are usually small and highly diversified, but errors in deciding which projects will be carried across the valley can bust the budget. That fact has led to the conventional wisdom that government should not commit the sin of "picking winners." (Analysts in other countries are never quite so worried about picking winners, but in the US the combination of a market culture and a long history of bad choices by government agencies has created a paralysis about this problem.) In reality, crossing the valley of death is all about picking winners because picking everything isn't viable. At this writing, although the US is rapidly increasing its spending on energy research – including demonstration projects – the paralysis about really expensive investments and about picking winners has made it very hard to get serious about unspringing the innovation trap. For example, the US government is relying heavily on loan guarantees for demonstration and first of a kind projects because loan guarantees have a much lower cost to the public budget. That approach has a role, but it also guarantees that demonstration will be the province of established firms that are most able to exploit the benefits of guaranteed loans. It also focuses too much attention on the financing effects of loan guarantees on individual projects – which for some companies, such as regulated utilities, is a small but important reduction in the cost of capital – rather than the whole portfolio of demonstration and commercialization of novel technologies.

Beyond the sheer level of spending needed, the tough questions for policy are how to pick winners in a smart way and, when possible, how to build a portfolio of possible winners and adjust the investment choices along the way.

The answers to these policy questions will vary by government because the capacity of governments to manage costly, risky portfolios varies so widely. While the strategies will vary, at least four criteria will determine whether the valley-crossing efforts are successful. First, it is important for government to stay focused on the central purpose of policy in this area: demonstration of the technology. Many projects set goals that are unachievable or not closely tied to the central purpose of a demonstration project. When the US government set up a corporation to back technologies that would make synthetic oil from coal starting in the late 1970s, it set output goals that could not be reliably achieved (2 million barrels of oil equivalent per day by 1990) rather than just measuring progress in the performance of the underlying technology. Actual output would depend on technological progress – which is usually hard to predict at the outset for a technology that is still at demonstration phase – and on market conditions such as the price of oil over which the demonstration project had no control. In the early 1980s when the price of oil collapsed due to other factors in the world oil market the government wisely shut down the program. Most observers see the synthetic fuels experience as an example of exactly what government should not be doing. But given what was known in the late 1970s and expected for the future supply of oil, the synfuels bet was probably a good one – albeit one that was often poorly executed and, unknown at the time, would ultimately prove unnecessary.[55] Most big demonstration projects embrace goals that seem wildly unrealistic, perhaps because the process of convincing political masters of the worthiness of such efforts requires inflated goals. What really matters for demonstration of technology is a focus on technical performance and a willingness to shut poorly performing projects. But the need to energize politicians may help explain why myths such as "energy independence" endure as goals in political debates even as most experts think it is neither achievable nor wise to pursue.[56]

Second, it is essential to provide reliable support signals. Big demonstration projects work not just by demonstrating technical feasibility but also by attracting commercial interest in the viability of the effort. The more engaged the commercial partners the fewer the risks for public funding and the more likely the technology will spread widely into commercial service because firms will invest to help steer the effort. Short and erratic funding cycles and other forms of market support – punctuated by big shifts in policy – are incompatible with the patient efforts needed to cross the valley of death. Some governments are able to make credible long-term commitments; for others, especially open democracies with a weak civil service, credibility requires a greater effort – such as through the creation of special government corporations with long time horizons built into their founding statute.

Third, strategic decisions about funding and organization must stay connected to expert assessment of technology performance. This lesson – that choices should be made by professionals rather than political hacks – is obvious yet extremely difficult to implement. The architects of PNGV knew this mattered and thus created an annual independent review of the PNGV research portfolio – perhaps the single most positive attribute of PNGV's design. But keeping management decisions tied to valley-crossing is much harder than it seems. Because of the cost involved and the desire to transfer funding to private investors as soon as possible, most governments fund demonstration projects through consortia with private investors who can shoulder some of the cost and also provide management. By playing a subsidiary role, government allows itself to become deskilled. That approach can make sense, but with a consortium comes all the risks already evident in industry-led decision-making in public–private partnerships. Established industries choose technologies that are most familiar and least risky to their incumbency. A particularly large political challenge for costly valley-crossing schemes is choosing a physical site and suppliers. When the money is big, many jurisdictions want a share of the spoils. Efforts by the US to site the FutureGen project for demonstration of advanced coal technologies, for example, was delayed by a tortuous process of selecting a final site. (And once the site was found, in Illinois, support from other congressional delegations in most of the rest of the country waned.)

Fourth, valley-crossing investments should be evaluated continuously against not just their own goals but also their role in a larger portfolio of low-emission technologies. If big progress is made on advanced nuclear plants then less spending will be needed on low-emission coal technologies since both kinds of power plants provide the same basic product: baseload electricity. If progress is made on lowering the cost of intermittent renewable electricity then more investment will be needed on technologies such as storage that will improve the odds that intermittent supplies will actually be useable at large scale. It has proved hard enough for governments to evaluate individual valley-crossing programs against their own internal criteria. Truly evaluating a portfolio is even harder because energy technology markets are global and the true frontier is often difficult to spot. This fact underscores the need for governments to craft technology strategies through international coordination, a topic to which I will return later.

While there are few good models in energy for such a portfolio management, models do exist in other fields. The Defense Advanced Research Projects Agency (DARPA) – the basic science and development arm of the US military – does this in a portion of its research that is focused on particular technological goals. DARPA is a particularly prominent and successful example of good administration of basic research and of valley-crossing investments but it has been hard to emulate in the rest of government. DARPA's budget, because it resides in the Department of Defense, is more insulated than in other federal agencies. That insulation boosts its capacity to make credible funding commitments and to manage its portfolio professionally. And because DARPA has one main customer – the military – it faces fewer challenges in crossing the valley of death when compared with technology development schemes that must survive in commercial markets where there are many competitors and attention to real costs is more laser-like.[57]

I have drawn many examples from the US, but in other countries the approach to meeting these four criteria will vary. In China, state-owned power companies and their research laboratories are probably the best institutions for crossing the valley of death, for only these institutions have access to the capital and expertise needed to manage the commercial risks that will arise. China is already organizing its R&D system to help provide the needed focus by nominating lead companies whose R&D efforts will concentrate on key technologies. For advanced coal gasification electric plants, state-owned Huaneng is the national lead for demonstrating advanced technology. For advanced coal plants that generate liquid fuels (which can be used to replace oil), state-owned Shenhua (the world's largest coal company) is the lead. And so on. The lead company system makes it easier for government to set clear priorities, make credible commitments, and delegate R&D management. However, it complicates efforts by the country, overall, to devise and manage an overall protfolio of technologies. Lead companies encourage stovepiping.

Where China is in much more flux today is in pre-commercial research. Until about a decade ago, most relevant research was done in laboratories that were connected directly to state-owned companies. Long innovation pipelines started in the laboratories and ended with technologies deployed by state firms; ideas outside that pipeline had little chance of success. Today many of those laboratories are now independent and more competitive – a direct result of government policies to provide more R&D funding through competitive grant-making focused on national priorities. (The practical effect of that policy is not yet clear. More competition should make the labs more relevant and capable, but it may also encourage them to pursue innovations that require less patience.) University researchers also play an increasing role, as in the US system, in pursuing pre-commercial ideas. China, today, is focusing its formidable R&D system on the challenges of green energy. That has analysts in many other countries worried that China will overtake the rest of the world in R&D, just as it has done in manufacturing. It is still unclear, however, whether the R&D system that China has built will be capable of making the difficult portfolio management choices that are essential to successful technology policy in green energy.[58]

In Europe the innovation system is split between the major EU member states (notably France, Germany, and the United Kingdom) and an emerging Brussels-centered system for funding continent-wide research. Each of the main member states has their own national systems for innovation. In France and Germany those systems have historically relied heavily on state-owned enterprises for valley-crossing investments. French and German companies could work patiently – with credible government support on advanced technologies, much as China seems to be doing today. In technology, however, the attributes that encourage patience – such as government-backed monopoly – can make mistakes just as readily as game-changing innovations. France backed the national "minitel" system for electronic communication for many years even as the Internet was proving itself superior. (Many internet-related innovations that might have existed in France now lag severely as a result.) The slow breakup of national champions in these countries is disrupting those R&D systems. But the big wildcard in European innovation is the growing Brussels-centered system for crafting and implementing policy. In Europe, only a few countries and research institutions really matter for fundamental innovation, and one danger is that the shift to Brussels will diffuse funding across many other EU members that are politically well connected yet practically much less relevant.

Thus the appropriability problem can be solved with two kinds of policies that are familiar. One is broad funding of basic research. The other is an active effort – tailored to each country's policy and regulatory system – to carry innovations across the valley of death. On both fronts one lesson is clear: promoting innovation will require governments that are highly capable of creating and managing portfolios of projects. And for governments that have struggled in performing such functions, the effort to build a low-carbon energy system could be extremely challenging.

Solving the lock-out problem

Lock-out problems will be much harder to solve because they are more sprawling in origin. There is no single, compact set of policies that governments can adopt to ensure that worthy new technologies have fair access to markets. Part of the solution is easy to anticipate: governments must adopt market signals, such as emission pricing and carbon regulations, that pull new technologies into service. Such signals are important not only because they get the economics right, but they are also a sign of credibility. Adopting visibly costly rules is one of the hardest things for governments to do, and when those decisions have been made the rest of the policy enterprise, including efforts to promote investments in low-emission technologies, becomes instantly more credible. The practice of government is filled with cheap talk and all the efforts to promote investment in innovation and in valley-crossing demonstration projects will be more effective when private investors, inventors, and government bureaucrats all believe that what they are doing is not ephemeral.

Lock-out problems come in many varieties, and here I focus on the two that are most important: informational and regulatory. The informational problems are the easiest to understand and fix. Consumers often do not know which technologies are best, and in the absence of information they understandably stick with the status quo. Programs such as labeling and energy audits help fix such problems by making it easier for consumers to obtain usable information. In general, such troubles arise mainly for small consumers such as individuals who are not expert and often are wisely unwilling to spend the time needed to research the performance of new technologies because they have other weightier priorities like showing up to work and raising their kids. By contrast, informational problems are relatively rare when technological choices are made by large, professionally managed organizations. Few electric utilities, for example, are unaware of the technologies available for purchase to make their power plants run more efficiently. Many homeowners, by contrast, are unaware that the old refrigerator in the garage dedicated to keeping a few beers cold is an energy hog.

A second source of lock-out is regulatory. Much of the energy industry is highly regulated – especially in electric power, which is particularly important for the problem of regulating warming gases because it offers some of the easiest places to make large dents in emissions. In most countries, power companies are either owned by governments or regulated by independent commissions. Historically, regulated industries have not been a hotbed of enthusiasm for new technologies. In the telecommunications industry, for example, the major inroads by low-cost microwave long-distance communications came from small independent start-up companies rather than regulated monopoly national phone companies. And regulatory barriers that monopolists helped erect to protect their markets dramatically slowed the spread of these microwave innovations.

The same process of lock-out through regulation has been feared in electricity, and over the last three decades federal and state regulators have adopted a host of rules designed to make it easier for favored new technologies to gain a share of the market. For example, in 1978 the US adopted the Public Utility Regulatory Policies Act (PURPA), which required many utilities to purchase expensive renewable energy supplies at favorable rates. Today, all major industrialized countries and many developing countries are repeating the experience with policies such as renewable energy mandates. There is little doubt that renewable energy technology is much further advanced due to the experience gained in these guaranteed markets.

The problem with "fixing" regulatory barriers is that many of those barriers have legitimate purposes that are difficult to disentangle from their impact of tilting the field of competition. For example, renewable energy suppliers often found it difficult to get dispatched if they faced the same standards for power reliability that apply to other electricity sources. Most renewable energy – notably wind and solar – is intermittent and thus intrinsically unreliable without major innovations in grid management. Many jurisdictions have relaxed those standards, which helps explain (along with other factors) the rapid rise in renewable power – to the point where in some settings the integrity of the electric grid may be in question because renewable energy accounts for such a substantial share of the power supplied in some parts of the US grid. The North American Electricity Reliability Council (the power industry's reliability watchdog) has documented growing fears of the electric grid becoming unreliable as investors build more renewables.[59] In Texas on February 28, 2008 a sudden drop in wind power took the near equivalent of two coal plants offline in a period of ten minutes, almost causing massive outages across the state. While some have blamed these troubles on the Texas grid operators and the lack of planning for more reliable standby power supplies, the reality is that this event is a harbinger of things to come anywhere engineers try to integrate large amounts of wind into power grids. Bigger investment in storage, more intelligent "smart grids" that could seamlessly switch power to where it is needed, and better designed market incentives to match suppliers and users of power could help solve these problems. But these technologies and markets are not appearing as rapidly as policy makers are pushing renewable power, and in most power systems the pricing regimes for renewable energy do not create adequate incentives for such investments.

Moreover, regulatory fixes create new interest groups that are hard to dismantle once the fix has served its original purpose. On the Texas power grid, which has the largest penetration of wind power in the United States, the various subsidies offered to wind generators are so valuable that power prices are, at times, negative. (Most of those subsidies come from the federal government while the consequences for managing the grid fall mainly to state and regional institutions.) Wind generators are happy to keep running even when they sell their product at a loss because the subsidies for production are so valuable. Much of the European renewable energy industry thrives on feed-in tariffs that greatly reduce the risk for investors in these favored technologies. In Spain, the risks have been so low that a scheme to encourage wind and solar power investment produced a bubble when many more investors signed up for the special tariffs than the government was willing to pay.[60] The PURPA program in the US had the positive effect of encouraging a focus on new energy sources such as wind and geothermal as well as more efficient energy systems such as cogeneration – all of which had a hard time getting access to customers prior to PURPA – but it also saddled utilities with massive costs that were an especially large burden as utilities tried to prepare for a more competitive, deregulated electric market.

In addition to these lock-out problems, markets are often tilted in many other ways. One is the perennial problem of price distortions, such as energy subsidies. The obvious remedy for that problem is removal of subsidies, but politically that has proved very difficult in many countries and not all subsidies are necessarily without merit.[61] Some barriers to market adoption also arise because of the structure of the market. In some countries there is only a single electric firm, which makes it difficult for the owners of the firm and their regulators to know which practices are most cost-effective. In other countries, notably the US, exactly the opposite problem prevails: the US has 3,271 electric companies, most of them tiny municipalities and co-ops that are poorly equipped to test and adopt risky new technologies.[62]

Fixing these structural barriers that lock out new technologies is important, and there aren't any general rules for what governments should do. Every country and market is different. One place to start is for each country to map out how it would craft a technology strategy. That mapping would include attention to how the country could solve its appropriability and lock-out problems. Most of those solutions lie within national governments, but some could benefit from coordination with other important countries. Next I turn to when and how that coordination might be useful.

The need for international coordination

So far I have shown that markets, left alone, will lead to under-investment in low-emission research and development for two major reasons. One is that ideas leak and thus individual firms may not be able to appropriate the benefits from their investments in R&D. The other is that new technologies may be blocked from gaining market share due to an array of regulatory, informational and other barriers. In effect, when firms evaluate whether it makes sense to invest in R&D they will be too miserly and myopic. But when a government, which represents the broader social interest rather than just the parochial concerns of an individual firm, makes the calculus it finds that investing in R&D along with demonstration of novel technologies is a wiser investment.

Even if individual national governments follow all the advice given so far they are still likely to underinvest in R&D. That's because ideas leak globally. Moreover, the markets for new technologies are also global and thus lock-out problems in one country affect the incentives for others to invest in R&D. For example, if advanced low-emission coal-fired power plants – so-called carbon capture and storage (CCS) units – prove hard to site in Europe and the US because local populations don't want CO_2 injected under their backyards then the incentives for innovators who want to export CCS technology (e.g., China) will wane. Twenty to thirty years ago if you visited power plants around the world you would tend to see technologies such as boilers and turbines that were supplied by local vendors. Today you see technologies from global suppliers. The globalization of energy technology markets is terrific news for efforts to spread the best technologies quickly through normal market channels. It will make the global warming problem a lot easier to solve when commercially viable low-emission technologies exist. But that news is also a reminder that a technology strategy must have a global element. As economies have become more global and as people and ideas move more freely it has become clear that many public goods, including knowledge, are actually global in scope.[63]

A global approach to addressing public goods does not require moving key decisions about the funding and management of R&D to international bodies. The international system doesn't have much capacity to do that, and governments are generally wary about allowing such decisions to be made fully by international institutions. Instead, what is needed is a mechanism for coordination so that individual nations develop their own R&D plans in a way that is mindful of what other nations are doing. If the key innovating governments are better informed of each other's efforts they are more likely to engage in useful coordination. They are also likely to expand their own national effort since the markets for advanced technologies will be larger. Chapter 8 will lay out a vision for how governments could organize international coordination of policy plans in many areas, including R&D.

The international system has lots of experience coordinating national policies. To date, however, very little of that experience has guided what countries do on R&D to lower warming emissions. The relevant international experience includes efforts to design and fund collaborative international scientific experiments. The most successful of those was the 1957–1958 International Geophysical Year (IGY) – a multinational effort to study the world's polar regions. (The IGY, among many other things, marked the first time that atmospheric data on CO_2 concentrations was collected systematically.) That same model has since been used for massive multinational programs in ocean drilling, atmospheric experiments, and some satellites such as LANDSAT. Most large physics experiments such as the collider at CERN and the ITER facility, which is still being planned, are conceived and funded through collaborative mechanisms. (The physicists are particularly good at coordination because they have no choice. Big machines are physically located in just one place and that focuses minds on the need for collective action.) Of course, one of the attributes that's different about low-carbon R&D is that funders also hope to gain commercial advantages from the effort, and thus whatever is done in collaboration will have a heavy dose of national and firm-level competitive interest.

What's interesting about a global approach to R&D is that the effort would need to engage only a very small number of countries. Twenty years ago a big push on innovation in energy technologies would require enlisting the support of a tiny group of like-minded industrialized countries – the United States, Japan, France, Germany, and the United Kingdom. The rest of the planet could be safely ignored. These countries varied in their national systems of innovation, but all had a similar outlook on the role of R&D investment in economic growth. All were members of institutions such as the OECD that helped countries coordinate; however, one country, the US, was so dominant that it had a strong incentive to organize coordination where that aligned with US interests. Today the picture is changing, notably with the rise of China, but the numbers are still small.

Actually measuring investments in knowledge – and thus which countries and firms are most important to engage, is difficult. One strategy is to look into history and trace the origins of important ideas, and from that gain a picture of which policies and decisions by firms and governments mattered most. That's what the National Research Council did in their careful review of the history of the information technology revolution, and it is what the best economic historians have done in many other studies.[64] But the backward-looking approach doesn't necessarily tell us much about the future.

So here I try to look forward to get a sense of which countries are likely to matter most for energy R&D. And because the low-carbon revolution will come from many quarters I will look broadly at innovative effort rather than just at particular kinds of energy technologies. Ten years ago if I had done this study and focused on particular devices, I might have concentrated on hydrogen energy for vehicles. Today, most visions for hydrogen futures have evaporated as the needed technologies have proved difficult to deploy while hydrogen's chief rival (gasoline) has proved highly competitive.[65] Today's visions center a lot on smart grids and electric vehicles. Much of that may, too, evaporate with the harsh reality of experience. Just as policy makers should not pick winners unless absolutely necessary, so too the analysts of technology policy should avoid too much focus on a particular technology.

Here I will look at the major input to innovation – the funding of R&D. And I will look at the outputs, which are harder to measure. For lack of better alternatives, when measuring output I will look at patents. Until a few years ago, patent studies had the major flaw that nearly all of them focused on the US. The US is the largest market for technology (and the largest economy) and the US Patent Office has particularly good records on the geographical origins of inventors. From those records analysts could map out the geography of innovation and could also look at how often a patent was cited as the source of an inspiration, which gave a measure of which innovations were most important. But one flaw in all that work was the US focus; some innovators would not bother to file for a US patent. That flaw is now being fixed, to some degree, by looking at two other patent offices – in Europe and in Japan – and at families of patents. This triadic view of innovation – US, Europe and Japan – helps to correct some of the host country bias that existed when analysts focused only on the US. It doesn't solve all of the bias, of course, because inventors in Brazil, China or other markets are still less likely to file for measured patents than inventors who live in the triad. But it's a start.

What I show is that today's innovative effort is concentrated in a handful of countries. Figure 5.4 shows data on R&D spending. Ideally I would gather data on energy R&D, which is the area of R&D that offers the most leverage on emissions of warming gases. But most countries outside the OECD don't measure energy R&D with much precision, and even inside the OECD the definitions vary so widely that it is hard to compare across countries. Thus here I look at total expenditure on all forms of R&D as a proxy for total innovative effort. If the goal is to create an international system for coordinating R&D, the countries in Figure 5.4 probably must be in the room – especially the US, Japan, and China that, together, account for more than half of all R&D spending. One of the wildcards in figuring out a global R&D system is the role of the European Union. Together, the twenty-seven members of the EU account for nearly one-quarter of all R&D spending – making them the world's second biggest investor in innovation after the US. If the EU were a truly coherent institution for government it should sit at the global table. My assessment, though, is that EU innovation policy is still highly fragmented and the EU does not speak with a single voice.

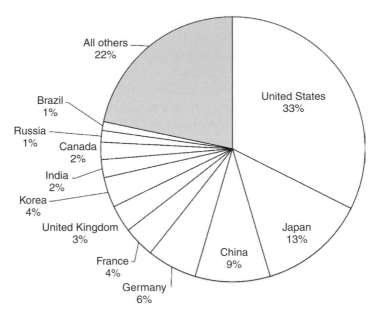

Figure 5.4 Top investors in innovation, 2007
Data are gross expenditures on research and development (GERD) from public and private sources in US dollars, converted using purchasing power parities (PPP).
Sources: UNESCO Science Report (various years) and UNESCO databases.

Better than having the EU join the table would be to have the top three innovators within the EU – Germany, France, and the United Kingdom (13 percent of world R&D) rather than the less reliable EU voice. One challenge for Europe is that its diplomacy emphasizes the EU but its competence in R&D is still largely a national affair.

Over the last decade the top innovators haven't changed much. The top OECD countries still play a central role, but new entrants are arriving. Most notable is China, whose share of global R&D has risen from about 2 percent in 1991 (the first year of reliable total R&D spending data by mainland China) to 9 percent today.[66] In less than two decades, China has gone from being a world player in R&D on the scale of Italy to, today, a country that spends nearly as much as France and Germany combined. Over the last decade, no country has risen faster in the innovation spending ranks than China. And in relative terms, no country has fallen further than the US.[67] Innovative effort worldwide appears to be in the midst of fragmenting somewhat. As shown in Table 5.1, the concentration of innovation in the

Table 5.1 *The world's top inventors and emitters*

	R&D spending		Patenting of innovations				Emissions	
			Total patents	Renewable energy	Nuclear energy	Fuel cells		
	1996	2007	2005	2003–2005	2003–2005	2003–2005	1996	2006
Top 5	72%	68%	88%	61%	74%	83%	44%	57%
Top 10	84%	82%	95%	79%	85%	90%	54%	67%
Top 15	91%	89%	97%	88%	91%	..	60%	74%
Top 20	95%	94%	99%	..	..	..	64%	80%

Sources: R&D spending from UNESCO databases; patents are OECD triadic families of patents (US, European, and Japanese patent offices) and reported in OECD's databases and in OECD, Compendium of Patent Statistics (2008). Emissions are for carbon dioxide from the burning of fossil fuels and exclude emissions from land use changes, drawn from the Carbon Dioxide Information and Analysis Center (CDIAC) via World Resources Institute's CAIT databases.

top countries has declined a bit from the mid-1990s (the earliest time there is reliable cross-country data) to today. Nonetheless, the concentration of innovative effort is remarkable. Since innovation is the main long-term engine of economic growth and environmental quality, in effect the future for what is often called "sustainable development" largely rests in the hands of the top 5–10 innovating nations.

Looking at the outputs of innovation produces a similar story. Table 5.1 reports the concentration of patenting activity. Whereas the top ten spenders on innovation accounted for 82 percent of the world total, the top ten patenting countries accounted for 95 percent of all the practical outputs from innovation activity. (This result may be a bit biased by the host country problem, but as it becomes easier and more important to patent innovations in the biggest markets the host country bias in patenting probably becomes less severe.) The top producers of patents do not correlate perfectly with spending, as seen in Table 5.2. Switzerland is big in patents (6th) but not as big in spending, thanks to an innovation strategy that focuses on pharmaceuticals where patenting is essential (perhaps to excess) and because Switzerland as a small nation, with barely any home market, hosts multinational companies that spend many of their R&D dollars in other countries. (A high ranking for the Netherlands and Finland reflects similar forces. In an open world economy there are big advantages for small, nimble, and focused countries.) India's prominence in innovative output is over-stated because much of patenting activity by Indian nationals probably relates to information and communication technologies – areas where India's science parks, modeled on their counterparts in Silicon Valley, are particularly well organized and prone to patent.[68]

The big spenders who are not big producers reflect, in part, shifts in the innovation landscape. Russia is still a big investor in R&D (10th in the ranking) but its patent rank is so abysmal (23rd) that it does not appear on Table 5.2. Some of this is the host country bias that triadic patent data can't fully fix, but most reflects the collapse of Russian science. China is ranked 3rd in spending, but it has risen so quickly in the ranks that its innovative output has not yet caught up and ranks at just 15 in patents. But quickly I reach the limits of what can be interpreted reliably from patenting data. In particular, interpreting trends over time is very difficult because true patterns in innovative effort commingle with trends in the incentives to file for patents. Data from

Table 5.2 *National rankings for innovation inputs (R&D), outputs (patents), and emissions*

Rank	R&D spending	Patents	CO_2 emissions
1	United States	United States	China
2	Japan	Japan	United States
3	China	Germany	Russia
4	Germany	Korea	India
5	France	France	Japan
6	Korea	Switzerland	Germany
7	United Kingdom	Canada	Canada
8	India	United Kingdom	United Kingdom
9	Canada	Netherlands	Korea
10	Russia	Italy	Iran
11	Italy	Sweden	Italy
12	Spain	Israel	Mexico
13	Brazil	Belgium	Australia
14	Australia	Finland	France
15	Sweden	China	Indonesia
16	Netherlands	Austria	Brazil
17	Israel	Chinese Taipei	Spain
18	Austria	India	Saudi Arabia
19	Switzerland	Australia	South Africa
20	Belgium	Ireland	Ukraine

Sources: same as Table 5.1.

1999 to 2005 (the longest time series for the triad patent data) show the US share rising 12 percent (from 33 percent to 45 percent), which probably reflects rising incentives for global patenting by US innovators and greater ease in global patenting as the administrative arrangements for filing patents in multiple jurisdictions are worked out.

For taking the pulse of basic research, the broadest data on R&D spending and on patenting are useful because basic research that is relevant to energy isn't the special province of any single field of research. But as ideas progress within a field more specialized data are needed to track progress and identify the leading centers of innovation. Table 5.3 shows the top ranking producers of patented innovations in three of the many areas that are relevant to the energy

Table 5.3 *Top innovators in three selected clusters of low-emission energy technologies*

Rank	Renewable energy	Nuclear energy	Fuel cells
1	United States	United States	Japan
2	Japan	Japan	United States
3	Germany	Germany	Germany
4	Denmark	France	Canada
5	UK	UK	France
6	Spain	Russia	UK
7	Australia	Sweden	Switzerland
8	Canada	Netherlands	China
9	China	Italy	Korea
10	France	Israel	Denmark

Sources: OECD 2008, sections 2.4, 2.5 and 2.6.

problem: renewable energy, nuclear energy, and fuel cells.[69] As I look at specifics, particular policies and markets have a big influence on rankings and the concentration of innovative activity. Patenting related to renewable energy is much more widely diffused around the world because policy interest is spread among a large number of countries. Denmark ranks 3rd in renewable energy patenting although it is only 22nd in overall patenting. Nuclear energy and especially fuel cells, by contrast, are much more highly concentrated although the top players differ. In fuel cells, about half of all innovative output comes from just one country (Japan) that has a long history of aggressive policies and organization of the research enterprise around those innovations. Japanese and US policy makers have been particularly enamored of fuel cells – in part because of their key role in a possible hydrogen-based energy system – and have poured money into those innovations while all other countries are much further behind. Whether the fuel cell race is one worth winning is another matter.

Putting it all together

I have explored three things in this chapter. First, technology innovation is extremely important in rewiring the politics of climate change.

To be sure, new technologies are essential to actually achieving deep cuts in emissions, but in tandem they help make the costs and the effort more politically palatable. As each nation becomes more convinced that the costs will be manageable then not only will it be easier to muster the support for national policies but governments will also become more confident that other nations will take similar steps. That confidence will brighten the prospects for meaningful international cooperation.

Second, I have made the well-worn yet still correct observation that innovation will require both the pull of market forces as well as the push of active "technology policies." The market pull arises from price incentives, such as emission taxes or cap and trade systems, as well as regulation that will require deployment of new technologies. Even when those market pulls exist, an active technology policy is needed because the market, left to its own devices, will fail in two ways. One is the well-known problem that private firms can't appropriate all the benefits from successful innovation for themselves and thus are prone to under-invest. That problem of appropriability is greatly magnified by the difficulties that important new technologies in the energy industry face when trying to gain access to commercial markets - so-called "valleys of death." The other problem is much less discussed by analysts but probably more important: new technologies are often locked out of the market because incumbents are well organized politically to protect their market share and because technologies that are used within large infrastructures often require a wide array of complex changes to standards and practices before the new technology can take a large share of the market. Changing a whole infrastructure is almost always a lot harder, slower, and less reliable than changing just a particular widget.

Fixing these problems requires an active technology policy consisting of at least three elements. One is funding – probably from national governments – for basic research across a wide array of fields. A second type of policy is investment to take promising ideas across the "valley of death" – the period of high risk, uncertain reward that kills most promising ideas. A third type of policy is a careful look across the economy at the lock-outs that keep new technologies from gaining market share.

Third, I have suggested that how countries will perform these functions is likely to vary substantially. Serious technology policy must

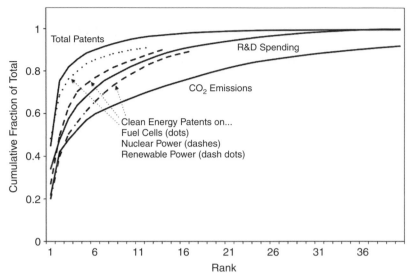

Figure 5.5 The concentration of innovation and emissions
The chart shows the cumulative fraction (vertical axis) from the largest innovators and emitters (horizontal axis).

align with national priorities and capabilities, and thus countries will
focus on different clusters of technologies and fields of research. And
countries will vary in the competence of their policy. These national
differences matter because the problems of appropriability and lock-
out that give rise to the need for an active technology policy in the
first place are ultimately global problems.

A global technology strategy must be crafted in a way that hon-
ors the wide national variations. That task is not quite so daunting
as it initially appears because luckily only a small number of countries really matter for innovation. Indeed, the concentration is quite
extraordinary, as shown in Figure 5.5. Tailoring international cooperation around the interests and capabilities of this small group will
require individual nations to craft their own innovation plans and
then coordinate. While working in a small group will greatly ease
the task, such a system of international cooperation will still require
flexibility and also a system of accountability. The outlines of such a
system will be the subject of Chapter 8.

6 | Preparing for a changing climate: adaptation, geoengineering, and triage

Avoiding global warming impacts is a game of chance. And the dice are increasingly loaded for nasty outcomes as the stock of warming gases accumulates in the atmosphere. Already the planet has warmed, on average, about 0.8 degrees Celsius since the onset of the industrial revolution.[1] Another 0.3–0.6 degrees of warming is already built-in to the planet but not yet measured by thermometers because the planet's big oceans are slow to warm.[2] Because human and technological systems are slow to change, even a crash program to regulate emissions probably wouldn't prevent another 0.5–0.7 degrees of warming on top of the warming already built into the planet. I'll call this total – 1.6–2.1 degrees – the *inevitable warming*.[3] That's bad news not just for the planet but also for the posse of diplomats that trot the globe signing communiqués claiming their goal is to stop warming at 2 degrees. The hard truth is that after two decades of dithering, the 2 degree goal is probably already history.[4]

This chapter is about how to brace for the large impacts that will accompany large changes in climate. I look at two kinds of impacts: those that are easy to predict and highly likely and those that are a lot harder to pin down. In my view, the really big dangers with warming lie in the latter variety. They lie way out in the "tails" of the probability distributions. The events in those tails appear to be a lot more probable ("fatter") than experts imagined even a decade or two ago. These fat tails worry me a lot, not just because they could be nasty but also because policy responses to them involve playing God with the planet. Humans probably aren't very good at that.

Luckily, the changes in climate that are easiest to predict are within the realm of what many human societies can probably manage. Humans are highly adaptive by nature, and most of the likeliest effects are broadly within the range of environmental changes that humans have already experienced. The adjustments needed in the future won't happen automatically and humans must rapidly gear up their adaptation skills. Many policies are already pointed in this direction. At best, however, aggressive adaptation policies will lower the damages from global warming but they aren't like a vaccine that inoculates humans from harm. Some triage will be needed where adaptation is impossible or prohibitively expensive. And adaptation isn't readily available to everyone. In general, wealthier societies are more adaptive than poorer ones, which explains why most analysts expect that the poor will be particularly hard hit by warming. I struggle with the challenge of how to help make poorer societies more adaptive, and I arrive at some unsettling news. There isn't much that outsiders can do to help.

If that news isn't unsettling enough, there's even worse news in the fat tails. Climate change could produce truly horrible outcomes. Sea levels could rise radically. A big shift in the monsoons could appear, with severe harm on countries such as India and Pakistan that depend on monsoons for water supplies and fear monsoonal storms when they cause flooding. Species already living on the edge could face mass extinctions. Individually, such impacts are worrying. But they could also combine in unexpected ways. Nobody knows the odds of these extreme outcomes because many are in the realm of "unknown unknowns." The world might get lucky and find interesting good news in the tails, but most of the science has focused on the really bad news.

Life in the tails could be terrible, but it could be a lot worse if humans don't start preparing for these unlikely but horrific outcomes. Part of the arsenal should include "geoengineering" – the ability to intervene directly in the climate system to blunt the effects of extreme warming. Geoengineering, itself, is full of risks. It isn't a substitute for fixing global warming at its root by controlling emissions. But root fixes take a long time, and nasty climate outcomes could appear much faster. In the face of a climate emergency a well-designed geoengineering plan will be better than doing nothing.

Many studies have looked at the logic in favor of investing in adaptation and geoengineering.[5] My focus here is on how societies should manage the politics of designing and implementing those policies. My starting point is to look at how important nations are likely to view adaptation and geoengineering policies. For adaptation, the incentives already clearly align in favor of countries adopting the right policies because most benefits from adaptation accrue locally. The big challenges will arise in weak, small and failed states whose governments are unable or unwilling to anticipate the harms from global warming and prepare their societies for the likely changes in climate. For geoengineering, the political logic that leads to national action is even more extreme. One nation, at small cost, could launch a geoengineering program that affects the whole planet. Indeed, that is the central political challenge in geoengineering: nations will become tempted to geoengineer on their own. If rogue nations choose improper geoengineering technologies, it could make the planet an even less hospitable place. While these geoengineering temptations are severe and could result in terrible outcomes, in this chapter I will show how they can be managed.

I will close this chapter with a fresh look at how humans relate to nature. If the climate changes in extreme ways then the options examined in this chapter imply a totally different relationship between humans and natural ecosystems. At the extreme, with geo-engineering and difficult triage decisions, humans will become direct managers of much of the planet's ecosystem. That God-like role is inevitable in a world of extreme climate impacts. The dice are loading in that direction.

A framework for analysis

My starting point is uncertainty. The climate system is a coupling of chaotic and imperfectly understood systems. The ultimate consequences of climate change arise through long and complicated chains of cause and effect. More emissions of greenhouse gases cause an ever-larger stock of those gases to accumulate in the atmosphere. More accumulation leads to more trapping of heat. More heat, in turn, causes changes in weather systems and climate. Still further down the chain of cause and effect, new weather and climate affects humans and ecosystems. Altered temperature and rainfall, for example, affects how crops and timber grow; they determine which natural ecosystems thrive or wither. Most links in the long chain of cause and effect are shrouded in uncertainty, and many of the uncertainties multiply along the way. Some of the impacts are relatively easy to measure and compare because they affect products, like food, that are already traded in markets. But many of the most dire impacts are felt in ways that humans don't value directly, yet nonetheless would lament if lost. What, for example, is the value of a pristine rainforest?

Putting all this together – the long chains of cause and effect and the difficulty in measuring impacts in markets – explains what I think is the central insight from three decades of research on climate impacts. Despite massive investment, scientists haven't really narrowed their estimates. That's not because they have wasted the public purse on café lattes and junkets. Rather, the inability to pin down climate impacts is intrinsic to the science. As scientists look more closely at climate impacts, they often find new uncertainties just as they find ways to render earlier forecasts more precise and accurate. Because scientists are looking at coupled complex systems with somewhat unpredictable properties, the tenor of their research has been to find new uncertainties faster than they close old ones. As the science proceeds the tails in the distributions get longer. That tail-lengthening is especially evident when scientists look at climate stresses that arrive rapidly. It is usually harder to predict the behavior of a complex system that is in the midst of rapid change from equilibrium.

To illustrate what's at stake, consider one of the climate impacts that will be most visible and already has many governments worried: rising sea levels. Sea levels affect coastal areas; higher seas along with stronger storms (another likely impact of global warming) are generally bad news. The central "best guess" estimates are based on two well-known mechanisms. One is expansion – ocean water expands when it warms. Relative to other climate impacts, this thermal expansion, as it is known, is fairly easy to measure and predict. A second mechanism is the effect of water from glaciers that melt when they are warmer. (Only glaciers that sit on land cause higher sea levels. Floating ice that melts has no impact on the sea level, just as an ice cube bobbing in a glass of water has no impact on the water level as it melts.) The quantity of meltwater is tricky to predict because the net effect of melting isn't just a function of temperature; it also depends on precipitation. If a warmer world leads to more snow falling on glaciers then sea levels might decline as glaciers expand. Indeed, the best guess today is several of the big glaciers in Antarctica will grow in size in a warmer world while Greenland's ice cap will shrink. Yet precipitation and temperature are still wildcards. A warmer world could lead to a lot more rain on some glaciers, which would accelerate the melting. Just as a stick of butter melts faster when cut with a warm knife, glaciers melt faster when hosed with warm rainfall than just basking in warmer weather.

These two factors – thermal expansion of sea water and glacial melting – explain why there's so much disagreement about today's best guesses for how much the seas will rise. When the United Nations Intergovernmental Panel on Climate Change (IPCC) summarized the published literature with its assessment of the most likely change in sea level, it found that sea level was already rising 2.8 cm per decade – mainly from thermal expansion.[6] Over the next century, depending on the scenario for warming emissions, sea level would rise 0.2–0.6 meters – again, with most of the increase due to thermal expansion.[7] That degree of sea level rise could be bad enough – an extra half meter of water along with stronger storm surges will already be terrible news for many unprotected coastal areas. But this assessment is conservative, and more recent studies suggest those estimates should be raised by perhaps a factor of three.[8]

The IPCC's conservatism reflects that, by design, the institution works only with highly reviewed published studies. And, by design, the IPCC reports aim to reflect the range of outcomes on which nearly all experts can agree. Often the IPCC relies on integrated models to project climate effects. Such models allow "apples to apples" comparisons of different scenarios, but some of the more worrisome futures for sea level are not found in these areas where it is possible to organize a consensus view using "apples to apples" techniques. For example, what will happen if ice sheets start to slide rapidly?

When the first big studies of global warming were done in the 1970s, the assessment of impacts on sea level included just the most likely effects from melting glaciers and expanding sea water. In 1978 one expert, J. H. Mercer, published a paper suggesting that a warmer world might cause the West Antarctic ice sheet to slide into the ocean leading perhaps to a 5 meter (16 foot) rise in sea level.[9] As research on ice physics and on climate science improved during the 1980s and 1990s, a new consensus view saw the West Antarctic ice sheet as much more stable. And then the pendulum swung again – seeing dangers there and also in other places, notably Greenland.[10] The new science foresaw not just a single (highly improbable) event of great sliding but a series of possible outcomes – partial slides and melts, each operating over different time-scales and each making their own contribution to sea level. For analysts, the central challenge has been to understand how ice sheets move, not just melt. Many glaciers initially appeared unlikely to melt quickly based on temperature and precipitation alone, but experts now think that once melting begins, perhaps they will slide more quickly. Some glaciers could melt underneath where the ice encounters warmer sea water – making sliding a lot easier. Others may be less penned up once the floating "tongues" of ice shelves that stick out into the sea disappear – as seems to be happening right now in both Greenland and parts Antarctica. All these forces, which require a close look at the physics and geometry of each glacier individually, add up to higher odds for swifter slides into the ocean than originally thought. When the IPCC issued a big consensus report on climate science in 2001, it found that scenarios that led to accelerated sea level rise from these forces were very unlikely.[11] Six years later, when the IPCC released its most recent report, it could not be so dismissive. While its total estimates for sea level rise could not reflect all these possible forces, the new report offered a host of observations and theories suggesting that ice sheets may not be so stable. Even that was criticized as too conservative by some scientists. Indeed, studies published since point to higher odds for higher sea levels and also much more uncertainty about exactly how much the seas will rise. Put differently, today's best guesses see a wider distribution of possible outcomes with fatter tails.[12]

Pity the planners in coastal cities who must build sea walls and water intakes with an eye to future sea levels. In the 1970s experts gave them a projection for possible future sea levels that was sufficiently small and narrow that few planners noticed. Summarizing what was known by the early 1980s for a National Academy of Sciences assessment of climate change, Roger Revelle concluded that sea levels would likely rise 70 cm over the next century – with an error of perhaps 25 percent either way – and noted that that rate compared with the current level of sea level rise at 10–20 cm per century and the average over the last few centuries of 100 cm per century. Sea level would change but probably not catastrophically. (Revelle also looked into the much more remote possibilities of catastrophic melting and sliding of ice sheets in Antarctica.) Economist Thomas Schelling, in the same report, noted that it would be easy to defend such a rise in sea level.[13]

Today, the projections for likely changes in sea level are larger and harder to ignore, but the range of outcomes is even wider than before. This odd outcome – that uncertainty seems to have gone up despite three decades of research – reflects that many "unknown unknowns" have been discovered along the way. In the late 1970s few experts much worried about Greenland's ice cap; today, most studies see Greenland as a bigger contributor to rising seas than Antarctica. Previously, most studies focused on the balance between precipitation and direct melting of ice; today, the frontier in ice research is the dynamic processes that govern how ice slides and how slides could dump a lot more water into the oceans than through simple melting. New thinking has not only led to a fuller range of predictions – the "known unknowns" – but also a new appreciation for how many other unknown unknowns are probably lurking in the climate system. Along the way, the mean and the variation in plausible outcomes for sea level have risen substantially.

I have focused here on sea level, but a similar story can be told for essentially all climate impacts. Indeed, the list of possible unpleasant surprises lurking in the warming world is growing longer. One reason for this apparent decline in confidence in how climate change will unfold is that assessors have become much better at talking systematically about what they don't know. In the first IPCC assessment of climate change, published in 1990, terms such as "likely" were used loosely with no clear meaning.[14] Today, IPCC has specific guidance on the terms; that, in turn, has inspired a generation of much more careful probabilistic assessments of inputs and outputs from climate models.[15]

The apparent confidence in predictions of climate impacts has also declined because experts are also much more aware today, unlike three decades ago, of the many ways that climate impacts could interact. Early impact assessments usually looked at each effect in isolation. But the really nasty impacts arise through interactions that multiply harm. Higher sea levels matter to humans mainly because more water means more flooding in coastal areas. But floods arise from the combination of high seas and the surges that accompany storms. Rapid warming could cause much stronger storms and bigger storm surges, which would amplify the dangers of flooding from higher oceans.

Similar interactions are evident throughout climate impacts research. For example, a warmer world will see more rainfall overall, but the extremes could be more pronounced – more rain where it already rains and more drought where dryness prevails. In drying regions, one worry is wildfires that rage longer and more furiously as ecosystems adjust to the new scarcity of moisture. Wildfire dangers are most pronounced when drying combines with other factors. In California, for example, a careful study has found that the odds of fire will rise in a warming world and the patterns of wildfires will be especially sensitive to how natural vegetation shifts with climate.[16] The margins between ecosystems are most vulnerable since those are areas where large shifts – for example from one tree species to another – are most likely to be felt with even small changes in climate.[17] Across western Canada, warmer winters are allowing pine bark beetles that kill trees to survive the winter, which has produced a much larger supply of tinder than if drying were the only force at work. The dying trees are converting a reliable sink for warming gases into a major source because the decaying biomass is converted back to CO_2 and a dead tree doesn't suck CO_2 from the atmosphere through photosynthesis. In the worst year already recorded, beetle-killed trees in British Columbia alone accounted for emissions equal to about three-quarters of Canada's typical total annual emissions from all forest fires.[18] Analysts are looking at a host of other pests that might become more voracious in a warmer world.[19] Three decades ago, none of the mainstream climate impact assessments examined such scenarios; today they are the cutting edge in climate impacts research.

Getting serious about managing climate impacts requires starting with fundamentals, which revolve around uncertainty. The most certain impacts of climate change are generally the least consequential. And the most consequential impacts, such as a sharp rise in sea level, are the most uncertain. Thus climate impacts come in two varieties. I will call the predictable variety "normal" because those climate impacts are all but certain, familiar, and generally well understood. Any country that envisions the future without estimating those impacts is engaging in reckless policy. The other impacts are the less likely, extreme effects. (The more that governments dither in controlling emissions, the more that "extreme" becomes the norm.) Other people call these extreme effects "abrupt" or "catastrophic." Abrupt impacts are particularly troubling because they are very costly to handle.

		Climate Impacts	
		Normal	**Extreme**
Human Responses	**Adjust Human Behavior**	(1) Adaptation	(2) Triage
	Adjust Nature's Behavior	(3) Plastic Surgery	(4) Geoengineering and Triage

Figure 6.1 Climate impacts and human responses

The other fundamental dimension, shown in Figure 6.1, is response. Will humans adjust to climate impacts by changing their own behavior and becoming less vulnerable? Or will they try to off-set or mask the impacts of climate change by changing the natural climate system? In the former case, policy is about crafting institutions and creating incentives that ultimately affect the behavior of many people – perhaps all of the billions of people on the planet, such as through the crops that farmers grow, where people live, and the design of climate-sensitive infrastructures such as coastal cities. The task for policy is familiar since nearly all policies are designed, in one way or another, to alter human behaviors. In the latter case policy is quite different. It is about intervening in nature, which is an activity that necessarily occurs on a large scale. In the former case, governments must be highly skilled at influencing the behavior of diverse human populations. In the latter case, governments must be highly skilled at manipulating nature. The skill sets are different and thus so are the policies. And so are the roles for international cooperation.

These two dimensions lead to four possible responses to climate impacts. I start by looking at the two opposites. In the upper left corner of Figure 6.1, box 1, is human adaptation to the normal effects of climate change that are likely to arise. In the lower right, box 4 is efforts to mask the extreme consequences with technologies such as geoengineering. In box 1 the goal of policy is to help humans adjust to the highly likely effects of changing climate; those effects are likely to be small and predictable enough that, in most societies, adaptation will be possible without fundamentally reorganizing society. Indeed, humans probably won't notice many climate impacts because humanity's adaptive capacity is massive.[20] In box 4, as I will show, that view of climate impacts and the pliability of human institutions is not nearly so hopeful. After looking at the two opposites I will briefly consider the other boxes.

Box 1: getting serious about adaptation

Nearly all the discussion about managing climate effects fits into the upper left box. That's because it is easier for governments to plan for outcomes that are likely, and because, as I shall show, all the other boxes imply policies that are unpleasant to contemplate, highly controversial, or both. Even so, until just the last couple years, it has been rare for politicians to talk about climate adaptation at all. There are no adaptation agencies. Few street demonstrations demand adaptation. And while there is growing awareness of the need for adaptation, talk far outstrips action.

Today, more governments are talking about adaptation because some of the effects of climate change are already visible. More are on their way. And many of the future impacts require efforts today to anticipate the changes. When building an ocean-front housing complex, for example, it is smarter to plan for higher sea levels from the outset than to worry about the problem in a few decades when waves are lapping the buildings.

The central challenge in crafting adaptation policy is that adaptation depends on human capabilities. That means that the most important adaptation policies are rooted in making humans and their institutions more aware and flexible. "Policy," for the most part, is not a discrete event or a particular set of actions.

As a general rule, adaptive capacity grows with income. Societies that are rich and full of capabilities to anticipate change and invest to manage change in their environment are much less vulnerable. But people living on the edge find themselves in deep trouble when the edge shifts even a bit. Wealth has its troubles, to be sure, but as the great political scientist Aaron Wildavsky put it bluntly in a proposition three decades ago, richer is safer.[21]

The wealth proposition explains the central finding from the last three decades of research into climate change effects. For most of the "normal" effects of climate change, the rich (highly adaptive) societies probably won't notice much. And the poor (less adaptive) societies are in deep trouble. The poor countries know this, which is one reason they are consistently organized at climate diplomatic conferences with the aim of pressuring the industrialized nations into making deeper cuts in emissions and also providing much more money to help the poor nations adapt. When global warming talks first began in the early 1990s nearly all the discussions about income transfers were focused on helping developing countries control emissions. Today that is shifting as those countries realize just how vulnerable they are (and how little real progress has been made in slowing global warming). For the poorest countries, especially, money to help with emission controls isn't very useful since most of those countries don't have high emissions. Yet adaptation is inevitable and not surprisingly they have shifted their demands to focus on adaptation assistance.

Studies on climate impacts began in the mid-1970s during the debate over supersonic aircraft (see Chapter 2). The early studies usually concluded that any change in climate caused human suffering because societies had optimized themselves for their current climates. In the 1970s the worry was cooling; studies on the impacts of cooling found bad news. Today, the worry is warming, and not surprisingly most studies find that a warming departure from today's cozy equilibrium is costly. That approach to climate impacts research, scholars soon learned, was completely wrongheaded. Change isn't costly if societies are always changing. If farmers keep planting the same crops with the same methods, then a changing climate would hit them hard. But if they could look forward and adjust their behavior – through purchasing new seed varieties, switching crops altogether, adjusting irrigation technologies, and such – the impact of a changing climate would be much smaller, at least up to the point where adaptation becomes very difficult. Dumb farmers, as the economists who did this research called them, would be hit hard. Smart farmers, who were more agile, could roll with the punches. The dumb versus smart distinction applies to foresters, coastal planners, and just about everyone who is exposed to climate impacts. But the single greatest focus of climate impacts research is on agriculture because farming is usually the human activity that is most exposed to climate change. Nearly all farming occurs outdoors and is exposed to the vagaries of weather and climate.

Armed with this insight – that it matters whether farmers are dumb or smart – in the 1980s analysts started rewiring the computer models used to estimate climate impacts. It transformed climate impact assessment because when impacts affect people who are smart and adaptive, the outcomes are a lot less dangerous. To be sure, there are limits to this insight. Iowa's soils and people would not readily shift from corn to tropical fruit. Farmers might be smart, but it was impractical to assume that all were Einsteins who had perfect fore-sight, although so-called "precision agriculture" is forcing analysts to grapple with the prospect that some farmers (with the help of profes-sional advisers and GPS units that allow fields to be managed to very fine resolution) could become extremely smart and nimble. Other lim-its include the cost of becoming smart. Getting information about future changes in climate may be expensive, and thus the farming world might be slow to smarten. And lots of other pesky real world factors might get in the way. Across much of the world, farming is highly subsidized and often regulated; those institutions, if not man-aged by smart bureaucrats, could blunt the ability of even the Einstein farmer to adapt to a changing climate. Inflexible property rights – such as property rights that govern access to water or the uses for land – might also impede change.

The first major study to look closely at smart farmers was a careful assessment of possible climate impacts in four states of the American farming Midwest – Missouri, Iowa, Nebraska, and Kansas. Dumb farmers would experience huge losses from a changing climate – to the order of $10 billion per year – but smart farmers meant that a cli-mate change had an economic impact that was roughly zero.[22] Pretty much every study since then has found a similar result when climate effects are modest and populations are adaptive. (The most recent studies tend to find, nonetheless, that substantial adaptive efforts will still be needed, partly because the effects of climate change are pro-jected to be more substantial than in the 1990s when the first inte-grated assessments of climate change were first done.) At first, these studies were done in the industrialized world, mainly America, where it isn't too hard to be adaptive if you are a farmer. Only later did ana-lysts look to developing countries where farmers were poor and thus faced many other obstacles to adaptation such as weak infrastructure and predatory governments.[23] Smarts aren't everything.

The policy implications of the central finding from this research – that smart farmers are less vulnerable – are straightforward. Help farmers become smarter and more adaptive. Markets should be encouraged since they are usually more flexible when circumstances are changing. New seeds and crops designed for likely new climates should be tested, and the lessons from these experiments should be disseminated widely. (The CGIAR network of agriculture research centers and agriculture extension stations discussed in Chapter 5 can help. Indeed, the CGIAR is a particularly attractive model for serious collaborative research and policy implementation on adaptation.) And the same logic applies to most other activities that are exposed to the effects of a changing climate. Planners in coastal cities should learn about likely rises in the sea level and changes in storm tracks so they internalize those risks when they plan and build new infrastructures. Following this logic, adaptation isn't so much a policy but a process of making it easier for all climate sensitive parts of humanity to anticipate and adjust.

For the most part, societies that are highly adaptive are already responding to this policy insight. The people of the Netherlands and Venice have long battled the seas and have settled large areas below sea level. Both are now battling harder – mainly by building bigger walls and other protective barriers. These efforts are not cheap. The system of seventy-eight floating gates designed to protect Venice will cost more than €4 billion (and surely will have cost a lot more once the project is fully finished in 2014). But they can be justified when needed to protect existing assets. Disastrous floods in the 1950s convinced planners around Britain's Thames River that a moveable barrier would help manage occasional high sea levels; that barrier now exists and is deployed more often as the seas rise. While the effects of adaptation planning are most visible around rising seas because the responses usually include tangible hardware to contain the water, in fact adaptive efforts are becoming pervasive. Since 2005 the State of California has required a regular assessment of climate impacts of all types. Those assessments have, in turn, helped the state adjust its planning to reflect both the likely impacts of climate change and even the possible extreme impacts.[24] (Better planning doesn't guarantee better policy. Policy changes that are costly and harm well-organized interest groups are usually difficult to adopt.)[25] Many developing countries are also following this insight. For example, India is setting up its own system for climate research, including studies on climate impacts tailored to India's special circumstances. And the government also recently announced plans for a major new weather forecasting system that will help the country's farmers anticipate key weather events such as the monsoon; the same capacity will also help them become more adaptive to a changing climate.[26]

The growing awareness of climate impacts is evident not only in governments but also in other large, well-managed institutions. The World Bank, for example, has begun an effort to assess the exposure of its lending and grant portfolio to changing climate. In 2006 it reported its first careful assessment, finding that 20–40 percent of the traditional development projects it manages are subject to climate risk. Now that the Bank is aware of these risks, it appears to be doing a better job managing them.[27] The Bank also has its own projects explicitly focused on adaptation – more on that below – but they are dwarfed by the effort of making all Bank lending and expert advice to developing countries more fully aware of climate risks.

Thus, for the most adaptive countries and institutions, "adaptation policy" is starting to happen. A lot more is likely as governments and other policy institutions become more aware of the growing impacts of climate change. What is clear is that serious adaptation policy isn't a discrete activity. There is no over-arching framework or strategy for adaptation. There is no shortlist of initiatives that signal a serious adaptation policy. Rather, serious adaptation among the countries that have flexibility and resources is about thousands of initiatives melded into existing planning and economic practices that ease the task of anticipating and adapting. Those efforts can be helped along with careful studies on likely climate impacts, and, on that front, the advanced industrialized countries and the large emerging markets such as Brazil, China and to some extent India are doing quite well. Adaptation isn't an event but a mindset.

The big challenge for adaptation policy is in the societies and institutions that are less fortunate. The wealth proposition helps us explain why. Lower incomes usually mean that fewer resources are available to help society adjust in times of change. Indeed, countries with lower incomes generally have less flexible economies. And in nearly every country, the least fortunate engage in economic activities, notably farming, that are highly sensitive to climate. In the United States, the agricultural sector comprises only about 1 percent of GDP, employing about 3 percent of the country's 154 million people in the labor force.[28] By comparison, in India agriculture makes up 18 percent of the country's GDP and employs about half the country's 467 million workers.[29] In the poorest African countries the role of agriculture is even higher. As incomes rise, people generally shift away from working the land because it is easier to control economic activity that is indoors and, in general, the opportunities for adding value (and thus earning incomes) are more attractive in manufacturing and services than in the raw production of commodities from the land.

Adaptive ability is not purely a national affair because income and governance often vary within countries. Within the United States, which is generally rich and highly adaptive, the flooding of New Orleans after hurricanes Katrina and Rita was a reminder that poverty and bad government can create maladapted societies even within the richest nations. Even if the federal government in the United States had been better organized for crisis, the local impediments in New Orleans assured disaster. In India, gated communities with their own water and electricity supplies are likely to adapt to climate changes much better than poor, rural Indian farmers living on the margin. China's cities, such as Shanghai and Hong Kong, are already planning for a world with higher sea levels, but China's marginal farmers will keep struggling with floods and crop failures and seem likely to fare even worse with a changing climate. Even the rich of Bangladesh – the canonical country cited whenever analysts point to the dangers of rising sea levels – live in a more adaptive cocoon within a much larger and less adaptive broader society. Singapore is becoming largely invulnerable to most of the world's nastiest diseases, such as malaria, even as the microbes ravage Malaysia just across the border – where incomes are lower and governing institutions generally less capable.[30]

Thus follows the most disturbing fact about climate policy. The countries with the highest incomes tend to cause the most harm to climate because they have the highest emissions, and they also have the greatest ability to adapt. The countries with the lowest incomes are least responsible for the warming problem yet are also most vulnerable.

What could the industrialized countries, which are responsible for most of the warming emissions that have already accumulated in the atmosphere, do to help the more vulnerable nations? This question has loomed over climate talks from the very beginning. Around 1990, just when the talks leading to the United Nations Framework Convention on Climate Change (UNFCCC) were getting started, two British lawyers with funding from the Ford Foundation catalyzed the creation of the Alliance of Small Island States (AOSIS) – a coalition of the most vulnerable countries. AOSIS pressed for tight limits on emissions as well as for mechanisms to help the most vulnerable adapt to climate effects such as higher sea levels and stronger storms.[31] As a political coalition, AOSIS has been a tremendous success. Diplomatically the group is now omnipresent in the UN talks; the original five official regional groupings that dominate most UN negotiations were expanded to include a new group of vulnerable low-lying island nations. At the Copenhagen conference, tiny Tuvalu stopped the formal talks with its demand (unacceptable to the big countries) that the big emitters not leave without agreeing to a binding treaty that would force lower emissions.[32] Two years earlier, Papua New Guinea's representative (another AOSIS member) famously told the Bush administration's diplomats to get out of the way.[33] AOSIS is articulate and has a compelling case, but these nations are nonetheless not powerful. With AOSIS backing, climate diplomats created a voluntary tax on international emissions offsets with the proceeds earmarked for a special fund that would help poor and vulnerable countries (such as most AOSIS members) adapt to the changing climate. Until Copenhagen, where these countries (and other vulnerable poor nations) forced industrialized nations to make vague new promises for adaptation funding, at most about $448 million was raised from this tax and all sources for adaptation assistance.[34] Politically, international funding for adaptation has been tough to mobilize and sustain. One of the difficulties is that such funding is generally drawn from public budgets; aside from the voluntary offsets tax, which was very small (2 percent), adaptation funding has none of the attributes that lends itself to private sector financing.

Although not much real adaptation assistance has been forthcoming, should rich countries do a lot more? In Copenhagen the unequivocal answer to that question was yes. Although the final outcome in Copenhagen was ambiguous, one of the clear points of agreement is that industrialized countries would supply massive new funds for adaptation. This response has deep moral roots, for the rich nations are causing serious harms that fall on the poor. I am not a professional philosopher, but I have grown skeptical that the moral argument has been framed correctly. If big funds are mobilized, how would the money be spent? The moral argument needs a firmer foundation in practical answers to that question – a morality of consequences.[35]

On the surface, the moral argument about climate consequences is straightforward and compelling. In the ideal world, polluting countries would stop their pollution. But that outcome may be immediately infeasible. Until not long ago, nobody really knew that warming would be so harmful; new technologies do not yet exist widely to cut the pollution. Even with serious effort, many decades will be needed until pollution is cut and the environment recovers. During that period, the polluters have a responsibility to help the harmed, especially when the harmed are much poorer. The basis for this line of thinking comes, in part, from the classic question that Rawls posed in his theory of justice: imagine you are sitting behind a veil of ignorance about exactly where you will end up in life. What kind of rules and obligations would you want? To Rawls, the answer was a set of rules that protected the least fortunate.[36] Other philosophers have extended that argument to international justice, and a similar line of argument underlies an ethics of climate change.[37]

If the big emitters actually followed this moral logic, what could they do to help the poor in other countries adapt? My concern is that there aren't likely to be practical, helpful answers to this question. The problem in helping the vulnerable poor adapt to climate change is that for them, like all countries, adaptation policy is a mindset rather than a discrete activity. Only the most blatant, last-ditch efforts – such as building a sea wall around a submerging island or buying one-way tickets for a fleeing population – can easily be identified as adaptation and ring-fenced for special funding by the emitters who caused the problem. Everything else, which is the vast majority of what will be most effective in responding to the most likely effects of a warming planet, must be integrated into the process of economic development. It is impractical to disentangle "adaptation" policies from ordinary policies aimed at managing the economy and infrastructure.[38]

The task of helping countries become more adaptive to climate change is quite similar to economic development, and track record with efforts by outsiders to help countries boost their economic development is mixed. Development assistance works when it is applied in the right contexts – where investment and advice by outsiders reinforce good governments and sound fiscal management.[39] The same logic applies to adaptation assistance – it will work when it reinforces national systems of government that are adaptive. The central problem with adaptation assistance is that nobody yet knows how to measure which national contexts are adaptation-friendly, and the countries with the contexts where adaptation assistance could be most effective are those where societies are already adaptive on their own. There are growing sums of money earmarked for adaptation in the countries that need adaptation assistance the most, but nobody really knows how to spend those resources wisely.

This logic helps explain why careful reviews of "adaptation policy" arrive at the conclusion that very little is being done on this front.[40] In fact, political systems around the world are gearing up for adaptation. But little of what they do is a discrete project that is easy to spot. And in the societies that are not gearing up the actions that are most needed are pervasive and internal to the society rather than particular events or activities that outsiders can easily fund. Adaptation is not a discrete project; rather, like serious development assistance, it is a pervasive and multi-pronged activity whose success depends on the host country's local institutions.

One implication of this practical problem in providing adaptation assistance is that the moral challenge in global climate change hasn't been framed in the right way. To date, most of the moral debate has been anchored in guilt and focused on the argument that emissions cause climate change and thus emitters have a moral obligation to clean up their mess and to help those harmed by the effluent. That line of moral reasoning has animated a burgeoning literature on how to measure the harm and allocate burdens.[41]

But this line of moral thinking is misplaced because it focuses on the wrong starting point for policy. Many of the moralities around climate policy start with the assumption, echoing the insight of Rawls, that it is useful to imagine a setting where individuals do not know what station they will occupy in life. Rawlsian thinking is helpful in imagining moral end-states, but it isn't necessarily useful in charting the *process* for getting to those end-states in a world that already exists. On the climate change problem, this matters because the policy question surrounding adaptation isn't whether rich countries should impose harm on poor nations. They shouldn't. But the real policy question is what should be done from today's perspective with industrial systems already built that are causing harmful pollution that was largely unknown when the foundation for those systems were laid. Answering that question isn't so straightforward because polluting nations don't just pollute. They also generate economic activity that, through trade, affects economic activity in the rest of the world. And when the rest of the world is richer and more engaged with the world economy it is also more adaptive.

Looking at the adaptation question through this lens – one of process and consequences, not end-states – leads to a different way of thinking about morals in the era of global warming. The polluting nations have an obligation to help less fortunate countries. But there are many entries in the ledger of benefits and costs that rich nations transfer to the poor. A righteously clean nation that adopts costly emission control policies – and thus harms economic development globally – is probably pursuing a less moral policy than the nation that did little to control its pollution but invested more efficient policies at home or effective development assistance policies abroad. Simple morality looks to emissions and their harm when assessing scores. Complex morality looks at the whole ledger of ways that a polluting nation affects the welfare of vulnerable nations.

The question of complex morality isn't just an academic one. Thinking about morality in this way could transform the relationship that the rich polluters have with the poorer, vulnerable nations. One dimension (pollution) becomes three (pollution, economic development, and overt policy assistance). If rich countries adopt climate change policies that cause excessive economic harm at home, then that harm also hurts the poor through trade – especially the poor that export to the rich. And if rich nations adopt policies that include predatory trade sanctions that punish poor nations, then they magnify the immoral harm. If noble sounding climate funds earmarked for nonexistent adaptation projects undercut the money that flows into well-managed development assistance programs – either because donor nations are poorer or perhaps because, politically, the moral pressure for aid is sated by new efforts in greenery – then the immoral damage multiplies still further.

For the most part, none of the public debate about global warming obligations has looked at these other dimensions to morality. When arguments along these lines have been raised it is often to raise questions about whether it is wise to spend money controlling emissions when other uses of those funds could have a bigger impact on the welfare of poor nations. That kind of questioning is important, not least because emission control policies will have an impact on global warming only in the distant future while the benefits of economic growth in the most vulnerable countries is more immediate.[42] But the full analysis requires looking at the whole ledger.

This more complex way of thinking about adaptation and morality could lead to some profoundly different priorities for policy. Here I focus on three. First, people who care about morality need to rethink the role of international transfers. A bigger transfer program doesn't fix the moral problem, especially if a country's adaptiveness is difficult for outsiders to influence – even outsiders that offer huge transfer programs. Transfers to help developing countries adapt to climate change are popular these days because poor countries are well organized to demand them and government in industrialized countries, perhaps due to guilt, are not shy about promising them. Such transfers are steeped in suspicions that they will not be "new and additional," which has created pressure to make discrete adaptation funds whose activities are not fungible with other purposes. If adaptation money is to be well spent then exactly the opposite approach then would be better. Adaptation must be integrated into well-administered development assistance programs not walled off as a separate activity. The contexts that make a country adaptive overlap heavily with those that encourage economic development. Mainstreaming adaptation into traditional well-managed development assistance is probably the most effective and moral strategy.

A second implication for policy is that the rich industrialized countries have a moral obligation to adopt policies that impose the least deadweight cost on the world economy. If such losses arise, a special effort is needed to minimize losses to the most vulnerable countries. Ironically, this line of moral thinking might lead some countries to dampen their enthusiasm for mitigation. The United States, for example, is on the cusp of spending several tens of billions of dollars annually from its gross domestic product to mitigate a small fraction of its emissions through new regulatory programs.[43] Devoting a portion of that, on the scale of billions of dollars per year, to well-conceived programs for economic development in poor countries would probably be a much more moral policy. Political choices are usually not made this way, but moral thinking requires considering such trade-offs.

A third implication is more sobering. The very poor, vulnerable countries will be in deep trouble. These countries already generally live on the edge. Global warming is more terrible news for them.

And the ability of outsiders to make much of a difference is quite constrained. A central element in the moral calculation, looking at the process of policy change rather than ideal outcomes, will be triage of which countries can benefit from development and adaptation assistance. The blunt fact is that in very poor countries infrastructure is not that valuable; long-lived infrastructures are rare. Indeed, these countries are poor in large part because they lack the governing institutions needed to encourage stable, long-term investment in infrastructure and public goods. Thus in crass economic terms, there isn't much that is worth protecting in comparison with higher value assets elsewhere in the world. Outsiders, attentive to costs and benefits in a moral calculation, will find there isn't much they can do to be helpful. Triage doesn't necessarily mean walking away, but it will require looking into new policy options. For countries that have consistently failed to create the right context for economic development (and adaptation) a range of new approaches – such as receivership or migration – merit attention. I will come back to triage later.

Box 4: masking the horrors with geoengineering

Quite distinct from the normal, likely effects of climate warming in box 1 are possible extreme and horrific outcomes. By "extreme" I mean outcomes for which adaptation is exceptionally difficult and costly. By "horrific" I mean outcomes so unpleasant that they are hard to tolerate and adaptation is impractical. For the next few decades, such extreme and horrific outcomes are unlikely, although the odds they will appear are rising along with the concentration of warming gases in the atmosphere. In a world with a lot of warming, extreme will become commonplace.

In theory, it is possible to engineer nature to offset some of the impacts of global warming. Ideas of that ilk usually travel under the name of "geoengineering" – that is, large-scale interventions in the climate system to offset the effects of warming gases.[44] Most geoengineering policy debates have focused on various strategies for managing the amount of incoming energy from the sun by tinkering with the reflectivity of the planet, also known as "albedo." By dialing up the albedo – and thus dialing down the sun, in effect – it might be possible to offset crudely some effects of climate change. (Nobody has found a practical way to dial down the sun directly.) At present, about one-third of the incoming sunlight is reflected back to space. Increasing that amount by just a few percent could crudely offset the higher temperature caused by the build-up of greenhouse gases. In theory, there are many ways to change the albedo. One is by shooting rockets or using large guns or airplanes to inject reflective particles in the stratosphere about 10–50 kilometers above the earth's surface.[45]

(Other options that don't involve tinkering with the balance of solar radiation are also often called "geoengineering" but I won't focus on them here. They appear to be harder to deploy and work more slowly, which means they are less useful in an emergency although they may also have fewer nasty side effects.[46] To avoid confusion, most experts call the emergency measures solar radiation management (SRM) and eschew the term "geoengineering" because it has lost concrete meaning.)

Making a more reflective stratosphere is the most widely discussed geoengineering concept in part because it is familiar. Nature offers periodic tests of the approach by blasting off volcanoes. Familiarity is helpful because, as I shall show, tinkering with nature is fraught with dangers, and many of the most worrisome side effects are hard to assess. A geoengineering system that is already familiar and tested may cause fewer unanticipated side effects, which would make the dangers easier to assess and the public more comfortable with the option. Making people comfortable playing God is never easy.

Whole books have been written about geoengineering, and a burgeoning scientific literature is examining the opportunities and dangers.[47] The range of options is already large and growing. The stranger the idea, the more media attention it seems to garner. For our purposes, however, what matters is that these options exist and, while crude, probably work.

Managing solar radiation is interesting, at least in theory, because it allows a quick response if climate change turns ugly. In contrast with adaptation (box 1), which requires changing the whole process of economic development and the management of infrastructures, geoengineering is fast and blunt. That's why the most likely scenarios for deploying geoengineering start with a climate emergency. Fast, blunt options are particularly useful in such settings, much as a tourniquet is handy to have ready if you accidentally cut off your arm. (A few analysts are also looking at the possibility that geoengineering systems might work so well that they would be useful not just in an emergency but also as part of a more general strategy to dampen the likely effects of climate change and perhaps even create designer climates.[48] My sense is that most societies won't tolerate such tinkering except in case of emergency.)

Unlike adaptation, which requires altering millions of behavioral decisions by all of humanity that is affected by global warming, geoengineering is a more centralized activity. Only a few capable actors are needed to design and deploy a system. By tinkering with albedo, these systems allow humans huge leverage on the climate. Small changes in reflectivity have large impacts on climate, just as small changes in the planet's heat balance due to the build-up of warming gases cause huge impacts on climate. High leverage and centralization also explains why a crude geoengineering system might cost only a few tens of billions of dollars to deploy, which makes this option essentially free when compared with the trillion dollar price tag for deep cuts in emissions.[49] Those crude systems are probably quite flawed and likely to yield many nasty side effects. More realistic geoengineering systems that include serious efforts to fix some of the side effects – what I have called in other writings "cocktail geoengineering" after the more costly (but more effective) drug cocktail strategies used to combat AIDS and other complex diseases – will be a lot more expensive.[50]

The attributes that make geoengineering attractive – namely, the ability to have large, quick leverage on the climate system for small cost – also create huge policy challenges. I will focus on two of the most important. First, geoengineering works by making small alterations in the planet's highly leveraged, complex climate system. Almost always, alterations to highly leveraged, complex systems produce uncertain outcomes as the full effects ripple through the system – whether it is the world's financial markets, accidents on congested roadways, or the global climate. And in highly leveraged, complex systems, not only are outcomes hard to predict, but the odds of extreme outcomes – good and bad – are higher than in simpler and more stable systems. Geoengineering is most likely to be used in the face of a climate emergency when extreme climate impacts are already evident. Policy makers, faced with the decision of whether to deploy geoengineering systems in that setting, will wisely ask whether geoengineering a system that is already coming unhinged will make matters worse. They will also ask what kind of geoengineering will be safest to deploy – a simple system that is also cheap or a "cocktail

geoengineering" scheme that is more costly, perhaps harder to predict and manage because it is more complex, and yet designed to offset some of the likely side effects of simple geoengineering. The first
task for any serious policy strategy on geoengineering is, therefore,
learning about possible side effects and management strategies before
actual deployment. That kind of research is far outside the normal
type of research familiar to climate scientists, and its odd characteristics will require different types of institutions.

The other challenge for geoengineering policy is governance. Even
if it proves possible to obtain reliable information about the benefits
and consequences of deploying geoengineering systems, whose hands
will be allowed on the thermostat? The question is a familiar one to
scholars of nuclear weapons proliferation. Once the genie is out of
the bottle, many countries want the ability to make weapons. For the
dozen or more countries that can already contemplate deploying at
least crude geoengineering systems, what would stop them from acting alone? As climate impacts mount and the most vulnerable countries become frustrated by the lack of progress in worldwide emission
controls, this question must be contemplated. Acting alone could
be trouble if unilateral geoengineers deploy systems that are poorly
designed and cause even more harm. That danger has led some analysts to demand that geoengineering not be used except with prior
international agreement. But requiring too much consensus is a recipe
for gridlock not governance.

I look at each in turn – first learning and then governance.

Learning more

The scientific research on solar radiation management is still in its
infancy. Often the experts are asked whether geoengineering will
"work." That's the wrong question. Almost certainly, crude programs
that tinker with the albedo will have an effect on climate because the
basic physics are relatively easy to master and volcanoes provide ready
tests of the theory. The real questions hinge on the side effects and the
cost of systems to reduce or eliminate those side effects.

Already, studies have pointed to an array of possible side effects.
Geoengineering systems might alter rainfall or even cause greater
risks of drought.[51] Geoengineering could cause massive ozone depletion if the albedo scheme includes injection of particles into the

stratosphere since some of the chemical processes that destroy ozone are particularly speedy when the stratosphere is rich in particles.[52] Geoengineering might alter ecosystems if, for example, dimming affects light-sensitive plants or if changing rainfall patterns alters the availability of water.[53] None of the geoengineering schemes under discussion is likely to exactly offset the change in climate caused by warming gases because the physical processes in geoengineering and climate warming are different.[54]

The biggest problem is perhaps that tinkering with the albedo will still leave in the atmosphere the CO_2 and other warming gases that caused global warming in the first place. CO_2 is a particular worry because it interacts with ocean chemistry to make a mild acid. Already the oceans are becoming measurably more acidic, and as that process continues, it is likely to be extremely harmful to marine ecosystems that depend on shell-forming animals. (In a more acidic environment these animals find it more difficult or even impossible to make shells. The base of most marine ecosystems depends in large part on such organisms, and some particular marine ecosystems such as coral reefs are thoroughly dependent on shell formation.[55])

In the ideal world, analysts would gather information about the costs and benefits of a policy option such as geoengineering. Decisions could be made about deployment by comparing costs and benefits. So far, there hasn't been much progress on that goal because geo-engineering does not lend itself to normal cost-benefit analysis. The cost of actually deploying crude geoengineering systems doesn't really matter because it is so small.[56] But the cost of geoengineering systems that include extra schemes to counteract all the side effects of crude geoengineering will be extremely hard to assess. For example, some analysts have suggested systems that could be deployed to counter-act ocean acidification.[57] And all the other side effects of crude geo-engineering might be amenable to similar kinds of solutions – extra fixes added to a basic albedo management system, each with a cost. This kind of complex set of arrangements – "cocktail geoengineer-ing" – is the option that governments would likely face in a climate emergency. Nobody knows what the many variants of such options will cost and nobody knows which extra fixes will be needed because the side effects from possible geoengineering systems are so poorly understood. More social science research that looks into the design and costing of these systems is urgently needed.

An effective research program in this area will need special teams of analysts to look not just at the most likely costs and effects of geoengineering systems but also at the unknown unknowns – the odd, unexpected, and possibly extreme side effects of geoengineering. Over the last two years, several academies of science have organized to assess the prospects for geoengineering and have called for more research of exactly this type.[58] But significant funding has not yet followed. Based on my own experience, the community of geoengineering scientists probably still spends more time fielding calls from reporters writing stories about the oddball ideas around geoengineering than doing actual research. The ratio of think tank reports to actual research is high and rising. And this kind of research ultimately requires support from government or public interest foundations because, at present, there are few ideas that lead to viable private sector opportunities. Getting the private sector centrally involved too early will create too much secrecy and unhelpful pressures to deploy such systems.

A serious geoengineering research and assessment program should not just explore the unknown unknowns but should also be international in its orientation. An international approach will help make the findings more widely accepted, which will ease the task of governance in ways I will explore later. An international approach will also make geoengineering a more legitimate topic, which will make it politically easier for governments to spend public resources on this topic. Especially in open democracies the public will be skittish about research that seems aimed at playing God with the planet; huge pockets of public opposition are likely to arise. Already some environmental groups, at present, oppose such research on the belief that merely studying geoengineering makes it more likely that governments will lose focus on the urgent need to control emissions. (My view is the opposite. The more people study geoengineering the more the public will understand that climate dangers are so serious that they require contemplating such radical responses. When the public started seeing governments preparing for ugly futures after the use of nuclear weapons, they, for the most part, realized that the dangers were real. The same, I expect, will happen with geoengineering.)

The standard models for international scientific research and assessment probably won't work for geoengineering. In the past, the most visible international scientific assessments have aimed at building consensus around important questions such as "is the world warming?"

or "will more warming be dangerous?"[59] The Intergovernmental Panel on Climate Change (IPCC) is a testimony to the importance of these activities. Even when doubts are raised about the integrity of climate science, the IPCC offered a consensus view that has been hard to assail. Similar approaches to consensus science have included the international assessments done on ozone depletion (linked to the Montreal Protocol on the ozone layer) and on acid precipitation. Indeed, in some areas of international environmental regulation, governments largely defer to scientific bodies to determine expert consensus on technical issues. In the Montreal Protocol, technical bodies largely determine which uses of ozone-depleting substances are truly "essential" and thus exempt from regulation; in endangered species, a highly influential "red book" system largely managed by NGOs helps determine which plants and animals are subjected to the tightest regulations. These existing models work best when there are well-established methods for scientific assessment; where the knowledge is relatively well structured; and where experts can resolve controversies. But they don't work well when the knowledge is so scattered and uncertain that scientists can't agree. For example, even as the IPCC has historically done a good job estimating the most likely impact of climate warming on sea level it has struggled to force a useful consensus view on the possibility that sea levels could rise much more rapidly than the mainstream scientists traditionally estimated.[60] For normal science, consensus-oriented assessments are useful; for scientific questions where paradigms are weak or highly contested, such assessments produce either pabulum or silence.

Scientific assessments of geoengineering must reflect that the fact that nearly all the important questions of impacts and side effects will concern research where consensus is unlikely. Extreme side effects, in particular, will be steeped in controversy. Yet it is the extreme side effects – and how they might be managed – that will be of most importance for policy.[61] Moreover, such research will require a large role for the social sciences – looking at questions such as how societies will respond to geoengineering and how useful norms for governance can emerge. Most interesting research in the social sciences is not prone to useful consensus.

Rather than a single comprehensive international assessment, which has been the standard approach in other areas of international environmental law, a better strategy would encourage a variety of assessments working in parallel. Academies of science are probably the best place to begin the process because they are usually well connected to the setting of research priorities and political decision-making. Russia is a good candidate because of that country's long history of dreaming about (and studying) climate modification and its role in heavy space lift (which is important for some geoengineering options). So is the US, which must play a central role because most geoengineering science is, at the moment, American. The UK is well positioned to play a helpful role since its Royal Society is already in the lead with a recent careful assessment and is playing a central role in crafting a research program.[62] To that small group, China must be added, as that nation is building the capability to understand the issues and possibly deploy geoengineering systems. Maybe other countries should be added, with an eye to evaluating special options – for example, Brazil or other forested nations, if tinkering with the forests is envisioned. Throughout, the goal of these assessments would be a plurality of ideas and new evaluations, not consensus. Elsewhere, several colleagues and I have explored how such an academy-based assessment process could operate.[63]

At this stage, almost none of the research that will be needed to make geoengineering a politically viable option is being done. The option exists in the realm of science fiction. But in reality – where real governments are able to assess risks and debate which systems might be deployed – geoengineering is still a fantasy. This is a bigger problem than the lack of attention to adaptation because adaptation will prove relatively easy to mainstream. Indeed, that is happening already as publics and governments become more worried about climate impacts. By contrast, mobilizing careful assessments of geoengineering options and side effects will require governments to make politically controversial decisions, such as to fund and test candidate geoengineering systems and debate how to assess the results. If the worst case scenarios for climate impacts are to be believed, geoengineering might be needed very soon.

Governing the geoengineers

Although careful assessments of geoengineering are still elusive, it is not too early to start worrying about governance. That's because geoengineering is full of temptation. The technologies needed for crude geoengineering systems are already widely available and affordable. Imagine the choices facing Nigeria or Saudi Arabia – two countries whose coastal areas will suffer from the higher sea levels that are likely with global warming. Neither country has much ability to control global emissions and both actually benefit from unchecked use of fossil fuels. For them, the easier economics and organization of geoengineering may be enticing. Indeed, the same logic probably presents itself to every vulnerable nation. The smallest and poorest of them – pity Tuvalu and its drowning neighbors, for example – might find a rich friend willing to help: a "greenfinger" self-appointed protector of the planet who channels his personal fortune into geoengineering for the benefit of the least adaptive nations.[64]

Thus it is not too fanciful to imagine a country or a person getting started on geoengineering. And once a geoengineering scheme begins it will be hard to stop. Unlike collective efforts to control emissions, which are plagued by the constant threat of defection, once geoengineering has been underway for a few years, it is likely to continue because failure to keep even a crude geoengineering mask in place will lead to exceptionally rapid (and dangerous) climate change.[65] Thus, the most difficult regulatory questions arise right at the beginning when a government first reaches for the thermostat. It is hard to predict when that might happen and it is not too early to begin preparing. Once geoengineering begins, so does a brave new world.

An obvious answer to the governance problem is adoption of a taboo. Indeed, fears that geoengineering could run amok have led to growing calls for a taboo against geoengineering – or, barring that, a new regulatory treaty that would give all nations a say in the use of geoengineering (and thus provide a de facto taboo since universal agreement on anything controversial is rare).[66] In fall 2010 the Convention on Biological Diversity (CBD) adopted a taboo-like decision discouraging many kinds of field research in these technologies.

A taboo would be the worst policy. That's because a taboo is likely to be most constraining on the countries (and their subjects) who are likely to do the most responsible testing, assessment, and (if needed) deployment of geoengineering systems. In general, the most responsible governments will be those with the most open societies and thus exposed to the greatest public scrutiny; the legal and political systems in those same countries are also most likely to enforce a taboo that is enshrined into international law. It is not impossible for an open society to contravene a widely held international norm – as the United States has demonstrated by its decision to continue use of landmines despite a treaty signed by 156 other nations banning their use – but such decisions are extremely costly and rare, except in cases of clear national preference and security. Meanwhile, a taboo would leave less responsible governments and individuals – those most insulated from scrutiny and prone to ignore or avoid inconvenient international norms – to control the technology's fate. Most examples of governments developing technologies that are seen, in hindsight, as reckless and contrary to established norms concern programs that are pursued by institutions insulated from scrutiny. Examples include the secret US and Soviet military programs to develop weather modification techniques for use in war time. (Putting more rain on the battlefield, for example, would advantage armies that were better equipped for the mud.) These programs so horrified other countries when they were discovered that the rest of the world organized a treaty, signed in 1977 and entered into force in 1978, against hostile uses of environmental modification.[67]

The same logic that argues against a taboo also suggests that launching a negotiation on geoengineering treaty would not be much better. From today's vantage point, a treaty negotiation would yield inconclusive outcomes. Most nations in a treaty negotiation would probably favor a ban on geoengineering because they don't immediately have the capability to geoengineer on their own and they fear that countries with geoengineering technologies will run wild – exactly the outcome observed in the convention on Biological Diversity.[68] A few countries, though, would want to preserve the option because geoengineering could prove extremely useful. The stalemate would yield vague language designed so that both sides can agree yet offer no useful guidance. Or, countries that were considering geoengineering and were unhappy with a more demanding treaty could simply reject the agreement. For example, exactly this kind of inconclusive outcome followed the hotly contested negotiations leading. Originally to the CBD in 1992, which contained European-inspired language that was hostile to genetically engineered crops along with language demanded by developing countries that wanted complicated revenue-sharing for some kinds of germplasm collections. Getting universal agreement was nearly impossible, so diplomats focused their efforts on crafting language that, by design, offered no clear guidance. And the US, world leader in genetically engineered crops, simply refused to join the treaty. Facing these new legal uncertainties, private investment in genetic engineering for crops slowed, despite the large potential benefits from such innovations.[69]

A treaty negotiation at this stage would also raise some questions that could become highly contested without purpose. For example, one interesting geoengineering option involves putting diffraction gratings in space at a special orbit between Earth and the Sun. A formal, binding treaty negotiation might raise the unanswerable question of who owns the orbit. The question is hardly hypothetical. Earlier treaty negotiations about outer space raised difficult issues of who owned geostationary orbits that were particularly useful for communications satellites. And treaty negotiations around the Law of the Sea were stalled for many years by the hypothetical question of how to allocate rights to deep-seabed minerals through the Law of the Sea.[70] In both those cases – geostationary orbits and deep sea mining – imagined riches never appeared, despite intense wrangling over revenue-sharing agreements. Such negotiations can be distracting and are probably irrelevant if underlying circumstances make the deal that is reached inconvenient for important players.[71]

A more effective approach to building a relevant regulatory system would concentrate, today, on laying the groundwork for future negotiations rather than attempting to codify immature norms now. Meaningful norms are not crafted from thin air. They can have effect if they make sense to pivotal players, if they provide a useful function, and if they then become socialized through practice. A lot more social science research is needed on how these norms could arise related to geoengineering and what kinds of international arrangements could facilitate their spread. In doing that work, scholars might find it useful to look especially at the spread of norms in human rights – an area where the relationship between international agreements and national norms and political mobilization has received much scrutiny.

What can be done to craft sensible norms? At this stage, the main answer is scientific research. A decentralized process of research and assessment can generate the information needed to assess different geoengineering options. If done openly with extensive review as well as complementary funding to examine scenarios for actual geoengineering deployment, then such a process will likely create a base of accepted, shared information that could inform later formal efforts to create norms. National academies of science might be engaged to review that research and sponsor dialogs about how geoengineering systems could be tested and deployed.

The process should be open enough so that scientists from prospective geoengineering nations see it as the main source of useful knowledge about geoengineering and, at the same time, become socialized with the prevailing norms and best practices. CERN and ITER come to mind as models, as do the halting joint efforts during the Cold War by Soviet and US scientists to conduct joint seismic research (which was relevant for monitoring of underground testing and helped governments craft workable test ban agreements). All of these efforts were designed to create norms through experience and dialog. This approach does not guarantee that all nations will adhere to the emerging norms, but it is interesting to note that often it is the scientists who are in the midst of international scientific assessments and collaborations who become the strongest advocates for regulation and also best positioned within their governments to press for responsible national policies. This norm-building approach would aim at creating not just the knowledge needed for effective regulation in the future but also transnational partnership of experts and government officials who can manage national research programs and eventually international coordination.[72] Along the way, enough may be learned from this "bottom-up" process to create more formal treaties or other regulatory institutions. At this writing, geoengineering is a topic ripe for use of flexible, nonbinding agreements because the costs and benefits of coordination as well as the best kinds of regulatory instruments are still unknown.[73]

As these norms develop, the threat of unilateral action will loom large. That worries me, but it has the advantage of creating strong political pressure on governments that want effective norms. Governance in geoengineering is a race between the slow, bottom-up, essential process of conducting research and crafting usable norms and the blunt temptations for some countries to geoengineer on their own without regard for the side effects. I worry that the liberal democracies don't understand that race and will adopt policies, such as taboos, that will make those countries irrelevant to the real decisions about deployment. A better understanding that a taboo is a dangerous policy because it cedes defeat in this race will help realign the politics in the liberal democratic countries in favor of supporting a research program.

Some more inconvenient problems

So far I have looked at two extreme scenarios that may arise as the climate changes. In one, the effects of climate change are so horrific that society tries to fight back and mask the effects with geoengineering (box 4). In the other, the effects of climate change are sufficiently gradual that humans, at least in adaptive societies, are able to adjust without much overt effort (box 1). Here I briefly consider two other scenarios that also, logically, could arise.

In one, the effects of climate change arise gradually and humans nonetheless try to mask them (box 3). This outcome is unlikely to exist in the real world because the side effects of such schemes are probably unknowable in advance. It is hard to see how societies will tolerate a world of nips and tucks to the climate unless the situation were so dire that there was no choice but to accept the risks and side effects from masking. I'll call this box "plastic surgery." A few analysts have written papers that envision designer climates that could be tailored to local circumstances, but plastic surgeries for the planet are probably impractical.[74]

While that world is unlikely, it may sound enticing to some governments – especially those that can easily avoid dissenting voices. This could be the scenario that leads to unilateral geoengineering. Because climate change affects different ecosystems and societies in variable ways, it is unlikely that there will be a single planetary agreement on when a climate emergency has arrived. The very rich countries tend to place much higher value on nature for nature's sake, and they may be prone to see emergencies when extinctions begin en masse. The less wealthy countries, which are generally less able to adapt, may be prone to declare emergencies when a changing climate affects their economies even though those same changes may have relatively little impact on wealthier and more adaptive countries. Climate change will affect some areas of the world more than others – high-latitude countries, such as Greenland or New Zealand, may ring the emergency bell more readily than rich countries in the tropics, such as Singapore, that are climatologically more immune. One country's emergency that requires radical intervention might be seen by others as unnecessary plastic surgery.

The most worrisome scenario is box 2: extreme effects of climate change that are beyond the capacity to adapt and for which society will not fight back. Geoengineering, for all its intrigue, may not be available as a practical option. It might be too scary for most societies to stomach. It might not work. That will leave triage. Humans will be forced to respond to extreme climate impacts by adjusting what they value – by spending large sums to protect some assets and letting others go. Even if a large dose of geoengineering is applied, quite a lot of triage may remain as well.

Box 2 has received very little attention because it is an ugly scenario. It is familiar in Hollywood in movies such as *Waterworld* and *Blade Runner* – dystopias where extreme changes in climate and technology forced new organizations on humans. As a practical matter, triage questions are likely to arise first in the least adaptive countries and, especially, in nature. Even with modest changes in climate some ecosystems will fail; extinction is likely. Mass extinctions, while still seemingly remote, are a possibility. That world will force tough choices.

Box 2 is a world of aggressive adaptation and triage. Whole ecosystems might be abandoned while societies pour resources into others. So-called charismatic megafauna – polar bears, eagles, whales, and other green darlings – will become magnets for efforts to manage ecosystems, much as the societies spent handsomely to lime special ecosystems when acid rain put their survival in danger.

Mankind and nature

The topic of this chapter is rarely discussed in environmental policy. Bracing for change is viewed as a distraction from the central goal of avoiding environmental harm in the first place. It is seen as a signal of defeat. Politically, the groups that are most mobilized in favor of environmental policy are usually focused on fundamental solutions rather than on the adjustments that environmental damage will require. And as a practical matter, societies have not had to devote much attention to environmental adaptation and masking in the past. They have solved most of their environmental problems without the need for much adjustment. And in the cases where they have failed – such as the loss of passenger pigeons and other animals through extinction – the outcome has been lamented but has not altered human organization much.

Adaptation and masks, in fact, are familiar aspects of most environmental management. Adaptation is the norm whenever underlying problems are not readily solved. In smoggy cities, a system of smog alerts and decisions by asthmatics and other sensitive people to stay indoors, away from the pollution, are examples of adaptation. Despite the highly successful international treaties to protect the ozone layer, the long delay from when ozone-eating pollution has been regulated to when the ozone layer fully recovers later this century has made adaptation inevitable. Countries that sit under the worst hit holes in the ozone layer, such as Australia, have been forced to adapt. Sun-blocking shirts and creams have been added to the nearly clothes-free Australian beach scene. Skin cancers and their treatments have also become more prevalent. As proof that adaptation is politically toxic, when the Reagan administration first grappled with the need to regulate the pollution that causes ozone depletion, Interior Secretary Donald Hodel dissented with the claim that adaptive hats and sunglasses would be all that was needed. Hodel earned the ire of environmentalists, which was more lasting than any grace he might have been due by the hat and sunglass lobby. Yet, in some respects, Hodel was right. Hats and sunglasses would be essential, at least as a transition. Where he erred was to claim that adaptive measure was the only response needed.

Masking is less familiar because few externalities lend themselves to effective masks. In the 1980s, regulators in Europe and North America discovered that it would be hard to tame acid rain quickly; for the most sensitive ecosystems, such as mountain lakes, they neutralized the acid with lime. Liming, along with adaptation, bought time and eventually became less necessary as regulation stemmed the pollution problem and nature recovered. In most cases, however, it has proved difficult to create masks that work reliably within poorly understood, complex systems. A farmer in Australia released rabbits for hunting but the rabbits soon took over the countryside and created one of Australia's greatest ecological catastrophes. One of the remedies invented was a calicivirus that might obliterate the feral rabbits; instead, interactions with another virus made the rabbits immune. In open and poorly understood ecological systems, masks are hard to apply. When choosing between adaptation and masking, the former almost always wins. Adaptation is about putting the burden mainly on humans to respond and adjust; masking requires the cooperation of nature, which is harder to predict and usually less pliable.

Global warming is likely to force much closer attention to adaptation and masks. Even with a crash program to control emissions, massive adaptation will be needed. Most of that adaptation, I have suggested, will arise not as a specific policy but through building awareness of global warming effects into existing institutions. If the effects of global warming are modest, that strategy will work in adaptive societies. Less adaptive societies will be much worse off. And while outsiders will struggle to help them, I am skeptical that much can be done.

The biggest political challenges will arise if severe climate impacts appear. These will be so disruptive and costly that triage will be needed. And they will force societies to face the hard truth that schemes to mask the effects – "geoengineering" – could be worth the many risks that will certainly travel along with playing God. Scenarios where geoengineering systems are deployed are not far off; getting ready for them probably means starting to test and evaluate systems today. The Brave New World is here.

PART III

Putting it all together

7 | Explaining diplomatic gridlock: what went wrong?

For twenty years the international diplomatic community has held continuous diplomatic talks on global warming but those efforts have produced very little. This chapter explains why.

My starting point is the fact that global warming is a hard problem to solve. As I showed in Chapter 2, one of the central reasons for the difficulty is that the chief pollutant, CO_2, is an intrinsic by-product of the modern fossil fuel-powered economy. Deep cuts in CO_2 are needed, but making those cuts will influence the economic competitiveness of nations. National policies must be interdependent. That is, what one country will be willing to adopt depends on the efforts its trading partners are making. The benefits from successful cooperation – less global warming – are abstract and arise mainly in the distant future. In the best of worlds it was never going to be easy to manage this problem.

My argument in this chapter is that when the global warming problem appeared on their radar screen the world's top diplomats opened a toolbox that had all the wrong tools for the job. They thought global warming was just another environmental problem, but the standard tools of environmental diplomacy don't work well on problems, such as global warming, that require truly interdependent cooperation. The diplomats took a hard problem and made it even harder to manage by choosing the wrong strategy. Here I will focus on the four tools that were the centerpiece of that toolbox. Diplomats with the most experience negotiating climate treaties are proud of those four tools. Yet each was exactly the wrong tool for the job. Before turning to that critique, I start with a brief history of global warming diplomacy that helps explain why such wrongheaded choices were made and why it has been so difficult to shake the conventional wisdom that leads to diplomatic gridlock. The next chapter will pick up where this one ends and offer an alternative vision.

How did we get here?

From the mid-1980s policy makers – at least a few of them – have been struggling with the question of how to control emissions. It didn't take long for a few NGOs and concerned governments – such as Canada, the Netherlands, and Norway – to hold formal talks on emission controls. The most prominent was the 1988 World Conference on the Changing Atmosphere held in Toronto, which ended with a non-binding call for governments to cut emissions 20 percent below 1988 levels by 2005.[1] Nobody really knew if 20 percent – the so-called "Toronto target" – was achievable, but it was bold and designed to draw a line in the sand. A year later two European summits and then the 1990 Second World Climate Conference echoed similar sentiments.[2] The Toronto targets set up a pattern that has guided most climate talks ever since: governments set ambitious goals with no real idea how they might be implemented. (Indeed, nearly every government blew through its Toronto targets, and there is little evidence that these wild goals had any real impact on emission policies.) It was one thing for enthusiastic countries and some NGOs to set bold goals, but reluctant countries – at the time, the US and essentially all developing countries who feared that expensive new mandates would arise from global warming regulation – feared that all these bold proclamations were getting out of control. Into that fray stepped the United Nations.

The UN talks originated with two major decisions by the United Nations General Assembly, the institution's broadest decision-making body. The first, in 1988, created the Intergovernmental Panel on Climate Change (IPCC), charged with assessing the science of climate change.[3] It is hard to remember today that the late 1980s was a period of chaos in the public understanding of global warming science. It was hard to know which facts were credible. More importantly, most of the large industrialized countries had their own major national assessments under way, and the problem was that a German or US assessment wouldn't necessarily have much credibility in other nations – especially in the developing countries where there was generally little indigenous scientific capacity focused on the global climate and even less ability to assess the state of the world's science. The IPCC was designed to fix that problem and it has performed extremely well.

One of the models for the IPCC was the network of experts that had assessed the science around the ozone layer and helped speed effective international treaties to regulate ozone-depleting substances. But the IPCC was different in two major ways. By design the IPCC gave clearer and firmer final approval of its assessments (and also line-by-line approval of its widely read "summary for policy makers") to governments who were keen to keep tighter control on the process. And from the outset the IPCC focused not just on the underlying physical driving forces and evidence for climate change but also on the impacts and possible social responses. Its influence has been much greater in the physical sciences where the science is more airtight and knowledge is better organized. By contrast, the realm of the social sciences, which are central to assessing climate impacts and responses, is marked by much less agreement over what experts really know. Not only do social scientists have a hard time agreeing but the implications of their research wander deeply into the territory of government policy, which helps explain why governments have tended to keep them on a short leash.[4] Over four major assessments (the last published in 2007) the IPCC has been extremely successful. (Full disclosure: I have been heavily involved in IPCC studies over the years and in the next major IPCC study am co-convenor for the opening chapter in the volume that looks most closely at the social science aspects of climate.) Today the IPCC is in hot water over questions such as whether its review process is fully airtight (it isn't and can't be) and whether it has misstated some of the facts (it has). That controversy reflects that the IPCC has taken the commanding heights in the debate about climate change science. Few people attacked the IPCC when it was a fledgling body; today it has a bullseye painted on its chest because it is relevant.

Originally, one purpose for the IPCC was to indicate whether formal diplomatic talks would be needed on warming gases. Everyone knew the answer would be yes, and when the IPCC finished its first assessment report in 1990 the clamor for formal talks to regulate emissions was unstoppable.[5] Even before the IPCC report was complete, entrepreneurial diplomats were drafting a second resolution that the United Nations General Assembly adopted in 1990 to launch formal negotiations.[6] They set the deadline for concluding those talks by the 1992 Rio Conference on Environment and Development, a date long on the UN Agenda to mark the twentieth anniversary of the 1972 Stockholm World Environment Conference. (Stockholm had marked the start of the UN's most active period of treaty-making on environmental issues.) More than half the multilateral environmental treaties ever negotiated arose in the fifteen years following the Stockholm meeting.[7] The Rio Conference also marked the deadline for several other treaty negotiations – on biological diversity and forests, in particular – but climate change was the marquis event. And when political disagreements put the biological diversity negotiations into gridlock and forced governments to abandon a forest treaty the spotlight focused even more brightly on climate change. The deadline of the Rio summit was immoveable and failure to reach agreement would be politically costly.

With a hurried negotiating schedule that would become typical of climate talks, diplomats achieved a final agreement by setting aside the most contentious issues. They agreed on what could be agreed. When 108 heads of state arrived in Rio in the summer of 1992, they signed the new treaty – the United Nations Framework Convention on Climate Change (UNFCCC).[8] Most policy advocates had hoped the UNFCCC would contain binding targets and timetables for emissions, but that proved too controversial. Instead, the strategy of agreeing on no more than what was agreeable to every nation on the planet produced a mealy-mouthed ambition of "limiting ... emissions ... by the end of the present decade to earlier levels."[9] Developing countries were exempt from all of the UNFCCC's obligations except to file occasional reports on their emissions and activities. The industrialized countries paid all the cost of those report-filing activities and most of the cost for developing country diplomats to attend meetings. By design, the UNFCCC would impose no extra burdens on developing nations. If it had, then those countries would have refused to sign their names or even show up at meetings.

Within two years the UNFCCC entered into force as a binding treaty, and once in force the parties could meet formally and make decisions about still more talks. The first time they did that, in 1995, their first major decision was to declare the treaty inadequate and launch another hurried negotiating process.[10] In less than two years the result was the 1997 Kyoto Protocol.

Once again, the strategy for reaching final agreement in Kyoto followed a familiar pattern. Diplomats agreed on what could be agreed and deferred everything else until later. Since the global treaty required nearly every nation on the planet to offer their consent, the final structure of the Kyoto Protocol was deeply conservative and avoided nearly all areas of controversy. The mealy-mouthed commitments of the UNFCCC were turned into crisp targets and timetables mainly because the presidency in the United States now embraced targets and timetables. (Bill Clinton's administration took over from the more conservative George H. W. Bush seven months after the Rio summit. The shift in perspectives was particularly evident in the summer of 1996 during negotiations over what would become the Kyoto Protocol. The lead US negotiator announced during these talks that the US would support binding targets and timetables and he earned a round of applause and a partial standing ovation.)

In Kyoto the US diplomats agreed to cut emissions 7 percent below 1990 levels by 2008–2012, but back at home the government soon discovered that such a goal was unachievable. After a few years of delay and another change in administration (to George W. Bush, whose team was a lot less keen to spend resources on global warming) the US abandoned the treaty. Most other industrialized countries did a better job of negotiating commitments they could actually honor, but the US was in a bind because the European negotiators were demanding a US commitment that it could not deliver, and the Clinton team was unwilling to bear the immediate political costs of walking away from the Kyoto talks. So they agreed on what could be agreed and hoped for the best. The very attributes that made targets and timetables so attractive to environmentalists – that they set clear, binding goals without much attention to cost – made the Kyoto treaty brittle because countries that discovered they could not honor their commitments had few options but to exit.

Targets and timetables applied only to industrialized countries. Russia, which had studiously avoided becoming a "developing country" in UN parlance, if not in reality, signed on to freeze its emissions at 1990 levels. That was hardly a concession since Russia's emissions were already about two-fifths lower by the late 1990s when the Kyoto treaty was taking shape – thanks to the country's economic collapse.[11] Countries that were already more concerned about global warming signed on for more ambitious goals that largely reflected what they would have done anyway. Japan adopted a goal that was far beyond what Japanese policy would have delivered on its own, but as host it was keen to ensure the Kyoto event was not a public relations disaster so it made a little extra effort. In general, the industrialized countries reached agreement by adjusting their targets and timetables to match local interests. And the developing countries were enticed by exemption from all commitments. It took a few more years to iron out the details, and in 2005 the Kyoto Protocol finally entered into force.

Two years later, in 2007, diplomats once again declared the efforts of the Rio Framework Convention and the Kyoto Protocol inadequate.[12] Another process with a hurried schedule and a hopelessly long list of issues to settle began anew. Slated to run from late 2007 through the Copenhagen meeting in December 2009, that new process was designed to create a replacement treaty well before the Kyoto treaty's most important commitments expired in 2012. But the Copenhagen event ended, instead, with a spectacular fizzle. The age-old strategy of reaching an agreement by avoiding testy issues had run out of steam. There was too much on the table; too many countries with diverse interests were unable to agree; and there was no clear plan for how to craft a practical agreement that would settle all the issues.[13]

Wrong tools for the job

Other studies have detailed the diplomatic history around these events.[14] My goal here is to identify attributes of diplomacy that will determine whether these talks and agreements have any real effect. My goal isn't to find ways for diplomats to reach agreements faster or with less controversy. It is clear that diplomats are already pretty good at that, which helps explain why there are so many international environmental accords. In fact, diplomats working on environmental issues may be more skilled at crafting agreements quickly than in any other area of international cooperation.[15] Nor is it my goal to find ways to boost compliance with the agreements that are reached. In fact, compliance with such accords is usually very high – partly because diplomats are skilled at negotiating agreements for which it is easy to comply.[16] Instead, my goal is to understand *effect*. That is, what are the attributes of the diplomatic process that ultimately determine whether the international agreements and institutions actually *influence* the behavior of governments and the individuals and firms that those governments regulate at home. Scholars have generated a huge literature on these questions, although very little of it has had much impact on the strategic choices that diplomats make. My hope is that this book may make a difference.

When boiling the diplomatic process on climate change down to its essential factors, four stand out as most important in influencing the style and content of diplomacy:

- *Universal membership.* From the outset, formal UN climate talks have been open to all countries. Key decisions usually require unanimous consent. I will call this the *geometry of membership*, for it is about the size and shape of the negotiating table. Big tables at which everyone has a voice are prone to produce agreements that are widely seen as legitimate, and legitimacy may help spread norms more widely and rapidly. But big tables also generate huge costs because agreements that reflect many voices are difficult to negotiate and usually tuned for the least ambitious member. In the extreme, such agreements earn consensus by imposing no extra obligation on countries.
- *Targets and timetables.* For the most committed governments and NGOs, the holy grail of climate talks has been agreement on emission targets and timetables. This obsession has been based on the belief that only with targets and timetables is it possible to be sure that climate agreements will produce benefits for the environment. I will call this the question of *instruments*. I will show that the choice of targets and timetables as the central regulatory instrument has come at the expense of other instruments that might work better.
- *Legally binding.* Nearly all the governments and NGOs most committed to slowing global warming are guided by the belief that binding agreements – also known as treaties – are better than various other kinds of nonbinding accords. I will call this the question of *legal form* and will show that once a decision has been made to pursue a treaty, many pernicious consequences follow. Legal form includes not just the binding status of a treaty but also various provisions for flexibility. In other areas of international law, treaties include flexibility, such as reservations, derogations and other systems for opting out of inconvenient commitments. Nearly all such provisions are excluded from all climate treaties on the theory – wrongheaded, as I will show – that absolutely bombproof treaties are the most effective legal forms.

- *Enforcement.* Oddly, one of the central reasons offered in favor of
  binding treaties with targets and timetables is that such commitments are much easier to enforce. Yet no climate treaty has actually
  included a system for enforcement, and serious systems for formal
  intergovernmental enforcement is extremely rare in all of international environmental law.

Understanding how these four attributes have come to dominate
climate talks – and why they make climate diplomacy much less effective than it could be – is an essential first step in devising more effective diplomatic approaches. I look at each in turn and then ask why
skilled diplomats could have made so many bad choices. The story
here is not a pleasant one, for under a bright spotlight of scrutiny it
appears that on every front the diplomatic process has been guided by
the wrong lessons from history.[17]

Geometry: who sits at the table?

In an ideal world, every country – or perhaps even every person –
would sit around a giant table and have its voice heard. That policy,
because it was guided by all voices, would be seen as fair and representative and thus legitimate. In turn, legitimate policy might be
more effective than policies crafted in other ways, such as through
back-room deals and tiny cabals.[18]

But that ideal world doesn't exist because policy making at the
international level is peculiarly vulnerable to gridlock. In a system
with many voices, the noise level is extremely high. And when the
subjects under debate are complex and multidimensional, lots of noise
makes it hard to craft meaningful agreements. In a universal system
that requires unanimous consent almost any pesky government can
slow or block efforts by the others. Indeed, it has been very difficult to design a highly effective climate change treaty while having
in the room not just the governments that are keen for the venture
to succeed but also those that will be harmed by success, such as the
world's largest oil exporters. It is no accident that when the members
of the UNFCCC tried to set voting rules to make decision-making by
the large group of treaty members more efficient, a handful of OPEC
nations blocked the effort. Nor is it hard to understand why those
same nations make the perennial demand (so far ignored in the rest
of the world) that climate talks include a compensation mechanism

for fossil fuel producers who would be harmed if climate diplomacy actually cut demand for carbon.

Experts call the rule of unanimous consent a "unit veto" system because one dissident can block agreement by the whole. The problems of decision-making under unit veto rules have been known for a long time, but most climate talks still proceed as if a big table is the best approach. That's because most of those talks take place in the UN system where it is nearly impossible to change the size and shape of the table and thus unit veto rules prevail. The UN's legitimacy is based in part on a strong norm of universality. Nearly all UN institutions – the Security Council (which not surprisingly is the most powerful UN body) is a notable exception – are open to all comers. And within the UN system a conventional wisdom thrives that bigger talks lead to more fair, legitimate, and effective outcomes. Most of that conventional wisdom turns out to be wrong.

The political scientist who has thought the most about this question is probably the Norwegian Arild Underdal. In the 1970s he puzzled over why so many fisheries agreements were useless. There was no shortage of agreements, but the fish kept declining. Underdal's chief answer was that fishery diplomacy was stuck in a death march. The countries whose fishermen were most rapacious were prominent members of fishery agreements. Yet the unit veto rules that governed most treaties meant that the weakest proposals always set the tune. Underdal called it the "law of the least ambitious program."[19] Working with many of Underdal's students in the 1990s, I ran a research program in Austria that was animated, in part, by the desire to find ways around the sober pessimism of Underdal's law.[20] Many of the remedies involved varying the membership in agreements – usually sidelining the laggards while encouraging countries that wanted more effective governance to form smaller groups to push for regulation.

Even when sidelined, laggards can cause a lot of trouble if their behavior is still pivotal to the common goal. It's often hard to stop them from plundering the high seas or releasing pollution that flows into other countries. Sometimes the mere act of sidelining and calling out a laggard helps shift behavior – as happened in Britain, which came under the harsh spotlight in the mid-1980s as the "Dirty Man of Europe" for its continued pollution of the North Sea. The spotlight changed British minds – especially prime minister Margaret Thatcher's – and today Britain is a reliable leader in most international environmental ventures. When the glare of the spotlight doesn't

work, other strategies are also available. They include paying polluters and fishers to change their behavior. Iceland's fishermen are paid
not to net so many salmon on the theory that smaller commercial
catches will help wild salmon stocks recover – a goal that sport fishermen in Canada are happy to finance. (The typical Atlantic salmon is
worth perhaps $500 when caught on the line of a sport fisherman in
one of Canada's rivers but one hundred times less when netted commercially in Greenland.) Along the Rhine river, downriver countries
such as the Netherlands have bribed upriver polluters such as France
to change their behavior – the bribe was cheaper than suffering the
consequences of a fouled river. And when bribing doesn't work – or
is unavailable, such as when the public finds it distasteful – then gun-
boats sometimes appear. Some of the most important efforts to solve
the decline of North Atlantic turbot (halibut), cod, and numerous
other species have ended with warlike actions such as boarding and
seizing of ships and even the occasional shot fired.[21]

The law of the least ambitious program helps explain many of
the troubles with climate diplomacy. Back in 1997 when the Kyoto
treaty was crafted, the world's largest emitter – the US – ultimately
withdrew because the treaty included more ambitious commitments
than US politicians would stomach. The countries that were keenest
to see Kyoto work – the European Union – adopted commitments
that weren't much more ambitious than what they, under strong
pressure from environmental groups, would have implemented anyway. A much more stringent regulation would have put the EU at an
economic disadvantage since EU industry knew that most other big
emitters wouldn't do much to control their effluent. The third largest
emitter at the time, China, joined the Kyoto treaty because as a developing country it was not required to adopt any real policy reforms.
The fourth largest emitter, Russia, joined only because its allowable
emissions were so preposterously high that it, too, faced no cost from
membership. And so on. In Underdal's parlance, the outcome is the
law of the least ambitious program. The diplomats agreed on what
could be agreed. And the resulting treaty has little or no real impact
on the underlying warming problem. Compliance for the countries
that are formal members of the treaty is perfect (so far) but effect is
nearly zero.

The Underdal law also helps explain why efforts to set a clear objective for climate talks have also faltered. Article 2 of the UNFCCC

calls for avoiding "dangerous anthropogenic interference in the climate system," and soon after the UNFCCC entered into force there
were many efforts to figure out what Article 2 meant in practice.
Scientists were asked to define "dangerous" and to identify thresholds
for unruly amounts of climate change. But none of these attempts
bore fruit because what's dangerous depends on lots of local factors
and on how every government evaluates benefits as well as costs.
Since nobody can agree on the exact threshold for danger the result is
Article 2: an obligation that is vague because it is designed to accommodate all interpretations. Today, the most widely accepted goal for
climate diplomacy is to limit warming to 2 degrees. That number
didn't arise from Article 2 of the UNFCCC. Instead, it was the product of a few European governments deeply concerned about climate
change writing the 2 degree number into the EU's own guidelines
and then pushing hard to have that number adopted in other forums.
Absent any other number that was more credible, 2 degrees stuck.

   Those historical experiences offer a compass for how to get around
the iron grip of the law of the least ambitious program. A lot more
attention is needed on the size and shape of the table. Big tables with
lots of voices – especially voices from players who want diplomacy
to fail – are usually a bad way to begin effective diplomatic talks
unless the only goal of those talks is legitimacy. Leaders must be given
flexibility so they can adopt more ambitious commitments. Laggards
must be sidelined and inoculated – or coerced and bribed if they play
essential roles. Doing all that will require crafting complicated deals
that are unlikely to be successful if pursued within a universal forum
where any unit can veto the outcome.

   The difficulty of negotiating complex deals probably rises exponen-
tially with the number of countries in the room. Each new member
creates a network of relationships (and thus complications) with existing members since all countries, to different degrees, are engaged in
international trade and concerned about how warming regulations
will affect their competitiveness. Yet leverage over the problem – measured by emissions – saturates quickly as numbers rise. The top six
emitters (counting the EU as a single emitter) account for 64 percent
of world emissions of CO_2 from burning fossil fuels; the top dozen
are responsible for about 74 percent. Gaining another ten percent of
emissions requires adding another ten countries (see also Figure 5.5).
Political scientists haven't worked out a tight, empirically grounded

theory to suggest the optimal number of countries to engage. My hunch is that it is about a dozen – the top ten emitters from burning fossil fuels, plus Brazil and Indonesia (two of the top emitters of CO_2 from changes in land use). At numbers greater than a dozen, negotiating complexity will overwhelm the advantages of additional leverage. If engaging fewer than a dozen members, the club will be too exclusive to gain leverage.

So far, it has been hard to follow this practical advice because the first twenty years of climate diplomacy have subscribed to a "broad then deep" philosophy. Advocates for broad membership claim that the climate problem is a long-term problem and the first steps must engage all players to confer legitimacy on the enterprise, promote shared understanding, and set standards that will spread globally. Testing this hypothesis with evidence is difficult, but my read of most of the history in other areas of international cooperation is that the hypothesis is wrong.

Starting broad risks staying shallow, as has happened with global warming. Getting to deep and demanding commitments usually requires starting with a narrow group. The World Trade Organization (WTO), notably, has emerged to be the most effective example of global cooperation by focusing, through the original General Agreement on Tariffs and Trade (GATT), on a limited number of countries whose interests (and capabilities) were sufficiently aligned to allow cooperation. Over time, experience and success have allowed deeper and wider cooperation (and have also led to more complex negotiations that extend over much longer time periods). By the GATT round that ended in the early 1990s with the creation of the WTO, the agreement included much more than simply the tariff bindings that were the core of the first GATT agreement. It is unlikely that WTO members would have arrived at that point of deep cooperation if they had not first worked out the most demanding commitments in smaller forums – originally in the GATT. Indeed, today's WTO is so large that it may be impractical for such a group to make much more progress. Similarly, the EU emerged from a more focused cooperation (on infrastructures and key industrial inputs such as coal, steel, and nuclear power) among a limited number of countries. With experience and the confidence of success, the original small European group expanded eventually to become the EU. The recent expansion to include twelve new countries, and the agenda for talks with Turkey may test the limits of EU expansion. Even when there is a long history of cooperation and well-established standards, an institution can falter if it gets too large and the complexity of all its nodes becomes overwhelming. Both the EU and the WTO owe their depth to strategies that started narrow.

Instruments: targets and timetables

Climate change agreements, like most accords in international environmental law, include many forms of commitments, such as requirements to report data and obligations for some countries (mainly the industrialized nations) to help others (mainly the developing countries). All these varied commitments work together as a system. But the central debate over substantive commitments has always focused on one issue above all others: targets and timetables for regulating emissions.

Why are governments are drawn to targets and timetables when there are lots of other ways to coordinate efforts to control emissions? Governments could agree to adopt common policies or to share information about policies. They could agree to make comparable efforts, measured as the cost of their policies rather than the actual level of emissions. Yet targets and timetables reign supreme.

What's puzzling about that choice is that governments actually have very little control over the particular level of emissions emanating from their territory. The quantity of emissions in any year is mainly the product of the health of the economy and other factors that governments affect only indirectly, such as the price of fossil fuels. In 2008, for example, emissions from the US economy declined 2.2 percent – not because of new US policy on warming gases but mainly because the economy was weak and because carbon-light natural gas became a lot cheaper to use, which meant that utilities fired their coal plants a bit less while relying more heavily on cleaner natural gas.[22] Britain famously found large caches of natural gas in the North Sea in the 1970s and production from those fields grew rapidly from the early 1980s.[23] That, along with new labor policies that accelerated the demise of Britain's coal industry, had a huge impact on reducing emissions of warming gases. A market-oriented reform of the electric industry also encouraged the more efficient operation of nuclear plants. From 1990 to 2000 British emissions of CO_2 declined 7.2 percent. In 1992 alone the country shut thirty coal mines and the dash to gas was well under way. Germany's emissions declined nearly one-fifth from 1990 to 2000 as high-pollution industries in the eastern part of the country were shuttered and rebuilt with more efficient western technologies.[24] Western Germany did not agree to absorb the east and Britain did not look for gas in the North Sea and reform its electric power market because they were trying to save the planet. These fortuitous events just happened. And fortune can cut both ways. When China grew unexpectedly rapidly and the Chinese economy swung back to energy-intensive manufacturing in the early 2000s, emissions rose 15–25 percent per year. Even as the government began an aggressive program to boost energy efficiency, emissions still rose far faster than state planners had expected. By contrast, the same economy saw its emissions shrink 1–3 percent annually in the late 1990s when other factors also largely beyond government control, such as the Asian financial crisis, were at work.[25]

All else equal, agreements are a lot more effective when they are based on credible commitments. Targets and timetables intrinsically make it hard for governments to offer credible promises because over the time horizons that are typical in international regulatory law – such as the five-year commitment period in the Kyoto Protocol – the main factors that influence emission levels are largely beyond government control. The standard practice in international environmental law of allowing a long delay between negotiation of commitments and their full entry into force further undermines credibility. A decade passed from the final negotiations in Kyoto until the beginning of the Kyoto compliance period in 2008, and a lot happened during that period that governments could not have anticipated. One reason the US withdrew from the Kyoto Protocol, for example, was that its emissions had grown unexpected rapidly in the late 1990s, which made it impractical for US policy makers to plan compliance with the 7 percent cut its negotiators had promised in Kyoto. When the new Bush administration took power in 2001 it was a lot easier to kill a treaty whose commitments could not be honored under any realistic scenario than if the Kyoto obligations had been more practical.[26]

Since it is so hard for governments to control pollutants according to exacting targets and timetables, why are nearly all the governments and NGOs that are most enthusiastic about slowing global warming obsessed with the idea that the emission targets and timetables are the best way to slow global warming? In the early 2000s, just as governments were putting the final touches on the Kyoto treaty, a colleague

Lesley Coben and I tried to answer this question. We suspected that governments chose targets and timetables because that is what they had done in every other major air pollution treaty. What we called a "herd mentality" had taken over. With the herd in stampede, nobody could stop to think about whether targets and timetables actually made any sense.

To test this hypothesis we looked at all multilateral air pollution treaties that had been crafted before 1995. We expected that air pollution agreements would be the likely body of law that would serve as the first point of reference for addressing a new air pollution problem – in this case, the problem of global warming. And 1995 marked the start of negotiations that led to the Kyoto treaty. We wanted to take the pulse of conventional wisdom up to the point when the Kyoto talks began. That left us with 21 agreements out of the 196 total multilateral environmental agreements ever signed.[27]

First we asked whether the main regulatory instrument used in each agreement was a cap on emissions or a requirement to adopt policies that affected emissions. Economists will recognize this question as the age-old puzzle of whether it is better to solve pollution problems by regulating the quantity (e.g., an emission cap) or by controlling the effort (e.g., by regulating the price of emissions such as through an emission tax).[28] This puzzle has already reared its head in Chapter 3 when we asked the same question at the national level: which regulatory approach is best? Economic theory has a simple answer. For most environmental problems that are caused by the build-up of pollution over long periods of time the best policy is usually to regulate prices rather than quantities. That's because the exact quantity of emissions in any given year doesn't have much impact on environmental damage. But many of these pollutants are difficult to regulate precisely, which makes it hard for firms or even the whole country to know exactly what it will cost to meet exacting emission standards. By contrast, setting the price – or level of effort – would make it easier for firms and governments to adopt rational, long-term investment plans.

What Lesley and I found, initially, was that most air pollution agreements actually focused on efforts, such as policies. Only a small fraction actually put caps on emissions. Our hypothesis seemed to be dead wrong.

So then we recoded the entire data set to look at one more factor: were the commitments specific or broad? Many attempts at international environmental cooperation begin with broad, general frameworks – often termed a "Framework Convention" – and then proceed to craft more specific commitments in later agreements. There is a strong premium for diplomats to reach agreements quickly because environmental issues come with relatively large rewards even for symbolic efforts. Governments and their diplomats need to show they are "doing something" about environmental degradation, so they hold many summits and usually set impossibly ambitious goals for diplomatic talks. (This is not the only issue-area where symbolism sometimes trumps real attention to impact. Much human rights diplomacy may be of the same type – good at boosting attention to an issue but mixed in actual impact on behavior.[29]) And the strategy of agreeing on what is agreeable usually produces generalities in the early stages of environmental diplomacy.

Global warming followed this pattern – early negotiations produced a general Framework Convention on Climate Change at the Rio Conference in 1992. Later talks delivered a more specific and possibly more consequential Kyoto Protocol. Still further talks, which had been slated to end by Copenhagen in 2009, were intended to develop even more specific and demanding commitments. Lesley and I thought that the specificity of commitments could be a good indicator of whether the parties are simply codifying platitudes because they are unable to agree on demanding commitments or whether a treaty might actually require some serious effort to comply. (Ideally we would have measured the level of effort that each agreement required, but there was no way to measure that reliably. Looking at the specificity was a simpler, second-best way to get the same information.)

Figure 7.1 shows the striking results. Nearly every agreement in which the dominant commitments are general in nature is focused on things that governments can readily control, such as the efforts they should make in adopting policies. Nearly every agreement with specific commitments contains a quantity instrument as the central obligation.[30] When negotiations turn from generalities to demanding commitments the herd always reaches for emission caps.

Figure 7.1 is a smoking gun. It suggests that the mentality in favor of emission targets and timetables has gathered strength over the years. But it couldn't tell us *why* diplomats kept turning to caps. Resolving that puzzle would require looking into each agreement.

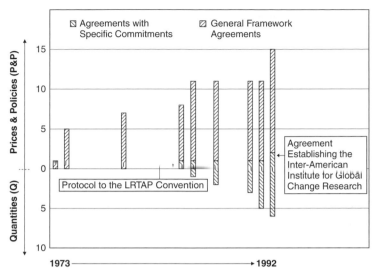

Figure 7.1 Specific vs. general agreements

Data shown are the cumulative number of international air pollution agreements. The practice of international environmental diplomacy favors the use of pricing and policy (P&P) instruments for general agreements; diplomats choose quantity instruments in nearly all cases where they craft specific (usually more stringent) commitments. Two exceptions don't affect the general rule: the 1984 Protocol to the LRTAP Convention and the 1992 Agreement Establishing the Inter-American institute for Global Change Research. Both of these include specific commitments but do not relate to regulating pollution – rather, they concern the funding of research institutions that provide information to other collective international efforts to address air pollution. Data from CIESIN analyzed by Victor and Coben (2005).

Leslie and I started with the most effective air pollution agreement in history: the Montreal Protocol on Substances that Deplete the Ozone Layer. We knew that the pollutants that deplete the ozone layer weren't identical to those that cause global warming, but surely the architects of the Montreal Protocol faced a similar problem: as they tightened the screws on emission controls, how could they square the fact that the promises in the Montreal Protocol were codified as specific caps on pollution levels even though governments didn't have direct control over the pollutants? Why had targets and timetables worked so well in protecting the ozone layer? It was important to learn the right lessons from the Montreal Protocol experience not only because the agreement was so successful but also because it was the leading guide for the architects of the international agreements on global warming. More than any other model, the herd looked to Montreal.

There are several very good histories of ozone-layer diplomacy, so it wasn't hard to start answering these questions.[31] Compared with global warming, slowing the emissions of ozone-depleting substances was easier because it required only a few dozen major firms to take the lead. Once political pressure forced at least a few firms to break ranks and support a shift to (more profitable) substitutes, it was easier to turn the rest. The substances that deplete the ozone layer also were not integrated into the very fabric of the economy, unlike fossil fuels which are integrated, and thus regulations were unlikely to engender as much political opposition. The cost of converting from ozone-depleting substances has been orders of magnitude lower than the likely cost of weaning the modern economy off carbon. Thus, from the outset, the ozone problem was a lot easier to handle. But the leading diplomatic history of the ozone layer has rightly pointed out that when diplomats set out to coordinate international regulation of ozone-depleting pollutants they didn't know that economics and industrial politics would prove so easy to conquer.[32] In fact, the early days of the Montreal Protocol negotiations looked a lot like the last two decades of diplomacy on global warming – governments were extremely sensitive to making commitments they could not honor, nobody really knew with certainty what alternatives would replace ozone-depleting substances, costs loomed large and uncertain, and the politics of reaching effective agreements were anything but easy.

The key to the success of the Montreal Protocol was a system of diplomacy that tailored commitments to what governments could be sure to deliver. At first the tailoring was crude and that meant that the real impact of the Protocol was pretty modest. The first commitments required only freezing and then cutting in half the emissions of the most noxious ozone-depleting substances – mainly two chlorofluorocarbons (CFCs) that were used in huge volumes for purposes such as propellants in spray cans and refrigerants but also halons that had a variety of industrial uses. For most industrialized countries it was easy to honor this blunt cap on emissions because alternative propellants were already available and new refrigerants soon arrived. In a few industrialized countries, such as the United States, governments had already adopted policies such as a ban on CFCs in most spray cans.

For these countries, cutting emissions in half would be tougher because they started with the screws already tight, but they were already much further along in their own national regulatory programs, had a better sense of what they could really achieve, and were more willing to do something about the thinning ozone layer. All the developing countries were initally exempt from controls and later paid to comply, so for them it was also easy to make reliable promises.

Over the years governments tightened the controls as they gained confidence about what they could implement at home. With confidence they also expanded the list of regulated substances. Unlike the Kyoto Protocol, which lumped all pollutants into a single basket, the Montreal architects kept pollutants in different baskets so they could tailor commitments according to their confidence. Because the politics and the engineering of substitutes varied, the Montreal Protocol regulated each of these new chemicals separately, which made it easier to ratchet tighter controls exactly as alternative substances came into production. After the CFCs and halons, the next biggest depleters of ozone were methyl chloroform and methyl bromide. For methyl chloroform, a solvent, regulations proved relatively easy to craft. For methyl bromide, a fumigant that plays an important role in controlling agricultural pests, it has been much harder to find more benign substitutes and thus governments have been much slower in agreeing to tighter international limits.[33] (Methyl bromide also implicated well-organized agricultural interests in developing countries that were particularly wary of costly regulations.) In the Kyoto negotiations the dominant theory that led governments to put all pollutants into one basket was that a single basket would give markets the maximum flexibility to find the cheapest pollutant to regulate. But that theory was blind to the more important prior condition – markets for pollution control are a function of government policy decisions, and those policy decisions are no better than what governments are confident they can reliably implement in the real world where politics shape what governments and markets actually do.

Although the Montreal Protocol history is celebrated as one where governments quickly rose to the occasion, it is also a reminder that rising too quickly can generate large mistakes. When CFCs were first being phased out, one of the most attractive substitutes was a chemical cousin: HCFCs. The cousin was a lot less noxious than the original CFCs but not fully benign, and once a few governments (led by

the US) had pushed their industry to invest heavily in these chemicals it was impossible to phase them out quickly when even more
benign substitutes appeared. Thus today CFCs are a much less serious
future worry to the ozone layer than HCFCs, and a full phase-out of
HCFCs won't be complete until 2030. Firms that had invested heavily in HCFCs were not keen to abandon what they had already sunk
into the new HCFC industry when governments learned that they had
travelled too quickly down the wrong regulatory path.

The political engine for all these efforts was public concern in the
advanced industrialized countries. The developing countries never
became very enthusiastic about spending their own money to control
ozone-depleting substances, but a special fund paid them the "agreed
incremental cost" of compliance. For them, reliable promises were
also easy to make – the promises matched the level of funding that the
industrialized nations would provide.[34]

Lesley and I found that emission caps and timetables worked so long
as it was relatively easy to match promises to policy efforts. Every two to
three years governments would ratchet the caps tighter. But that process ran out of steam when the ratchet was so tight that governments
needed to be sure they had a reliable substitute for every use. What
happened next is instructive, for the challenge that the architects of the
Montreal Protocol then solved is the one most similar to the problem of
global warming today – where even modest ratcheting of emission caps
and timetables raises severe questions about the credibility of the caps.

As governments tightened the caps on ozone-depleting substances
they realized that it would not be easy to eliminate all uses of these compounds according to an exact schedule. For some applications – what
became called "essential uses" – there were no known substances with
adequate cost and performance. Examples include some of the foams
used on the US space shuttle and some laboratory testing equipment.
By far the most important examples are metered dose inhalers (MDIs)
for asthmatics and others whose essential medicines must be inhaled.
Eliminating all ozone-depleting substances would cause untold harm in
these particular, narrow applications. The extraordinary success of the
ozone-layer agreements would have evaporated if the world's militaries,
astronauts, and asthmatics had organized against the effort.

To fix this problem – and thus make promised emission caps more
credible – the architects of the Montreal Protocol installed a safety
valve that prevented the burden of regulation from skyrocketing out of

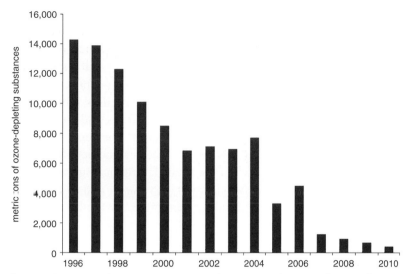

Figure 7.2 Essential use exemptions in the Montreal Protocol: a mechanism for containing economic and political costs

The Montreal Protocol allows for exemptions for certain "essential use" applications, such as drug inhalers. The chart shows approved exemptions for industrialized countries, as exemptions for developing countries (known technically as countries operating under paragraph 1 of Article 5 of the Protocol) began only in 2009.

Sources: 1996–2007: Ozone Secretariat, "Essential-Use Exemptions Approved by the Meetings of the Parties." http://ozone.unep.org/Exemption_Information/Essential_Use_Nominations/EUN_Approved_by_Parties.shtml.

Sources: 2008–2010: Reports of the Meeting of the Parties to the Montreal Protocol on Substances that Deplete the Ozone Layer, 18th, 19th, 20th, and 21st sessions.

control. Every year parties may nominate "essential uses," which an expert committee reviews to help determine which essential uses should be exempted from a nation's total allowable quota of ozone-depleting substances. Over time, as shown in Figure 7.2, the exemptions have been whittled away as new substitutes were found and tested.

The lesson from this experience isn't that the herd is right to favor emission caps and timetables. Instead, the proper lesson is that regulatory instruments must be matched to what governments can credibly deliver. For most of the history of international air pollution agreements, it has been relatively easy to deploy emission caps and timetables because most air pollution accords have not been very demanding. (In fact, as I shall show, compliance has been nearly perfect.) But as the obligations tighten so must the marriage between the design of regulatory instruments and what governments can actually deliver. In the Montreal Protocol, the most successful international air pollution accord in history, the shift to instruments designed for credibility – in that case, the system of essential uses – has meant, in effect, detailed coordination of national policies and technologies rather than blunt emission caps and timetables. The general lesson is that when governments don't know what they can achieve in advance a large measure of flexibility will be needed.[35] Achieving that flexibility requires rethinking another chestnut of conventional wisdom – the question of whether legally binding commitments are best – and to that I now turn.

Form: legally binding commitments

A third puzzle is the choice of legal form. Among most diplomats and environmental NGOs the conventional wisdom is that the best international agreements are legally binding. That assumption is based on the theory that governments are more likely to take binding law seriously. Most governments have elaborate procedures for ratifying binding international commitments – the US, for example, requires a positive vote by two-thirds of the Senate (a hard standard to meet these days) – and through such procedures governments are more likely to take steps to ensure they comply. In some national legal systems, binding international law has superior status even to domestic law and can be enforced directly by national courts. And although formal international enforcement systems are scarce, under some theories of international law a binding obligation is a lot more enforceable under international law than a woollier nonbinding accord. All the stars, it seems, align in favor of binding law.

In reality, the decision about legal status is just one of several design choices that affect outcomes. All else equal, binding law is almost always taken more seriously by governments than other, nonbinding accords. Under some circumstances – such as agreements that affect the security or survival of a nation – binding rules make it possible to achieve much more demanding, precise, and effective international accords. As revealed over the history of strategic nuclear arms talks, for example, governments have been willing to make bigger efforts at disarmament when they are confident of the detailed efforts that their adversaries are also making.[36] Disarmament yields security only when all sides disarm in tandem. Otherwise it breeds suckers.

But all else is rarely equal. The real problem with economic and environmental cooperation is that success requires changing the behavior of firms and individuals that are not fully under the government thumb. Indeed, by design the most successful world economies are usually those where the private sector is much larger than the government sector and where government controls are purposely weak. Thus it is not surprising that the toughest issues on the international agenda, among them global warming, are those that require governments to coordinate actions that are at arm's length (or even further) removed from government. In those settings, governments have incomplete information about what they can truly deliver. Shrouded in such uncertainties, agreements that are flexible – either because they are nonbinding and pliable or because they include specific flexibility measures such as opt-out clauses or schemes like the Montreal Protocol's limited exemptions for "essential uses" – are more attractive to governments and usually elicit broader membership and higher effectiveness. There's a lot more research that needs to be done on the use of flexibility measures in international environmental agreements. On the surface, it appears that formal flexibility is rare in international environmental law, although many other areas of law offer a lot more useful experience with flexibility provisions such as derogations and reservations that allow governments to tailor commitments to their own circumstances.[37] The paucity of such formal measures in international environmental law reflects, in part, that environmentalists and diplomats generally abhor flexibility systems because they fear flexibility will be used to undercut environmental protection. The Kyoto Protocol, for example, explicitly prohibits reservations and the Kyoto diplomatic process never gave much attention to other mechanisms that would make commitments more pliable.[38] The paucity of experience with flexibility measures means that scholars need to look to more obscure provisions in treaties (such as the essential uses exemption in the Montreal Protocol) and the body of soft nonbinding law to see how flexibility has actually worked in international environmental cooperation.

That leaves a trade-off between the supposed advantages of binding law (it is taken more seriously) and nonbinding accords (they are more flexible).[39]

It is possible to see the trade-offs at work by looking at legal form from two different angles. First, history provides a few well-controlled experiments where binding law has been used in tandem with other kinds of accords. Finding and selecting those historical examples is difficult and prone to all sorts of biases. But they are a good place to start. There aren't many such examples from the marquis areas of international environmental cooperation because binding law is so favored by international environmental diplomats that they almost always seek it exclusively, but some of the lesser known issue-areas provide interesting experiments where these two different forms of law have been used in tandem and we can explore which legal form works best and why.

The experiences with international cooperation to regulate pollution in the North Sea, the Baltic Sea and to regulate the emissions that cause acid rain in Europe are all examples where binding and nonbinding instruments were deployed side-by-side. In each, the nonbinding rules proved much more effective.[40] In all these cases nonbinding instruments helped governments avoid gridlock because they were more flexible at a time when governments did not know how to regulate the pollutants that caused the problem. In the North Sea and Baltic Sea regimes, a series of ministerial-level conferences focused on the most ambitious regulatory programs that governments were willing to implement and then codified the results in nonbinding agreements. By contrast, in both cases years of efforts that had concentrated on binding treaties had produced very little action. In the European acid rain regime, more ambitious nonbinding commitments to control NO_x (a leading cause of acid rain) were adopted by a smaller number of countries alongside a binding convention to address the same pollutant.

These cases don't prove that nonbinding agreements are better than binding treaties. None is a perfectly controlled experiment – those rarely exist in the real world – and none is a perfect analogy for global warming. However, they do suggest some conditions under which nonbinding approaches work better. One is that the problem at hand should be steeped in uncertainty about the real causes and effects of environmental damage and, especially, uncertainty about what governments can really deliver. Another condition that favors nonbinding approaches is sustained high-level attention – usually at ministerial levels – to improve the prospects that nonbinding accords would lead to real policy reforms. Visible participation by leaders helps solve the perennial worry that nonbinding accords, precisely because they are flexible and easy to adopt, will be taken less seriously by governments. Leaders create more visibility and therefore are prone to negotiate commitments that are more credible. Leaders also often interact with each other on a regular basis, often over long time periods. Experts on cooperation call this the "shadow of the future." When people interact with a long shadow of the future they tend to be more cooperative – even when there isn't a formal enforcement mechanism to keep everyone in line.[41] And still another condition is institutional. In all three of these cases, nonbinding commitments worked because they were embedded within institutions that could mobilize detailed performance reviews. Those reviews – akin to the Montreal Protocol's system for expert assessments of essential use exemptions – helped ensure that the parties narrowed the uncertainties over time and learned which strategies worked best. They also helped focus a spotlight on governments whose efforts fell short, which in turn made it easier for other governments to mobilize pressure (the shadow of the future) and adjust their own behavior since every government worried about being a sucker. In the European acid rain regime the most important review mechanisms were supplied by the European Union, which had built a large scientific research program to understand the problem of transboundary air pollution. In the North Sea and Baltic Sea regimes, review was an ad hoc affair. Whichever government hosted the next ministerial summit also sponsored a detailed performance review, and over time this ad hoc arrangement worked well because most of the governments were competent and faced political pressure to make serious efforts to control the polluted seas. Along both these seas, governments found it relatively easy to regulate pollution that was dumped directly into the oceans, such as from ships that incinerated solid waste at sea, but the review process helped them focus on the more difficult-to-manage problem of land-based pollution, such as run-off from fertilizers used in farms (North Sea) and paper mills (Baltic Sea).

A second angle for looking at the trade-offs around legal form is compliance. The case for binding law is that governments take it more seriously. If that is true then experts who study these accords should see evidence that when governments negotiate and ratify binding accords they pay close attention to compliance, and when they undertake nonbinding accords compliance is a less dominant concern.

It is very hard to measure precise levels of compliance because international accords are rarely like the speed limit that provides (in theory) a bright line to discern illegal speeding from compliant behavior. They have many different aspects and are often written to be vague because diplomats are skilled at finding agreeable words.

Nonetheless, the few studies that have tried to measure compliance with binding international pollution agreements generally find that compliance is just about perfect. By contrast, compliance with nonbinding accords is generally much lower. When the North Sea governments set ambitious nonbinding accords, nearly all fell short and failed to comply with one of the most visible nonbinding commitments: to cut in half land-based pollution. The Baltic Sea experience followed a similar path. And every European government that joined the binding agreement to freeze emissions of nitrogen oxides (NO_x, a major cause of acid rain) complied, but many of the subset "club" of governments that signed a more aggressive nonbinding accord to cut emissions 30 percent fell short.

Scholars have focused a lot of attention on compliance because it is a logical place to start when probing how law actually affects behavior. But in international law, perfect compliance is often the problem not the goal. Good news about compliance is often bad news about effect cooperation.[42] When dealing with problems marked by lots of uncertainty, a pristine record on compliance is an indicator that governments are setting commitments too modestly. Looking just at compliance, binding accords almost always perform better than nonbinding ones. But when correcting for the content of the accords – which is nearly always more ambitious in comparable nonbinding accords precisely because there are fewer penalties for falling short – often the nonbinding accords perform better. The diplomatic process that crafted binding international treaties on NO_x carefully moved the binding goalposts around to find an obligation that every nation would surely honor. So by design, compliance was perfect. But the nonbinding accord was much more demanding (initially a 30 percent cut in emissions rather than just a freeze) – compliance was a lot lower, but the actual impact on behavior was higher. This odd relationship – that effectiveness is high when formal compliance is low – is not always true. Later in this chapter I will examine when it does hold, for understanding that is one step to building a more effective diplomatic system to manage global warming.

The news that compliance with binding environmental accords is very high is one of the biggest problems for today's diplomacy on global warming. Deep cuts in emissions are needed, but the deeper the cuts in emissions the harder it is for governments to plan their emission controls to exacting emission standards. If governments are obsessed about compliance, as happens when international accords are binding, they will be prone to under-promise. A diplomatic process that is marked by under-promising can never arrive at agreements that will be demanding enough to make a dent in greenhouse warming. That will upset the countries that care most about solving the problem, so they will demand more – something that most other governments will be unable to promise reliably if promises are binding – and the result will be gridlock. More flexible approaches, such as nonbinding accords, can help governments avoid the resulting gridlock.

Incentives: rotten carrots and wimpy sticks

The odd relationship between compliance and effectiveness also helps explain a fourth puzzle: the absence of enforcement mechanisms. Most international environmental law hasn't included many incentives – sticks or carrots – because it revolves around commitments that largely mirror what governments would do anyway. And when incentives have been used, the experience is carrot-heavy because most international legal agreements don't have formal effect without the consent of the governed. (In Chapter 4 we saw how those carrots can work and we also learned that the current system of carrots for cooperation on the regulation of warming gases, based on the CDM, is much too small and poorly administered to make much difference.) It is difficult to organize coalitions to brandish sticks – even in cases where grave matters of national security are at stake, such as when North Korea or Iran developed rogue nuclear weapons programs. Rarely are the stakes so high that nations will organize big sticks to enforce legal obligations. Indeed, most of the experience with enforcement in international environmental law comes from unilateral action and much of that is in a shadow area where it is not clear whether countries have even violated formal legal agreements. The US, for example, has organized a system of sanctions against countries that refuse to stop commercial whaling regardless of whether they formally violated international law. In the case of Iceland those sanctions were quite effective because, with a small economy highly dependent on exports of sanctioned products (fish), Iceland's government had little choice but to buckle under US pressure. Canada has enforced fisheries agreements, periodically putting it into conflict especially with rogue Spanish fishing boats. And in a few cases, such as when a small number of countries successfully managed the pacific fur seals stock, enforcement has unambiguously been used as an integral part of international resource management agreements.[43] But what is most striking is the rarity of any enforcement procedures. When agreements must earn consent by the governed, brandishing sticks is usually a costly way to get consent.

Over the last three decades, a few diplomats have tried to fix this problem and plant the seeds for enforcement in international environmental agreements. So far, results of their efforts are quite modest. Most of these nascent enforcement systems are based on data that countries, themselves, report. An enforcement scheme based on self-reported data will sound like an odd system to people more familiar with the stronger, independent enforcement systems typical of national law. But international law is a lot weaker, and self-reported data is a good place to start looking to see if countries will be willing to invest in enforcement. About fifteen years ago I led an effort based at a research institute in Austria – the International Institute for Applied Systems Analysis (IIASA) – to figure out what was done with all the self-reported data in these agreements. What we found is that not much happens.[44] Only rarely are systems in place to check the quality (accuracy and comparability) of such data. Even one of the most effective examples of reporting and review in international environmental cooperation – the Montreal Protocol, which has a Non-Compliance Procedure (NCP) that functions a bit like an enforcement system – has suffered problems of poor data quality because the system was never designed with the capacity to obtain independent data nor to confront countries that might be lying.[45] In the case of the ozone layer these problems have not been particularly severe because the countries with the highest capacity to control ozone-depleting substances have been motivated to solve the ozone problem. And the countries with lower capacity and greater wariness are paid the "agreed incremental cost" of controlling emissions and are unlikely to have a strong incentive to report incorrect data. The tough cases are the ones that fall between the cracks, such as Russia which has had a strong incentive to make ozone-depleting substances (some of which end up on the black market) and is not eligible for any of the international funds that pay the cost of phasing out the substances.[46] Tough cases are a good test of the strength of enforcement mechanisms, and the Montreal Protocol's NCP has struggled mightily to keep Russia in line.

The exceptions to the rule that environmental agreements don't contain much enforcement are unusual and revealing. Usually they arise when international environmental law dovetails with other institutions that are powerful and have access to data on their own. In Europe there is a regional system of agreements that was originally designed to regulate acid rain – a quintessential international environmental problem because pollution from one country would waft downwind and cause harm in other nations as well. Today that treaty system – which is a collection of binding treaties under the Long Range Transboundary Air Pollution (LRTAP) Convention – also regulates other pollutants. (The example of NO_x pollution, discussed earlier, is part of this system.) Conveniently, the LRTAP treaties have access to data sets and models that are largely funded by the European Union, which has made the Convention a lot more capable in spotting and enforcing violations and in tuning commitments to what countries are really able to deliver. Most of the heavy lifting in LRTAP is done by the EU, which makes LRTAP a lot more effective than if it relied only on its own treaty-based international legal mechanisms.[47]

The most interesting exceptions are in wildlife law. Going back to the nineteenth century, much of the international effort to protect wildlife has been anchored in the work of NGOs. When governments got around to codifying commitments to protect wildlife, which started in the 1960s and gathered steam in the 1970s, they could rely on a network of well-administered NGOs to get information about which species were most threatened and which governments were falling short. Essentially all the NGOs were based in western countries and aligned their activities with the passions of colonial gentlemen, such as birding, fishing, and hunting. Some wildlife treaties even give formal agenda-setting authority to NGOs, notably the International Union for the Conservation of Nature (IUCN), which is actually a hybrid of NGOs and governments. As in most areas of environmental law, absent the NGOs, the wildlife would be a lot worse off. If all this could be done in wildlife, why couldn't more effective enforcement systems be created to help slow global warming?

When I was running the research group at IIASA we decided to take what we had learned and use it to help the parties to the UNFCCC build the kernel of an enforcement system. The question of enforcement had come up during the diplomatic talks that led to the UNFCCC, but since countries couldn't agree on how to handle this problem they pushed the issue into the future. In Article 13 of the UNFCCC they wrote in 1992 with the Rio deadline looming, what could be agreed – which was that in the future the Parties to the agreement might want to establish a Multilateral Consultative Process (MCP).[48] In the minds of the people who wrote that invitation was something like the Montreal Protocol's Non-Compliance Procedure. Naïvely, in our research group we looked closely at the Montreal Protocol experience and at relevant experiences from other areas of international law, such as the GATT, and offered an avalanche of unsolicited advice to the negotiators who were charged with creating the MCP. But from the outset the diplomatic talks on the MCP were stillborn. Governments that thought they might have trouble complying with the climate treaty didn't want such a system, and most governments didn't care. In 1995 the Parties to the UNFCCC adopted an anodyne decision to keep studying the issue.[49] To this date the MCP has no useful role in climate diplomacy.

For most academics who study international cooperation, the absence of enforcement mechanisms is a big problem. Without enforcement, many academics tend to think it will be hard to solve interdependent problems like global warming. And it will be hard to get the reluctant countries to do much if they know they can hold out for payments that cover the full cost of compliance (and then some perhaps). Oddly, the absence of strong enforcement mechanisms in environmental agreements doesn't seem to bother most diplomats nor even most international legal experts. Perhaps because I am an academic I think the academics are right to be worried.

This mismatch in views – between advocates for enforcement and those who think the need for enforcement is overstated – has spawned one of the big debates between international relations and international legal scholars of the last two decades.

There are at least four hypotheses that could explain the absence of formal enforcement mechanisms. One is that international legal agreements are enforced mainly by national pressure groups. By this logic, international legal processes are effective mainly by drawing attention to issues; interest groups mobilized at home then generate public pressure, file suits in national courts, and deploy other instruments to keep governments in line. For example, in the early 1990s political scientist Marc Levy (now at Columbia University) tried to figure out why international accords on acid rain had been effective in some countries – even countries whose governments didn't seem much worried about pollution. What he found was a process he called "tote board diplomacy." International diplomatic talks would negotiate targets and timetables for regulating emissions on large "tote boards" that would be carried from negotiation to negotiation and adjusted as the talks proceeded. (Today that would be done with PowerPoint, but in the early 1990s when Levy first tried to figure out why targets and timetables had an impact even in the absence of enforcement mechanisms, Sharpie pens and butcher paper were still favored technologies.) Once norms were written on the board (and in a treaty), it was easier for NGOs to call out the violators and to mobilize public concern.[50] Obviously this mechanism didn't work in all settings. This process of setting norms didn't have much impact in the countries whose behavior already exceeded the norms. And it didn't work in nondemocratic governments or when there wasn't a free press, as the engine for this process is public and peer pressure.

Scholars working in other issue-areas have found similar effects. For example, human rights treaties can have a big impact on government behavior even in the absence of formal international enforcement mechanisms because once the norms are codified into international law it is easier for other actors, such as human rights NGOs and other national groups (as well as courts in some countries), to pressure for compliance.[51] There are many ways that international law affects domestic politics and, in tandem, shifts the odds in favor of higher compliance. By this logic, international enforcement is a lot less necessary because the existence of these interest groups changes the preferences of governments to make them more inclined to comply.

This logic suggests that targets and timetables might be more useful for climate change agreements than I have implied. But one insight from the scholarship on domestic mobilization is that the targets are useful when they can be used to focus resources on practical changes in behavior. Levy's "tote board" diplomacy was most influential in countries such as the UK, where the targets on tote boards had some plausible relationship to real policies that the British government might adopt. Human rights mobilization has benefitted from the fact that government behavior can plausibly be expected to align with international norms, such as on torture. Even then, the supposed impact of naming and shaming countries to honor human rights norms is often over-stated.[52] These logics have a place in the regulation on global warming, and in tandem with the policy-focused system for cooperation that I will advocate there is also a need for clear emission benchmarks. But national policies on emissions are a lot harder to influence by focusing on emission targets and timetables. So far, the experience has been that targets are usually divorced from real policy options and thus they mobilize political energy around goals that can't be achieved. They encourage the kind of behavior evident under the UNFCCC (and the Toronto target system of the late 1980s) where governments set ambitious goals while real national policies drift far off course.

A second logic is that enforcement isn't needed because once an agreement exists – especially a binding agreement – there is an automatic "pull" towards compliance. Enforcement isn't needed because every lawyer learns in law school that treaties are to be obeyed.[53]

A third logic, closely related, is that most violations of treaties don't arise in malice but from ambiguous commitments and poor capacity. If this hypothesis holds then the best way to promote compliance isn't through enforcement but with procedures to clarify the law and help countries comply.[54] Carrots and information, not sticks, are best according to this logic. Certainly this hypothesis holds in some settings, and one of the important functions of international funds such as the Montreal Protocol's Multilateral Fund has been to help countries build their regulatory capacity.

In my view, a fourth hypothesis dominates all others in explaining why environmental diplomats ignore enforcement. Nearly all environmental agreements are pre-wired to make compliance easier. I have already shown this hypothesis at work in explaining why high compliance rates with formal treaties don't reveal whether those treaties actually work. It's not that the academic experts who are keen to see more enforcement mechanisms are wrong. It is just that, by design, enforcement isn't needed because diplomacy moves the goalposts. In the few cases where heftier incentives to comply have been needed it has been fairly easy to offer carrots. So far, the carrots have been pretty effective because they haven't needed to be very large or very complicated to organize. Training programs have helped governments do a better job of regulating trade in specimens from endangered species – such as tusks, horns, and pelts – and that has made international wildlife law more effective. The EU has had an extremely effective program to help less wealthy European countries – especially those that are not EU members and thus prone to have poorly conceived and administered pollution laws – build their capacity, and that has made LRTAP more effective at clearing the European air. The largest and most effective of these so far is the $2.3 billion spent under the Montreal Protocol to help developing countries pay the full extra cost of compliance.[55] By most accounts that money has been very well spent. Altruism may play a role in the decisions by governments to fund such carrot programs, but the real factors at work are self-interest. Countries that care the most about solving environmental problems have a strong self-interest in strengthening other governments that are weaker links.

These arguments have been swirling around for at least two decades and so far it has proved very difficult to pin down exactly when they explain compliance. From the research that has been done, each of these hypotheses plays a role in explaining why compliance has been high. But if the fourth hypothesis is the dominant one – as I am fairly certain is true – then most of the body of experience with international environmental law is silent about what to do when there are stronger incentives to cheat. That makes most of that canon an unhelpful guide for how to slow global warming.

The absence of any serious enforcement procedure is a sign that diplomacy is on the wrong track. That the UNFCCC system has survived for two decades with no enforcement procedures says nothing about whether serious international cooperation on global warming will require enforcement. When governments really tighten the screws on emissions and thus expose their countries to costs that will affect their economic competitiveness, governments won't just view enforcement as castor oil. They'll demand it and put energy into building enforcement systems because the countries that undertake the most costly commitments will be most keen to ensure that other countries are also honoring their commitments. Indeed, exactly that outcome is evident in the history of the GATT and WTO – as commitments became more demanding and worries about poor implementation rose so did the demand for formal enforcement. The demand for enforcement also rose once countries started negotiating trade commitments that were less tangible and thus harder to enforce through simple reciprocity. Much of what the WTO now regulates concerns so-called "nontariff barriers" that are much harder to spot and regulate; pivotal countries knew that and demanded a formalized system to make enforcement of such obligations easier. Policy coordination on global warming will look a lot like the efforts to manage nontariff barriers – it will focus on actions that will be hard to enforce through reciprocity and will require a formal, institutionalized system to help governments spot and respond to violations efficiently.

Reading the scholarship about international trade alongside that on the environment is like reading about two different planets. The absence of any worry about enforcement in the canon of international environmental law helps explain why naïve young scholars try to invent enforcement mechanisms for global warming treaties and find no demand. Because most of the models that have guided global warming diplomacy are drawn from international environmental law, by design the global warming diplomats have never seen much need to invest resources in building an enforcement system. Agreements absent enforcement reinforce the tendency to focus on shallow commitments that automatically lead to compliance. The experience in trade has been the opposite.

In addition to encouraging shallowness, the absence of any prospect for enforcement sticks has also put global warming diplomacy on a track that is too dependent on carrots. Compared with earlier international environmental accords that have paid reluctant countries for the extra cost of compliance, the global warming problem is a lot more expensive to solve. With no prospect of credible sticks the carrots that reluctant countries demand will be large. The economic activities that cause emissions sprawl across the entire economy, making it hard to draw clear lines around what should be funded. By contrast, the Montreal Protocol's fund was effective because it addressed a discrete set of industrial processes and relied on a group of independent experts to set the boundaries and review every national funding proposal for merit.[56] And for some of the biggest emitters – such as China and Brazil – the western nations that always fund the carrots in other international environmental accords will be especially wary of letting their funds be used for cleaning the energy systems in their most formidable economic competitors.

For global warming the price tag for a full carrot strategy is hard to pin down, but it is probably at least $100 billion per year, or about two orders of magnitude larger than the experience with the ozone layer.[57] A team at MIT recently calculated the value of the carrots that would be needed to meet the goal of cutting world emissions in half by 2050 while fully compensating developing countries for the cost of their efforts. That team concluded that the transfers would start at $400 billion per year in 2020 and rise to $3 trillion in 2050.[58] For comparison, total government-to-government foreign aid was about $84 billion in 2008.[59] With such a large price tag and politically toxic transfers to economic competitors, governments have never seriously looked at paying for carrots directly. They have created some small funds modeled on the Montreal Protocol fund to help low-income governments build capacity, but those were mainly designed to boost weak governments' ability to collect and report data and to attend diplomatic meetings on global warming. The big dollars aren't in filing reports and visiting summits. They are in paying for new energy and agricultural systems that allow for deep cuts in emissions.

The political solution to the problem of giant carrots, as I showed in Chapter 4, was to shift the cost to private industry through the Clean Development Mechanism – something that had never been done on a large scale in international environmental law. In the past, funding programs worked not just because they were small and focused but also because governments kept control. In theory, relying on industry to provide the resources was good politics and good policy. Since some of the biggest money transfers would flow to countries that were also potent economic competitors, governments would find it politically toxic to make such visible transfers on their own. In Copenhagen, for example, the chief US climate change diplomat took pains to underscore that none of the US government money pledged for overseas assistance would flow to China.[60] But private money could flow to China much more easily. Indeed, within the CDM China is, by far, the largest recipient of private sector transfers.

Relying on private sector transfers has been politically expedient, but it is hard to see how it will expand to the scale needed for a carrot-only approach to slowing global warming. The CDM is already struggling to manage private sector investments on the scale of $10 billion per year and is under pressure to adopt a much stricter administration. Without any sticks, the carrot-only approach leads to diplomatic outcomes that are impractical at the scale actually needed to make deep cuts in warming emissions.

Toward a new approach

In the next chapter I will outline an alternative strategy. But here it's worth noting that just doing the opposite of what has been tried for the last two decades won't fix the gridlock on global warming. In fact, that's been tried. On all four fronts – geometry, instruments, legal form, and incentives – governments have run individual experiments. All have failed.

On geometry, governments have taken up the global warming issue in high-level clubs. Ever since 1990 the issue has been regularly on the agenda of the G8 industrial nations, and when the G8 expanded to have regular meetings with the five most important developing countries (the so-called G8+5) global warming was on that agenda as well.[61] So far, the G8 has adopted increasingly precise declarations about the need to control emissions and limit warming to 2 degrees although most of the G8 has little ability to make that goal a reality. The G8 is a forum for talking that works when talking is what's needed in diplomacy. In global warming, however, talking is the problem – it rewards diplomacy that tilts at bold promises (such as stopping global warming at 2 degrees) but invests little effort at the reality of implementation.

On instruments, in the 1990s the EU pushed for a regulatory approach called "policies and measures" that would let countries choose among a variety of policies that could control emissions. But the EU never invested much effort to figure out how to ensure that other countries would actually adopt new policies nor how to measure the practical effect of its approach, so it abandoned the scheme in favor of emission targets and timetables. The vestige of that system is in Annex A of the Kyoto Protocol.[62] The instincts that led EU diplomats to focus on concrete policies and measures were the right ones. But just making long lists of policies and measures – as in Annex A – does not automatically lead to effective international coordination.

On legal form, all of the G8 efforts have been nonbinding – as have the declarations of other talk shops such as the Asia-Pacific Partnership (APP) and the Major Economies Forum on Energy and Climate. But in all these institutions, nonbinding has not just been an invitation to flexibility; it has also meant that governments haven't worked hard to meet their obligations. That helps explain why environmental NGOs and the governments most committed to doing something about global warming have viewed nonbindingness as an excuse for inaction. A nonbinding system focused on complex policies and measures works only when it is married to sophisticated institutions that can check up on whether each country is honouring its promises and whether the effort, in total, is adequate.

On incentives, a few governments have even mooted the idea of using sticks to force stronger emission controls. The holy grail in this effort is a system of trade sanctions, and legal scholars have been working overtime to see whether such sanctions might actually be compliant with the World Trade Organization.[63] Most trade lawyers are suspicious because rules favoring free trade have been painstakingly created over many decades, and that progress could easily unravel if lots of new issues are added to the agenda – especially issues such as environmental goals that are worthy yet easily used as cover for protectionism. Trade measures will be needed as part of a serious system for enforcement, but nearly all attention to trade measures has focused on the penalties alone rather than how sanctions fit into a larger system for a more effective system for climate diplomacy.

The problem isn't the lack of experience on each of these four fronts. Rather, it is a lack of strategy in combining the best choice on each front into an integrated approach. More flexible, smaller groups won't have much impact on the problem unless the group members see a benefit from success. "Clubs" must produce incentives that encourage members to do more and, over time, encourage outsiders to join. A focus on policies and measures makes sense because that's what governments actually control, but if the effort isn't combined with a mechanism to check on whether governments are making real efforts then the results are usually meaningless. The same is true for nonbinding agreements, for the benefit of flexibility is also an invitation to laziness unless there is a way to enforce obligations. And sticks are useful only within a larger framework for cooperation that includes carrots and which, over time, lets countries demonstrate that their efforts to implement policies to control warming emissions are credible and effective.

Conclusions

The last twenty years of diplomacy on global warming have been guided by lessons drawn from the wrong histories. The lessons from international environmental law are mostly irrelevant to the problem of global warming. And the most relevant lessons from that experience – such as the need to fine-tune treaty commitments according to capabilities and costs, as was done in the Montreal Protocol's system of exemptions for essential uses – have been ignored. Guided by the wrong lessons, climate change diplomats have led themselves into a cul-de-sac of global, binding treaties sponsored by the United Nations. The gridlock on global warming arises in part because the tools that climate diplomats have used are not well suited to the problem at hand.

8 | *A new strategy*

So far, I have left four loose ends in this book. Here I tie them up.

In Chapter 3 I concluded that the countries most enthusiastic about slowing global warming are likely to adopt quite varying national strategies for regulating emissions. It is unlikely that any of them will adopt simple economy-wide cap and trade programs that would let them make credible international promises to regulate their emissions at particular levels. That conclusion points to the need for flexibility when these countries negotiate their international commitments and also suggests that those commitments could become quite complex as these governments tighten the screws and implement highly diverse policies whose exact impact on emissions are hard to measure. But I have not shown how international negotiations can manage that complexity.

In Chapter 4 I argued that the success of efforts to slow global warming will hinge on engagement of countries that are, today, reluctant to spend their own resources on controlling emissions. I showed that these countries could make a much bigger dent in emissions with very little extra effort but that the current system of incentives – the Clean Development Mechanism (CDM), notably – is not well matched to the real barriers that slow action. But I have not shown how a different system of incentives could work.

In Chapter 5, I showed that efforts to control emissions must be married to an active technology policy. I also showed that only a handful of countries need be engaged. But I did not show why technology leaders would have an incentive to develop and implement cooperative technology policies.

In Chapter 7 I showed that when the global warming issue arose on radar screens the governments that were most keen to act reached for the wrong toolbox. They chose strategies based on the history of international environmental law that were prone to gridlock when applied to the problem of global warming. As governments tried to tighten the screws on emissions the diplomatic problems compounded.

Inflexible targets and timetables were poorly matched to the commitments that governments could credibly honor. The involvement of such a large number of countries with diverse interests has yielded diplomatic chaos. Yet even in the aftermath of the Copenhagen meeting, which so far is the high-water mark for chaos, alternative ideas have not gained traction. (As this book goes to press the world is gearing up for the next global warming summit – in Cancun, Mexico, in December 2010. It might yet prove even more chaotic than Copenhagen, although expectations are so low that practically any outcome from Cancun will be branded a success.)

Now I tie up those loose ends by offering a new strategy. Before I begin, a reminder that diplomacy must be realistic. Even a diligent effort to implement the strategy offered here won't erase the sobriety check of Chapter 6. Adaptation to climate change will be essential, and there is very little that the international community can do to help countries adapt. All countries, especially the poorest with the least capable public institutions, must focus urgently on adaptation. In addition, emergency geoengineering may also be needed. Knowing that, investments in geoengineering technologies to ready the options are overdue.

There are very few analogies in the history of international cooperation that can guide efforts to solve the global warming problem. Here I will focus on one that is the closest – the effort to create strong and effective rules to govern international trade, notably through the GATT and the WTO – and draw on other examples along the way.[1]

Clubs, commitments, and incentives

My strategy is based on three central ideas. These ideas reflect the three central questions that must guide any serious negotiation: who is at the table, what are they promising, and what will encourage them to honor their promises?

The first is what I will call the carbon club. Demanding commitments will be difficult to negotiate because every country's circumstances are different. The interests and capabilities of countries will vary and so will the policy instruments – such as direct regulation and emission trading. Some countries will be enthusiastic and capable; others will be more reluctant to bear the national cost of policies that deliver global benefits. When negotiations are complex there is a strong premium on starting with a small number of countries that matter most. In small clubs it is easier for negotiators to craft more complex deals. And when groups are small it is easier to channel the benefits of cooperation to other club members, which creates a stronger incentive for the countries that are in the club to sustain cooperation.

The second central idea is that diplomacy must concentrate on crafting useful commitments. Rather than focus on targets and timetables that are largely unhelpful because governments don't have much control over emission outcomes, negotiations must focus on governmnent effort not just emission outcomes. Useful commitments will be contingent. As the screws are tightened and the costs of these policies rise, what one government offers to implement will depend on what it thinks other governments will adopt. And what governments promise and deliver will depend on many factors, such as the price of fuel and the availability of technology, that government can't anticipate and plan perfectly. The tighter the screws the more contingent and unpredictable will be every government's policy effort.

The process of crafting useful commitments must start with what each government is willing and able to deliver. That process can't run top-down by starting with abstract global goals (e.g., limiting warming to 2 degrees) and then work backwards to optimize every government's contribution. It must start "bottom up" with governments themselves. At best, global goals are benchmarks rather than starting points for crafting policies. I will call the starting point for this bottom-up process a "bid" – that is, an offer from each of the key countries about the policies and measures it might adopt. For enthusiastic countries, those bids might include cap and trade schemes, direct regulation of emissions, technology policies, and programs to help spread low-emission investments in developing countries. For developing countries those "bids" might include a host of policies that the country already finds in its interest – in Chapter 4 I provided a few examples – as well as the packages of external funding and other resources that would lead them to do more.

Serious bids will be complex and lengthy, but all must share key attributes. One is the inclusion of metrics for assessing whether the bid actually reflects what the country can deliver. (More on this below.) Another attribute is a contingent schedule, which is less familiar yet crucially important. That is, bids are not just declarations of what the country *will* do – they are also promises of efforts *contingent* on what others might do. For enthusiastic countries that are concerned about economic competitiveness, those contingent offers might include regulatory efforts that explicitly vary by the cost of policies that other countries impose on their economics. For reluctant countries, contingent offers might include a menu of efforts that the country would like to make along with the requirements (if any) for external assistance. That assistance might be money, although the examples I offered in Chapter 4 suggest that other resources, such as technology cooperation, market access, and security guarantees, may usually be more valuable and also politically easier for outsiders to mobilize and administer. Put differently, the reluctant countries' bids can include their list of policies that belong in box II (see Figure 4.3) as well as the foreign resources and actions they would need to make those policies work.

Contingency will help ensure that the bids are not too miserly. When every country thinks about its offer as an island and assumes that other countries will do the same then few governments will find it worthwhile to make much effort. That's the situation the world is in today. But when countries see credible contingencies that will magnify their own efforts then each will be more willing to do more. This won't guarantee serious, interdependent cooperation. And it won't stop global warming if big polluters see no interest in that outcome. But designing a system for international cooperation that focuses on contingency is an essential first step to improving the prospects for international cooperation because it orients each nation to the collective effort and not just its own interests as an island.

The experience with trade law offers a good model for how to construct these bids. When new countries join the GATT/WTO they assemble an "accession" package of promises. Those promises are the starting point for negotiations over what the country will do to become a member in good standing and the starting point for diplomacy on what existing GATT/WTO members will offer in exchange. Commitment packages in climate change can follow the same model. I call them "climate accession deals" (CADs). Cooperation begins with a club of important countries that are also most willing and able to control emissions. And the club deepens and expands through periodic rounds of bidding and negotiating CADs.

Third is incentives. I have already argued, in Chapter 4, that the existing system of incentives could be reformed to make it much more effective. Special purpose funds can be expanded – though doing so will be politically challenging – and better targeted. The administration of the CDM could be tightened. Competition between offsets schemes could be encouraged so there is a market force favoring high-quality efforts to reduce emissions. In time, sticks such as trade sanctions can be added.

All these incentives can help encourage cooperation, but much more will be needed as well. The incentives need to be built into the schedule of promises that governments make and the CADs they negotiate. For enthusiastic countries that means that bids should include resource promises that are linked to specific efforts by reluctant countries. Since publicly funded resources are particularly difficult to mobilize, as a practical matter those promises might include offers of access to the host country's national emission trading markets and national technology markets. Portions of these markets can be opened for offsets credits, and the size of that portion linked the counter-offers from other nations.

These three elements work in tandem. Negotiations begin with the carbon club and they focus on policies that countries can reliably implement. Those policies, which will be offered to other club members as bids, will be contingent. If many countries are willing to adopt strict limits then each nation individually will be willing to ramp up its own effort. The outcome of these negotiations will be a series of interlocking deals with incentives to comply rooted in the contingency of bids and efforts. In the GATT/WTO system those interlocking deals are called "rounds" – trade law has advanced through eight big rounds of deal-making, each producing a new package of interlocking deals, as well as a stream of parallel negotiations to bring in new members.

The system in action

The goal of this approach is to shift the focus of climate talks from abstract promises that are hard for governments to honor, such as targets and timetables, toward promises to implement policies that are more credible. And by making commitments more interdependent, this shift would encourage governments to coordinate around policies that are a lot more effective in controlling emissions.

The good news is that climate diplomacy has already taken some early, tentative steps in this direction. The European Union, long the real leader in global warming diplomacy, offers a partial model. Early in the talks that were convened to negotiate a successor to the Kyoto treaty, it promised to boost its planned 20 percent cut in emissions to 30 percent if other industrialized countries made a similar reduction.[2] Yet outside that tantalizing offer only a few other countries have made contingent offers that would lead to more action. One reason the EU offer didn't gain more traction is that it was hard to assess because it focused on emission levels and included few details on the real policies that would lead to deeper cuts in emissions. Thirty percent didn't encourage more action in part because it wasn't seen as credible. And the EU made little effort to reveal the exact circumstances under which their own effort would magnify from 20 percent to 30 percent.

Doing better will require that climate diplomats push countries to make contingent offers and realize that the form of contingency will vary with the interests and abilities of governments. For example, some governments find it particularly difficult to adopt policies that have long-term effects. Their political institutions may be new and their authority uncertain. In those cases, as in the EU today, contingent bids might take the form of time-limited promise for emission controls and an offer to do more if other countries make similar offers. That's what the EU did during the run-up to Copenhagen by offering to boost its emission cuts to 30 percent if other countries followed. But that effort was wisely focused on 2020, for in the EU long-term promises, such as out to 2050 or 2100, are much harder to make believable.

For countries where the legislative process is filled with veto points and it is extremely difficult to pass new legislation, contingent promises will probably take the opposite form. In those instances, the difficulty is assembling a winning political coalition to make major changes in policy, but once the policy is in place it is hard to undo. The United States is that kind of government, and the main US policy proposals reflect that. The Waxman–Markey legislation adopted in the House of Representatives opened with the statement that the US may weaken its already miserly plans if big developing countries fail to make comparable efforts.[3] Draft legislation sponsored by John Kerry and Joe Lieberman in the Senate offers more detail on how US efforts would be contingent upon similar efforts in most of the rest of the world's economic activities that are heavy users of energy and sensitive to trade, such as steel. In this kind of country, legislation would define the maximum effort that the country could make under ideal conditions and then carve out exceptions if other countries don't make comparable efforts. In the US that maximum effort is probably roughly an 80 percent cut in emissions by 2050 – the benchmark in both the Waxman–Morkey legislation and the Kerry–Lieberman draft.

More demanding commitments will require better systems for assessing whether promises are credible. The biggest of the industrialized and developing countries – the United States, European Union, Japan, China, and India – can set the right tone by nominating themselves for an intensive, open review of their contingent promises. Although global warming diplomats are wary about any effort that could be intrusive, such across-the-board policy reviews are becoming common. The IEA, for example, has recently finished a careful review of China's options for cleaning coal, done with the full cooperation of China's most important economic planners (and with funding, in part, from the British government).[4] Eventually this approach will make verification and enforcement more familiar and easier to organize, but initially its main purpose would be to shine a spotlight on which national policy proposals are the most credible and thus make it easier for governments to negotiate contingent deals. Mavens of the climate process will recognize this idea as "pledge and review" – a concept that gained traction in the early 1990s but was then abandoned by climate diplomats who were deluded by the idea that legally binding targets and timetables set on hurried negotiating schedules would be more effective.

The central idea behind bidding is to arrive, country by country, at a collection of individual promises that outline what the country will do at home to slow global warming and also collective deals that determine what each country will do in tandem with other countries. In modern economies these deals, what I am calling CADs, will ultimately affect millions of actors – notably firms that play the central role in making industrial investments that account for most warming emissions. However, the process of assembling CADs must begin with governments in each host country. National governments have three advantages that no other actor enjoys. First, governments can make the most credible long-term commitments on behalf of their territory. Second, nearly always, the host government is able to mobilize the most reliable and widely accepted information about the actual baseline of policies and efforts that are planned, and it can best contemplate how those might be adjusted as part of a CAD. The host government usually knows the most about what it can actually implement in different sectors of its economy.[5] And third, there is rarely any other actor that can better assemble the complex array of stakeholders needed for high-leverage CADs – the industrial and economic development ministries, state-owned power corporations, and important private sector players.

The strategy in making bids and negotiating CADs is not new in international cooperation. It is analogous to the accession problem in any international institution that imposes demanding obligations on its members. The key task in accession is to entice a new member into the club (and thus create broader benefits for the club) while not over-paying (or under-charging) the new member. As each new member joins the obligations on existing members change as well. When a club is small – as I propose for global warming today – each of these deals can be tailored to particular individual interests. As the club grows in size and deepens in influence then some general rules and patterns will be needed to make negotiations more tractable.

The WTO offers a model through its accession process.[6] Potential new members assemble bids of promises that they will offer in exchange for external benefits. In the WTO case those promises vary with each nation's circumstances and include tariffs as well as an array of other policies that affect trade, such as export subsidies, protection for intellectual property, and government procurement. Governments that seek membership put those policies on the table because they want the benefits of successful membership, such as particular tariff concessions and most favored nation status that are hard to obtain without joining the WTO club. Many governments also join because they know that policies they favor at home will be easier to implement and harder to reverse if membership in a prominent international agreement ties their hands.[7] Negotiations then proceed with any interested WTO member allowed to join the "working party" that shapes the final accession agreement, which includes a plan for transition since accession deals often require radical changes in host government policy that can't happen overnight.[8] In every significant case of WTO accession those first bids are not accepted – rather, each interested WTO member begins bilateral negotiations with the candidate and through the normal process of bargaining arrives at a final, agreed package. The negotiation process focuses on what the host country is willing to concede and also what WTO members think the host country is actually able to deliver.[9] Negotiation elicits information about how each country's actions related to trade affect the interests of other WTO members, and that information makes it easier for the working party to focus on accession deals that are most practical and deliver the largest collective benefits. A sign of the complexity of the process is the time that accession requires. On average, WTO accession negotiations require about five years. For big countries, such as China and Russia, WTO accession negotiations have taken longer because the stakes are larger, the policy adjustments more complex, and many more countries join the working party.

What I will propose here will seem overly complicated to global warming diplomats and stakeholders used to focusing on targets and timetables and lamenting the lack of "political will" by governments to promise deeper emission cuts. The complications are unavoidable if governments get serious about coordinating their policies. The WTO experience is a useful model because it reveals that the international community can organize such a scheme for bidding and deal-making. Many other models, such as coordination of financial regulation, involve similar complexity although I think they are somewhat less germane because what the global warming issue shares with trade is the need to focus on credible policies that affect long-term, capital investments such as the creation of whole new industries and infrastructures.

It is striking how little attention climate diplomacy gives to the important details of national policy and the credibility of national proposals. By contrast, diplomacy in other areas, such as trade and finance, is much more steeped in the important details and thus much better connected to the realities of what governments might actually implement. In global warming, so far the incentives have favored speedy negotiations, high-profile summits, and a focus on simplistic emission targets. The result has been the illusion of action but not much impact on the underlying problem. In trade, the benefits from pure symbolism are fewer and negotiations are allowed to be more complex. Such negotiations are consequently much more ponderous but also a lot more relevant to real coordination of national policies and real patterns of capital investment.

The WTO accession experience applied to climate change suggests that two types of benefits will create strong incentives that will encourage countries to join. One is the general benefit afforded to all club members in good standing. For global warming, those general

benefits could include access to the carbon markets in the enthusiastic
nations for CDM-like offset trading as well as access to government-
to-government funding for emission abatement projects, adaptation,
and capacity-building. The other benefits would be tailored to each
member. I will focus the rest of this chapter on those particular benefits because in the early days of creating a club general benefits are
likely to be few and probably diffuse. Particular benefits tailored to
each country will be a more powerful inducement to action. Indeed,
the central challenge in creating effective global warming cooperation
is that the general benefits from cooperation are highly diffused – they
accrue only slowly and globally in the form of less warming. The
club approach makes cooperation easier by, in effect, creating new
benefits – such as lucrative new markets for low-emission technology and access to lucrative national emission markets – and concentrating those benefits exclusively on club members. As the club effort
works and establishes credibility then more general benefits become
a stronger draw.

   In practice, these deals will take many different forms. Here,
though, I will focus on the deals that will be hardest for diplomats
to craft: the deals with large, reluctant countries. These countries are
indispensable yet wary about taking on costly obligations. And they
know they are indispensable, which means they can drive a hard bar-
gain. Some of the deals that result from this process might be grand
and interlocking – requiring a major intervention by a complex array
of countries. For example, one of the many initiatives that China
might include in its bid is the creation of an East Asian gas pipeline
grid that connected Russia's continental gas supplies with markets in
China and South Korea. (That grid, in turn, would facilitate greater
use of gas for power generation and thus lower CO_2 emissions, as
I discussed in Chapter 4.) Initially, however, most deals with these
countries would probably rest on less complex proposals that will
be easier to organize and less fragile politically. For example, India
might bid to test and deploy more efficient (and thus less polluting)
ultra-supercritical power plants through its state-owned power company. (At present, India has just commissioned its first supercritical
power plant. Ultra-supercritical technology, already widely used in
China, would be even more efficient.) Enthusiastic countries that har-
bor the relevant technologies and the interest in engaging the reluctant
countries would then negotiate – and compete – to provide financing,

training, and other elements that help realize a greater deployment of these advanced power plants.

Competition on both sides – between reluctant countries offering many bids and enthusiastic countries searching for the best deal – would help ensure that bids stay in line with reality. Where these deals produce private benefits for enthusiastic countries – such as larger markets for technology exports – few other forms of "credit" may be needed. A recent $23 billion deal between France and China to deploy nuclear reactors is an example. Where the benefits are more diffused then "credit" may take the form of fewer obligations to adopt costly regulations at home. Part of the CAD negotiation would include the appropriate credit that the donor country would earn. Countries such as Japan that are already highly efficient and have few opportunities for local emission control might make most of their effort through CADs – just as they are, today, heavy users of the CDM. This approach would not eliminate the CDM and other offsets markets, but it would allow those markets to focus where they work best – on the limited subset of projects that involve marginal changes in technology for which it is relatively easy to establish baselines.

To a small degree, these kinds of initiatives are already under way through the normal process of bilateral and multilateral development assistance. Norway, for example, is far along in implementing a deal with Indonesia to protect forests and is negotiating with other forest-rich countries as well. Those efforts will create models as well as incentives for other countries that are concerned about controlling emissions to negotiate their own deals with forest-rich nations before the good forest protection opportunities disappear. Those competitive pressures are encouraging. Multilateral banks have also organized to make many investments in reluctant countries that would lower emissions.[10] What's different about my proposal, however, is that the CADs framework – the system of bids, the deal-making, and the credit that countries would earn for CADs – would be integrated into the legal framework on climate change. That would create much stronger incentives for reluctant and enthusiastic countries, alike, to participate. At present, for example, neither Norway nor Indonesia directly gains much from their efforts to protect Indonesia's forests. (Both think they might gain in the future if a viable forest crediting system – known as "REDD+" in climate change parlance – comes into full effect. But those benefits are highly uncertain and abstract.)

Absent any serious mechanism for credit, not surprisingly such efforts at deal-making are scant despite abundant evidence that there are huge opportunities for reluctant countries to make deep reductions in emissions at little or no extra cost.

The really difficult negotiations, of course, will focus on the credit that enthusiastic countries should earn from these deals, the obligations that reluctant nations would undertake in exchange, and the mechanisms for tracking whether counties actually honor their pledges. Such discussions are unavoidable because the international initiatives that will matter most in global warming will have the most unpredictable outcomes. For example, how much credit should be awarded to EU initiatives (led by Britain) to develop and test advanced coal combustion technology in China? Several US firms, partly with support from the US government, have similar initiatives under way in China. Should both the European and US efforts earn credit, and what metrics should be adopted so that credits encourage the ventures that are most likely to yield commercial success? Negotiations focused on these questions will help encourage competition between projects, provision of accurate information, and transparency that can help encourage coordination where that is appropriate.

The absence of credit and accountability help explain why the system of pledges adopted at the close of the Copenhagen conference in December 2010 has not led to much deeper cooperation on climate change. In that system, countries make public pledges about the efforts they will undertake. In theory, the guidelines for pledging are so flexible that countries could make the kinds of contingent offers I envision. But the Copenhagen pledging system, in reality, was an afterthought and is not integrated into the real diplomacy over climate change. Countries don't earn credit if they make realistic pledges and there are few incentives for ambitious contingent offers. There is also no system for accountability, and thus wildly unrealistic pledges stand alongside genuine offers and the Copenhagen system doesn't generate much useful information that would make it easier for diplomats to discern viable offers from the bogus.

I have focused here on the WTO accession process as a model, but of course there are many other examples that offer similar guidance. The EU arose from a core group of countries that focused on collective management of a few of the "commanding heights" of the 1950s economy (coal, steel, and nuclear power) and then expanded to address other topics with new members.[11] EU accession occurs through a similar process of negotiation, although the resources mobilized are much larger and the scrutiny much more intense because much more is at stake. And the EU has a system for administration that is much more sophisticated than what is likely to emerge on international global warming coordination for many decades. The original formation of the OECD arose through a process of negotiation among recipient states – the war-ravaged economies of western Europe – for the Marshall Plan funds provided by the United States. Each European member bid for a share of the pie by proposing a complex array of policy reforms that it would implement; its peers evaluated the bids and negotiated a full package of resources and policy efforts that all the members would implement.[12]

The WTO and other models suggest that care will be needed not to rely only on diplomacy. The governments that care most about slowing warming can help push global diplomacy with some hard-nosed unilateral decisions. Europe and the US have a pivotal opportunity. The EU's carbon market is the world's largest, and the eventual US market will be even bigger. Both are slated to rely heavily on international offsets to help lower the cost of compliance while engaging developing countries in efforts to control emissions. Both could set tough rules to govern which offsets are most prized while also promising full linkage to other markets that have comparably tough provisions.

Those actions, which only the EU and US can decide at home, would transform the international politics of climate change by creating a planetary competition for quality.[13] By contrast, most of today's offsets systems – such as the CDM that governs most EU offsets as well as the schemes taking shape in the US – are geared mainly to produce high volumes of credits without much serious attention to quality. (I welcome efforts, under way at this writing, to tighten the rules governing the CDM, but that tightening process is cumbersome in part because it unfolds in the intergovernmental setting where the countries that create most of the value in the CDM, notably the EU and Japan, have relatively little influence.) The real arbiters of offset quality are the prices in the markets where offsets are purchased.[14] A unilateral tightening of offset rules would encourage investors to seek higher quality projects, and a credible plan for further tightening would magnify the flight to quality.

At present, the framework for international cooperation on climate change doesn't give room for such hopeful unilateralism. It confers on the CDM a monopoly on international offsets and thus guarantees that unless the CDM works efficiently – which is unlikely since nobody yet knows how to design and implement an efficient international offsets system – investors will have no incentive to experiment with projects outside the CDM framework. One of the benefits of competition is that it produces information about which approaches work best, but inside the CDM monopoly there is little competition over quality.[15]

Constructive unilateralism could also help create a credible subset for the CDM and other international offsets schemes. Offsets have a role to play, but if they are seen as perpetual promises then they also create perverse incentives for reluctant countries to adopt even emission-reducing policies that align with their own local interests. Chapter 4 outlined in more detail how subsets could work in practice.

International institutions and convergence

The backbone of this approach is the process of offering bids and negotiating CADs. The process of agreeing on policies that will lead to deep cuts in emissions will run no faster than countries are willing to make an effort. While the success of this effort rests with key governments – especially governments that are most enthusiastic to slow global warming – their endeavors will be more effective with the help of international institutions. Some elements of these institutions already exist – such as in the data reporting system of the UNFCCC – but will require reforms. Building and reforming institutions is not easy and thus a clear strategy is needed so that efforts can focus on the institutional functions that will be most essential. And a strategy is needed so that the governments and private actors that have the strongest interest in building and reforming these institutions will mobilize for the effort.

Broadly, international institutions can help in three ways. First, institutions can manage the process of bidding, negotiating, and codifying CADs. This function of hosting deal-making efforts by governments requires a wide array of legal and administrative capabilities. On the topic of climate change, many of those talents have already been assembled in a secretariat that manages the UN process. However, getting started on the club approach outlined here will probably require a new institution since the UN secretariat has neither the legal authority nor the interest in building a more effective, smaller rival club. There are several other forums that might offer these services, such as the G20 or the MEF, but so far none of those institutions has invested in building the skills that would be needed to host a serious negotiation of the type needed. Crafting CADs, as in successfully running a WTO negotiation round, requires standing capabilities. Making the club approach work would require a few sympathetic governments – ideally the largest beneficiaries of an effective climate club, such as the EU, US, China, India, and Brazil – to make a contribution. (Much smaller countries that are nimble and strategic might also play a role – such as Norway has illustrated with its pioneering efforts on forests – although they are not pivotal since their emissions are relatively low.) Those large countries are already engaged in active negotiations through the G20, MFF, and the UN process so focusing those efforts on practical deals would not require heroic extra efforts and would align with their interests. (Of this list, the EU is probably the most wary because it has invested so heavily in the UN process on climate change, and thus other countries may need to get this rival institution started to demonstrate to the EU that it will advance the goal of slowing global warming rather than just threaten the UN.) Since the initial focus of this club effort will be on crafting major national deals with content that will be hard to predict, probably the best legal form is a flexible system of nonbinding accords. In time, however, binding agreements may be needed for particular topics such as standards for international emission trading that require a firm legal basis.

Second, institutions can help club members (and potential entrants) negotiate more effective deals by providing information. Within the existing UN climate change process, information-gathering activities have focused on emissions and national policies. Those efforts have been helpful because while there are many databases on national emissions (some probably more accurate than the UN data) there is no official common data set. Those common data are essential for monitoring progress and, where quantitative emission controls are part of national commitments, in assessing compliance. What's missing is useful information about national policies and their possible impacts on emissions. The system for data reporting under the UNFCCC requests countries to report information on their policies, but almost no serious effort has been made to generate useful data of this type. Such data are difficult to organize and analyze (a problem that can be surmounted with effort). But the chief obstacle to developing useful policy data systems is that at present nothing useful is actually done with that information. Promoting serious policy coordination – such as I propose here with the CADs approach – requires the ability to focus on the policy efforts that really matter. Some of the needed information will emerge through the normal process of competition between bids and during negotiations over CADs. But a more active focus on getting data about policy efforts and possible outcomes is needed.

A new institution is needed to provide regular assessments of policy implementation. Such institutions are rare in environmental negotiations and thus it is not surprising that, twenty years ago when diplomats started working on climate change by using models from international environmental cooperation they didn't pay close attention to the need for detailed and useable data on policy implementation. But the need for such data is an increasingly common aspect of international cooperation on economic issues. The creation of the WTO in 1995 included an agreement to launch a trade policy review mechanism (TPRM) that would regularly review nations' compliance with WTO commitments. That model is imperfect, however, because its architects could not agree on whether the TPRM would connect to the WTO's real enforcement system (its dispute resolution process). In the end, there was no connection nor any other prominent role, and thus TPRM has withered in its practical influence.[16] Important countries didn't want a TPRM probing their national policies unless the probing had a clear purpose that produced benefits to the country. Better precedents are probably found in the OECD, IEA, and IMF. From the outset, the OECD included an intensive review process because the original members wanted to hold each other accountable to the commitments they had made collectively. (Some of those commitments – such as on public budgets, exchange rates, and customs – were interdependent and prone to deteriorate unless each country had confidence that the others were in compliance.) That OECD review process continues today with regular reviews of its members' economic, science and technology, and environmental policies. While the economic reviews have atrophied in importance, the OECD's environmental reviews remain an area where the institution has particularly high visibility and, in many cases, influence. IEA, an independent arm of OECD, conducts regular reviews of its members' energy policies that are also often influential.[17] The IMF's Article IV process includes an intensive review of policies when members are allowed to suspend some of the institution's norms. Through an intensive process of review the IMF (and its members) learn about the political and economic forces that lead to a member's noncompliance which makes it easier to work with the target country to outline a path back to compliance.[18]

These experiences suggest design of an assessment institution that could look broadly at each country's promised efforts and then probe in detail where those efforts seem to be falling short. Benchmarks and milestones promised during the negotiation process could be used to measure compliance. Perhaps even more important would be the ability of such a review process to identify the efforts needed in cases where countries are falling short of full implementation – a goal that the architects of the WTO had envisioned for the TPRM. With experience and demonstrated competence, the review process might make assessments on the degree to which efforts have fallen short (and thus suppliers of external resources should not earn credit for their contributions) and also where efforts have exceeded expectations (thus leading perhaps to bonuses). As a practical matter, this under- and over-compliance might not take the form of quantified emissions but would be an assessment of effort that could feed into negotiations among the enthusiastic countries about whether each is meeting its obligations.

As governments tighten the screws on emissions and become more sensitive to costs the availability of transparent performance reviews will be essential to sustaining confidence that each country is making its agreed effort. And it will allow countries that have made contingent offers to adjust their efforts in line with what other countries are actually implementing. Serious emission control policies will be expensive and are likely to be steeped in suspicions that other countries are shirking. More transparency can dampen the suspicions and also create a stronger foundation for deeper cooperation. These insights help inform the politics of creating a serious review mechanism. The countries with the largest ambition to control global emissions will have the strongest incentives to invest in creating a review mechanism – even to the point of volunteering themselves for early reviews. And the ability to spot efforts that fall short of promises will create a context in which individual countries can enforce compliance through reciprocity. Such capabilities will not eliminate the eventual need for formal enforcement systems, but they can reduce the need to rely on formal systems to perform all the difficult enforcement tasks.

A third role for institutions is in providing particular functions delegated by governments. For example, several countries will include investments in innovation with their pledges. I have suggested in Chapter 5 that a handful of countries, in particular, should be encouraged to make a big concerted push on technological innovation. Under the current Kyoto-style system of emission targets and timetables such investments are welcome but countries get no credit for their efforts. Leading innovators might delegate the function of crafting an international technology strategy to a special purpose institution. And the members of that institution could follow the same club logic already described: the group would start with small numbers of governments that are most relevant, and they would negotiate a package of promises – such as funding for R&D as well as field deployment of new technologies – while providing private benefits that are initially available to club members, such as access to advanced technologies and deployment funds as well as markets for new technologies. Indeed, the countries that are already among the world's top innovators are also large markets for low-emission energy – for example, China, Germany, Japan, the UK, and the US – which means they will be well positioned to channel exclusive benefits in the form of market access to other members of this innovation club. That institution could also help determine the credit that each country should earn for its national technology strategy.

Performing many of these functions will require many new institutions that are dedicated to tasks related to climate change as well as reforms at existing institutions. As these efforts mature they can be stitched together into a general set of expectations and approaches. Much as the early reciprocal trade agreements from the late 1940s matured as the General Agreement on Tariffs and Trade (GATT), serious deals on climate change could become a General Agreement on Climate Change (GACC) with a core body of legal expectations and codified norms. A common, central body of law will eventually be necessary so that there are clear minimum standards – for example, governing the crediting and trading of emission offsets. A common body of law and expectations will also make rules, such as decisions to sunset offset crediting and other benefits as countries develop economically, more credible.

In addition to dedicated institutions, efforts to craft climate deals will also include instructions and demands for other institutions. For example, some of the gases that cause global warming are also regulated by the agreements that were initially designed to protect the ozone layer. Some of these gases may prove easier to regulate under the Montreal Protocol than in the more sprawling UNFCCC system.

The biggest challenges in linking to other institutions are likely to concern trade. Serious efforts to control warming gases will affect trade in at least two ways. One is widely discussed and has already appeared many times in this book: the use of trade sanctions and border tariff adjustments. The other may prove more important. Clubs work best when they produce private benefits, and for climate change that will include special market access (and exclusions for non-club members). As the club commitments become more demanding the need for those special trade rules will rise, and that will eventually conflict with the norms of free trade and equal access that are extended to all 153 members of the WTO.

Convergence

As governments begin regulating warming gases there will be strong pressure for convergence. If countries adopt similar approaches then it will be easier to link their markets, and that will offer gains from collaboration – such as larger markets for emission credits and technologies. With convergence there will be less pressure from reluctant nations for large income transfers because the different economies will operate according to more similar rules.

Expectations of convergence and continued cooperation will also create helpful pressure on governments to adopt a broad array of policies that align with national interests while also helping reduce global warming. If governments see CADs as single one-off deals then they will be reluctant to make the investments and adjustments needed to put the country on a different development trajectory. As the CDM experience has revealed, one-off deals with no vision for the future create perverse incentives for reluctant nations to avoid sensible policies, including putting a positive price on carbon, because once those policies are in place the host country can no longer earn credit for the additional effort. A solution to this problem is to ensure that the individual, tailored elements of each CAD are coupled to a broader set of expectations and a clear transition path for the country to adhere to general norms. (Those general norms might be codified into the UNFCCC or a protocol – akin to the general norms that were codified into the GATT and later enforced with the WTO legal system.) That transition process could include milestones as well as visible commitments to extinguish external support as a country develops. By combining these transition commitments into a broader agreement, their enforceability will rise because the commitments will be coupled to the broader benefits of membership.[19] Enforcement through formal institutions and reciprocity is more efficient when benefits can be witheld readily rather than mustering new penalties.[20]

While there will be an incentive for convergence, the rates of change may still be very slow because convergence in policies that are intimately tied to a nation's industrial organization has never been fast. In the 1990s many analysts forecast a political and economic convergence around the idea of "globalization" – that is, market-oriented economies managed by democratic governments. Today, much of the deregulation and privatization that was the backbone of that vision is in tatters; democracy, while on the rise, is hardly the only form of government. The same kinds of forces that have preserved (even encouraged) fragmentation in political and economic organization will have similar effects on convergence in the regulation of warming gases.

The efforts to reduce trade barriers through the GATT and the WTO offer a guide for what to expect.[21] Back in the 1950s through the early 1960s when trade issues involved the relatively simple task of adjusting border tariffs between about two dozen countries, each "round" of negotiations was short (less than a year in duration) and could be finished reliably on time. Today, negotiations are a lot more complex because the issues they cover, such as subsidies and food safety rules, are politically and administratively more difficult for governments to regulate reliably. And earlier successes mean that trade issues left unsolved – such as access to agricultural markets – are politically the hardest ones to solve. Trade talks thus linger longer with outcomes that are more indeterminate. The trade talks that began in the mid-1980s and created the WTO, required eight years to finish and engaged 123 countries. The current "Doha Round" of talks, with an agenda that includes nearly impossible issues such as the paring of agricultural subsidies while engaging more than 150 countries, has no end in sight. Doha is a warning to climate diplomats that sprawling agendas and memberships can produce diplomatic zombies that hold endless meetings yet never succeed or die.

Even as massive global trade talks stall, trade diplomacy has made progress in smaller forums that are easier to manage and by focusing on agreements rooted in national self-interest. Thus bilateral trade and investment treaties and regional "clubs" have advanced the trade agenda – a bit at the expense of global institutions but mainly in ways that advance the global agenda. A few countries even unilaterally reduce trade barriers, such as India in 2008,[22] with the goal of spurring similar actions by others. Purists heap scorn on these clubs and special deals because they are not universal. By design they are fragmented. They are, in part, a strategic use of clubs that concentrates benefits on club members and thus creates stronger incentives for cooperation. The practical reality is that complex and demanding negotiations usually fail, as with Doha, when the agenda is too big and every country has a seat at the table.

Conclusions

The alternative strategy offered here is based on the central lessons from the experience in trade. Commitments must match what governments can actually deliver. Serious cooperation must start with a small group of countries that is most relevant to the problem – what I call the carbon club. Small groups have big advantages over the global geometry of the UN because they are better suited to the complex, interdependent bargaining that is necessary for getting serious about slowing global warming. Small groups make it easier to channel particular benefits to members of the club, which gives countries a stronger incentive to cooperate.[23] Well-designed international trading systems can do the same by channeling incentives to firms and governments that make the biggest efforts at controlling emissions and thus fetch the highest prices.

Why would any nation – in particular in the developing world, which has been wary of becoming entangled in climate commitments – agree to this scheme? The answer lies in conditionality and contingency. The enthusiastic nations have large resources to offer – technology, funding, linkages to valuable carbon markets and the like – that that they can offer conditionally only to club members in good standing. And the enthusiastic nations can also threaten the eventual use of sticks – such as trade sanctions – to large countries that avoid such commitments. (Eventually, depending on how the climate and trade regimes evolve, the two areas of international cooperation could merge in some respects.) And the regime would evolve as quickly as possible to a system that includes linkages between carbon pricing systems and technology markets so that the "most favored" provisions that offer general benefits to club members have real value. The deeper the linkages the greater the benefits from membership.

Long-time observers of the climate scene will recognize some of these ideas in an early 1990s proposal from the Japanese government for "pledge and review." The idea was that governments would make pledges for emission control policies and then review the efficacy on a periodic basis. Pledge and review was pilloried by the environmental community and most European governments because it deviated from the conventional wisdom that the best way to slow global warming, like all environmental problems, was to set binding targets and timetables. But the real reason it never gained traction is that Japan never invested in efforts to show how it would work. The same troubles are likely to befall the Copenhagen Accord, which also (using different language) offers a pledge and review system. After nations could not agree on much in Copenhagen they created a system for each nation to pledge what it would offer as its national policies. Yet, just as with the Japanese proposal in the early 1990s, no nation has invested much effort into showing whether their pledges are viable and there is no institutional framework for facilitating informed negotiations between countries that uses the Copenhagen pledges as a starting point. Little of today's diplomacy concentrates on the most central need for interdependent cooperation – linking the promises in different national pledges into packages that lead countries to make bigger efforts by working in concert.

After two decades of effort the system of climate diplomacy has made strikingly little progress. This chapter has offered a different model for how diplomacy could be organized to be a lot more effective – in many cases by working with the same institutional building blocks that climate diplomats have already created. The engine for this new model is a small group of countries that can tailor commitments more readily around their interests and abilities. Those club efforts can run in parallel with the broader, global framework that already exists. As the club becomes more effective it will also help make the global regime more relevant and, in time, the two may merge.

Climate change and world order: implications for the UN, industry, diplomacy, and the great powers

CO_2 is a tough pollutant to manage. It is long-lived and most of its emissions are intrinsic to burning fossil fuels, which industrialized economies depend on. Any serious plan for taming CO_2 will require intense international cooperation, but no country acting alone has much incentive to control its pollution. Worse, no country will adopt costly emission controls without confidence that its economic competitors are doing the same. These simple factors make the problem of global climate change a really hard one to solve.

This book has advanced six arguments. First, gridlock on global warming exists, in large part, because governments have adopted the wrong models to guide their diplomatic efforts. They have relied too much on the history of international environmental accords. But those models mostly don't work well for problems such as regulating CO_2 that require complicated coordination of policies that are costly and thus affect national economic competitiveness. The hallmark of the CO_2 problem is the need for interdependent commitments. What one country is willing to adopt depends on what its economic competitors are implementing. None of the history of international environmental cooperation offers robust models for that kind of cooperation. And in the few instances where international environmental diplomacy offers relevant precedents the community of global warming diplomats have largely drawn the wrong lessons. Following the wrong models has made a hard problem even harder to solve.

By following the wrong models, over the last two decades the community of diplomats working on global warming have become highly skilled at reaching agreements, action plans, and communiqués. But their efforts haven't actually done much to protect the climate. For example, diplomats have sought global treaties with legally binding emission targets and timetables. Yet they have largely ignored the fact that governments have little direct control over emissions and that serious cooperation should focus on policies that governments actually master. They have created incentive schemes such as the Kyoto Protocol's Clean Development Mechanism (CDM) that offer the illusion of encouraging emission reductions but are mainly just shell games because few governments have invested much in the institutions needed to administer such systems effectively.

A radically different strategy is needed. Getting started on that new strategy requires looking to new models. I have looked to many other models, mainly from international economic coordination, and drawn particularly heavily on the experience with the GATT and WTO.

Second, getting started on a new approach requires working in smaller groups – "clubs." Global warming policies are hard to coordinate because the range of policies that each country adopts will be highly varied. Flexibility will be essential. And yet the incentive for countries to be serious is weak because the benefits from success – less global warming – arise so far in the future. A club approach makes it much easier to manage those challenges. By focusing initially on the countries that matter most, the number of voices will be fewer and it will be easier to craft complicated deals. Within a smaller and more exclusive group it will be easier to channel benefits such as preferential access to clean energy markets and carbon credits to other club members. Those exclusive benefits will create more tangible incentives for club members to lead. As club members cooperate and generate exclusive benefits the incentives for further cooperation will grow and so will the interest of other countries to join the club.

A club approach intrinsically requires working outside the global United Nations (UN) system that has dominated climate talks so far. But success with the club approach can, in time, make the global UN-based approach to climate change more effective. It will create competition for the UN approach and be a helpful incentive for the UN system to perform better. It can also offer a useful compass. Models for effective cooperation worked out inside these small clubs will be easier to apply globally once countries see that they are effective and once the big countries are already invested in them. One of the largest political challenges in making this shift to the club approach is that the countries with the greatest interest in effective climate change regulation are also, at present, those most invested in the UN approach.

Success with the club approach will require a ruthless and strategic focus on which countries are truly essential members. I have suggested that a handful of enthusiastic nations from the industrial-ized world along with a few of the most rapidly growing reluctant nations – notably Brazil, China, India, Indonesia, and South Africa – are essential. Other countries should be engaged where they can be useful, but large clubs that face complicated tasks are prone to become unwieldy. Success will also require attention to avoiding, at least ini-tially, possible club members who will steer negotiations into gridlock because they don't mind global warming or their economies thrive on carbon exports. Russia and much of OPEC fall into that category.[1] Particularly careful attention must be paid to the problem of Russia, for it not only has historically blocked serious emissions regulations but it is also a large emitter. One danger is that without a smart strat-egy more countries, including big emerging markets such as China, could fall into that hostile category.

In looking to new models, climate diplomats need to get a lot more serious about national interests and abilities. Every successful inter-national agreement starts with the interests of the most powerful coun-tries. Those interests can change, of course, as has happened over the last two decades as news about global warming dangers has spread and most countries have become more willing to spend resources to control emissions. But efforts at cooperation that stray far from national interests don't last long and won't be seen by most govern-ments and investors as credible. Credibility is especially important in global warming because it is impossible to fix the warming prob-lem without whole new energy systems, and the investment in those systems requires a long-term perspective and confidence that the sup-porting policies will be durable.

Third, enthusiastic industrialized countries have the strongest incen-tive to lead this effort. And the best way to lead is with contingent offers. Those offers would consist of detailed promises of the policies they would implement as well as extra efforts they would make if other countries participate. Contingency is crucial because when policies are costly the actions of one country depend on what it expects others will do. And contingency will create a strong incentive for more effective diplomacy since every government will see its own national efforts multiplied through contingency. These national offers would be the starting point for negotiations over the actual packages of policies that these countries will implement. The outcome of those negotiations is a series of deals that I have called climate accession deals (CADs).

This approach of focusing on packages of contingent policy commitments will seem a lot more complicated to negotiate and administer than the schedules of emission targets and timetables that have occupied most diplomacy on climate change over the last two decades. That complexity is unavoidable, and it is explicitly intended to move negotiations beyond simple commitments that look nice on paper yet have had little impact in reality. Most governments will adopt a medley of policies that, together, can't credibly assure compliance with country-wide emission output targets. As the screws are tightened on emissions the exact emission levels will become even harder to predict. By refocusing diplomacy on coordination of policies rather than just emission targets and timetables the odds will rise that diplomatic outcomes will actually reflect what governments are willing and able to implement.

Fourth, developing countries – what I prefer to call "reluctant countries" – should be engaged through the same kinds of deals. But negotiating these CADs will be a lot more difficult because these governments have fewer incentives to invest in global public goods such as slowing global warming. (The current approach of paying them the full extra cost of controlling emissions, such as through the CDM, has weakened their incentive for action even further. A credible sunset for those payments would help.) Getting started with these countries requires tailoring deals to their national circumstances. The complexity of doing that well demands that efforts focus, initially, on just a few countries and on the sectors of their economies where national governments can make the most credible commitments.

I have shown that there is a huge potential for reducing emissions through policies that align with these reluctant countries' national interests, but these "win-win" policies have been misunderstood by most analysts. They won't happen automatically. Outside help will be needed and must be tailored to each country's national circumstances. The starting point for that effort would be offers from each reluctant country that include not just policies that make sense for them to pursue on their own but also the kinds of external assistance that would be needed. A fruitful competition between enthusiastic countries to promise that assistance will help generate deals that provide the most leverage on emissions. The biggest leverage will come from large-scale policy and infrastructure reforms. High leverage policies are essential because CADs will be difficult to negotiate. Indeed, the kinds of policy reforms that offer the largest leverage on emissions are quite poorly suited for funding through discrete, market-based offset schemes such as the CDM.

Several of the enthusiastic and reluctant countries, alike, will want to concentrate some of their effort on technological innovation so that over the long term new and less costly options for emission control are available. Innovation and testing of new technologies is a complement to policies, such as cap and trade and direct regulation, that have a more immediate effect on emissions. Unlike the current approach to climate diplomacy, countries should get credit for such national technology strategies and should also be held accountable for ensuring that their national efforts are actually effective. And while most innovation policy occurs at the national level, the markets for low emission technologies are increasingly global and thus a measure of international coordination will be required.

Fifth, this club approach – focused initially on the most important enthusiastic and reluctant countries – will require institutional support. New institutions will be needed to help analyze the policies that governments actually put into place so that it will be easier to identify areas where governments are falling short. More transparency will also help build confidence that CADs are being honored. Transparency will also ease the task of enforcement, which will become an essential function as cooperation becomes more demanding.

None of these institutional functions will be easy to create, but one advantage of the club approach is that the countries most centrally involved in creating the needed institutions will be those with the strongest incentive to make them work. As the CADs become more demanding and the institutions more effective the exclusive benefits available to club members will be larger. That will not only reinforce the incentives to cooperate but will also make it easier for existing club members to make large demands of new members.

Sixth, under any scenario a serious system for international coordination will take a long time to build and even longer to transform the energy and agricultural systems that cause most warming emissions. The climate will change, and those changes could be huge. Thus in tandem with creating a system for managing emissions – which will include investments in new technologies as well as detailed coordination of national emission policies – governments must also brace for a warmer world. The core of that effort must be adaptation, and unfortunately nearly all adaptation efforts must come from within countries. That means that the poorest countries that are most vulnerable and least able to adapt will face very difficult circumstances because there is relatively little that outsiders – notably the big emitters that caused most of the harm – can really do to help. Bracing for change must also include investments in geoengineering technologies that can crudely mask climate change so that the technology and governance systems are familiar in case a climate emergency appears.

Some broader implications

In this final chapter I don't review the argument from the whole book in more detail. Chapter 1 did that already. Instead, I speculate on four broader implications of the ideas I have presented.

First, if these ideas are taken seriously what would be the consequences for the UN? From the earliest days of diplomacy on global warming most countries have looked to the UN as the only international forum for negotiations. The UN brings formidable assets to this problem. All else equal, it is the most legitimate international institution. It also has a secretariat that can be tapped to help manage negotiations and codify agreements and thus speed up the process of coordinating national policies to slow global warming. The UN General Assembly is the ultimate expression of one country, one vote – not quite direct democracy, but the closest thing the international system has to offer. Those assets are valuable, but they come with large costs that are intrinsic to an open global forum.

The ideas in this book, and most of my earlier writings on the topic of global warming, will be resisted in part because they appear to threaten the UN's role as the central forum for managing global issues. For a US scholar it is particularly difficult to write analytically about the UN because criticism that originates in the US is seen globally through the rocky relationship that the American people have had with the UN over many decades. The US, unlike nearly all other countries on the planet, can get things done without the UN, and that luxury allows many Americans to see the UN as a bothersome constraint on American freedom of action. I don't fully share those views. But I do think the UN's role in most global problems, including global warming, should be measured functionally. Does the UN help get the job done?

Expecting the UN to make much headway on the warming problem is unhelpful to both the UN and global warming. The gridlock that has already appeared in the global UN-sponsored climate talks has, over time, degraded the credibility of climate negotiations and that has also harmed the UN's reputation. Deadlines are set and ignored; promises are not kept; countries that are already skittish about costly emission control programs see their fears confirmed. The Copenhagen Accord is merely the latest in the string of incredible promises that this process is geared to offer but not honor. Commitments such as providing $100 billion of new funding for developing countries annually by 2020 and stopping warming at 2 degrees – the two most prominent elements in the Copenhagen Accord – are hard to believe. Yet such promises are easy to make in global forums where accountability is widely diffused and the benefits from adopting serious policies to honor such promises are hard to internalize.

A shift in institutional forms – away from an exclusive role for the UN – can make promises of regulation action a lot more credible. Credibility is important because it is the catalyst for investment. When governments and firms believe that regulatory commitments are credible they start investing in anticipation of new rules. They put financial and political resources into low emission technologies and institutions. They invest in research and development (R&D) to expand their options because they know that tighter emissions are inevitable. The bravest spend money to create whole new industries that will thrive in a world with ever-tighter screws on CO_2. Governments invest in building better international institutions because they know that institutions perform important functions that help, among other things, keep the cost of regulation tolerable. The central argument in this book is that choice of institutional form – the design of clubs, the kinds of legal instruments they negotiate, and such – can have a big impact on credibility. By embedding national regulations in a more credible and contingent system for international coordination it will be harder for governments to backslide even when those commitments become inconvenient.

In tandem with finishing this book I have started working with other scholars on both fronts – on the value of credibility and on institutional form. Working with Valentina Bosetti, an economist at Italy's leading public policy think tank, we have set out to quantify the impact of credibility on investment. We modified a standard climate economic model by adding a dial that allows us to vary the time horizon over which firms and governments can anticipate regulations. Turning up the dial to create long time horizons mimics the effect of highly credible regulations that can be set far in advance and which allow firms to invent and install new technologies with the normal turnover of the capital stock. (Credibility is particularly important for energy-related regulations because most of the stock of energy-related capital has a long lifetime and is slow to change.) Turn down the dial, making firms more short-sighted, and we simulate what happens when companies don't know which regulatory promises to believe. We then compared the impact of credibility on the total cost of regulating warming gases. When we started this work economists had already looked at some other real-world factors that often lead to regulations that are more expensive to implement when compared with optimal "first best" policies. For example, regulations might only apply to one sector of industry rather than the whole economy. Or some countries might be able to avoid regulation for a time. Valentina and I showed that, of all those second-best factors, credibility is by far the most important. Even when governments design economically perfect policies, if firms don't think they are credible they sit on their hands and the eventual cost to everyone in society explodes.[2] By starting with a small group of countries that can make credible promises, the cost to all countries – inside and outside the club – is a lot lower when compared with diplomacy that starts globally and gets stuck in gridlock.

Many diplomats know that the UN-based approach hasn't earned much credibility. Some are thus investing in other efforts. Today, rather than a single, unified treaty on global warming enshrined within the UN system, the real world is creating a multitude of institutions. There are efforts such as the Major Economies Forum on Energy and Climate (MEF) and the G8 to create clubs. The largest emission trading system – Europe's Emission Trading Scheme (ETS) – is making links to overseas markets that, in practice, are a lot deeper with some countries than others. A few donor governments and even firms are working with a few forest-rich nations to craft new deals to protect trees. Many of these efforts are linked formally to the universal UN warming talks but they thrive because they are small and focused rather than general and diffused. (They are club-like.) Within a sea of general obligations and norms, there are islands of serious efforts to control emissions and develop new technologies. Rather than a single, central over-arching treaty under which all of these efforts sit – which works well when diplomats can focus on a well-contained problem, such as the depletion of the ozone layer – there are many different legal institutions and no clear hierarchy. Robert Keohane and I have explained this institutional outcome as something we call a "regime complex."[3] Our argument is that regime complexes – instead of focused, hierarchical regulatory regimes – are likely for problems such as global warming that are, by nature, sprawling. Because getting started on cooperation is easier and more credible with small groups of countries and at the outset nobody knows which "clubs" will prove most effective, the institutional forms that tend to emerge are decentralized, nonhierarchical, and viral. Once cooperation generates benefits in one forum then governments and firms invest money, expectations, and other resources around those rules. Cooperation expands. Bob and I think this is not just an accurate prediction for how governments try to manage these kinds of problems, but it can also be a lot more effective than trying to craft global omnibus agreements at the outset. In such settings, a Cambrian explosion of diverse attempts at cooperation followed by an aggressive winnowing out is probably more effective than trying to find that single grand design from the outset. Evolution through a diverse and fragmented system is not just a realistic description of what we observe but it could be a lot more efficient than hoping that a single UN-based treaty system can be designed and adjusted to fit the many difficult tasks that serious climate management requires.

On implication of the arguments that Valentina, Bob and I are examining is that it is unwise to treat the UN as a monopoly. Global warming is one of a class of problems that includes financial regulation, coordination of energy policies, and probably many others where the functional test demands many different forums rather than a monopoly approach. For the parts of the climate problem that lend themselves to a single, global strategy – such as the effort to create a single consensus view of global warming science through the IPCC – the UN has played an extraordinary role. For the rest, the monopoly is unhelpful. By making it harder for diverse regulatory approaches to be tested and for the best to gain traction, the monopoly lowers the credibility of international regulatory coordination. That leads to more global warming and also higher regulatory costs over the long term.

Second, I speculate on the future of industry. Most scholarship on international cooperation is written by political scientists and international lawyers. By training and sentiment we focus on governments and policies. We don't spend enough time studying firms and the interaction between industrial organization and regulation.

If successful, global warming regulation will be one of the largest, planned reorganizations of the industrial economy. (The winner for the prize of the largest reorganization will probably still go to the Soviet Union's 70-year run with central planning. Hopefully the outcome in global warming is better.) Inevitably, that reorganization will have a large impact on firms. Some, such as big carbon suppliers, could face extinction. Others, such as the inventors of technologies that remove carbon from the atmosphere, could rise from oblivion to become major players in the world economy.

The conventional wisdom is that the best role for government in this transformation is to set clear limits on emissions and incentives such as carbon taxes and then stand back while industry responds. I share that view. Decarbonizing the economy has all the hallmarks of a policy goal that is best left to the private sector. Nobody knows which technologies and business models will perform best. The stakes are huge – a few percent of the economy, or even more if decarbonization is handled badly. Government is likely to make many mistakes – and to recover from them sluggishly – if it led and dominated the effort. The private sector and competition should play the central role.

Over the three years it has taken me to write this book I have grown deeply skeptical that the ideal market-oriented approach is the likely outcome. I still think a market-led approach is best. But my confidence that market forces will predominate in decarbonization is waning. In a world where regulations are often not credible and interest groups organize to advance policies to channel benefits to themselves, as I showed in Chapter 3, the role of government will be a lot more intrusive. Deep cuts in emissions could lead to massive new and intrusive roles for government. Government will be the master of a technology policy – a role that even a market-led approach envisions for government because markets, on their own, won't invest adequately in public goods such as new knowledge. But the role of government won't stop there. It will also channel subsidies to favored technologies, and once those subsidies are in place whole industries will organize to preserve them – a pattern already evident in the fact that massive, unproductive, and environmentally harmful subsidies for biofuels in the US and Europe have so far proved nearly impossible to reform.

Libertarians will be horrified by this new role for government, and that fact may help explain some of the persistent difficulties in getting broad public support for climate regulation in the United States where libertarian views of government are particularly influential. (More on the US later.) The role of government is rising not just because government helps hide the cost of policy but also because private firms have little confidence that low-carbon regulation is credible. Governments are under pressure to deliver the goal of climate protection but few are able to create credible long-term market signals that would really catalyze the low-carbon revolution. And essential efforts to coordinate those policies internationally, which would make it easier for national governments to impose credible rules at home, have not delivered much. Firms are understandably skittish about a world where government regulations are fickle and they face the prospect of major deployments of capital for low-carbon technologies that are more expensive than their rivals and create massive financial risks.

One of the great unanswered questions is whether this outcome will simply persist – leading to a lot more global warming – or whether governments will do something about it. I wrote this book with the goal of offering a way to make international cooperation more credible. That, in turn, could make national policies – including market-based policies – more credible. There is encouraging news on that front to which I return shortly. But that news is thin. My worry is that in the absence of credible market signals governments will try to fill the gap themselves – not by crafting more market-based emission policies – but by intervening directly in energy markets with subsidies and special rules to speed innovation and deployment of favored low-carbon technologies. Already, in all the countries that have made the largest efforts at decarbonizing their economies the role of government in the energy industry has risen sharply as a result of low-emission policies. This new role for government – which actually isn't that new across the history of energy policy in most countries – is evident not just at the national level but also within states, provinces, and localities where powerful political forces understandably want action on climate change and are using direct government intervention to make that action more credible because wise market-based approaches that span the whole broader economy are politically so difficult to craft. This role involves shifting costs and risks – in most cases to rate payers and tax payers. Done well, this could be a fitting and proper role for government. Done poorly it will create a whole new class of energy subsidies and regulatory interventions. These days it is fashionable to bash the energy industry for the varied subsidies it obtains. My guess is that if societies get serious about deep cuts in carbon emissions they will look back on the present era as a period of very low subsidization.

If the world is entering an era where competition in the energy industry depends on regulation and subsidy rather than just competition through markets, then the role of management at firms is also likely to change. As the leaders of regulated industries know, the most important relationships in a firm are those with the regulator. The whole of the energy industry is headed in this direction. In earlier research with colleagues at Stanford I looked closely at the implications of this kind of shift for managers in the electric power sector – one of the most heavily regulated (often government owned) sectors of the economy. One of the things we found is that the most successful firms in this kind of industry were "dual firms" – that is, companies that were managed simultaneously to be good at commercial functions and also good at managing the more political regulated and subsidized relationships with government.[4] It isn't easy to perform both functions side by side, and very few firms are really good at it. In new research we are looking at the same issues in an even larger industry – the oil business, where all the world's largest companies are owned or controlled by governments, and the best of that group are skilled dual firms.[5] The world may be headed toward an industrial outcome in which the champions of the low-carbon economy are like today's state-owned oil companies – politically inspired, viable only with a close link to government, and especially varied in their performance. This outcome suggests that decarbonization will proceed a lot less quickly and perhaps at much higher social cost when compared not just with an ideal market-led strategy (which is fun to think about but impractical politically in most countries) but also politically feasible approaches that rely heavily on market forces alongside traditional government regulation.

The search for credibility may create a second wind for carbon taxes. In Chapter 3 I outlined a theory that would explain why governments would choose a hybrid of emission trading and direct regulation. When compared with taxes, trading systems have a huge political advantage because they start with a huge pile of assets – emission credits – that government can award for free to politically well-connected groups. Once those groups own their credits they will mobilize to protect their assets.

Those political advantages for trading are powerful but they arrive only at the beginning – when the assets are first allocated – and only if well-organized groups think the allocations will be durable. The experience with the US effort to create an emission trading system shows that if the first stage drags on a growing array of interest groups will discover how valuable emission credits could become and will organize with the goal of obtaining a share of the assets. Those new political entrants and their demands may erase some or all of the political advantages of trading. And the experience in Europe, which is shifting away from free allocation toward a system of auctions, suggests that governments can't make credible promises to firms that allocations will always be free. These are early signs that the political advantages of trading may not be durable. Moreover, regulated firms have learned, especially in Europe's ETS, that the prices for emission credits can be volatile, which makes long-term investment planning harder and creates incentives for firms to mobilize in favor of safety valves and floors that constrain prices to predetermined bands. Such a shift, in effect, transforms an emission trading system into something that operates more like a tax. Cap and trade systems in Australia and New Zealand are both evolving in this manner. And the growing awareness that emission trading doesn't offer durable political advantages may add to the momentum for taxes.

Social scientists need to take a fresh look at the politics of taxation. Although most analysts favor cap and trade systems – in part for the kinds of political arguments I advanced in Chapter 3 – the politics of emission taxes may not be as ugly as originally expected. Indeed, there are many pressures on governments – especially fiscal pressures – that may lead them to adopt rules that will tilt the odds in favor of taxes. For example, more sensible public finance rules should treat emission credits as valued public assets, making it harder to allocate them for free and creating incentives for governments to auction these assets, which will erase the political advantages of emission trading. Smarter political engineering may also focus on how to build a coalition of tax supporters by focusing on how tax revenues could be spent. And once a tax system is in place and the revenues are allocated to valued public purposes a broad array of political forces will mobilize to keep the tax in place. A tax approach – or a scheme that begins with emission trading and then is transformed to something more tax-like through the use of safety valves and price floors – could be a lot more politically durable and credible than conventional wisdom today suggests.

Third, I speculate on the consequences for the climate talks if the ideas I advocate in this book are taken seriously. My impression is that the world is already evolving in the direction I advocate. The global UN talks have not stopped, but most likely they will never stop. It is hard to halt a huge diplomatic machine. Over the last five years the message that global talks are prone to gridlock has become more widely accepted, and the outcome at Copenhagen reinforced that view. Also rising in prominence is the need to focus on policies rather than just emissions. After Copenhagen, governments created a mechanism for any country to pledge the policies it will adopt. Climate experts will recognize this idea from the early 1990s when the Japanese government advocated a "pledge and review" system that focused on policies rather than emission targets and timetables. At the time, that idea was too innovative and most other countries were too enamored with approaches that they had used for most earlier environmental treaties, which included a flagship role for emission targets and timetables. After two decades with few accomplishments the ground is ripening for new ideas.

Unfortunately, the climate talks are evolving in this direction by default rather than strategy. That default does not bode well because very little effort is being made on all the major elements of the strategy. For example, following the climate summit in Copenhagen governments have done the easy things, such as letting every government "pledge" whatever policies it wants. Yet almost no effort has been made to create a mechanism that would evaluate those pledges. Very few governments have made contingent pledges. Almost none of the diplomatic talent around the negotiating table at climate talks is focused on deep package deals among small numbers of countries. Clubs have emerged in abundance but few club members have devoted much effort to making their club effective. One of the first attempts at creating a club was the Bush administration's Asia Pacific Partnership (APP), which was a good idea but has faltered as other governments viewed the Bush club as a way to avoid the Kyoto treaty rather than actually do something about climate change. Clubs will work only if governments invest resources in making them capable.

Fourth, and finally, it is hard to see a big shift in strategy without leadership. And who does the heavy lifting is an open question. Twenty-five years ago, on most matters of international environmental policy the US was usually the leading voice for action. Today, the US itself is stuck in political gridlock. US policy makers are advocating many of the ideas in this book, such as the APP and other clubs. They are making some forays into crafting the kinds of deals with reluctant countries that will be needed – such as with India on access to fissile material (which will make low emission nuclear power more viable in that country) and with China on research concerning advanced energy technologies. But the US voice is a lot less credible than it was a few decades ago. In my view, this is the chief argument in favor of swifter US national policy on climate change. Even for a big emitter like the US most of the leverage over global warming comes from what other countries do. More credible action at home along with more prominent contingent offers will make it much easier for the US to shape international institutions to be more effective – hopefully along the lines discussed in this book. Oddly, though, most of the national debate in the US focuses on the national impact of global warming regulations. It is the international impact that really matters, and most US domestic policy on mitigating emissions should be seen through the lens of how it influences the shape of the international effort.[6]

Other great powers can play more central roles in reforming international climate institutions along the lines discussed in this book. For now, the most credible voice comes from the European Union. Alas, the EU is also the most invested in the UN-based approach of negotiating global, legally binding treaties focused on emission targets and timetables. One of the most important immediate questions about the future of climate institutions concerns whether the key players in the EU will see that the current approach does not work and invest in alternatives. The Japanese voice, too, is a credible one. That country has made major investments in controlling emissions and has a credible voice. But so far the experience with Japan in diplomacy on climate change (and most other topics) is that the country is unwilling to swim much against the international diplomatic current.

The great power wildcards are the reluctant countries such as Brazil, India, and especially China. All these countries are in the midst of an encouraging shift in how they engage with the world. Many observers are frustrated by these countries' lack of more aggressive action to control emissions. And in the US the perceived inaction by these countries, especially China, is often used as an excuse for inaction by the US. But the real story is very different. All three countries, and many other emerging markets such as Indonesia, are doing a lot more that will contribute to global goals when compared to the turn of the century when nearly developing countries were uniform in their belief that they should bear no cost to slow global warming. These countries have a strong interest in an international approach that is flexible and which gives them the space to focus, initially, on policies where local goals such as energy security and pollution control align with global benefits of fewer warming emissions. That approach won't lead to deep reductions in emissions, but it is a credible way to start.

The western countries seem to be stuck in gridlock on global warming – whether through inaction at home as in the US or through excessive faith in the wrong models for international coordination such as the EU. The emerging countries have a strong incentive to invest in alternatives, and after many years of professing no interest in global warming they might be the best hope for charting a better path.

Notes

Hard truths about global warming: a roadmap to reading this book

1 UNFCCC 2010a.

2 For example, see Rogelj et al 2010.

3 Energy Information Administration (EIA) *International Energy Statistics* (2008 data on CO_2 emissions from fossil fuels, ad hoc query at www.eia.doe.bov/emeu/international/contents.html).

4 This difference was calculated for the EU-15 countries. GHG emissions without land use change in CO_2 equivalent was 4,244.7 million metric tons in 1990 and 3,970.5 million metric tons in 2008. Emissions decreased over that time period by 274 million metric tons (European Environment Agency 2010).

5 For example, Pearson and Worthington 2010. Of course, measuring the impact of the ETS at this stage is difficult since impact requires an assessment of the baseline emissions that would have occurred and also analysts expect that the biggest impacts will be further in the future. Nonetheless, their finding that the ETS has lowered emissions less than 1 percent is striking.

6 The only official GHG emissions data published by the government of China was for the year 1994. Figures for China are estimates by the International Energy Agency. See Leggett and Logan 2008. For US emissions see US Environmental Protection Agency, 2009.

7 For a prediction of Copenhagen's woes see Victor 2009c.

8 For the two-year timetable see UNFCCC 2008.

9 UNFCCC 2009a; 2009b; 2009c.

10 The clubs approach here relies heavily on Victor 1991 and Victor 2007a, but it is hardly new to the study of cooperation. See Buchanan 1965; Olson 1965; and applied to international cooperation see Keohane and Nye 1977 as well as Keohane and Nye 2001.

1 Introduction and overview

1 To be sure, these marginal players can help slow the rate of warming and shift the most intense periods of warming by decades. A big effort to regulate strong but short-lived warming gases such as black carbon or methane can help slow the rate of warming, but there is no viable strategy for making deep reductions in the rate of warming or stopping warming altogether without a central focus on CO_2. For multi-gas studies that explore such issues see, among many, notably Wigley *et al.* 2009 and Ramanathan and Xu 2010.

2 Ausubel, Grubler, and Nakićenović 1988.

3 For example, IEA 2009a and EIA 2010a.

4 See, for example, Paltsev *et al.* 2009 which analyzes the economic costs of an ideal policy and also policies that are implemented in more fragmented Potemkin-like ways. The latter are a lot more expensive to society.

5 Among the exceptions – a study that looks at "win-win" policies with a close eye to whether and how such policies are actually implemented effectively – is World Bank 2009.

6 Some analysts say that emission trading fixes that problem because it guarantees that emission caps are honored. As I will show in Chapter 4, that view is largely a fiction because much of international trading concerns CDM credits that are designed to create the illusion of compliance with emission caps while not actually reducing emissions.

7 For example, see Hoffert *et al.* 1998.

8 The EU, for example, is attempting to mobilize funding for its multi-billion dollar effort to build a dozen projects to test carbon capture and storage – a promising route for lowering CO_2 emissions from coal-fired power plants – by setting aside several hundred million metric tons of emission credits. It is finding, in reality, that real investors have a hard time assigning value to those credits since the market price for credits fluctuates so wildly.

9 Nobody is really sure of the exact timetable over which regulatory efforts will lead to climatic outcomes. The timescales for change I quote here come from combining the slow rate of turnover in energy infrastructures (see Grübler, Nakićenović, and McDonald 1998) with the slow rate of change in atmosphere conditions (e.g., Wigley, Richels, and Edmonds 1996).

10 Belatedly there is now much more public attention to preparations for the large coming changes in climate. For a thoughtful essay on this see Pielke *et al.* 2007.

11 There is a growing literature on climate-induced extinction. See, for example, McLaughlin *et al.* 2002 and Root and Schneider 2006.

12 Among the exceptions, Richardson *et al.* 2009.

13 The geoengineering intelligentsia actually call this "solar radiation management (SRM)" because their definition of geoengineering is much broader and includes any large-scale intervention in the climate system. Here I will use the term in a narrow way to mean climate interventions that produce quick results, such as sprinkling reflective particles in the stratosphere to mimic the behavior of volcanoes. What matters is that these systems produce very rapid and large-scale climate impacts – that's why they are interesting to investigate as options in case a climate emergency appears on the horizon and why they are also scary. Whenever one messes with a complex system in ways that produce large-scale and rapid change it is hard to predict all the consequences.

14 The argument here is based on the original logic of clubs (i.e., cooperation in small groups) in Buchanan 1965 and Olson 1965. This line of thinking is applied to international affairs in Keohane and Nye 1977 and in Keohane 1984 who looks at clubs anchored around the interests of one dominant member, the hegemonic USA.

15 For example, see Martin 2005; Stern and Antholis 2007. Initiated by Paul Martin's interest in this idea, in the early 2000s I spent a lot of time fleshing out the ideas around how global warming could be addressed in a small forum. From the first time I looked at the global warming problem in detail I was skeptical that universal treaties that were commonplace in environmental problems would work. See Victor 1991, which used the GATT as a model for how to get started on global warming. I think it still reads well today, but its practical influence on the negotiations then and now has been nil.

16 For more on that argument see Victor 2009c.

17 Notably Stigler 1971. With complex and intrusive social regulation the regulatory state has faced a wide array of problems as it has learned about the dysfunctions of the regulatory process. For a review see Moran 2002.

2 Why global warming is such a hard problem to solve

1 On the question of why we disagree about climate change I commend Hulme 2009 especially. He looks at the underlying scientific debates and puts them into historical context and shows how they inform the political debates. Control over rhetoric is a big part of political debate, and Hulme has mastered the field.

2 On the radiative strength of different greenhouse gases see, especially, section 2.3 in Forster *et al.* 2007. In terms of total impact on the heat balance of the atmosphere, water vapor is actually the most important

gas. But humans don't have much direct impact on the amount of water in the atmosphere, which is regulated mainly by the climate system itself. Similarly, there are many natural processes that emit and absorb CO_2 such that humans are not even the main players in regulating that gas. But what really matters is how these gases are affected at the margin, which is where the human influence is enormous. One of the many red herrings in the climate change debate is that humans are not at fault for rising concentrations of greenhouse gases because the effect of natural processes is so much greater. In the volume of gas, nature is more important. But in altering the overall level of the gas in the atmosphere, which is what matters for climate warming, human action is decisive.

3 Callendar 1938.

4 There are a few histories of climate science in print. I have found two particularly useful: Fleming 1998; Weart 2008.

5 Bush 1945.

6 See McDougall 1997, pp. 118–23.

7 See especially chapter 5 in McDougall 1997.

8 Revelle and Suess 1957.

9 Weart 2007.

10 Jacobson and Stein 1966.

11 Carson 1962.

12 For example, SCEP 1970 and SMIC 1971.

13 For a history of the supersonic transport debates, see Horwitch 1982.

14 CIAP 1975.

15 For the basic history of the ozone issue and an introduction to the science see Benedick 1998 and Parson 2003.

16 Hansen *et al.* 1981. Hansen was not the only person writing about the end of cooling worries and the onset of warming. Notably, see a much earlier paper by Wally Broecker (Broecker 1975).

17 Hansen worked at NASA, home to many of the best planetary scientists. As a government employee his public statements required government approval. As a public figure, Hansen would have been a lot less famous if the White House had not intervened, but as often happens efforts to bury a message actually make it salient.

18 Some of the processes that remove CO_2 run on short timescales, such as the rapid absorption of a fraction of CO_2 in the atmosphere into the surface of the oceans. But these processes run in equilibrium and thus CO_2 that cycles out of the atmosphere into the surface oceans also results in CO_2 cycling from the surface oceans back to the atmosphere. Similar short-term processes with little net effect are at work with surface soils on land. But the processes that ultimately remove all the excess CO_2 from the atmosphere – cycling into the deep oceans and also the

weathering of rocks – are geologic in their slow pace. For more on the carbon cycle, see Denman *et al.* 2007.

19 Indeed, the lifetime of CO_2 is so long that for planning purposes what matters most in determining warming are the cumulative emissions of CO_2; total warming is a lot less sensitive to exactly when those emissions were put in the atmosphere. This point has been known for a long time – see, for example, Manne and Richels 1992 among others that lead logically to this conclusion – but for a recent careful analysis based on detailed climate models see especially Allen *et al.* 2009. While this point is correct in its geophysics it has led many policy advocates to argue that the world should simply set a "budget" for total cumulative emissions and then allow countries (and firms) to optimize within that budget. That idea, unfortunately, is impractical in international law because a long-term budget strategy works only if the budget constraint is credible, and in international law it is particularly difficult to create credible long-term commitments unless they are self-enforcing. A budget constraint of this type is highly unlikely to be self-enforcing. In an effort to keep my main text focused on a central argument, I will set aside this appealing but impractical approach here in the notes, but for more commentary see Victor 2009b and Victor 2009c.

20 A signal of the shift in concerns is found in the ways that experts measure carbon. When I first learned basic geophysics in the 1980s, the best papers on this issue – also known as the carbon cycle – measured the flows in tons of carbon. The scientists were less interested in the exact form of the carbon – whether bound up in long chains of carbon and hydrogen as plants or fossil fuels, or free in the atmosphere as carbon dioxide gas. Their focus was on getting the numbers right for the whole cycle. As policy concern about CO_2 has risen, the prized unit has become carbon dioxide.

21 Based on data from CDIAC, fossil fuel CO_2 emissions have risen on average 2.75 percent per year from 1900 to 2006 (Boden, Marland, and Andres 2010).

22 For example, the International Energy Agency projects a 40 percent increase (above 2007 levels) for world CO_2 emissions by 2030 (IEA 2009a, p. 623).

23 The fractions of CO_2 emitted from burning fossil fuels are coal (42%), oil (38%), and gas (20%). Data are 2007 as reported by EIA 2009b.

24 Hoffert *et al.* 1998; Jaccard 2005.

25 Parson 1993; Benedick 1998.

26 See, for example, the findings of the Ozone Assessment Panel, based heavily on modeling studies by EPA scientists: US Environmental Protection Agency 1988; WMO 1990.

27 Of course, the full story is more complicated; here I just focus on the main elements. Among the interesting complexities are those that arose in countries, such as China, that manufactured CFC-using and CFC-containing products for export to industrialized countries – such as refrigerators. Because regulation in their export markets was changing these countries also changed their interest in controlling ozone-depleting substances (and their ability to implement those controls) more rapidly than other reluctant countries.

28 Our particular focus was on the legal no-man's-land that arose between signature of the first global warming treaty – the United Nations Framework Convention on Climate Change (UNFCCC) – and the eventual entry into force of the treaty as a legal document. We worked as the UNFCCC was being negotiated through 1991 and early 1992, and we were mindful that the gap between signature and entry into force could be a long time. Our solution, known as "prompt start," was a scheme that would allow the new institutions to start operating immediately after a treaty was signed – before formal entry into force.

29 UNFCCC 1992, Article 2.

30 G8 Summit 2005; 2006; 2007; 2008; 2009.

31 Commission of the European Communities 2007.

32 Broecker 1987.

33 For more on extreme effects see Chapter 6 in this book.

34 Notably see McKibben 1989.

35 Victor 1999. Obviously fairness interacts with other factors to determine when regulatory instruments have an impact. For a recent treatment that looks at that variable alongside others see Mattli and Woods 2009.

36 For example, see Low 1992, Jaffe *et al.* 1995, and James 2009. I also commend studies that have detailed the role of firms in the regulatory process, which also point to the general (but not complete) lack of "race to the bottom" dynamics. Notably see Braithwaite and Drahos 2000 and Vogel 1995.

37 Victor 1990.

38 The critique of learning curves I suggest here is just the beginning. The learning curve approach is useful for policy only if it is based on a causal theory that links experience to improved performance. Yet much of what is lumped together under the heading of "learning" is actually other forces at work. And because learning curves compound in importance they lead to policy strategies (and efforts to model those strategies) where wrong early choices for technologies lead to massive financial support for learning at the expense of other technologies that might prove more viable at scale. For an overview see Nordhaus 2009.

39 Grübler 2009.

3 Regulating emissions part 1: the enthusiastic countries

1 The experience varies a lot, however and in some settings – such as when it is hard to obtain reliable information about performance and to administer a market system – command-and-control policies perform better. For a recent overview, including some reviews of the cost advantages of market approaches, I particularly recommend Freeman and Kolstad 2007.

2 Weitzman 1974.

3 For a rigorous exploration of instrument choice with special attention to the problem of global warming see Newell and Pizer 2003.

4 Of course, there are other cases where government has no option but to choose regulation. Some problems are impractical to regulate with market instruments, such as when it is difficult to measure pollution sources and thus enforce market compliance or when many different activities interact in complex ways to cause environmental harms. Much noise pollution is of this type.

5 There are cases, of course, where firms have actually favored command-and-control regulation because politically well-connected firms can use regulation as a way to block competition and other market outcomes that can be harmful to their interests. Such a logic helps explain why barbers favor licensing even though it adds extra costs to their business. It explains why coal companies were thrilled by command regulations that barred, until 1987, the use of natural gas for generating electricity in the United States. It may explain why so many electric power utilities don't mind strict regulation and why they are trembling as Google and other companies try to change regulatory rules to make it easier for any company, utility or not, to enter the electric supply business. But it does not seem to explain how most firms behave when they face environmental regulation. Few environmental rules are well suited to blocking competition, and badly administered command-and-control regulations can impose massive unnecessary costs on firms.

6 Of course, the details in this political argument depend on many local circumstances – not least because this political argument hinges on other groups not recognizing the value in emission credits and not organizing quickly to seize some of the largesse for their own purposes. All else equal, trading systems that are created quickly are probably the most painless because many new groups have not had time to organize and claim a share of the new assets from existing emitters. That may help explain why the US has had such a hard time forging agreement on a national emission trading system – once the process was under way and drags on the claims on these free new assets multiply.

7 For the best single review of how Europe designed the ETS and the practical experience with trading see Ellerman, Convery, and de Perthuis 2010.
8 See Frondel *et al.* 2010.
9 There are many terrific ideas for general clean energy standards, such as Morgan, Adams, and Keith 2006.
10 Formally, those goals were written into the "Berlin Mandate," which is the main decision from the first official conference of the parties to the UN Framework Convention on Climate Change (see UNFCCC 1995).
11 Formally, the legal obligation to comply with an emission target accrues to the government and thus formally under the CDM governments must exchange the credits. In practice, most governments have created special funding windows through which these purchases occur, in part because those windows help assure that these transfers are not comingled with other foreign aid programs – a move that is not just administratively wise but also helps governments assure they will comply with the Kyoto rules and also sustains political support for CDM funding.
12 The exact volume and value of Japan's purchases is not reported; the $10 billion here is intended to indicate the scale. Japan has been widely reported as the largest government trading in the CDM although "nationalities" are misleading especially for EU-destined trades since so much of that activity runs through private markets (mostly based in the UK, which is why that country appears on trading statistics to be the largest buyer in the late 2000s of CDM credits). For composite data on trading activity see especially Kossoy and Ambrosi 2010.

4 Regulating emissions part 2: engaging reluctant developing countries

1 In general, as economies grow so do the administrative capabilities of the government – in part because a more capable administration abets economic growth and in part because greater wealth yields larger tax resources that can be spent on public administration.
2 For example, Morris and Hill 2007 propose a sanction-like mechanism targeted against developing countries that could be included in US legislation. The 2009 Waxman–Markey bill in the United States House of Representatives, which was the only complete and politically viable draft for US warming legislation at the time this book was written, includes a sanction-like system of border tariff adjustments (US Congress 2009). The Kerry–Lieberman draft legislation, which reflected the Senate's efforts on this topic, also included a sanction-like system. Numerous studies have explored the legality, practicality, and wisdom of such an approach (see Pataki and Vilsack 2008; Hufbauer,

Charnovitz, and Kim 2009). A few other governments have mooted such ideas, but none has elaborated them as much as in the US – which is not surprising since unilateral sanctions on commodity products are very hard to design and if any country is to take the lead on this question it will be the one with the largest market.

3 For example, see Winchester, Paltsev, and Reilly 2010 who show that border adjustments reduce leakage (i.e., the flight of investment to less regulated countries) but have minimal impact on global emissions and could impose large costs (losses in welfare) on the economy.

4 See National Research Council of the National Academies 2010c and Pataki and Vilsack 2008.

5 While more analysts are calling for trade sanctions fewer have actually done the spadework on how these systems could work. Important exceptions include Hufbauer, Charnovitz, and Kim 2009.

6 My argument is not that providers of development assistance should ignore these possible sources of leverage, and some initiatives are under way that might gain some leverage. More should be done if such initiatives work. In the Congo, several western governments have developed a regional forest protection initiative that might lessen deforestation. Other examples are worth considering as well. Most of Indonesia's emissions come from deforestation, and officially funded government programs might yield large leverage on that pollution – an example I consider in more detail later in this chapter. A huge wildcard in the question of whether the poorest nations have much impact on warming and thus whether traditional development assistance can be rejiggered to make a dent in warming is "black carbon." For example, it appears that a significant part of India's warming emissions takes the form of "black carbon" emanating from primitive cookstoves used in rural areas, especially in the cooler northern parts of the country. Programs to change how very poor people cook are classic tasks for government funding, and there may be a role for ODA in that as well.

7 See Multilateral Fund website (www.multilateralfund.org). In tandem with the UNFCCC fund the World Bank and other international development agencies also created a Global Environment Facility (GEF) to perform a similar role. Through the GEF, these agencies play the central roles in administering the official UNFCCC financial mechanism. Today, there are many official institutions that are organizationally distinct yet perform closely related functions. In addition to the central funding mechanism there are many other special funds and initiatives, although none of those add up to much. For example, a special tax on the Kyoto Protocol's Clean Development Mechanism (CDM) has delivered a trickle of resources into a special fund to help poorer countries adapt to the effects of warming. In addition to all this funding earmarked for

warming, many traditional development funding agencies have looked
for ways to make their existing programs more climate-friendly. That
process of mainstreaming climate change is important and must continue, although it is very hard to pin down just how much extra leverage
arises from mainstreaming or the costs that mainstreaming is imposing
(World Bank 2009). The Copenhagen Accord calls for large additional
contributions to these financial mechanisms as well as new financial
mechanisms, although in practice those new resources (a few billion
dollars per year) are likely to be small compared with private sector
funding that is expected to flow ($100 billion per year).

8 On the dominant role of coal-fired energy (mainly electricity) from
developing countries (mainly China and India) in projections for future
emissions see IEA 2009a. The calculation here is to illustrate scale and
considers a power station of about 3 Gigawatt capacity.

9 This figure was compiled using an average of less than $10 billion per
year in new investment under the CDM over a lifetime of about eight
years. For more detail see citations below and original data on annual
investment flows in Seres 2008; Violetti 2008; Capoor and Ambrosi
2009; Violetti 2010; Kossoy and Ambrosi 2010.

10 The real world of the CDM is a bit more complicated. Because CDM
credits must travel officially through governments there is a large role
for government regulation (and even funding in some cases) in the transaction. And in most developing countries, politically visible activities
such as energy supply are usually dominated by state-owned firms –
which gives those actors a central role. But the main point here is that
the engine for investment in the CDM is an incentive that works on the
private sector, notably private firms in the west that are keen to get low-
cost emission credits.

11 In 2008 forward purchase prices were about $12–20 per ton CO_2. For
more on the volume of CDM credit usage in Europe see Commission of
the European Communities 2009.

12 Wara 2007. See also, notably, Schneider 2007 who was also a pioneer
in criticizing the CDM.

13 For cost estimates, see Wara 2008 and see Wara and Victor 2008.

14 Victor and MacDonald 1997.

15 The fraction quoted here is primary CDM sales through 2012. See
Kossoy and Ambrosi 2010.

16 Wara and Victor 2008.

17 He and Morse 2010.

18 See, for example, Ball 2008; Kintisch 2008; Forelle 2008; Vidal 2008;
Kempf 2008.

19 Nobody knows what fraction of emission credits doesn't represent
emission reductions, and getting serious about that question requires

looking also at the degree of additionality not just the binary question
of whether a project caused some change in behavior or not. The range
of fractions I quote here is based on our finding (Wara and Victor 2008)
that essentially all of the renewable energy and natural gas projects
in China (which is the largest host country for CDM projects of all
types) were unlikely to be additional and the view from earlier work
(Wara 2007) showing that perverse incentives in industrial gas projects
were encouraging firms to avoid installing emission control technologies unless their projects were awarded CDM credit. Because industrial
gas projects account for such a large fraction of total credits (see Figure
4.1) one's view of the total fraction of projects that are not additional
is highly sensitive to one's view of whether the CDM has created the
right incentives for truly additional investment in that area. My view on
that question is highly negative, as I explain in the main text. For well-
informed, independent reporting that arrives at the same conclusion see
Gronewold 2010.

20 I explored buyer liability in some detail in Victor 2001. Also, notably
see Keohane and Raustiala 2009.

21 Blanford, Richels, and Rutherford 2009.

22 The numbers I cite here – $10 billion for the CDM and $50 billion
potential for all offsets schemes – are intended to indicate the scale
of low-carbon investment tied directly to offsets. These numbers are
not total trading volume in offsets, which of course will be larger.
Investment numbers are very hard to pin down because they depend
on whether investments are truly additional (see above) and on leverage. From 2003–2009, on average, the estimated investment per year
ranges from $3.0 billion to $7.2 billion. In 2003–2004, investment
was <$1 billion but in 2007, estimated investment was as high as $33
billion. For data see Seres 2008; Violetti 2008; Capoor and Ambrosi
2009; Violetti 2010; Kossoy and Ambrosi 2010. CDM investment is
now waning due to uncertainty about the future of the mechanism.
Actual investment under a US offsets scheme is hard to predict since
such a mechanism does not yet exist, so my upper estimate of $50b
may be too high.

23 IEA 2009a.

24 China does not report reliable total investment numbers in the power
sector, and thus the number I quote here indicates the order of magnitude. It reflects 60 gigawatts of power plants built per year at an average
of about $800 per kilowatt for the plant and an equal sum for transmis-
sion and distribution as well as infrastructure for delivering primary
fuels (mainly coal) to plants. These numbers are based on experience
in the Chinese power sector over many years. In most of the rest of the
world building 60 GW of power supply capacity would cost a lot more

than $100 billion, but in China infrastructure is particularly inexpensive to build.

25 The rules on carbon capture and storage may yet change since those decisions rest with the CDM Executive Board. The prohibition on nuclear power is written into the language that created the CDM. The bias against large hydro will also be very difficult to overcome.

26 Victor 2009a.

27 Rai and Victor 2009.

28 Adding the figures from Victor 2009a and Rai and Victor 2009 yields 1.82–1.92 billion metric tons. (Note: the Victor 2009a assessment goes to the year 2025.)

29 Projecting from 2008 data, EU emissions are likely to be about 274 million metric tons per year lower than 1990 levels and Japanese emissions about 75 million metric tons higher. These are crude measures of the actual impact of the Kyoto Protocol; total reductions may prove larger once the Protocol has fully run its course, or they may be smaller since many such reductions weren't actually due to the presence of the Protocol (European Environment Agency 2010; UNFCCC 2010b).

30 EIA 2009a.

31 Rosen and Houser 2007.

32 On efficiency efforts as they related to coal, especially, see IEA 2009c.

33 Jiang *et al.* 2008.

34 Russia's less reliable supplies in 2006 and 2009 are rooted in pricing disputes with Ukraine. When the Soviet Union existed, gas exports required crossing few transit countries before they reached lucrative western markets. The collapse of the Soviet Union yielded many more independent transit countries, notably Ukraine, and is a lesson that China knows it must heed. A direct gas export route from Russia is likely to be much more reliable than one that depends on transit countries. That logic helps explain China's interest in circumventing Mongolia with a possible gas pipeline from Russia and its keen interest in direct export of gas and other products from Kazakhstan in the west.

35 Here I have focused on conventional gas supplies, but the same logic could apply to improving the ability of countries to tap unconventional gas supplies, such as coal-bed methane and shale gas. There have been some international initiatives on the former, although so far they have attracted minimal serious government or private sector attention, and initiatives on the latter are just now taking shape.

36 For more on coal pricing and its fundamental driving forces see Victor and Morse 2009.

37 UN FAO 2005.

38 See generally www.wri.org/stories/2010/07/whats-next-indonesia-noeway-cooperation-forests.

39 This proposal for a peat-focused program is inspired by Tacconi, Jotzo, and Grafton 2008.

40 See Page *et al.* 2002 which estimates that between 0.81 and 2.57 Gt of carbon were released during the 1997/1998 forest fires.

41 Injection rates for particular projects and for the totality of world efforts in carbon storage are reported in Rai *et al.* 2008. Rates at which the technology can plausibly expand are explored in Cullenward 2009.

5 Promoting technological change

1 For a closer look at the scale of the effort needed see, among many good reports in this area, IEA 2008a.

2 As we saw in Chapter **4**, countries that are getting serious about fixing deforestation are doing so by creating much clearer systems for regulation and enforcement of public laws and private property rights on forest land and reducing corruption in public administration. Some of that effort is aided by technology – such as remote sensing satellites – but most of the innovations are institutional rather than technological. The exact fraction of world emissions caused by land use changes is hard to pin down; here I use the IPCC data (17 percent of total emissions as CO_2 from deforestation and decay of biomass; 57 percent as CO_2 from fossil fuels). These numbers are approximate as there are no highly reliably data on deforestation and changes in biomass. See Barker *et al.* 2007.

3 Many people who hold this view look to the "wedges" theory and start counting wedges. See Pacala and Socolow 2004.

4 It is very difficult to make these calculations, which depend on a wide array of controversial assumptions. The numbers here are intended to illustrate the scale of effort needed by about the year 2050. The five-fold expansion in *useful* energy is based on a one-to-one relationship between energy services and growth in human demands. With a world population rising at 1 percent per year and economy at 3.1 percent per year (assumptions per IEA 2009a, for the period to 2030 which I extend to 2050), the rise in demand for useful energy is about fivefold by 2050. In practice, useful energy actually rises faster than human demands, but measuring useful energy is very difficult and thus most studies measure energy inputs (e.g., barrels of oil). Looking at energy inputs, IEA sees a rise of 1.5 percent per year (Table 1.2) and a rise of CO_2 emissions of 1.5 percent per year. Compounded to 2050, 1.5 percent per year is roughly a doubling in primary energy demand and emissions.

5 Good analysts don't believe that technology is the only element of warming policy, but it is easy to misread many studies that advocate a central role for technology policy. See, for example, Prins and Rayner 2007; Shellenberger *et al.* 2008. Prins and Rayner, for example, argue

that technology is one of seven principles for which they advocate. As the energy-generating capacity in the industrialized world nears the end of its useful life and needs to be replaced, an internationally competitive program to modernize energy is urgently needed. For any emissions reduction strategy, new investment in energy R&D is needed. Investment is needed to make existing technologies economically competitive. For them, technology is part of a flexible, multi-option strategy, which they call their "silver buckshot approach." For a helpful overview of studies that are focused on the technological challenge see Milford and Morey 2009.

6 I am hardly the first person to point this out. On the need for complementary (push and pull) policies see many other studies, such as de Coninck *et al.* 2008, which focuses on international technology-oriented policies.

7 For an earlier recounting of such failures in energy-related technologies see Cohen and Noll 1991. Their argument focused on the political forces that lead technology policy to degenerate into rent-seeking activities rather than a proper focus on innovation, but many of their most egregious examples arose in the absence of market-pulling forces.

8 Among the innovations was the first ever use of Portland cement for water pipes, which made the pipes much more resilient and reliable when compared with traditional cement technologies that dated back to the Roman empire. The story of London's sewers relies heavily on Solomon (Solomon 2010).

9 The role of evidence and agreement on underlying causes is particularly well developed by Richard Cooper (Cooper 1989). According to Cooper, one reason that effective international cooperation on public health was slow to emerge was that the main diseases were not understood. When news of an epidemic arose, it created panic but not policy responses that would be effective. It is hard to build international cooperation on folklore.

10 Experts on US environmental laws will be horrified by this paragraph, but here's why it is true using the example of the Clean Air Act in the United States. In 1970 Congress amended the CAA to set very tough air pollution quality standards and mandated compliance by 1975 with the threat of refusing to approve additional industrial activities in states whose implementation plans fell short. Yet in reality, when those standards proved unattainable no state implementation plan was outright rejected, and in 1977 Congress amended the CAA again to stretch out the timetables to 1982 (and to 1987 for areas with stubborn pollution problems). And when those deadlines were missed, an array of "nonattainment" regulations was created to balance the need for economic development with the slower pace of pollution control. Indeed, most of

the impact of the CAA takes the form of technology standards that are interpreted by the EPA, state regulators, and the courts as not requiring excessive costs. (The exact technology-cost balancing depends on a wide array of circumstances.) And most air pollution rules in the CAA were written in a way that gave regulators much tighter authority over new sources – to the point that the question of what is a "new source" became one of the most important issues for planners in the electric power industry in recent years. For an overview of the statutes, their interpretation by the courts and some of the regulatory administration see, for example, Findley, Farber, and Freeman 2003. In particular, see the discussion of state deference under State Implementation Plans on pp. 322–34. Similar political forces help explain the ratcheting up of pollution laws on much cleaner areas of the country – notably the rules on the prevention of significant deterioration (PSD) that were popular among dirtier states who supported such rules that helped keep industry from migrating to clean locales.

11 The US was a notable exception, and for that country a 50 percent cut was more expensive because the nation had already eliminated most of the sources that were very inexpensive to control. Public concern was higher in the US at the time and thus the extra cost was tolerable. On the leading role of the US in crafting the regime see, especially, Benedick 1998.

12 On the role of media coverage in spreading the idea that regulation of ozone-depleting substances was worth the cost see Social Learning Group 2001.

13 For more detail on the essential uses of exemptions and their importance, see Victor and Coben 2005 and see Technology and Economic Assessment Panel (TEAP), various years.

14 On the financial mechanism see DeSombre and Kauffman 1996 and also Parson 2003.

15 Oye and Maxwell 1994.

16 The 2 percent estimate is not much better than a guess, but it is probably about right. Some studies suggest that emissions controls are feasible at zero or negative cost. That line of thinking is seen, for example, in Lovins *et al.* 2004. It is hard to see how that would be true, although a lot can be done at low cost with focus and attention to detail. The Stern Review (Stern 2007) suggests that costs by 2050 for an emission trajectory that is consistent with stabilizing concentrations of warming gases would be about 1 percent of GDP. (The Stern Review also points to a wide range, up to 3.5 percent of GDP.) The IEA *World Energy Outlook 2009* (IEA 2009a, p. 203) estimates that the macroeconomic cost of a global policy to stabilize concentrations of warming gases at 450 ppm (about 2 degrees of warming, which by 2050 means a cut in

world emissions roughly by half) would be 0.9–1.6 percent of GDP by 2030 (the last year of their projection) and rising higher in later years. Such estimates are controversial and based, in part, on the assumption that governments will largely adopt economically efficient policies. If real policy is a politically inspired hodgepodge rather than an efficient market-oriented system (as I argue in Chapter 3) then actual costs will be higher, but nobody is sure how much higher since the models that are used to examine costs are unable to represent the frictions and inefficiencies that arise in most "second best" policies that real governments are likely to adopt. (It is much easier to model efficient, pure policies than actual regulations that real governments tend to adopt.)

17 In 1863, the US government estimated that the civil war cost $2.5 million per day (www.civilwarhome.com/warcosts.htm). Later estimates put the total direct cost of the war at about $6.7 billion in 1860 dollars (Goldin and Lewis 1975). To put into perspective the magnitude of this expenditure, the relative value of the total cost in today's dollars is $21 trillion, or approximately 145 percent of the current GDP. This amount does not even include the indirect cost of the disruption to the economy or the resulting loss of future production. According to some estimates, accounting for direct and indirect costs, the total cost is about $45 trillion in current dollars (data and calculations available at www.measuringworth.com/uscompare/).

18 See, for example, CNA's study that argues that climate change will become a "threat multiplier" (CNA Corporation 2007). I am skeptical of the underlying social scientific basis for such claims (see Victor 2007b). But it is hard to deny that reframing climate change as a security problem has made regulation of warming gases attractive to a broader community. Linking issues to security is an age-old strategy used in many national projects, such as Eisenhower's program to build national highways.

19 Since the 1990s many countries have deregulated some energy prices, especially oil prices, but price regulation remains a dominant aspect of most energy markets.

20 Specker 2009.

21 On the history of the power industry and its industrial organization, see generally Victor 2002.

22 On the G8 request see IEA 2009a. On the scenarios see IEA 2008a, chapter 2.

23 See IEA 2008a, Box 2.6.

24 For example, Heller and Eisenberg 1998. There is no shortage of ideas for how to fix patent thickets and related problems of congestion in the assertion of intellectual property rights. For example: Shapiro 2001; Burk and Lemley 2009. One of Shapiro's central arguments is that the

varied solutions to patent thicket problems can be costly to implement, and those extra costs impede innovation.

25 Amazon.com debuted online in 1995 and went public in 1997. Calculations were made based on financial reports filed with the SEC from 1995 to 2009. Cumulative net earnings were calculated from net income and total cumulative investment was calculated from cash used in investing activities. Based on these definitions, in its debut year, Amazon.com reported a $303,000 loss in net income and $52,000 in total investment. When the company finally reached a positive cumulative net income of almost $186 million in 2009, its total cumulative investment had reached $6.2 billion. It must be noted that this calculation is simply to demonstrate that the company has actively invested back into the company and that sometimes the expense and risk of investing in innovation can pay off.

26 For many energy technologies the key to understanding lock-out effects lies in the regulatory process. Much of the energy industry – including nearly all of the world's electric power industry – is highly regulated by governments. In many countries, regulation takes the form of direct state ownership. In a few, mainly in the advanced industrialized countries, the function of regulation is separated from ownership – private owners of electric utilities, for example, are regulated by public agencies. Regulation is a highly political process and usually favors incumbents who are better connected to regulators than new entrants. Thus new technologies that are well aligned with the interests of incumbents often find it easy to gain market share – for example, the US quickly built many new nuclear and large coal plants in the 1970s because the large capital expenditures needed for such projects aligned well with a regulatory system that prized companies that made massive capital investments. Today, in some states, the regulatory system has swung to an opposite extreme where utility-style investments in large new generating plants are nearly impossible to approve while all manner of unproven decentralized technologies and off-grid applications that remove market share from traditional utilities gain regulatory blessing.

27 The potential for still further improvements in sugar cane ethanol appears to be large. See Goldemberg *et al.* 2004.

28 Obviously these two dimensions are not the only two aspects of technology that affect innovation. Others include the reward structure, the perception of risks and the like. My argument is that these two explain much of the variation and help illustrate why policies that work for one cluster of technologies often fail for the problem at hand: energy. On other dimensions see, e.g., National Research Council 2004.

29 Performing this task is proving very difficult because the standard tools for determining whether a market is contestable – for example,

measurement of market share – do not seem to work for technologies that are prone to serial monopolies. Norms about cross-market relationships are also difficult to apply since many of the benefits from IT arise when systems are readily connected, but such connections also create larger risks that dominant firms will abuse their position in one market to favor their innovations in another. Such troubles have bedeviled Microsoft in its two largest markets – the US and Europe – and a coherent strategy for addressing them has not yet emerged from governments on either side of the Atlantic.

30 For an overview of the innovation model in pharmaceuticals see Pisano 2002. Biomedical research is typically one of the most R&D-intensive industries, with much of the research focused in areas that are often thought of as basic research because viable products come directly from the frontier of knowledge whereas in other industries (including energy) there is a much longer innovation pipeline and a larger role for development and demonstration investments. My statement here that private sector research exceeds public sector is based on total research spending (of which 57 percent is private sector); more fine-grained assessments about the private/public breakdown for basic versus applied research are much more difficult to draw because the data are not organized in a way that allow for consistent comparisons. For a careful look at the data see Moses *et al.* 2005.

31 For example, the Bayh–Dole Act of 1980 allows universities and other government-funded researchers to license innovations based on the theory that if they have an incentive (licensing fees) they will work harder to get ideas out of the laboratory and into the hands of commercial investors who will take them to the market. (For the biggest universities that theory has worked. Smaller ones, though, have struggled to justify the cost of maintaining the offices, lawyers, and other paraphernalia needed to make Bayh–Dole actually work.) Mowery *et al.* 2004, p. 241.

32 Given these incentives it is not surprising, therefore, that R&D spending for agriculture is highly fragmented. Across the world, total spending on agriculture R&D is roughly evenly divided between the public and private sectors. But about 95 percent of all private sector agriculture R&D is done in the industrialized nations and concentrated on crops that earn large private returns. Out of all R&D done in developing countries, only 6 percent was conducted by private firms and they focused on a few cash crops that are generally grown for export such as cotton and sugar. Money is pulsing into agriculture R&D in a few areas just as crops and agricultural activities that are most relevant for the world's least fortunate farmers remain orphans. Places where crops are least lucrative and the institutional elements needed

for private investment are weakest see the lowest share of private sector investment. In sub-Saharan Africa only 1.7 percent of all agriculture R&D comes from private sector resources. Globally, about $34 billion was spent on all forms of agriculture R&D. The entire CGIAR system, which is the main publicly funded mechanism for cooperation on R&D funding in developing countries, spent only about $547 million and is periodically wracked by funding crises since the vast majority of its resources come from governments. (Half of CGIAR's funding comes from European governments alone; only 2 percent comes directly from foundations.) Broad trends in agriculture R&D spending are from National Science Foundation 2008 as summarized in Pardey and Alston 2010. The CGIAR budget is from CGIAR 2009.

33 For a history of this in the US see Swanson, Bentz, and Sofranko 1997. For a recent review worldwide see Swanson 2008. For insights on the international system see Horsch 2009. For a particularly helpful overview of the incentives to invest in innovation in agriculture, see Pardey and Alston 2010.

34 Today, farmers who use the most advanced agriculture technologies – such as genetically engineered seeds – sign complicated contracts that include large payments in the form of technology fees with the seed companies. The farmers nonetheless tolerate this because these innovations produce even larger revenues, such as through more productive crops that need fewer costly pesticide and herbicide inputs. It is not surprising therefore that private sector money for innovation has poured into innovations that produce a readily measured surplus for farmers. When Monsanto introduced genetically engineered soybeans in 1995 the innovation spread more rapidly than any major innovation in the history of agriculture because farmers saw an immediate benefit from more productive crops that required less costly weed controls; these new crops had much higher technology fees than traditional soybeans but, for most farmers, were worth every penny (Carpenter and Gianessi 1999).

35 Victor and Runge 2002; Paarlberg 2008; Pollack and Shaffer 2009.

36 Data here are from the United States' three-digit industrial (NAICS) classification and should be treated with some caution. Actually measuring R&D investment in industries is tricky because some industries internalize R&D and thus look like big investors in new ideas while others tend to purchase innovative products from other industries. Moreover, R&D intensity is usually measured as a fraction of sales, and thus industries that are in their early stages of development with few sales look like big innovators while industries that are mature look like laggards. Mindful of these caveats, all of the biggest R&D spenders have this internalization mode of research (often coupled with low

commercial sales) while also being industries where R&D is the key to commercial success: pharmaceuticals (12.7% of sales spent on R&D), communications (14%) and software (21%). By contrast, the petroleum industry (which is combined with coal production in the NAICS three-digit data) spends just 0.4% of sales on R&D and utilities get the gold medal for low R&D intensity at just 0.1%. For the data, see National Science Board 2008, volume II appendix Tables 4–22.

37 Among the notable exceptions is the President's Committee of Advisors on Science and Technology (PCAST). See Holdren *et al.* 1999. In recent years there has been growing attention to technology policies for energy, and the vision that I outline here is broadly compatible with the most thoughtful and detailed of the visions for an energy technology strategy that others offer. I commend six studies in particular: Alic, Mowery, and Rubin 2003; DTI 2003; Edmonds *et al.* 2007; Ogden, Podesta, and Deutch 2008; Mowery *et al.* 2009; and American Energy Innovation Council 2010. Many of these studies also draw on National Academy of Sciences *et al.* 2007 and on National Research Council 2001. In terms of my intellectual evolution on this issue, I owe a lot to John Deutch who convinced me that government was not always bad at promoting innovation. For thoughtful cases in innovation see The Breakthrough Institute (2009) and for international cases see Levi *et al.* 2010. See also Hayward *et al.* 2010 for an argument in favor of an innovation-led climate strategy.

38 Griliches 1992; Jones and Williams 1997. Applied to energy issues see Margolis and Kammen 1999a; Alic, Mowery, and Rubin 2003.

39 On the logic for energy policy that supports public investment in R&D see, among many others: Johansson and Goldemberg 2002; IEA 2008a; Holdren *et al.* 1999. For a recent study that makes the argument generally and globally see Witte 2009.

40 See National Research Council 1999, pp. 3–5.

41 Many factors are at work, and it has proved quite difficult to establish a clear cause-and-effect relationship between deregulation and the decline in energy R&D. for a particularly important argument on the dangers see Morgan and Tierney 1998; among many other essays on this theme notably also see Dooley 1998.

42 On the logic that explains why some styles of innovation lead directly to final products see Stokes 1997.

43 Under special circumstances of good administration this approach may work through patent buyouts. See Kremer 1998.

44 The number of truly competitive electricity markets remains surprisingly small. Of major countries, such markets exist only in Britain, parts of the United States, and Australia. No developing country except Chile has successfully liberalized its power market, and the Chilean

case reveals that deregulation remains a policy only so long as it is convenient. For more on why deregulation in power has been so difficult, see Victor and Heller 2007.

45 The actual design of the policy might not be strictly a tax credit since such credits are useful only when companies are making a profit. Thus tax credit schemes tend to create volatile policy signals since their value is low or nonexistent in times of economic recession and low profitability.

46 Notably, see Hall 2002; and see David, Hall, and Toole 2000. Actually measuring these effects is very difficult, however, due to sampling bias (firms that seek R&D credits tend to be the ones that would do R&D anyway) and other factors. See Klette, Møen, and Griliches 2000. For similar work in other countries and settings, see, for example, Czarnitzki, Hanel, and Rosa 2004.

47 The statements here are my assessment of the program's accomplishments, but there is a wide array of views on whether the program worked. For a more positive assessment see Sperling 2001. One of PNGV's good design elements was a regular, independent review by the Transportation Research Board (an arm of the National Research Council). For the most useful of the TRB reports, see National Research Council 2001.

48 In particular, see Nalebuff and Stiglitz 1983. Applied to the question of climate change see, in particular, Newell and Wilson 2005.

49 Sobel 1995.

50 On the broad patterns in energy R&D see Dooley, Runci, and Luiten 1998; Dooley 1999. See also Margolis and Kammen 1999b; Sagar and van der Zwaan 2006; Zhang, Fan, and Wei 2006. The Zhang *et al.* paper makes the cogent point that energy R&D spending is correlated with energy shocks. In a recent study, Hillard Huntington and Christine Jojarth update that observation and show a particularly striking relationship between oil prices and spending on renewable energy (Huntington and Jojarth 2010). On actual R&D spending and the stimulus, see *The Economist* 2009, which reprints data from Kelly Gallagher and the Office of Science and Technology Policy.

51 I have not done a detailed assessment of funding levels, but the goal of doubling energy-related research is consistent with other surveys such as Holdren *et al.* 1999. And, in particular, see the recent study by Richard Newell (Newell 2008). A recent commission chaired by Bill Gates and Jeff Immelt called for a tripling of energy research spending along with a variety of institutional reforms that would help ensure the money could be spent wisely (see American Energy Innovation Council 2010).

52 Freeman and van Reenen 2008.

53 For the announcement of Venter's private venture and the nearly universal scorn it received at the time see *Issues in Science & Technology* 1998.

54 One of the uncertainties with the technology is, in fact, the cost. This number is based on a very large reactor design built as a pair with a capital cost on the scale of $5000/kw.

55 My bias before starting this project was that the synfuels corporation was an example of wrongheaded winner picking. John Deutch, who helped shepherd the program through Congress as undersecretary at the Department of Energy from 1979–1980, has convinced me otherwise. For more on Deutch's views about setting the right kinds of goals see Yergin, Johnston, and Deutch 2009. See also Deutch 2005.

56 Deutch, Schlesinger, and Victor 2006.

57 On the DARPA model and its potential application to energy see Bonvillian 2006.

58 This assessment of the Chinese national system for innovation is drawn heavily on the assessment by Valerie Karplus (Karplus 2007) and also Changlin *et al.* 2004; Osnos 2009. It is hard to analyze energy R&D in isolation from major reforms in the rest of the nation's economy and R&D system. On that point, see especially OECD 2007.

59 NERC 2008.

60 Alvarez *et al.* 2009.

61 Victor, 2009d.

62 See EIA website "Electric Power Industry Companies by Name, Code, and State," www.eia.doe.gov/fuelelectric.html.

63 For more on global public goods see Kaul, Grunberg, and Stern 1999.

64 See, for example, Ruttan 2001 and Mokyr 2002. And for a broad sweep of history see Landes 1999.

65 Victor, Heller, and Victor 2003.

66 See UNESCO 2005.

67 To make such assessments it is necessary to look at data starting in 1996 (prior to that year UNESCO, which has the best international data collection on R&D spending, does not have complete records). From 1996 to 2007 (the most recent year for which there is nearly complete data) the US share of total world R&D spending has declined 4% (from 38% to 34%) and Japan's share has dropped 2%. China's share has risen 7%. These shifts may be colored, a bit, by UNESCO's use of purchasing power parities (PPP) for converting local spending into common units (US dollars). For the US and Japan there is essentially no difference between market exchange rates and PPP, but for China (like all developing countries) the difference is substantial and that difference has changed (narrowed) as the Chinese economy has grown. PPP effects can cut both ways and it is not clear if any substantial bias has appeared in the world comparisons due to the use of PPP conversions. The alternative – market exchange rates – would probably be worse due to fact that a dollar of effort goes a lot further in most developing countries that have

big innovation programs (which is why so many companies have moved R&D operations to China, India, and other rising innovation stars) and official exchange rates (notably in China) often misrepresent the currency's real buying potential.

68 Even this statement is hard to pin down, however. Much of the Indian strength in innovation relates to software, and the favored methods for software protection are not patents but copyright and secrecy.

69 The OECD *Compendium of Patent Statistics 2008* (OECD 2008) identifies renewable energy patents into one of the five categories of wind, solar, geothermal, ocean, and waste technologies. These patents include technologies such as biomass combustion, and improved geothermal systems. Nuclear energy patents are divided into two main categories: nuclear reactor techniques, which include fusion reactors and protection against radiation; and radiation acceleration/detection techniques, which count radiation filters and measurement of nuclear or x-radiation. There is one main fuel cells patent classification, considered "pure" fuel cells, which a large majority (73 percent) of the patents fall into. The remainder of fuel cell patents can be categorized as batteries, which count unclassified fuel cells, or other techniques, which includes chemical processes and hydrogen.

6 Preparing for a changing climate: adaptation, geoengineering, and triage

1 0.8 degrees is based on the nonlinear warming estimate (0.76°C above pre-industrial) reported by the IPCC plus its average annual warming (0.013°C) for the four years (2006–2009) since the end of the IPCC observation period (2005). For the IPCC summary see Trenberth *et al.* 2007.

2 The 0.3°C estimate comes from the IPCC's consensus (i.e., probably conservative) projection of warming that would occur if atmospheric concentrations were held constant at current (2000) levels. That number is reported at about 0.3°C with little variation across climate models. See Meehl *et al.* 2007, p. 749. For higher numbers see Hansen *et al.* 2005. There has been a lot of work on this question of committed warming. For a few key papers see: Ramanathan 1988; Wigley 2005; and Hare and Meinshausen 2006.

3 The basic idea here is hard to refute, but the concept of "inevitable warming" is not a scientific one and is based on assumptions that are hard to nail down exactly. I get "inevitable" warming as the central estimate of the warming that essentially all models project for the "early twenty-first century" (2011–2030), which IPCC estimates at 0.64–0.69°C. (For simplicity I use 0.66, as there is very little variation across models and

scenarios due to the built-in warming and the fact that emission scenarios do not vary much in the near term. Of that 0.66, about 0.3 is
inertia in the climate system and 0.36 is warming from extra emissions.) On top of that estimate I add *half* of the projected *extra warming* from early twenty-first century to mid-century (i.e., 2046–2065).
The total extra warming (i.e., without the 0.66°C of warming that will
be evident by early century) is 0.64–1.14°C. Half of the total extra is
0.32–0.57°C. By mid-century, projections for emissions and accumulation of gases in the atmosphere vary more markedly than the early
twenty-first-century estimates for warming, which is a sign that policy
(and other factors) could alter outcomes. Because the variation is about
as large as the total extra warming, I use half the total extra as a good
indicator of the inevitable warming over this period. That leads us to
inevitable warming from additional emissions that is the sum of the
inevitable warming in early century (0.36°C) plus the range of inevitable extra warming from emissions by mid-century (0.32–0.57°C),
which totals 0.68–0.93°C. Finally, I reduce all these figures by 0.2°C
because the increased warming reported here is against a base of
average temperature in the 1980s and 1990s whereas the warming I
reported above is against the IPCC base year of 2005. Fifteen years of
average warming from 1990 to 2005 is 0.5°C. I have made no extra
allowance here for the additional thermal inertia that will come from
extra greenhouse gases in the atmosphere nor for the possibility that
many large emitting countries may find it impossible to make much
dent in emissions in the next few decades, and thus what I call "inevitable" here is intended to be a highly conservative estimate. The warming estimates are drawn from IPCC (see Meehl *et al.* 2007).

4 For simplicity I have discussed just simple ranges for future temperature,
but a proper analysis would examine the probabilities of meeting targets in
light of all the major uncertainties in emission and climate models. For one
particularly thorough study see Webster *et al.* 2009. Total warming depends
on at least three factors, and none is easy to pin down. Humans control one
factor: emissions. Even then, many governments – as I showed in Chapters
3 and 4 – don't have much direct control over emissions once you account
for the administrative and political factors that are hard for policy makers
to master. A second factor, the "carbon cycle," determines how much of
the emitted gas actually lingers and accumulates in the atmosphere. The
cycle might change in future – becoming more or less effective in removing
the excess CO_2 from the atmosphere where it causes warming. And a third
factor, climate sensitivity, describes how a particular build-up of warming
gases causes actual changes in climate. If the climate is highly sensitive to
warming gases then the inevitable warming could be 3 degrees or more. With

luck, climate may not be sensitive and much less warming could unfold. In addition to the Webster *et al.* 2009 study see also another 2009 study by a different team that varied all three of these factors – emissions, the carbon cycle, and climate sensitivity – and found that even if governments adopted a crash program to cut world emissions in half, there would be as much as a 45 percent chance that global warming would top 2°C (Meinshausen *et al.* 2009). In a very unlucky world, even cutting emissions in half would create a 5 percent chance that warming would approach 3°C. And if emissions kept rising such that they were at least one-quarter higher than 2000 levels by 2020, then the odds of blowing through 2°C would be much higher than 50/50. For commentary on the Meinshausen *et al.* 2009 study see Victor 2009b. The Meinshausen *et al.* study's strength is its attention to the climatic factors; their scenarios for emissions controls are at the outer boundaries of what is plausible. For comparison, the International Energy Agency's most recent projection for emissions of warming gases sees the world total rising by one-third from 2000 levels by 2020 (IEA 2009a, Figure 4.2). Ramanathan and Xu 2010 arrive at a similar pessimism about holding warming to 2 degrees but note that aggressive action on radiatively stronger, short-lived species could raise the odds of keeping warming to less than 2 degrees. For a look at the economics of 2 degrees (and the implausibility of keeping warming at 2 degrees) see Nordhaus 2010.

5 The literature in this area has grown rapidly. For some early comments on the need for adaptation see Schelling 1983; for the most recent extensive review of adaptation see IPCC 2007b. For a recent review of adaptation in economic models see Patt *et al.* 2010. There is growing attention on these issues in developing countries as well (e.g., see Chipanshi, Chanda, and Totolo 2003; Sanghi and Mendelsohn 2008; Kumar, Shyamsundar, and Nambi 2010). On the politics of adaptation (and a call for long overdue attention to adaptation) see Pielke *et al.* 2007; Stern 2007; National Research Council 2010a; 2010b. On geoengineering, see Keith 2010. There are several detailed efforts under way to develop geoengineering experiments and to flesh out the technologies and research programs. For one particularly thorough recent review see Blackstock *et al.* 2009. On geoengineering see especially Victor *et al.* 2009 and The Royal Society 2009a; for an accessible history of the geoengineering technologies see Goodell 2010.

6 Bindoff *et al.* 2007; IPCC, 2007a.

7 See Meehl *et al.* 2007, Table 10.7.

8 Vermeer and Rahmstorf 2009.

9 Mercer 1978.

10 For example, see Oppenheimer 1998.

11 Church *et al.* 2001.

12 I am grateful to Walter Munk, Helen Fricker, and Julienne Stroeve for tutorials on some key recent issues in ice science; I hope my overview has done justice to the underlying science.

13 Revelle 1983; Schelling 1983.

14 See generally IPCC 1990.

15 Among the many benefits from more careful thinking is closer attention to surprises that are truly a surprise and those that can be imagined and predicted probabilistically (Schneider, Turner, and Garriga 1998). And on uncertainty more generally see: Morgan and Henrion 1990; Schneider 2002; and Kandlikar, Risbey, and Dessai 2005. On the IPCC guidance see IPCC 2004.

16 Westerling *et al.* 2009.

17 Allen and Breshears 1998.

18 Kurz *et al.* 2008.

19 Rosenzweig *et al.* 2000; Gutierrez, Ponti, and Cossu 2009. For nearly all climate impacts that affect human systems one of the chief difficulties is to project not just the climate impact (e.g., change in pest range) but also human responses. Ignorance of the latter often leads to projections that are overly pessimistic. For more on this question see Victor 2007b and for recent commentary on this challenge focused on the particular problem of malaria see Ledford 2010.

20 Ausubel 1991.

21 Wildavsky 1980.

22 Rosenberg and Crosson 1991; Rosenberg 1993.

23 See, for example, an early effort at a global assessment of climate impacts on agriculture: Parry 1990.

24 See California State 2005. For the most recent impact report, see Moser *et al.* 2009. On sea-level rise, especially, see California State 2008.

25 See, for example, Service 2007.

26 Mishra 2009; see also Misquitta and Anand 2009.

27 In the parlance of development assistance these are ODA and concession-financed projects. See World Bank 2006.

28 Labor force figures are from the Bureau of Labor Statistics using 2008 data (US Department of Labor 2009). GDP figures are from the CIA, The World Factbook: United States (CIA 2010b).

29 Data for India come from the CIA, The World Factbook: India (CIA 2010a).

30 Schelling 2006.

31 See Heileman 1993 and McMahon 1993 – on the history of AOSIS.

32 See Vidal 2009.

33 See Harris 2007. Kevin Conrad, representing Papua New Guinea at the 2007 Bali climate talks, addressed the United States representative

saying, "We ask for your leadership. We seek your leadership. But if for some reason you are not willing to lead, leave it to the rest of us. Please get out of our way."

34 There are five funds dedicated solely to adaptation, although the World Bank administered fund refers to "climate resilience." Contributions into each fund since fund creation total as follows: Adaptation Fund $33.03 million; Special Climate Change Fund $100.53 million; LDC Fund $135.45 million; Strategic Priority on Adaptation Fund $50 million; Pilot Program for Climate Resilience $128.6 million. Some of the contributions to the Adaptation Fund come from sales of CERs, with governments contributing about $3.3 million to the fund and some of those governments have asked to be reimbursed. These amounts are much less than was pledged ($965 million), and even less has actually been disbursed ($253 million) (Climate Funds Update 2009).

35 Thanks especially to Robert Keohane for help in rethinking my argument here on the morality of consequences. For more, see Weber 1918/2004 and Wolfers 1962.

36 Rawls, of course, imagined his justice experiment within a coherent society. Others have tried to extend that logic, however, to global problems of justice such as foreign aid, arms control, and now environmental protection. See Rawls 1971.

37 There is a growing literature on the international ethics of climate change. For an example see Singer 2002.

38 Perhaps there are a few areas where special efforts at adaptation might be merited. A fuller effort might be needed to make development agencies and local officials aware of climate dangers so that they don't encourage, for example, settling of lands that will become inhospitable with higher sea levels or a changed climate. Those efforts, also known as "mainstreaming," are exactly what is already under way in the advanced industrialized countries; some developing countries are doing the same, and more can do a better job. But outsiders will have little impact on this process since, as with the industrialized nations, mainstreaming concerns about climate impacts requires changing the internal operations of national institutions. In addition to this effort, outsiders might help with specific projects such as building higher sea walls around high-value assets like cities or designing crops that can better handle new climates. Looking practically, however, it is hard to see what outsiders can do to help on these fronts. Particular adaptation projects will have little impact unless they are implemented within the context of a nation's broader plan for managing how it will respond to a changing climate. Simply parachuting particular new adaptation projects into countries that don't have those institutions in place will

simply reproduce the problems already seen with costly development projects. The external aid will become a curse – an inspiration to corruption.

39 Since at least the 1990s, there have been careful studies assessing whether foreign aid for the purpose of promoting economic development actually works (Dollar and Pritchett 1998). The central result of that research is that providing money to poorly governed countries doesn't help much, but targeting funds and other resources to countries that have the right governing institutions in place can make a big difference. Countries already have plenty of reasons to apply that wisdom, and they have plenty of excuses for why the wisdom is often ignored. The problem for foreign assistance is that the countries that are the most needy for development assistance are nearly always those that can least use the help effectively. This does not mean that foreign development assistance is a doomed enterprise, but it works best when donors make their aid conditional on policies that will better ensure the resources are not squandered. In most foreign aid programs those threats are not credible because little effort is made to tailor foreign aid to make it available where it is most useful. The money flows for many reasons, not simply for a detached goal of development, and once it flows it is hard to stop. In the late 1980s, I lived in Nairobi, Kenya, and watched a parade of World Bank officials threaten the government with a cut-off in aid absent reforms to tame corruption; those reforms never came yet the aid money kept flowing. These are not new problems; awareness of climate change will not fix them.

40 See, for example, McGray *et al.* 2007 who look at 135 projects, policies, and initiatives that are supposedly aimed at adaptation.

41 See, for examples, Meyer 2001 and Böhringer and Welsch 2004 on contraction and convergence. See also Patt *et al.* 2010 on estimating the vulnerability of least developed countries to climate-related extreme events.

42 Schelling 1992.

43 EPA analysis used two models to project GDP in 2020 of $17.4–$17.7 trillion with a total cost of abatement ranging from $28 billion to $30 billion (US EPA 2009). Pinning down exactly how much the US will spend to control emissions is particularly difficult since the country won't soon adopt the market system that EPA analyzed but an array of (probably costlier) direct regulation. So far, investments in the US for GHG mitigation technologies totaled $132.9 billion between 2000 and 2008, a number that will rise sharply as the whole country faces credible limits on emissions. Source: www.environmentalleader. com/2009/06/18/us-spends-133b-for-emission-mitigation/.

44 For reviews see especially Keith 2000; Lane *et al.* 2006; Ricke *et al.* 2008.

45 There are many kinds of reflective particles. Sulphate particles have attracted most attention because volcanoes already naturally inject large quantities of emissions that yield sulphate when they erupt, offering natural analogs for envisioning and studying possible man-made geoengineering systems. In addition to these ideas, other imagined schemes include putting diffraction gratings in outer space (which can deflect a bit of incoming sunlight away from the planet) or installing machines on the ocean that could blow water vapor into the atmosphere, which increases the cover of reflective bright clouds. As people focus more on the options, there is little doubt they will find still more intriguing strategies. They will also find ways to cut the cost. For example, the chief cost in stratospheric injection programs is lofting large amounts of material into the stratosphere and replenishing it. David Keith has suggested that those costs might be reduced with designer particles that are lighter (and thus less expensive to loft) and self-levitating in the Earth's magnetic field (and thus less needy of replenishment). Particles that steer themselves might be interesting as well, so that geoengineering masks are concentrated where they are most useful.

46 Consider just two examples of many that are being explored. One involves planting more reflective crops (or painting the roofs of structures a brighter color), which could make the planet overall more reflective. That proposal is intriguing, but the effects on ecosystems are hard to assess and the increase in albedo hinges on the rate at which the plants or painting can proceed. Another option would suck CO_2 from the air. That might be done by coaxing the oceans or forests to absorb more CO_2; two companies have been created to explore the ocean option, which would involve fertilizing oceans with a scarce nutrient (iron) and then watching the algal blooms that follow suck CO_2 from the surrounding waters and the atmosphere. One of those companies went bankrupt. Tinkering with the oceans is not popular, and serious questions have been raised about whether fertilization makes much difference. See Martin 1990 and Riddell 2008. Another air capture option involves constructing machines that remove CO_2 with a catalyst and then turn it into an inert substance or inject it safely under ground. So far, this latter air capture option appears to be very expensive, but if it works, it would be the closest geoengineering inverse to emissions and could conceivably operate largely without side effects (Keith 2009).

47 On side effects see studies such as Bala 2009; Lenton and Vaughan 2009; and Thompson and Launder 2010. For recent, accessible overviews see especially The Royal Society 2009a and Goodell 2010.

48 See, for example, Teller, Wood, and Hyde 1997. This view is a minority. Most experts doing the best work on geoengineering see the option as fraught with dangers and hubris and thus envision using it only in case of emergency. In the absence of more precise information about risks and benefits, a full-blown analysis of when and how different geoengineering options should be deployed is still premature. See, for example, Robock *et al.* 2009.

49 For an early cost estimate see National Academy of Sciences *et al.* 1992. For attention to the ways that the low cost of geoengineering and the potential unilateral use of the technology changes international cooperation, see Schelling 1996.

50 Victor 2008.

51 Liepert *et al.* 2004; Oman *et al.* 2006; Trenberth and Dai 2007.

52 See Crutzen 2006. That's why the hole in the ozone layer appeared – the ozone-destroying chemicals mixed with natural particles that were particularly prevalent in the stratosphere over Antarctica. If humans inject particles throughout the stratosphere, those reactions might be more prevalent.

53 See, for example, Stanhill and Cohen 2001; Govindasamy *et al.* 2002; Naik *et al.* 2003; Mohan *et al.* 2006; D'Arrigo *et al.* 2008.

54 Govindasamy and Caldeira 2000; Oman *et al.* 2005.

55 For more on acidification see Lane *et al.* 2006 and Doney *et al.* 2009.

56 For efforts to quantify the cost see National Academy of Sciences *et al.* 1992; Robock *et al.* 2009; Levitt and Dubner 2009.

57 For example, see House *et al.* 2007.

58 See G8+5 National Academies of Science 2008. Notably, see The Royal Society 2009b.

59 For more on the importance of consensus statements and assessments see Mitchell *et al.* 2006; National Research Council 2007.

60 Oppenheimer *et al.* 2007. Similar arguments apply to the IPCC assessments of the effects of aerosols on climate forcing (for example, see Morgan, Adams, and Keith 2006).

61 Geoengineering is also particularly ill suited for standard assessments, such as through the IPCC, because some of the most important issues involve the evaluation of trade-offs, which is the realm of the social sciences. Outside of economics, the social sciences do not have strong enough and sufficiently well-accepted intellectual paradigms to yield usable knowledge through standard international assessments. The IPCC particularly struggles where paradigms are contested because it is, by design, an open and weak institution. Without the aid of a strong paradigm, weak institutions have a hard time embracing novel ideas and conveying the true diversity of opinions in the "tails" while, at the same time, keeping charlatans at bay.

62 The Royal Society 2009a.

63 Victor *et al.* 2009.

64 The arguments in this section about geoengineering draw heavily on Victor *et al.* 2009 and Victor 2008.

65 Some estimates suggest that once a geoengineering scheme is in place, failure to sustain it could lead to climate warming at a pace twenty times greater than the warming evident today (Matthews and Caldeira 2007).

66 For more detail on the argument against taboo see Victor 2008. At the time of writing there are various proposals that would yield a taboo, such as through the science working committee under the Convention on Biological Diversity.

67 For the best history of weather control see James Fleming, 2010, *Fixing the Sky: The Checkered History of Weather and Climate Control* (Columbia University Press).

68 Those dynamics explain, for example, the 1978 taboo treaty on environmental modification – nearly all nations abhorred a technology they did not use while the US and Soviet Union did not want to incur the political cost to block them. Their calculus was aided, certainly, by the fact that environmental modification also didn't work well. A similar logic unfolded in the late 1990s with the building momentum behind banning landmines of all types. In that case, however, important players (notably the US) made a different calculation and opposed landmine bans because the technology was much more useful.

69 Raustiala and Victor 2004.

70 Sebenius 1984.

71 The issue for geoengineering is the Lagrangian point L1 – an orbit that affords uninterrupted position between Sun and Earth and thus could be an ideal site for space-based sunshades. At the moment, nobody knows how to assign property rights at L1, but surely some governments will imagine great riches and demand their share. At this stage, attempting to allocate L1 would not be useful. It is not clear whether L1 is uniquely special because jostling hardware at that slot could be hazardous for the planet as a whole. Or perhaps L1 will become like geostationary orbits – once imagined to be scarce and thus highly valuable, but today much less scarce thanks to innovation in low-power satellites and higher gain antennas. Disputes over ownership of L1 could lead governments to question whether systems could ever be placed in that orbit, and that would lead them to forgo possibly useful investment in L1-based geoengineering options.

72 Haas 1990; Slaughter 2004.

73 Victor, Raustiala, and Skolnikoff 1998; Victor 2007a.

74 Teller, Hyde, and Wood 2002.

7 Explaining diplomatic gridlock: what went wrong?

1 WMO (World Meteorological Organization) 1988.

2 Ministerial Conference on Atmospheric Pollution and Climatic Change 1989; The Hague 1989.

3 United Nations General Assembly 1988. For a more detailed history of the early years of the IPCC see especially Hecht and Tirpak 1995. Although the main resolution creating the IPCC arose from the UN General Assembly, the responsibility for overseeing IPCC fell jointly to the United Nations Environment Programme (UNEP) and the World Meteorological Organization (WMO). Those same two organizations had jointly run the highly successful panels that assessed the state of ozone science.

4 There is more research to be done on why the sciences have performed so differently in the IPCC and other international environmental assessments. My impression is that the strength of the "paradigm" plays a big role because in well-organized fields (where paradigms are strong) it is easier for scientists to map out where they agree and disagree, but in poorly organized fields scientists often don't even share core assumptions. Most of the social sciences, outside mainstream economics, are poorly organized. Interestingly, the most famous study of scientific paradigms (Kuhn 1962) opens with a musing on this lack of agreement in the social sciences and the problems that poor paradigms create for allowing efficient scientific progress as well as the role of strong paradigms in setting a field up for scientific revolution.

5 United Nations General Assembly, 1988. This resolution says: 1) The IPCC is "to provide internationally coordinated scientific assessments of the magnitude, timing and potential environmental and socio-economic impact of climate change and realistic response strategies." 2) The General Assembly "Encourages the convening of conferences on climate change, particularly on global warming, at the national, regional and global levels in order to make the international community better aware of the importance of dealing effectively and in a timely manner with all aspects of climate change resulting from certain human activities." The latter mandate probably was not enough to begin formal UN talks on climate change and, instead, was a signal that the UN would not quash other talks that were under way, such as the follow-on to the Toronto talks.

6 United Nations General Assembly 1990.

7 This assessment is based on dating treaties in the CIESIN ENTRI database. In 1972 there were about 50 treaties on the books; by 1987 that number had grown to about 150. Today, multilateral treaty-making has saturated at about 200 treaties – in part because diplomats are running out of topics to regulate and in part because treaties are getting a lot

more complicated and thus slower to negotiate. The hope for a pulse of treaty-making from the 1992 Rio Conference was realized, and 1992 was the most active year for treaty-making in the history of the planet (thirteen new treaties were finished that year). But the pulse was short-lived. For more see Victor and Coben 2005.

8 172 governments including 108 heads of state signed on with three major agreements at the Earth Summit. See United Nations Department of Public Information 1997.

9 UNFCCC 1992, Article 4.2(a).

10 UNFCCC 1995, Decision 20/CP.1.

11 By 2000 Russian emissions were down 39 percent from 1990 levels (see official Russian data, excluding land use change, reported to UNFCCC at http://unfccc.int/di/DetailedByParty.do).

12 See the "Bali Action Plan," UNFCCC 2008.

13 While writing this book I tested out most of the theories offered here with some predictions for the Copenhagen conference (and some advice on how to make the event less of a diplomatic disaster). For the results, see Victor 2009c.

14 In particular, I commend Bodansky's history of the process leading to the UNFCCC: Bodansky 1993.

15 When scholars working on different issue-areas get together to compare notes, one of the things they usually remark is that "environment" is one of the most highly institutionalized areas of international cooperation.

16 This is a quite controversial statement, and later in this chapter I will justify the point. There are many different factors that explain compliance, but it is hard to avoid the fact that compliance with binding accords is easy for nearly all governments because the accords are tuned to assure compliance (for more, see Downs, Rocke, and Barsoom 1996). Of course, in some circumstances, other forces are at work to create pressures for compliance as well (see Mitchell 1994; Chayes and Chayes 1995).

17 Political scientists will recognize that these four attributes overlap with the three aspects of "legalization" that have been the focus of a productive effort by scholars in international relations and international law to study jointly how international law works. Those three aspects are obligation (binding versus nonbinding), precision (flexibility of commitments), and delegation (enforcement) (see Goldstein *et al.* 2001). In addition, political scientists have long studied the numbers and choice of countries that participate – what I call geometry (see for example Kahler 1992; Keohane and Nye 2001; Underdal 1980). To this standard list I add instruments – in particular, targets and timetables – because

that is such a central part of environmental diplomacy. (For a review on why targets and timetables are so central in air pollution diplomacy see Victor and Coben 2005.)

18 This view is so widespread yet so absurd in the extreme that there is very little research to test whether fully inclusive policies are, in fact, seen as more legitimate or whether more legitimate policies are more effective. For a careful look at the legitimacy of multilateral institutions see Buchanan and Keohane 2006. Some philosophers have addressed the question of representation in the allocation of obligations to address global problems, in general concluding that special voice should be given to less advantaged groups and individuals – drawing on a principle that dates at least to the early 1970s and John Rawls arguing that just societies are organized to avoid harm to the least advantaged. For a modern application to climate change see, for example, Peter Singer (Singer 2002). In climate change policy circles, for a long time there has brewed the argument that if climate change policy is "fair" it will be more effective. Pinning down what is meant by "fair" has proved hard, but often analysts have in mind agreements that reflect the full range of voices. For some general views along these lines see, for example, Tóth 1999 and my skepticism in the same volume.

19 Underdal 1980.

20 See, generally, Victor, Raustiala, and Skolnikoff 1998 – especially part II. Notably, see the studies of Andresen, Skjærseth, Stokke, and Wettestad.

21 On the Rhine river notably see Bernauer 1996 and on turbot see DeSombre and Barkin 2000.

22 Total GHG emissions in 2008 were 2.2 percent below the 2007 total. The EIA also recently released the 2009 data showing a large decline in US energy-related CO_2 emissions of 7 percent (EIA 2010b).

23 For a brief history of discoveries in the UK North Sea, see "An Analysis of the UK North Sea Production" (http://home.entouch.net/dmd/north-sea.htm).

24 The exact decline was 18.3 percent. Data was retrieved from UNFCCC flexible GHG data queries and calculation was performed using time-series data for Germany (http://unfccc.int/di/DetailedByParty.do).

25 China's total CO_2 emissions from the consumption of energy during the late 1990s and early 2000s: 1998 emissions were 2,991.4 million metric tons. By 2004 they rose to 5,131.8 million metric tons. Source: EIA "International Energy Statistics" ad hoc data query.

26 For a fuller discussion of the predicament, written long before the Bush administration took power but anticipating the decision to withdraw from Kyoto, see Victor 2001.

27 CIESIN data set; Victor and Coben 2005.
28 Weitzman 1974; Roberts and Spence 1976. There have been several applications to warming emissions. See, for example, Pizer 1998 and 2002.
29 For a review see especially Hafner-Burton and Ron 2009.
30 The two exceptions are so unique as to underscore the power of the finding. One is the 1984 protocol to the LRTAP (Long-Range Transboundary Air Pollution) Convention, establishing the funding arrangements for two research centers (in Oslo and in Moscow). The other is a 1992 agreement establishing a global change research institute that ultimately was located in São Paulo, Brazil (the Agreement Establishing the Inter-American Institute for Global Change Research). Neither of those two cases – the only examples of specific commitments that take the form of P&P instruments rather than quantity limitations – actually concerns regulation of an air pollutant. Rather, they both provide ancillary services to air pollution agreements – in the former case, the other protocols to the LRTAP convention (all of which contain quantity instruments), and in the latter case, the international attempts to address global warming.
31 In particular, see Benedick 1998 and Parson 2003.
32 Benedick 1998.
33 Of course, the full story is a lot more complicated than our brief history here. After the first CFCs the next class of chemicals was halons and a second group of CFCs. And in addition to methyl chloroform and methyl bromide, one other individual chemical (carbon tetrachloride) also got special treatment – in that case because it was a feedstock for producing other chemicals and not always released to the atmosphere.
34 For more, see Chapter 4 and also DeSombre and Kaufmann 1996; Benedick 1998; Parson 2003.
35 This lesson has been examined in some detail in other areas of international cooperation (see, for example, Rosendorff and Milner 2001) but the optimal use of flexibility and the relationship between flexibility and credibility have not been topics that have attracted much attention of analysts who study environmental agreements, partly perhaps because those agreements are not very demanding and thus the need for flexibility has been lower. The Montreal Protocol experience reveals, in fact, that flexibility is essential as commitments become more demanding.
36 This history of the SALT and START talks broadly support this proposition, but we must be mindful that other factors were at work as well. Over time, adversarial governments learn about each other and about the types of arms control that will work, which also helps them negotiate more precise and demanding agreements. And over time adversaries

also pay the costs of failure – namely big arms budgets – which also produces more tangible pressure for success.

37 For sake of clarity I will focus on the canonical cases here – strict, binding law versus more flexible nonbinding agreements. In some areas of international cooperation that trade-off has been managed, rightly, with binding agreements that include well-tailored escape clauses such as reservations, opt-out provisions, derogations. These so-called "flexibility measures" allow for deep cooperation while giving governments confidence that they can avoid (often temporarily) highly inconvenient commitments. In time, such provisions will be needed in the area of climate change, but at present not enough is known about when such inconvenient commitments may arise and how to constrain the use of flexibility measures that I will set this issue aside. Oddly, one of the conventional wisdoms in international environmental law is that such measures degrade treaty effectiveness even though the evidence from other issue-areas is pretty much entirely the opposite. That wrong-headed logic explains, for example, why the UNFCCC (and nearly all major international environmental treaties) prohibits governments from entering "reservations" when they join the treaty. On the good experience with flexibility measures in other areas of international law and how such measures are part of the "rational design" of treaties see Koremenos, Lipson, and Snidal 2003, which reprints essays from a 2001 special issue of International Organization – notably see Rosendorff and Milner 2001. See also Raustiala 2005 and Koremenos 2005. For an empirical look at these questions in the GATT/WTO, where there is the most experience with flexibility measures, see Kucik and Reinhardt 2008. There has been very little such research on the use of flexibility measures in environmental agreements, with a few exceptions, such as Raustiala and Victor "Conclusions" in Victor, Raustiala, and Skolnikoff 1998; Boockmann and Thurner 2006; Marcoux 2009; and Böhmelt and Pilster 2010. The lack of attention to flexibility measures in environmental agreements is symptomatic of the fact that most environmental agreements have not given much attention to the challenges of crafting demanding commitments in a context where governments are unable to make credible promises concerning exactly what they will implement. I note that the question of what governments can promise is closely related to the burgeoning field of political science research that looks at the relationship between domestic politics and international commitments since domestic politics – that is, the interests, organization, and influence of different national interest groups on national policy making and implementation – usually has a dominant effect on what governments actually promise and deliver.

38 With formal flexibility measures off limits, pressure for flexibility arose in other ways in the Kyoto Protocol. Three, in particular, dominated most of the negotiations. One was the time horizon (five years instead of one). A second was the basket of gases (all gases instead of regulation gas-by-gas). And a third, the most important, was emission trading – both within Annex I nations (notably the so-called "hot air" allowances from Russia and Ukraine) and between industrialized and developing countries (the CDM). I do not address these in more detail here, although elsewhere in this book I show that all of these supposed points of flexibility have proved to be an illusion. The CDM has been the largest source of flexibility, and it has worked by creating the illusion of emission controls in developing countries when, in fact, actual emission reductions have been more scarce.

39 A few scholars have worked through these trade-offs and offer some theoretical guidance. Notably, see Abbott and Snidal 2000. In addition, for elements of a theory that concentrates more on the role of nonbinding agreements see Raustiala 2005.

40 On the North Sea see Skjærseth 1998; on acid rain in Europe see Wettestad 1998; and on the Baltic Sea see Roginko 1998. See also generally Victor, Raustiala, and Skolnikoff 1998.

41 The canonical study is Axelrod 1984. For a particularly thoughtful review of this concept and others that help explain cooperation see Seabright 2005.

42 Downs, Rocke, and Barsoom 1996.

43 See Barrett 2003, chapter 2.

44 See part I of Victor, Raustiala, and Skolnikoff 1998.

45 See chapters by Greene and Victor in Victor, Raustiala, and Skolnikoff 1998.

46 Victor 1996.

47 On LRTAP see especially Levy 1993 and Wettestad 1998.

48 UNFCCC 1992, Article 13.

49 UNFCCC 1995, Decision 20/CP.1.

50 See Levy 1993.

51 Notably, see the careful study by Beth Simmons who looks at how international norms mobilize various kinds of domestic actors that, in turn, expand the political possibilities (Simmons 2009). Many scholars have explored this pathway through which human rights norms gain influence. See, for example, Finnemore and Sikkink 1998 and Keck and Sikkink 1998. In legal scholarship, such ideas are developed for example in Goodman and Jinks 2004 on how international law might change state behavior (as well as in Goodman and Jinks 2005 that responds to criticism of the original argument).

52 For example, Hafner-Burton 2008.

53 Put more formally, the norms of *opinio juris* (a sense of legal obligation) and *pacta sunt servanda* (treaties are to be obeyed) normally prevail. For more on this, see Franck 1990, and Koh 1997.

54 See especially Chayes and Chayes 1995.

55 Amount as of May 27, 2009. UNEP 2009.

56 DeSombre and Kauffman 1996. I am focusing here on the Montreal Protocol's carrots, but experts will also note that the Protocol does include a system of sticks – trade sanctions against countries that fail to join the treaty (or at least implement comparable measures). That system is smart, but it is less consequential than it initially seems because the approach of compensating countries for the full extra costs of compliance guarantees (roughly) that every country will join the treaty. Situations of noncompliance, by design, will be rare because the carrots are so large. (As I noted earlier, the exceptions to this are rare – such as Russia, which has an incentive to violate the treaty but was not formally eligible for the carrot of MLF funding under the treaty.) The inclusion of trade sanctions is encouraging, but in practice less important than initially seems.

57 The Montreal Protocol fund has spent on average less than $1 billion per year in carrots. Deep cuts in warming emissions – consistent with stabilizing global warming at about 2 degrees – might require transfers at about $100 billion per year, which is the number used as a benchmark at the Copenhagen conference for transfers by 2020. That number includes public and private transfers (mainly the latter), but it is the total size that matters for our purposes here. In the Montreal Protocol case essentially all the transfers that held the agreement together were public funds.

58 Jacoby *et al.* 2009.

59 Data retrieved from OECD DAC1 Dataset: Official and Private Flows (OECD.StatExtracts "DAC1 Official and Private Flows" Development data. Development Co-operation Directorate (DCD-DAC), OECD website. http://stats.oecd.org/Index.aspx).

60 During a press briefing in Copenhagen, Todd Stern, Special US Envoy for Climate Change, said, "I don't envision public funds – certainly not from the United States – going to China." He said, "(T)here is inevitably a limited amount of money. The amount ought to be as high as it possibly can be, but it's necessarily going to be limited. That's just life, and the real world. So we would intend to direct our public dollars to the neediest countries, and China – to its great credit – has a dynamic economy, and sits on some two trillion dollars in reserves. So we don't think China would be the first candidate for public funding" (US 09

Copenhagen 2009). That said, there are many ideas for international funds of various types and also many ideas on how to raise the needed money. For the most creative see the line of proposals starting with Bhagwati 2006. I remain skeptical that big "green funds" are practical because I don't see how governments will make credible commitments to fill them with money. As in most matters related to foreign aid, the Scandinavian countries and a few other Europeans are exceptions, but their efforts don't add up to the tens or hundreds of billions of dollars that advocates for big green funds imagine.

61 The global warming issue was discussed in the Houston Summit in 1990.

62 UNFCCC 1998.

63 In particular, see Hufbauer *et al.* 2009.

8 A new strategy

1 The challenge of liberal, rule-governed international trade is not identical to global warming, but it shares many similarities. There are large collective benefits from success but there are also strong individual incentives to cheat. Commitments are interdependent, which means that what one country is willing to implement depends on its confidence that others are making comparable efforts. International commitments have become more demanding and complicated over time. In engaging more countries and eliciting more demanding commitments, both carrots and sticks have played important roles. At the same time, there are important differences, of which three are notable. The first is that trade agreements are intrinsically easier to enforce than the more diffuse obligations that are likely to arise around global warming. That's because trade is a tangible, reciprocal activity. It is relatively easy to know who is cheating and to concentrate penalties on the violator. (As the trade regime has focused on nontariff barriers it has addressed problems more analogous to the challenge in coordinating global warming policies – a point I explore in the main text.) The second, related, is that it is often easier, in trade, to create "private goods" – that is, benefits that only members of the club can receive, such as special trading zones and privileges. Private goods make it much easier to form useful clubs in the first place – as happened in the early days of the GATT – and to craft incentives so that other countries will do what is needed to gain membership in the club. Special care is needed in the creation of private goods around global warming, but they will exist – such as markets for clean energy and special access to lucrative emission trading markets. And third is that with radical innovation many of the toughest problems

in global warming diplomacy will abate. By contrast, with innovation the need for a vigorous liberal trade policy grows even stronger because the temptations to protect national industries that are made uncompetitive through innovation will grow. These are important differences that affect diplomacy in these two areas at different extremes, but they are not decisive.

2 Commission of the European Communities 2008.

3 US Congress 2009.

4 IEA 2009b.

5 The exceptions arise mainly in failed states that, for the most part, fortuitously also have low emissions. Regulating emissions of warming gases will be easier to manage than other international problems, such as terrorism, that flourish when governments fail. Almost all the biggest emitters have highly capable governments.

6 Here, for simplicity, I will speak of the "WTO" although the relevant experience extends much earlier than the formal creation of the WTO in 1995.

7 On WTO accession broadly see Michalopoulos 2002. And for particular care in examining the wide array of commitments in accession agreements and their interpretation (and enforceability) see Charnovitz 2006.

8 The most recent and important example of such large changes is China. For reviews of the accession process and its real impact internally in China see, e.g., Farah 2006.

9 In other ways the WTO model is also not ideal. For example, open access rules for joining access working parties allow, in effect, veto membership. The climate process might eventually arrive at that state, but when launching the first round of accession deals it would probably be better to limit the number of negotiating forums by establishing voting rules that are more permissive – for example, countries that account for half of the enthusiastic countries' emissions could block approval of a country's accession deal. (Approximately that rule was adopted in the Kyoto negotiations, and such rules are important because they protect the enthusiastic countries from adopting strict emission controls only to find that their most important economic competitors do not face such regulations.) Such a rule would force the industrialized countries to negotiate in blocks rather than singly. It would also tilt the balance, initially, in favor of encouraging expansion of membership and then, as the rules tighten, toward more demanding accession talks. Encouraging larger early membership would help broaden the climate regime in helpful ways. The WTO, back in the 1960s when it was still the GATT, also had accession rules that tilted much more strongly in favor of approving new

members when compared with today's rules (which are not only tighter but also cover a much broader spectrum of trade-related activities).

10 I am particularly impressed by the efforts in the World Bank to develop a strategy for how scarce resources might be deployed strategically. See World Bank 2009.

11 Much of this thinking goes back to what used to be called "functionalism" – the argument that deep integration arises through technocratic cooperation between governments that then spills over into a broader need for cooperation. For an origin along those lines see Haas 1958; and for an assessment of the broader array of domestic political forces that shape which countries are willing to integrate (and under which terms) see Moravcsik 1998.

12 For other models see notably Chayes 1991 (on the IMF Article IV process of national review) and Schelling 1992 (on the Marshall Plan system for coordinating allocations of foreign aid).

13 Keohane 2007.

14 Wagner *et al.* 2009.

15 I have explored this issue in Victor 2002 in the context of buyer liability, which would complement effort to create a competition for quality by creating a strong, direct incentive for investors to seek quality over the lifetime of a project. On this point see also, notably, Keohane and Raustiala 2009. And recently I have focused on how a unilateral market-based approach could be adopted by the US to foster a competition for quality (see Victor 2010b).

16 Price 2007.

17 For example, see IEA's review of the EU's energy policy – which is an extraordinary event in revealing the extent to which large, industrialized economies will allow intrusive reviews of their policies by institutions that they trust for an even-handed assessment (e.g., IEA 2008b). The OECD's reviews occur in a much wider array of issue-areas – such as innovation and competition policy – which reflects the OECD's origins and functioning as a general purpose agency for international cooperation. The US is noticeably less engaged in OECD policy reviews than most other members, and one of the important challenges will be the design of an institution that is tolerable to the United States – a problem that arises in nearly every area of international institution-building. The OECD, increasingly, even reviews policies (by invitation) of non-members, notably China, where it has reviewed innovation policy (in 2008) and other policies, such as investment policy (OECD 2003).

18 Chayes 1991.

19 Such a broader norm-based process might make it easier, eventually, to apply stronger sticks in future, including trade sanctions. A general

agreement on climate change and the negotiated transition with each of the new entrants would create higher legitimacy (and expectation) of future enforcement than a series of one-off deals.

20 On legalization and enforcement in the WTO see for example Steinberg 2004.

21 Victor 1991.

22 Singh 2008.

23 The benefit of cooperation in small club groups is hardly a new topic in economic thinking. See Buchanan 1965.

9 Climate change and world order: implications for the UN, industry, diplomacy, and the great powers

1 I have not spent time in this book looking at the optimal size of the club. In the context of a large effort inspired by Paul Martin to develop a leaders-level G20 (see Martin 2005), many academics worked on questions such as which countries should be invited to the club and which topics would be "ripe" for attention. Richard Cooper offered the sage advice, based on the history of the G8, that the club needs to start very small so that leaders can actually coordinate. His advice was about ten countries or fewer, and that advice strikes me as correct. The current G20 has already revealed that it is too large to get much done; it also, partly because of its size, has imposed little discipline on its agenda.

2 See Bosetti and Victor, in press.

3 Keohane and Victor, in press.

4 See Victor and Heller 2007.

5 On the variation in state-owned oil companies and their management strategies see Victor, Thurber, and Hults, forthcoming.

6 For this argument applied to California see Victor 2010a.

References

Abbott, Kenneth W. and Duncan Snidal. 2000. "Hard and Soft Law in International Governance." *International Organization* 54(3): 421–56.

Agence France-Presse. 2007. "Climate Change: Sarkozy Backs Carbon Tax, EU Levy on Non-Kyoto Imports." October 25.

Alic, John A., David C. Mowery, and Edward S. Rubin. 2003. *US Technology and Innovation Policies: Lessons for Climate Change.* Arlington, VA: Pew Center on Global Climate Change.

Allen, Craig D. and David D. Breshears. 1998. "Drought-Induced Shift of a Forest-Woodland Ecotone: Rapid Landscape Response to Climate Variation." *PNAS* 95(25): 14839–42.

Allen, Myles R. *et al.* 2009. "Warming Caused by Cumulative Carbon Emissions Towards the Trillionth Tonne." *Nature* 458: 1163–6.

Álvarez, Gabriel C., R. Jara, J. Julián, and J. Bielsa. 2009. "Study of the Effects on Employment of Public Aid to Renewable Energy Sources." Universidad Rey Juan Carlos, March.

American Energy Innovation Council. 2010. *A Business Plan for America's Energy Future.* Washington DC: American Energy Innovation Council.

Ausubel, Jesse H. 1991. "Does Climate Still Matter?" *Nature* 350: 649–52.

Ausubel, Jesse H., Arnulf Grübler, and Nebojša Nakićenović. 1988. "Carbon Dioxide Emissions in a Methane Economy." *Climatic Change* 12: 245–63.

Axelrod, Robert. 1984. *The Evolution of Cooperation.* New York, NY: Basic Books.

Bala, G. 2009. "Problems with Geoengineering Schemes to Combat Climate Change." *Current Science* 96(1): 41–8.

Ball, Jeffrey. 2008. "UN Warming Program Draws Fire: Fund Designed to Spur Renewable Energy Subsidizes Gas Plants." *The Wall Street Journal*, July 11. http://online.wsj.com/article/SB121573736662544537.html.

Barker, Terry *et al.* 2007. "Technical Summary." In *Climate Change 2007: Mitigation. Contribution of Working Group III to the Fourth*

Assessment Report of the Intergovernmental Panel on Climate Change, eds. B. Metz, O. Davidson, P. Bosch, R. Dave, and L. Meyer, 25–94. Cambridge, UK and New York, NY: Cambridge University Press.

Barrett, Scott. 2003. *Environment and Statecraft: The Strategy of Environmental Treaty-Making*. New York, NY: Oxford University Press.

Benedick, Richard E. 1998. *Ozone Diplomacy: New Directions in Safeguarding the Planet*, 2nd edn. Cambridge, MA: Harvard University Press.

Bernauer, Thomas. 1996. "Protecting the Rhine River Against Chloride Pollution." In *Institutions for Environmental Aid: Pitfalls and Promise*, eds. Robert O. Keohane and Marc A. Levy. Cambridge, MA: MIT Press.

Bhagwati, Jagdish N. 2006. "A Global Warming Fund Could Succeed Where Kyoto Failed." *Financial Times*, August 16. www.cfr.org/publication/11311/global_warming_fund_could_succeed_where_kyoto_failed.html.

Bindoff, Nathaniel L. *et al.* 2007. "Observations: Oceanic Climate Change and Sea Level." In *Climate Change 2007: The Physical Science Basis. Contribution of Working Group I to the Fourth Assessment Report of the Intergovernmental Panel on Climate Change*, eds. S. Solomon *et al.*, 385–432. Cambridge, UK and New York, NY: Cambridge University Press.

Blackstock, Jason J. *et al.* 2009. *Climate Engineering Responses to Climate Emergencies*. Santa Barbara, CA: Novim, July.

Blanford, Geoffrey J., Richard G. Richels, and Thomas F. Rutherford. 2009. "International Climate Policy: A 'Second Best' Solution for a 'Second Best' World?" *Climatic Change* 97: 289–96.

Bodansky, Daniel. 1993. "The United Nations Framework Convention on Climate Change: A Commentary." *Yale Journal of International Law* 18: 451–8.

Boden, T. A., G. Marland, and R. J. Andres. 2010. "Global, Regional, and National Fossil-Fuel CO_2 Emissions." Carbon Dioxide Information Analysis Center, Oak Ridge National Laboratory, US Department of Energy, Oak Ridge, TN, USA doi 10.3334/CDIAC/00001_V2010.

Böhmelt, Tobias and Ulrich H. Pilster. 2010. "International Environmental Regimes: Legalisation, Flexibility and Effectiveness." *Australian Journal of Political Science* 45(2): 245–60.

Böhringer, Christoph and Heinz Welsch. 2004. "Contraction and Convergence of Carbon Emissions: An Intertemporal Multi-Region CGE Analysis." *Journal of Policy Modeling* 26(1): 21–39.

Bonvillian, William B. 2006. "Power Play: The DARPA Model and US Energy Policy." *The American Interest* (November/December): 39–43.

Boockmann, Bernhard and Paul W. Thurner. 2006. "Flexibility Provisions in Multilateral Environmental Treaties." *International Environmental Agreements* 6(2): 113–35.

Bosetti, Valentina and David G. Victor. in press. "Politics and Economics of Second-Best Regulation of Greenhouse Gases: The Importance of Regulatory Credibility." *The Energy Journal.*

Braithwaite, John and Peter Drahos. 2000. *Global Business Regulation.* Cambridge University Press.

Broecker, Wallace S. 1975. "Climatic Change: Are We on the Brink of a Pronounced Global Warming?" *Science* 189(4201): 460–3.

  1987. "Unpleasant Surprises in the Greenhouse?" *Nature* 328: 123–126.

  2010. *The Great Ocean Conveyor: Discovering the Trigger for Abrupt Climate Change.* Princeton University Press.

Buchanan, Allen and Robert O. Keohane. 2006. "The Legitimacy of Global Governance Institutions." *Ethics and International Affairs* 20: 405–37.

Buchanan, James M. 1965. "An Economic Theory of Clubs." *Economica* 32(125): 1–14.

Burk, Dan L. and Mark A. Lemley. 2009. *The Patent Crisis and How the Courts Can Solve It.* University of Chicago Press.

Bush, Vannevar. 1945. *Science: The Endless Frontier.* Washington DC: Government Printing Office.

California State. Governor of the State of California. 2005. *Executive Order S-3–05.* Office of the Governor, June 1. http://gov.ca.gov/executive-order/1861/.

  2008. *Executive Order S-13–08.* Office of the Governor, November 14. http://gov.ca.gov/executive-order/11036/.

Callendar, G. S. 1938. "The Artificial Production of Carbon Dioxide and Its Influence on Climate." *Quarterly Journal Royal Meteorological Society* 64: 223–40.

Capoor, Karan and Philippe Ambrosi. 2009. *State and Trends of the Carbon Market 2009.* Washington DC: The World Bank.

Carpenter, Janet and Leonard Gianessi. 1999. "Herbicide Tolerant Soybeans: Why Growers are Adopting Roundup Ready Varieties." AgBioForum. *The Journal of Agrobiotechnology Management & Economics* 2(2): 65–72.

Carson, Rachel. 1962. *Silent Spring.* Boston, MA: Houghton Mifflin.

CGIAR. 2009. *Global Recommitment to Agriculture, CGIAR Annual Report 2008.* Washington DC: CGIAR Secretariat.

Changlin, Gao *et al.* 2004. *China National Energy Strategy and Policy 2020 Subtitle 10: Policy Research on Energy Research & Development.* Development Research Center of the State Council and the Energy Research Institute, June.

Charnovitz, Steve. 2006. "Mapping the Law of WTO Accession." The George Washington University Law School Public Law and Legal Theory Working Paper No. 237.

Chayes, Abram. 1991. "Managing the Transition to a Global Warming Regime, or What to Do Until the Treaty Comes." In *Greenhouse Warming: Negotiating a Global Regime*, ed. Jessica Mathews. Washington DC: World Resources Institute.

Chayes, Abram and Antonia Handler Chayes. 1995. *The New Sovereignty: Compliance with International Regulatory Agreements.* Cambridge, MA: Harvard University Press.

Chipanshi, A. C., R. Chanda, and O. Totolo. 2003. "Vulnerability Assessment of the Maize and Sorghum Crops to Climate Change in Botswana." *Climatic Change* 61(3): 339–60.

Church, J. A. *et al.* 2001. "Changes in Sea Level." In *Climate Change 2001: The Scientific Basis. Contribution of Working Group I to the Third Assessment Report of the Intergovernmental Panel on Climate Change*, eds. J. T. Houghton *et al.* Cambridge, UK and New York, NY: Cambridge University Press.

CIA. 2010a. "The World Factbook: India." CIA website, April 26. www.cia.gov/library/publications/the-world-factbook/geos/in.html.

CIA 2010b. "The World Factbook: United States." CIA website, May 3. www.cia.gov/library/publications/the-world-factbook/geos/us.html.

CIAP (Climate Impact Assessment Program). 1975. *Impacts of Climatic Change on the Biosphere.* Monograph 5 Part 2 – Climate Effects. Washington DC: Dept. of Transportation.

CIESIN (Center for International Earth Science Information Network). "Environmental Treaties." Environmental Treaties and Resource Indicators. CIESIN website, Columbia University.

Climate Funds Update. 2009. "Climate Funds." Climate Funds Update website, December. www.climatefundsupdate.org/listing.

CNA Corporation. 2007. *National Security and the Threat of Climate Change.* Alexandria, VA: CNA.

Cohen, Linda R. and Roger G. Noll. 1991. *The Technology Pork Barrel.* Washington DC: Brookings Institution.

Commission of the European Communities. 2007. *Limiting Global Climate Change to 2 Degrees Celsius – The Way Ahead for 2020 and Beyond.* Communication from the Commission to the Council, the European Parliament, the European Economic and Social Committee and the Committee of the Regions. Brussels: COM. http://ec.europa.eu/environment/climat/home_en.htm.

2008. *20 20 by 2020: Europe's Climate Change Opportunity.* Communication from the Commission to the European Parliament, the Council, the European Economic and Social Committee and the Committee of the Regions. Brussels: COM. www.energy.eu/directives/com2008_0030en01.pdf.

2009. *Progress Towards Achieving the Kyoto Objectives*. Report from the Commission to the European Parliament and the Council. Brussels: COM/2009/0630 final.

Cooper, Richard N. 1989. "International Cooperation in Public Health as a Prologue to Macroeconomic Cooperation." In *Can Nations Agree?: Issues in International Economic Cooperation*, eds. Richard N. Cooper *et al.* Washington DC: Brookings Institution.

Crutzen, Paul J. 2006. "Albedo Enhancement by Stratospheric Sulfur Injections: A Contribution to Resolve a Policy Dilemma?" *Climatic Change* 77(3): 211–20.

Cullenward, Danny. 2009. "Carbon Capture and Storage: An Assessment of Required Technological Growth Rates and Capital Investments." Working Paper 84. Program on Energy and Sustainable Development, Stanford University, May.

Czarnitzki, Dirk, Petr Hanel, and Julio Miguel Rosa. 2004. "Evaluating the Impact of R&D Tax Credits on Innovation: A Microeconometric Study on Canadian Firms." ZEW Discussion Papers 04–77. ZEW – Zentrum für Europäische Wirtschaftsforschung/Center for European Economic Research, November.

D'Arrigo, Rosanne, R. Wilson, B. Liepert, and P. Cherubini. 2008. "On the 'Divergence Problem' in Northern Forests: A Review of the Tree-ring Evidence and Possible Causes." *Global and Planetary Change* 60(3–4): 289–305.

David, Paul A., Bronwyn H. Hall, and Andrew A. Toole. 2000. "Is Public R&D a Complement or Substitute for Private R&D? A Review of the Econometric Evidence." *Research Policy* 29(4–5): 497–529.

de Coninck, Heleen, C. Fischer, R. Newell, and T. Ueno. 2008. "International Technology-Oriented Agreements to Address Climate Change." *Energy Policy* 36(1): 335–56.

Denman, Kenneth L. *et al.* 2007. "Couplings Between Changes in the Climate System and Biogeochemistry." In *Climate Change 2007: The Physical Science Basis. Contribution of Working Group I to the Fourth Assessment Report of the Intergovernmental Panel on Climate Change*, eds. S. Solomon *et al.* Cambridge, UK and New York, NY: Cambridge University Press.

DeSombre, Elizabeth and Samuel Barkin. 2000. "The Turbot War: Canada, Spain and the Conflict over the North Atlantic Fishery." Pew Case Studies in International Affairs. Case Study 226. Washington DC: Institute for the Study of Diplomacy.

DeSombre, Elizabeth R. and Joanne Kauffman. 1996. "The Montreal Protocol Multilateral Fund: Partial Success Story." In *Institutions for Environmental Aid*, eds. Robert O. Keohane and Marc A. Levy. Cambridge, MA: MIT Press.

Deutch, John. 2005. "What Should the Government Do to Encourage Technical Change in the Energy Sector?" MIT Joint Program on the Science and Policy Global Change, Report 120.

Deutch, John, James R. Schlesinger, and David G. Victor. 2006. *National Security Consequences of US Oil Dependency*. Independent Task Force Report No. 58. New York, NY: Council on Foreign Relations.

Dollar, David and Lant Pritchett. 1998. *Assessing Aid: What Works, What Doesn't and Why? – A World Bank Policy Research Report*. New York, NY: Oxford University Press.

Doney, Scott C., Victoria J. Fabry, Richard A. Feely, and Joan A. Kleypas. 2009. "Ocean Acidification: The Other CO_2 Problem." *Annual Review of Marine Science* 1: 169–92.

Dooley, J. J. 1998. "Unintended Consequences: Energy R&D in a Deregulated Energy Market." *Energy Policy* 26(7): 547–55.

1999. "Energy R&D in the United States." PNNL-12188. Battelle, Pacific Northwest National Laboratory, April.

Dooley, J. J., P. J. Runci, and E. E. M. Luiten. 1998. "Energy R&D in the Industrialized World: Retrenchment and Refocusing." PNNL-12061. Battelle, Pacific Northwest National Laboratory, December.

Downs, George W., David M. Rocke, and Peter N. Barsoom. 1996. "Is the Good News about Compliance Good News about Cooperation?" *International Organization* 50: 376–406.

DTI (Department of Trade and Industry). 2003. "Our Energy Future – Creating a Low Carbon Economy." Energy White Paper. Dept. of Transport and DEFRA, February.

Edmonds, J. A. *et al.* 2007. *Global Energy Technology Strategy Addressing Climate Change: Phase 2 Findings from an International Public-Private Sponsored Research Program*. Global Energy Technology Strategy Program (GTSP). College Park, MD: Joint Global Change Research Institute, 118–129.

Ellerman, A. Denny, Frank J. Convery, and Christian de Perthuis. 2010. *Pricing Carbon: The European Union Emissions Trading Scheme*. New York, NY: Cambridge University Press.

The Economist. 2009. "Energiser Money: American Innovation Faces Its Biggest Test for Decades." March 26.

EIA (Energy Information Administration. "Electric Power Industry Companies by Name, Code, and State." Electric Power Industry Companies. US EIA website. www.eia.doe.gov/fuelelectric.html.

2009a. "Country Analysis Briefs: China." US EIA website, July. www. eia.doe.gov/cabs/China/Background.html.

2009b. *Emissions of Greenhouse Gases Report.* Report DOE/EIA-0573(2008). Washington DC: US Dept. of Energy.

2010a. *International Energy Outlook 2010.* Washington DC: US Dept. of Energy.

2010b. *US Carbon Dioxide Emissions in 2009: A Retrospective Review.* Washington DC: US Department of Energy.

European Environment Agency. 2010. *Annual European Union Greenhouse Gas Inventory 1990–2008 and Inventory Report 2010: Submission to the UNFCCC Secretariat.* EEA Technical Report No 6/2010. Luxembourg: Office for Official Publications of the European Communities.

Farah, Paolo. 2006. "Five Years of China WTO Membership: EU and US Perspectives About China's Compliance with Transparency Commitments and the Transitional Review Mechanism." *Legal Issues of Economic Integration* 33(3): 263–304.

Findley, Roger W., Daniel A. Farber, and Jody Freeman. 2003. *Cases and Materials on Environmental Law,* 6th edn. St. Paul, MN: Thomson/West.

Finnemore, Martha and Kathryn Sikkink. 1998. International Norm Dynamics and Political Change. *International Organization* 52: 887–917.

Fleming, James R. 1998. *Historical Perspectives on Climate Change.* New York, NY: Oxford University Press.

Forelle, Charles. 2008. "French Firm Cashes in Under UN Warming Program." *The Wall Street Journal,* July 23. http://online.wsj.com/article/SB121677247656875573.html?mod=hps_us_pageone.

Forster, Piers *et al.* 2007. "Changes in Atmospheric Constituents and in Radiative Forcing." In *Climate Change 2007: The Physical Science Basis. Contribution of Working Group I to the Fourth Assessment Report of the Intergovernmental Panel on Climate Change,* eds. S. Solomon *et al.* Cambridge, UK and New York, NY: Cambridge University Press.

Franck, Thomas M. 1990. *The Power of Legitimacy Among Nations.* New York, NY: Oxford University Press.

Freeman, Jody and Charles D. Kolstad, eds. 2007. *Moving to Markets in Environmental Regulation: Lessons from Twenty Years of Experience.* Oxford University Press.

Freeman, Richard B. and John van Reenen. 2008. "Be Careful What You Wish For: A Cautionary Tale about Budget Doubling." *Issues in Science & Technology* (Fall): 27–31.

Frondel, M., N. Ritter, C. M. Schmidt, and C. Vance. 2010. "Economic Impacts from the Promotion of Renewable Energy Technologies: The German Experience." *Energy Policy* 38: 4048–56.

G8 Summit 2005. *The Gleneagles Communique.* Perthshire, Scotland, July 6–8.

2006. *Global Energy Security.* St. Petersburg, Russia, July 15–17.

2007. *Growth and Responsibility in the World Economy.* Heiligendamm, Germany, June 6–8.

2008. *G8 Hokkaido Toyako Summit Leaders Declaration.* Hokkaido Toyako, Japan, July 7–9.

2009. *Responsible Leadership for a Sustainable Future.* From La Maddalena to L'Aquila, Italy, July 8–10.

G8+5 National Academies of Science. 2008. *Joint Science Academies' Statement: Climate Change Adaptation and the Transition to a Low Carbon Society.* Hokkaido, Japan, June 10.

Goldemberg, José, S. Coelho, P. Nastari, and O. Lucon. 2004. "Ethanol Learning Curve – the Brazilian Experience." *Biomass and Bioenergy* 26(3): 301–4.

Goldin, Claudia D. and Frank D. Lewis. 1975. "The Economic Cost of the American Civil War: Estimates and Implications." *The Journal of Economic History* 35(2): 299–326.

Goldstein, Judith L., Miles Kahler, Robert O. Keohane, and Anne-Marie Slaughter, eds., 2001. *Legalization and World Politics.* Cambridge, MA: MIT Press.

Goodell, Jeff. 2010. *How to Cool the Planet: Geoengineering and the Audacious Quest to Fix Earth's Climate.* New York, NY: Houghton Mifflin Harcourt.

Goodman, Ryan and Derek Jinks. 2004. "How to Influence States: Socialization and International Human Rights Law." *Duke Law Journal* 54(3): 621–703.

2005. "International Law and State Socialization: Conceptual, Empirical, and Normative Challenges." *Duke Law Journal* 54 (February): 983–98.

Govindasamy, Bala and Ken Caldeira. 2000. "Geoengineering Earth's Radiation Balance to Mitigate CO_2-Induced Climate Change." *Geophysical Research Letters* 27(14): 2141–4.

Govindasamy, Bala, S. Thompson, P. Duffy, K. Caldeira, and C. Delire. 2002. "Impact of Geoengineering Schemes on the Terrestrial Biosphere." *Geophysical Research Letters* 29(22): 2061.

Griliches, Zvi. 1992. "The Search for R&D Spillovers." *Scandinavian Journal of Economics* 94: 29–47.

Gronewold, Nathanial. 2010. "Offsets: CDM Critics Demand Investigation of Suspect Offsets." *ClimateWire*, June 14. www.eenews.net/public/climatewire/2010/06/14/2.

Grübler, Arnulf. 2009. "An Assessment of the Costs of the French Nuclear PWR Program, 1970–2000." Interim Report IR-09–036. International Institute for Applied Systems Analysis, October.

Grübler, Arnulf, Nebojša Nakićenović, and A. McDonald, eds. 1998. *Global Energy Perspectives*. Cambridge University Press.

Gutierrez, Andrew P., Luigi Ponti, and Q. A. Cossu. 2009. "Effects of Climate Warming on Olive and Olive Fly (Bactrocera oleae (Gmelin)) in California and Italy." *Climatic Change* 95(1–2): 195–217.

Haas, Ernst B. 1958. *The Uniting of Europe: Political, Social and Economic Forces 1950–1957*. Stanford University Press.

Haas, Peter M. 1990. *Saving the Mediterranean: The Politics of International Environmental Cooperation*. New York, NY: Columbia University Press.

Hafner-Burton, Emilie M. 2008. "Sticks and Stones: Naming and Shaming the Human Rights Enforcement Problem." *International Organization* 62: 689–716.

Hafner-Burton, Emilie M. and James Ron. 2009. "Seeing Double: Human Rights Impact Through Qualitative and Quantitative Eyes." *World Politics* 61: 360–401.

Hall, Bronwyn H. 2002. "The Financing of Research and Development." *Oxford Review of Economic Policy* 18(1): 35–51.

Hansen, J. et al. 1981. "Climate Impact of Increasing Atmospheric Carbon Dioxide." *Science* 213(4511): 957–66.

2005. " Earth's Energy Imbalance: Confirmation and Implications." *Science* 308(5727): 1431–1435.

Hare, Bill and Malte Meinshausen. 2006. "How Much Warming Are We Committed to and How Much Can Be Avoided?" *Climate Change* 75(1–2): 111–49.

Harris, Richard. 2007. "Climate Roadmap Emerges from Grueling Bali Talks." *NPR*, December 15.

Hawyard, Steven F. *et al.* 2010. *Post Partisan Power: How a Limited and Direct Approach to Energy Innovation Can Deliver Clean, Cheap Energy, Economic Productivity and National Prosperity*. AEI, Brookings: Breakthrough Institute.

He, Gang and Richard K. Morse. 2010. "Making Carbon Offsets Work in the Developing World: Lessons from the Chinese Wind Controversy." Working Paper 90. Program on Energy and Sustainable Development, Stanford University, March.

Hecht, Alan D. and Dennis Tirpak. 1995. "Framework Agreement on Climate Change: A Scientific and Policy History." *Climatic Change* 29(4): 371–402.

Heileman, Leo I. 1993. "The Alliance of Small Island States (AOSIS): A Mechanism for Coordinated Representation of Small Island States on Issues of Common Concern." *Ambio* 22(1): 55–6.

Heller, Michael A. and Rebecca S. Eisenberg. 1998. "Can Patents Deter Innovation? The Anticommons in Biomedical Research." *Science* 280(5364): 698–701.

Hoffert, Martin I. *et al.* 1998. "Energy Implications of Future Stabilization of Atmospheric CO_2 Content." *Nature* 395: 881–4.

Holdren, John P. *et al.* 1999. (President's Committee of Advisors on Science and Technology, Panel of Energy Research and Development). *Powerful Partnerships: The Federal Role in International Cooperation on Energy Innovation – Letter to Neal Lane*. Washington DC: Report for Office of Science and Technology Policy, Executive Office of the President of the United States, May 24.

Horsch, Rob. 2009. "Partner's Perspective: Back to Basics." In *Global Recommitment to Agriculture – CGIAR Annual Report 2008*, 18. Washington DC: CGIAR Secretariat.

Horwitch, Mel. 1982. *Clipped Wings: The American SST Conflict*. Cambridge, MA: MIT Press.

House, Kurt Z., C. House, D. Schrag, and M. Aziz. 2007. "Electrochemical Acceleration of Chemical Weathering as an Energetically Feasible Approach to Mitigating Anthropogenic Climate Change." *Environmental Science & Technology* 41(24): 8464–70.

Hufbauer, Gary C., Steve Charnovitz, and Jisun Kim. 2009. *Global Warming and the World Trading System*. Washington DC: Peterson Institute for International Economics.

Hulme. Michael. 2009. *Why We Disagree About Climate Change: Understanding Controversy, Inaction and Opportunity*. Cambridge University Press.

Huntington, Hillard and Christine Jojarth. 2010. "Financing the Future: Investments in Alternative Sources of Energy." In *Global Energy Governance: The New Rules of the Game*, eds. Andreas Goldthau and Jan Martin Witte. Washington DC: Brookings Institution.

IEA (International Energy Agency). 2008a. *Energy Technology Perspectives 2008: Scenarios and Strategies to 2050*. Paris: OECD/IEA.

   2008b. *IEA Energy Policies Review: The European Union 2008*. Paris: OECD/IEA.

   2009a. *World Energy Outlook 2009*. Paris: OECD/IEA.

2009b. *Energy Technology Roadmaps: Status Report.* Paris: OECD/ IEA.

2009c. *Cleaner Coal in China.* Paris: OECD/IEA.

IPCC (Intergovernmental Panel on Climate Change). 1990. *Climate Change 1990: Scientific Assessment of Climate Change. Contribution of Working Group I to the First Assessment Report of the Intergovernmental Panel on Climate Change*, eds. J. Houghton, G. Jenkins, and J. Ephraums. Cambridge University Press.

2002. *Climate Change Information Kit.* Châtelaine, Switzerland: UNEP and UNFCCC.

2004. "Guidance Notes for Lead Authors of the IPCC Fourth Assessment Report on Addressing Uncertainties." From IPCC AR4 Workshops & Expert Meetings, May.

2007a. "Summary for Policymakers." In *Climate Change 2007: The Physical Science Basis. Contribution of Working Group I to the Fourth Assessment Report of the Intergovernmental Panel on Climate Change*, eds. S. Solomon *et al.*, 1–24. Cambridge, UK and New York, NY: Cambridge University Press.

2007b. *Climate Change 2007: Impacts, Adaptation and Vulnerability. Contribution of Working Group II to the Fourth Assessment Report of the Intergovernmental Panel on Climate Change*, eds. M. L. Parry, O. F. Canziani, J. P. Palutikof, P. J. van der Linden, and C. E. Hanson. Cambridge University Press.

Issues in Science & Technology. 1998. "From the Hill: Private Venture to Sequence Human Genome Launched." Fall.

Jaccard, Mark. 2005. *Sustainable Fossil Fuels: The Unusual Suspect in the Quest for Clean and Enduring Energy.* New York, NY: Cambridge University Press.

Jacobson, Harold K. and Eric Stein. 1966. *Diplomats, Scientists and Politicians: The United States and the Nuclear Test Ban Negotiations.* Ann Arbor, MI: University of Michigan Press.

Jacoby, Henry D., M. Babiker, S. Paltsev, and J. Reilly. 2009. "Sharing the Burden of GHG Reductions." In *Post-Kyoto International Climate Policy: Summary for Policymakers*, eds. Joseph E. Aldy and Robert N. Stavins. New York, NY: Cambridge University Press.

Jaffe, Adam, Steven Peterson, Paul Portney, and Robert Stavins. 1995. "Environmental Regulation and the Competitiveness of US Manufacturing." *Journal of Economic Literature* 33: 132–163.

James, Sallie. 2009. "A Harsh Climate for Trade: How Climate Change Proposals Threaten Global Commerce." Trade Policy Analysis No. 41. Center for Trade Policy Studies, CATO Institute, September 9.

Jiang, BinBin, Chen Wenying, Yu Yuefeng, Zeng Lemin, and David Victor. 2008. "The Future of Natural Gas Consumption in Beijing, Guangdong and Shanghai: An Assessment Utilizing MARKAL." *Energy Policy* 36: 3286–99.

Johansson, Thomas B. and José Goldemberg, eds. 2002. *Energy for Sustainable Development: A Policy Agenda.* New York, NY: UNDP, IIIEE, and IEI.

Jones, Charles I. and John C. Williams. 1997. "Measuring the Social Return to R&D." Finance and Economics Discussion Series 1997–12. Board of Governors of the Federal Reserve System.

Kahler, Miles. 1992. "Multilateralism with Small and Large Numbers." *International Organization* 46: 681–708.

Kandlikar, Milind, James Risbey, and Suraje Dessai. 2005. "Representing and Communicating Deep Uncertainty in Climate-Change Assessments." *Comptes Rendus Geosciences* 337(4): 443–55.

Karplus, Valerie. 2007. "Innovation in China's Energy Sector." Working Paper 61. Program on Energy and Sustainable Development, Stanford University, March.

Kaul, Inge, Isabelle Grunberg, and Marc Stern, eds. 1999. *Global Public Goods: International Cooperation in the 21st Century.* New York, NY: Oxford University Press.

Keck, Margaret E. and Kathryn Sikkink. 1998. *Activists Beyond Borders: Advocacy Networks in International Politics.* Ithaca, NY: Cornell University Press.

Keith, David W. 2000. "Geoengineering the Climate: History and Prospect." *Annual Review of Energy and the Environment* 25: 245–284.

2009. "Why Capture CO_2 from the Atmosphere?" *Science* 325(5948): 1654–55.

2010. "Engineering the Planet." In *Climate Change Science and Policy*, eds. Stephen Schneider and Michael Mastrandrea, 494–501. Washington DC: Island Press.

Kempf, Hervé. 2008. "Un dispositif incitatif du protocole de Kyoto mis en cause par des experts et par des ONG." *Le Monde*, May 27.

Keohane, Robert O. 1984. *After Hegemony: Cooperation and Discord in the World Political Economy.* Princeton University Press.

2007. "Thinking Inside the Box and Out: Multilateral Institutions and Climate Change." Paper adaptation of talk given at the Departmant of Politics and International Relations, Oxford University, December 3.

Keohane, Robert O. and Joseph S. Nye. 1977. *Power and Interdependence: World Politics in Transition.* New York, NY: Little, Brown, and Company.

2001. "The Club Model of Multilateral Cooperation and Problems of Democratic Legitimacy." In *Efficiency, Equity, and Legitimacy: The*

Multilateral Trading System at the Millennium, eds. Robert B. Porter, Pierre Sauvé, Arvind Subramanian, and Americo Beviglia Zampetti. Washington DC: Brookings Institution.

Keohane, Robert O. and Kal Raustiala. 2009. "Toward a Post-Kyoto Climate Change Architecture: A Political Analysis." In *Post-Kyoto International Climate Policy: Implementing Architectures for Agreement*, eds. Joseph E. Aldy and Robert N. Stavins, 372–99. Cambridge University Press.

Keohane, Robert O. and David G. Victor. in press. "The Regime Complex for Climate Change." *Perspectives on Politics*.

Kintisch, Eli. 2008. "California Emissions Plan to Explore Use of Offsets." *Science* 321(5885): 23.

Klette, Tor Jakob, Jarle Møen, and Zvi Griliches. 2000. "Do Subsidies to Commercial R&D Reduce Market Failures? Microeconometric Evaluation Studies." *Research Policy* 29(4–5): 471–95.

Koh, Harold Hongju. 1997. "Why Do Nations Obey International Law?" *Yale Law Journal* 106(8): 2599–659.

Koremenos, Barbara, Charles Lipson, and Duncan Snidal, eds. 2003. *The Rational Design of International Institutions*. New York, NY: Cambridge University Press.

Koremenos, Barbara. 2005. "Contracting Around International Uncertainty." *American Political Science Review* 99: 549–65.

Kossoy, Alexandre and Philippe Ambrosi. 2010. *State and Trends of the Carbon Market 2010*. Washington DC: The World Bank.

Kremer, Michael. 1998. "Patent Buyouts: A Mechanism for Encouraging Innovation." *The Quarterly Journal of Economics* 113(4): 1137–67.

Kucik, Jeffrey and Eric Reinhardt. 2008. "Does Flexibility Promote Cooperation? An Application to the Global Trade Regime." *International Organization* 62 (Summer): 477–505.

Kuhn, Thomas. 1962. *The Structure of Scientific Revolutions*. University of Chicago Press.

Kumar, K. S. Kavi, P. Shyamsundar, and A. Arivudai Nambi. 2010. "Economics of Climate Change Adaptation in India." *Economic and Political Weekly* 45(18): 25–30.

Kurz, W. A. *et al.* 2008. "Mountain Pine Beetle and Forest Carbon Feedback to Climate Change." *Nature* 452: 987–90.

Landes, David S. 1999. *The Wealth and Poverty of Nations: Why Some Are So Rich and Some So Poor*. New York, NY: Norton & Co.

Lane, Lee *et al.*, eds. 2006. "The Ames/Carnegie Solar Radiation Management Workshop: Goals and Background." Report from Workshop at Ames Research Center. NASA and Carnegie Institution of Washington, Dept. of Global Ecology, November.

Ledford, Heidi. 2010. "Malaria May Not Rise as World Warms." *Nature* 465: 280–1.

Leggett, Jane A. and Jeffrey Logan. 2008. *CRS Report for Congress: China's Greenhouse Gas Emissions and Mitigation Policies*. Washington DC: Congressional Research Service, September 10.

Lenton, T. M. and N. E. Vaughan. 2009. "The Radiative Forcing Potential of Different Climate Geoengineering Options." *Atmospheric Chemistry and Physics* 9: 5539–61.

Levi, Micheal A. *et al.* 2010. *Energy Innovation: Driving Technology Competition and Cooperation Among the US, China, India and Brazil*. New York: Council on Foreign Relations.

Levitt, Steven D. and Stephen J. Dubner. 2009. *SuperFreakonomics: Global Cooling, Patriotic Prostitutes, and Why Suicide Bombers Should Buy Life Insurance*. New York, NY: HarperCollins.

Levy, Marc. 1993. "European Acid Rain: The Power of Tote-Board Diplomacy." In *Institutions for the Earth: Sources of Effective International Environmental Protection*, eds. Peter M. Haas, Robert O. Keohane, and Marc A. Levy, 75–132. Cambridge, MA: MIT Press.

Liepert, Beate, J. Feichter, U. Lohmann, and E. Roeckner. 2004. "Can Aerosols Spin Down the Water Cycle in a Warmer and Moister World?" *Geophysical Research Letters* 31: L06207.

Lovins, Amory B., E. Datta, O. Bustnes, J. Koomey, and N. Glasgow. 2004. *Winning the Oil Endgame*. Snowmass, CO: Rocky Mountain Institute.

Low, Patrick, ed. 1992. *International Trade and the Environment, World Bank Discussion Papers No. 159*. Washington DC: The World Bank.

Manne, Alan A. and Richard Richels. 1992. *Buying Greenhouse Insurance: The Economic Costs of CO_2 Emission Limits*. Cambridge, MA: MIT Press.

Marcoux, Christopher. 2009. "Institutional Flexibility in the Design of Multilateral Environmental Agreements." *Conflict Management and Peace Science* 26(2): 209–28.

Margolis, Robert M. and Daniel M. Kammen. 1999a. "Evidence of Under-Investment in Energy R&D in the United States and the Impact of Federal Policy." *Energy Policy* 27: 575–84.

1999b. "Underinvestment: The Energy Technology and R&D Policy Challenge." *Science* 285(5428): 690–2.

Martin, John H. 1990. "Glacial-Interglacial CO_2 Change: The Iron Hypothesis." *Paleoceanography* 5(1): 1–13.

Martin, Paul. 2005. "A Global Answer to Global Problems." *Foreign Affairs* 84(3) (May/June).

Matthews, H. Damon and Ken Caldeira. 2007. "Transient Climate-Carbon Simulations of Planetary Geoengineering." *PNAS* 104(24): 9949–54.

Mattli, Walter and Ngaire Woods, eds. *The Politics of Global Regulation.* Princeton University Press.

McDougall, Walter A. 1997. *The Heavens and the Earth: A Political History of the Space Age.* Baltimore, MD: Johns Hopkins University Press.

McGray, Heather, Anne Hammill, Rob Bradley, E. Lisa Schipper, and Jo-Ellen Parry. 2007. *Weathering the Storm: Options for Framing Adaptation and Development.* Washington DC: World Resources Institute.

McKibben, Bill. 1989. *The End of Nature.* New York: Random House.

McLaughlin, John F., J. Hellmann, C. Boggs, and P. Ehrlich. 2002. "Climate Change Hastens Population Extinctions." *PNAS* 99(9): 6070–4.

McMahon, Vanessa. 1993. "Environmental Nongovernmental Organizations at Intergovernmental Negotiations." In *Papers on International Environmental Negotiation*, vol III, eds. William R. Moomaw, Lawrence E. Susskind, and Adil Najam. Cambridge, MA: PON Books.

Meehl, Gerald A. *et al.* 2007. "Global Climate Projections." In *Climate Change 2007: The Physical Science Basis. Contribution of Working Group I to the Fourth Assessment Report of the Intergovernmental Panel on Climate Change*, eds. S. Solomon *et al.* Cambridge, UK and New York, NY: Cambridge University Press.

Meinshausen, Malte *et al.* 2009. "Greenhouse-Gas Emission Targets for Limiting Global Warming to 2°C." *Nature* 458: 1158–1162.

Mercer, J. H. 1978. "West Antarctic Ice Sheet and CO_2 Greenhouse Effect: A Threat of Disaster." *Nature* 271: 321–5.

Meyer, Aubrey. 2001. *Contraction & Convergence: The Global Solution to Climate Change.* Foxhole, UK: Green Books.

Michalopoulos, Constantine. 2002. "WTO Accession." In *Development, Trade, and the WTO: A Handbook*, eds. Bernard Hoekman, Aaditya Mattoo, and Philip English. Washington DC: The World Bank.

Milford, Lewis and Jessica Morey. 2009. *Climate Crash Course for Copenhagen: The Six Simple Reasons Why We Need Global Technology Collaboration.* Montpelier, VT: Clean Energy Group, December 6.

Ministerial Conference on Atmospheric Pollution and Climatic Change. 1989. *The Noordwijk Declaration on Climate Change: Atmospheric Pollution and Climatic Change.* Ministerial Conference held at Noordwijk, The Netherlands, November 6–7. Leidschendam, The Netherlands: Climate Conference Secretariat.

Mishra, Bibhu R. 2009. "India to Set Up Hub on Climate Studies." *Business Standard*, October 19. www.business-standard.com/india/news/india-to-sethubclimate-studies/373636/.

Misquitta, Sonya and Geeta Anand. 2009. "India Hopes for Rain, and an Accurate Forecast." *The Wall Street Journal*, August 13. http://online.wsj.com/article/SB125002552576623777.html.

Mitchell, Ronald B. 1994. "Regime Design Matters: Intentional Oil Pollution and Treaty Compliance." *International Organization* 48(3): 425–58.

Mitchell, Ronald B., W. Clark, D. Cash, and N. Dickson, eds. 2006. *Global Environmental Assessments: Information and Influence*. Cambridge, MA: MIT Press.

Mohan, Jacqueline E. *et al.* 2006. "Biomass and Toxity Responses of Poison Ivy (*Toxicodendron radicans*) to Elevated Atmospheric CO_2." *PNAS* 103(24): 9086–89.

Mokyr, Joel. 2002. "Innovation in an Historical Perspective: Tales of Technology and Evolution." In *Technological Innovation & Economic Performance*, eds. Benn Steil, David G. Victor, and Richard R. Nelson. Princeton University Press.

Moran, Michael. 2002. "Review Article: Understanding the Regulatory State." *British Journal of Political Science* 32: 391–413.

Moravcsik, Andrew. 1998. *The Choice for Europe: Social Purpose and State Power from Messina to Maastricht*. Ithaca, NY: Cornell University Press.

Morgan, M. Granger and Max Henrion. 1990. *Uncertainty: A Guide to Dealing with Uncertainty in Quantitative Risk and Policy Analysis*. Cambridge University Press.

Morgan, M. Granger and Susan F. Tierney. 1998. "Research Support for the Power Industry." *Issues in Science and Technology* 15(1): 81–87.

Morgan, M. Granger, Peter J. Adams, and David W. Keith. 2006. "Elicitation of Expert Judgments of Aerosol Forcing." *Climatic Change* 75(1–2): 195–214.

Morris, Michael G. and Edwin D. Hill. 2007. "Trade is the Key to Climate Change." *The Energy Daily*, February 20.

Moser, Susan, G. Franco, S. Pittiglio, W. Chou, and D. Cayan. 2009. *The Future is Now: An Update on Climate Change Science Impacts and Response Options for California*. California Energy Commission, PIER Energy-Related Environmental Research Program. CEC-500–2008–071.

Moses, Hamilton, E. Ray Dorsey, David H. M. Matheson, and Samuel O. Thier. 2005. "Financial Anatomy of Biomedical Research." *Journal of the American Medical Association* 294(11): 1333–42.

Mowery, David C., Richard R. Nelson, and Ben Martin. 2009. *Technology Policy and Global Warming*. London: National Endowment for Science, Technology and the Arts.

Mowery, David C., Richard R. Nelson, B. Sampat, and A. Ziedonis. 2004. *Ivory Tower and Industrial Innovation: University-Industry Technology Transfer Before and After the Bayh–Dole Act*. Stanford University Press.

Multilateral Fund for the Implementation of the Montreal Protocol. "Achievements." Multilateral Fund website. www.multilateralfund.org/achievements.htm.

Naik, Vaishali, D. Wuebbles, E. Delucia, and J. Foley. 2003. "Influence of Geoengineered Climate on the Terrestrial Biosphere." *Environmental Management* 32(3): 373–81.

Nalebuff, Barry J. and Joseph E. Stiglitz. 1983. "Prices and Incentives: Towards a General Theory of Compensation and Competition." *Bell Journal of Economics* 14(1): 21–43.

National Academy of Sciences, National Academy of Engineering, and Institute of Medicine of The National Academies. 1992. *Policy Implications of Greenhouse Warming: Mitigation, Adaptation, and the Science Base*. Washington DC: National Academies Press.

2007. *Rising Above the Gathering Storm: Energizing and Employing America for a Brighter Economic Future*. Washington DC: National Academics Press.

National Research Council of The National Academies. 1999. *Funding a Revolution: Government Support for Computing Research*. Washington DC: National Academies Press.

2001. *Review of the Research Program of the Partnership for a New Generation of Vehicles, Seventh Report*. Washington DC: National Academies Press.

2004. *Accelerating Technology Transition: Bridging the Valley of Death for Materials and Processes in Defense Systems*. Washington DC: National Academies Press.

2007. *Analysis of Global Change Assessments: Lessons Learned*. Washington DC: National Academies Press.

2010a. *Adapting to the Impacts of Climate Change*. Report in a series of five reports in *America's Climate Choices*. Washington DC: National Academies Press.

2010b. *Advancing the Science of Climate Change*. Report in a series of five reports in *America's Climate Choices*. Washington DC: National Academies Press.

2010c. *Limiting the Magnitude of Future Climate Change*. Report in a series of five reports in *America's Climate Choices*. Washington DC: National Academies Press.

National Science Board. 2008. *Science and Engineering Indicators 2008.* 2 volumes. Arlington, VA: National Science Foundation, vol. I, NSB 08–01, vol. II, NSB 08–01A.

National Science Foundation, Division of Science Resources Statistics. 2008. *National Patterns of R&D Resources: 2007 Data Update.* Arlington, VA: National Science Foundation, NSF 08–318.

NERC (North American Electric Reliability Corporation). 2008. *Special Report: Electric Industry Concerns on the Reliability Impacts of Climate Change Initiatives.* Princeton, NJ: NERC, November.

Newell, Richard G. 2008. "A US Innovation Strategy for Climate Change Mitigation." Discussion Paper. The Hamilton Project, December.

Newell, Richard G. and William A. Pizer. 2003. "Regulating Stock Externalities Under Uncertainty." *Journal of Environmental Economics and Management* 45(2) Supplement 1: 416–32.

Newell, Richard G. and Nathan E. Wilson. 2005. "Technology Prizes for Climate Change Mitigation." Discussion Paper RFF DP 05–33. Resources for the Future, June.

Nordhaus, William D. 2009. "The Perils of the Learning Model for Modeling Endogenous Technological Change." Cowles Foundation Discussion Paper 1685.

    2010. "Economic Aspects of Global Warming in a Post-Copenhagen Environment." *PNAS* 107(24): doi: 10.1073/pnas.1005985107.

OECD. 2003. *OECD Investment Policy Reviews – China: Progress and Reform Challenges.* Paris: OECD.

    2007. *OECD Reviews of Innovation Policy: China, Synthesis Report.* Paris: OECD.

    2008. *Compendium of Patent Statistics 2008.* Paris: OECD.

Ogden, Peter, John Podesta, and John Deutch. 2008. "A New Strategy to Spur Energy Innovation." *Issues in Science & Technology* (Winter): 35–44.

Olson, Mancur. 1965. *The Logic of Collective Action: Public Goods and the Theory of Groups.* Cambridge, MA: Harvard University Press.

Oman, Luke, A. Robock, G. Stenchikov, G. Schmidt, and R. Ruedy. 2005. "Climatic Response to High-Latitude Volcanic Eruptions." *Journal of Geophysical Research* 110: D13103.

Oman, Luke, A. Robock, G. Stenchikov, and T. Thordarson. 2006. "High-Latitude Eruptions Cast Shadow Over the African Monsoon and the Flow of the Nile." *Geophysical Research Letters* 33: L18711.

Oppenheimer, Michael. 1998. "Global Warming and the Stability of the West Antarctic Ice Sheet." *Nature* 393: 325–32.

Oppenheimer, Michael, B. O'Neill, M. Webster, and S. Agrawala. 2007. "Climate Change: The Limits of Consensus." *Science* 317(5844): 1505–6.

Osnos, Evan. 2009. "Green Giant: Beijing's Crash Program for Clean Energy." *The New Yorker,* December 21. www.newyorker.com/reporting/2009/12/21/091221fa_fact_osnos.

Oye, Kenneth A. and James H. Maxwell. 1994. "Self-Interest and Environmental Management." *Journal of Theoretical Politics* 6(4): 593–624.

Paarlberg, Robert. 2008. *Starved for Science: How Biotechnology is Being Kept Out of Africa.* Cambridge, MA: Harvard University Press.

Pacala, Stephen and Robert Socolow. 2004. "Stabilization Wedges: Solving the Climate Problem for the Next 50 Years with Current Technologies." *Science* 305(5686): 968–72.

Page, Susan E., F. Siegert, J. Rieley, H. Boehm, A. Jaya, and S. Limin. 2002. "The Amount of Carbon Released from Peat and Forest Fires in Indonesia during 1997." *Nature* 420: 61–5.

Paltsev, Sergey, John M. Reilly, Henry D. Jacoby, and Jennifer F. Morris. 2009. *The Cost of Climate Policy in the United States.* Report 173. Cambridge, MA: MIT Joint Program on the Science and Policy of Global Change, April.

Pardey, Philip G. and Julian M. Alston. 2010. *US Agricultural Research in a Global Food Security Setting: A Report of the CSIS Task Force on Food Security.* Washington DC: Center for Strategic and International Studies.

Parry, Martin L. 1990. *Climate Change and World Agriculture.* London: Earthscan.

Parson, Edward A. 1993. "Protecting the Ozone Layer." In *Institutions for the Earth: Sources of Effective International Environmental Protection,* eds. Peter M. Haas, Robert O. Keohane, and Marc A. Levy, 27–74. Cambridge, MA: MIT Press.

  2003. *Protecting the Ozone Layer: Science and Strategy.* New York, NY: Oxford University Press.

Pataki, George E. and Thomas J. Vilsack. 2008. *Confronting Climate Change: A Strategy for US Foreign Policy.* Independent Task Force Report No. 61. New York, NY: Council on Foreign Relations.

Patt, Anthony G. *et al.* 2010. "Estimating Least-Developed Countries' Vulnerability to Climate-Related Extreme Events Over the Next 50 Years." *PNAS* 107(4): 1333–7.

Pearson, Anna and Bryony Worthington. 2010. "Cap or Trap? How the EU ETS Risks Locking-in Carbon Emissions." London: Sandbag, September. http://sandbag.org.uk/files/sandbag.org.uk/caportrap.pdf

Pielke Jr., Roger, G. Prins, S. Rayner, and D. Sarewitz. 2007. "Climate Change 2007: Lifting the Taboo on Adaptation." *Nature* 455: 597–8.

Pisano, Gary P. 2002. "Pharmaceutical Biotechnology." In *Technological Innovation and Economic Performance*, eds. Ben Steil, David G. Victor, Richard R. Nelson. Princeton University Press.

Pizer, William. 1998. *Price vs. Quantities Revisited: The Case of Climate Change*. Discussion Paper 90–02. Resources for the Future, October.
    2002. "Combining Price and Quantity Controls to Mitigate Global Climate Change." *Journal of Public Economics* 85(3): 409–34.

Pollack, Mark A. and Gregory C. Shaffer. 2009. *When Cooperation Fails: The International Law and Politics of Genetically Modified Foods*. New York, NY: Oxford University Press.

Price, Victoria. 2007. "GATT's New Trade Policy Review Mechanism." *The World Economy* 14: 227–38.

Prins, G. and Rayner, S. 2007. *The Wrong Trousers: Radically Rethinking Climate Policy*. Joint Working Paper. James Martin Institute for Science and Civilization, University of Oxford and Mackinder Centre for the Study of Long-Wave Events, London School of Economics.

Rai, Varun and David G. Victor. 2009. "Climate Change and the Energy Challenge: A Pragmatic Approach for India." *Economic & Political Weekly* 44(31): 78–85.

Rai, Varun, David G. Victor, and M. Thurber. 2009, "Carbon Capture and Storage at Scale: Lessons from the Growth of Analogous Energy Technologies," Stanford Program on Energy and Sustainable Development, Working Paper 81.

Rai, Varun, N. Chung, M. Thurber, and David G. Victor. 2008. "PESD Carbon Storage Project Database." Working Paper 76. Program on Energy and Sustainable Development, Stanford University, November.

Ramanathan, Veerabhadran. 1988. "The Greenhouse Theory of Climate Change: A Test by an Inadvertent Global Experiment." *Science* 240(4850): 293–9.

Ramanathan, Veerabhadran and Yangyang Xu. 2010. "The Copenhagen Accord for Limiting Global Warming: Criteria, Constraints and Available Avenues." *PNAS* 107(18): 8055–62.

Ramanathan, Veerabhadran *et al.* 2007. "Warming Trends in Asia Amplified by Brown Cloud Solar Absorption." *Nature* 448: 575–578.

Raustiala, Kal. 2005. "Form and Substance in International Agreements." *American Journal of International Law* 99(3): 581–614.

Raustiala, Kal and David G. Victor. 2004. "The Regime Complex for Plant Genetic Resources." *International Organization* 58(2): 277–309.

Rawls, John. 1971. *A Theory of Justice*. Cambridge, MA: Harvard University Press.

Revelle, Roger. 1983. "Probable Future Changes in Sea Level Resulting from Increased Atmospheric Carbon Dioxide." In *Changing Climate*, ed. National Research Council Carbon Dioxide Assessment Committee, 433–48. Washington, DC: National Academy of Sciences.

Revelle, Roger and Hans E. Suess. 1957. "Carbon Dioxide Exchange between Atmosphere and Ocean and the Question of an Increase of Atmospheric CO_2 During the Past Decades." *Tellus* 9: 18–27.

Richardson, David M. *et al.* 2009. "Multidimensional Evaluation of Managed Relocation." *PNAS* 106(24): 9721–4.

Ricke, Katharine, M. Morgan, J. Apt, D. Victor, and J. Steinbruner. 2008. "Unilateral Geoengineering." Briefing notes for a workshop at the Council on Foreign Relations, Washington DC, May 5.

Riddell, Lindsay. 2008. "Climos Aims to Profit from Hungry Plankton." *San Francisco Business Times*, April 25.

Roberts, Marc J. and Michael Spence. 1976. "Effluent Charges and Licenses Under Uncertainty." *Journal of Public Economics* 5(3–4): 193–208.

Robock, Alan, Allison Marquardt, Ben Kravitz, and Georgiy Stenchikov. 2009. "Benefits, Risks and Costs of Stratospheric Geoengineering." *Geophysical Research Letters* 36: L19703.

Rogelj, Joeri *et al.* 2010. "Copenhagen Accord Pledges are Paltry." *Nature* 464: 1126–1128.

Roginko, Alexei. 1998. "Domestic Implementation of Baltic Sea Pollution Commitments in Russia and the Baltic States." In *The Implementation and Effectiveness of International Environmental Commitments: Theory and Practice*, eds. D. Victor, K. Raustiala, and E. Skolnikoff. Cambridge, MA: MIT Press.

Root, Terry L. and Stephen H. Schneider. 2006. "Conservation and Climate Change: The Challenges Ahead." *Conservation Biology* 20(3): 706–708.

Rosen, Daniel H. and Trevor Houser. 2007. *China Energy: A Guide for the Perplexed*. Center for Strategic and International Studies. Washington DC: Peterson Institute for International Economics, May.

Rosenberg, Norman J., ed. 1993. *Towards an Integrated Impact Assessment of Climate Change: The MINK study*. Dordrecht, The Netherlands: Kluwer Academic Publishers, reprinted from *Climatic Change* 24(1–2): 1–173.

Rosenberg, Norman J. and Pierre R. Crosson. 1991. *Processes for Identifying Regional Influences of and Responses to Increasing Atmospheric CO_2 and Climate Change: The MINK Project – An Overview*. Prepared for US Dept. of Energy. Washington, DC: Resources for the Future, DOE/RL/01830T-H5.

Rosendorff, B. Peter and Helen Milner. 2001. "The Optimal Design of International Institutions: Uncertainty and Escape." *International Organization* 55(4): 829–57.

Rosenzweig, Cynthia, Ana Iglesias, X. B. Yang, Paul R. Epstein, and Eric Chivian. 2000. *Climate Change and US Agriculture: The Impacts of Warming and Extreme Weather Events on Productivity, Plant Diseases, and Pests*. Boston, MA: Center for Health and the Global Environment, Harvard Medical School.

Ruttan, Vernon W. 2001. *Technology, Growth, and Development: An Induced Innovation Perspective*. New York, NY: Oxford University Press.

Sagar, Ambuj D. and Bob van der Zwaan. 2006. "Technological Innovation in the Energy Sector: R&D, Deployment, and Learning-by-Doing." *Energy Policy* 34(17): 2601–8.

Sanghi, Apurva and Robert Mendelsohn. 2008. "The Impacts of Global Warming on Farmers in Brazil and India." *Global Environmental Change* 18(4): 655–65.

SCEP. 1970. *Man's Impact on the Global Climate: Assessment and Recommendations for Action. Report of the Study of Critical Environmental Problem (SCEP)*. Cambridge, MA: MIT Press, 319.

Schelling, Thomas C. 1983. "Climatic Change: Implications for Welfare and Policy." In *Changing Climate*, ed. National Research Council Carbon Dioxide Assessment Committee, 449–482. Washington, DC: National Academy of Sciences.

   1992. "Some Economics of Global Warming." *The American Economic Review* 82(1): 1–14.

   1996. "The Economic Diplomacy of Geoengineering." *Climatic Change* 33(3): 303–307.

   2006. "What Makes Greenhouse Sense?" In *Strategies of Commitment and Other Essays*, 27–44. Cambridge, MA: Harvard University Press.

Schneider, Lambert. 2007. *Is the CDM fulfilling its Environmental and Sustainable Development Objectives? An Evaluation of the CDM and Options for Improvement*. Report prepared for WWF. Berlin, Germany: Öko-Institut, November 5.

Schneider, Stephen H. 2002. "Modeling Climate Change Impacts and Their Related Uncertainties." In *What the Future Holds: Insights from Social Science*, eds. Richard N. Cooper, and Richard Layard. Cambridge, MA: MIT Press.

Schneider, Stephen H., B. L. Turner, and Holly M. Garriga. 1998. "Imaginable Surprise in Global Change Science." *Journal of Risk Research* 1(2): 165–85.

Seabright, Paul. 2005. *The Company of Strangers: A Natural History of Economic Life.* Princeton University Press.

Sebenius, James K. 1984. *Negotiating the Law of the Sea.* Cambridge, MA: Harvard University Press.

Seres, Stephen. 2008. *Analysis of Technology Transfer in CDM Projects.* Report prepared for the UNFCCC, Registration & Issuance Unit CDM/SDM, December.

Service, Robert F. 2007. "Delta Blues, California Style." *Science* 317: 442–5.

Shapiro, Carl. 2001. "Navigating the Patent Thicket: Cross Licenses, Patent Pools, and Standard Setting." In *Innovation Policy and the Economy, Volume 1,* eds. Adam Jaffe, Josh Lerner, and Scott Stern. Cambridge, MA: MIT Press.

Shellenberger, Michael, T. Nordhaus, J. Navin, T. Norris, and A. Van Noppen. 2008. "Fast, Clean & Cheap: Cutting Global Warming's Gordian Knot." *Harvard Law & Policy Review* 2(1): 93–118.

Simmons, Beth A. 2009. *Mobilizing for Human Rights: International Law in Domestic Politics.* Cambridge University Press.

Singer, Peter. 2002. *One World: The Ethics of Globalization.* New Haven, CT: Yale University Press.

Singh, M. 2008. "Opening address by Dr. Manmohan Singh, Prime Minister of India, At the Plenary Session-I of India-Africa Forum Summit Vigyan Bhawan, New Delhi." Speech presented at the India-Africa Forum Summit, New Delhi, India. April 8. http://mea.gov.in/indiaafricasummit/mystart.htm.

Skjærseth, J. B. 1998. "The Making and Implementation of North Sea Commitments: The Politics of Environmental Participation." In *The Implementation and Effectiveness of International Environmental Commitments: Theory and Practice,* eds. D. Victor, K. Raustiala, and E. Skolnikoff. Cambridge, MA: MIT Press.

Slaughter, Anne-Marie. 2004. *A New World Order.* Princeton University Press.

SMIC. 1971. *Inadvertent Climate Modification. Report of the Study of Man's Impact on Climate (SMIC).* Cambridge, MA: MIT Press, 308.

Sobel, Dava. 1995. *Longitude: The True Story of a Lone Genius Who Solved the Greatest Scientific Problem of His Time.* New York, NY: Penguin Books.

Social Learning Group, W. Clark, J. Jaeger, J. van Eijndhoven, and N. Dickson. 2001. *Learning to Manage Global Environmental Risks – Vol. 2: A Functional Analysis of Social Responses to Climate Change, Ozone Depletion, and Acid Rain.* Cambridge, MA: MIT Press.

Solomon, Steven. 2010. *Water: The Epic Struggle for Wealth, Power, and Civilization*. New York, NY: HarperCollins.

Specker, Steven. 2009. "The Challenge of Sustaining the Law of Constant Real Electricity Prices." *EPRI Journal* (Spring): 2–3.

Sperling, Daniel. 2001. "Public-Private Technology R&D Partnerships: Lessons from US Partnership for a New Generation of Vehicles." *Transport Policy* 8(4): 247–56.

Stanhill, Gerald and Shabtai Cohen. 2001. "Global Dimming: A Review of the Evidence for a Widespread and Significant Reduction in Global Radiation with Discussion of its Probable Causes and Possible Agricultural Consequences." *Agricultural and Forest Meteorology* 107(4): 255–78.

Steinberg, Richard H. 2004. "Judicial Lawmaking at the WTO: Discursive, Constitutional and Political Constraints." *American Journal of International Law* 98: 247–275.

Stern, Nicholas. 2007. *The Economics of Climate Change: The Stern Review*. Cambridge, UK and New York, NY: Cambridge University Press.

Stern, Todd and William Antholis. 2007. "Climate Change: Creating an E8." *Brookings*, January 1. www.brookings.edu/articles/2007/01energy_stern.aspx.

Stigler, George J. 1971. "The Theory of Economic Regulation." *Bell Journal of Economics* 2(1): 3–21.

Stokes, Donald E. 1997. *Pasteur's Quadrant: Basic Science and Technological Innovation*. Washington DC: Brookings Institution.

Swanson, Burton E. 2008. *Global Review of Good Agricultural Extension and Advisory Service Practices*. Rome, Italy: Food and Agriculture Organization of the United Nations.

Swanson, Burton E., Robert P. Bentz, and Andrew J. Sofranko, eds. 1997. *Improving Agricultural Extension: A Reference Manual*. Rome, Italy: Food and Agriculture Organization of the United Nations.

Tacconi, Luca, Frank Jotzo, and R. Quentin Grafton. 2008. "Local Causes, Regional Co-operation and Global Financing for Environmental Problems: The Case of Southeast Asian Haze Pollution." *International Environmental Agreements* 8(1): 1–16.

TEAP (Technology and Economic Assessment Panel). Various years. *TEAP Annual Progress Report*. http://ozone.unep.org/teap/Reports/TEAP_Reports/.

Teller, Edward, Lowell Wood, and Roderick Hyde. 1997. *Global Warming and Ice Ages: I. Prospects for Physics-Based Modulation of Global Change*. Prepared for submittal to the 22nd International Seminar on Planetary Emergencies, UCRL-JC-128715. Lawrence Livermore National Laboratory, August 15.

Teller, Edward, Roderick Hyde, and Lowell Wood. 2002. *Active Climate Stabilization: Practical Physics-Based Approaches to Prevention of Climate Change*. Submitted to the National Academy of Engineering Symposium, UCRL JC 148012. Lawrence Livermore National Laboratory, April 18.

The Breakthrough Institute. 2009. *Case Studies in American Innovation: A New look at Government Involvement in Technological Development.*

The Hague. 1989. *Hague Declaration on the Environment, 1989.* Declaration of the Hague, March 11.

The Royal Society. 2009a. *Geoengineering the Climate: Science, Governance, and Uncertainty.* London: The Royal Society.

　2009b. *Science Policy Centre: 2010 and Beyond.* London: The Royal Society.

Thompson, J. Michael T. and Brian Launder, eds. 2010. *Geo-Engineering Climate Change: Environmental Necessity or Pandora's Box?* Cambridge University Press.

Tóth, Ferenc L. ed. 1999. *Fair Weather? Equity Concerns in Climate Change.* London: Earthscan.

Trenberth, Kevin E. and Aiguo Dai. 2007. "Effects of Mount Pinatubo Volcanic Eruption on the Hydrologic Cycle as an Analog of Geo-engineering." *Geophyscial Research Letters* 34: L15702.

Trenberth, Kevin E. *et al.* 2007. "Observations: Surface and Atmospheric Climate Change." In *Climate Change 2007: The Physical Science Basis. Contribution of Working Group I to the Fourth Assessment Report of the Intergovernmental Panel on Climate Change*, eds. S. Solomon *et al.* Cambridge, UK and New York, NY: Cambridge University Press.

Underdal, Arild. 1980. *The Politics of International Fisheries Managements: The Case of the Northeast Atlantic.* New York, NY: Columbia University Press.

UNEP (United Nations Environment Programme). 2009. *Report of the Executive Committee of the Multilateral Fund for the Implementation of the Montreal Protocol to the Twenty-First Meeting of the Parties.* UNEP/OzL.Pro.21/6. Port Ghalib, Egypt, UNEP, November 4–8.

UNESCO (United Nations Educational, Scientific and Cultural Organization). 2005. *UNESCO Science Report 2005.* Paris: UNESCO.

UN FAO (United Nations Food and Agriculture Organization). 2005. "Extent of Forest Resources." In *Global Forest Resources Assessment 2005: Progress Towards Sustainable Forest Management.* FAO Forestry Paper 147: Rome, Italy: United Nations, 11–36.

UNFCCC (United Nations Framework Convention on Climate Change). 1992. *United Nations Framework Convention on Climate Change.* FCCC/Informal/84, United Nations.

1995. 1st Session. *Report of the Conference of the Parties on its First Session, held at Berlin from 28 March to 7 April 1995*. Berlin, Germany, June 6, FCCC/CP/1995/7/Add.1.

1998. *Kyoto Protocol to the United Nations Framework Convention on Climate Change*. United Nations.

2008. 13th Session. *Report of the Conference of the Parties on its thirteenth session, held in Bali from 3 to 15 December 2007, Part Two: Action taken by the Conference of the Parties at its thirteenth session*. Bali, Indonesia, March 14, FCCC/CP/2007/6/Add.1.

2009a. 8th Session. *A Proposal for Amendments to the Kyoto Protocol Pursuant to its Article 3, Paragraph 9*. Bonn, Germany, May 14, FCCC/KP/AWG/2009/7.

2009b. 8th Session. *A Text on Other Issues Outlined in Document FCCC/KP/AWG/2008/8*. Bonn, Germany, May 14, FCCC/KP/AWG/2009/8.

2009c. 6th Session. *Negotiating Text*. Bonn, Germany, May 19, FCCC/AWGLCA/2009/8.

2010a. 15th Session. *Report of the Conference of the Parties on its fifteenth session, held in Copenhagen from 7 to 19 December 2009 – Decision 2/CP.15 Copenhagen Accord*. Copenhagen, Denmark, March 30, FCCC/CP/2009/11/Add.1.

2010b. "National Inventory Submissions 2010." Annex I Party GHG Inventory Submissions. UNFCCC website. http://unfccc.int/national_reports/items/1408.php.

United Nations Department of Public Information. 1997. "Earth Summit+5, Special Session of the General Assembly to Review and Appraise the Implementation of Agenda 21, New York, June 23–27, 1997: Backgrounder." United Nations website. www.un.org/ecosocdev/geninfo/sustdev/es&5sust.htm.

United Nations General Assembly. 1988. 70th plenary meeting. *Protection of Global Climate for Present and Future Generations of Mankind*. A/RES/43/53, December 6.

1990. 71st plenary meeting. *Protection of Global Climate for Present and Future Generations of Mankind*. A/RES/45/212, December 21.

US Congress. 2009. *American Clean Energy and Security Act of 2009*. H. R. 2454. 111th Congress, 1st sess., June 26.

US Department of Labor, Bureau of Labor Statistics. 2009. "Employment Projections: Employment by Major Industry Sector." Table 2.1. December 10.

US EPA (Environmental Protection Agency). 1988. *Future Concentrations of Stratospheric Chlorine and Bromine*. EPA 400/1–88/005. Washington DC: EPA, August.

2009. "EPA Analysis of the American Clean Energy and Security Act of 2009." US EPA Office of Atmospheric Programs, June 23. www.epa. gov/climatechange/economics/economicanalyses.html.

US 09 Copenhagen. 2009. "Press Briefing December 9. Todd Stern, Special Envoy for Climate Change." UN Climate Change Negotiations, Copenhagen, Denmark, December 9. US State Dept. website http:// cop15.state.gov/pressroom/133343.htm.

Vermeer, Martin and Stefan Rahmstorf. 2009. "Global Sea Level Linked to Global Temperature." *PNAS* 106(51): 21527–21532.

Victor, David G. 1990. "Liquid Hydrogen Aircraft and the Greenhouse Effect." *International Journal of Hydrogen Energy* 15(5): 357–367.

1991. "How to Slow Global Warming." *Nature* 349 (February 7): 451–456,

1996. "The Early Operation and Effectiveness of the Montreal Protocol's Non-Compliance Procedure." Executive Report ER-96–2, International Institute for Applied Systems Analysis. Laxenburg, Austria.

1999. "The Regulation of Greenhouse Gases – Does Fairness Matter?" In *Fair Weather? Equity Concerns in Climate Change*, ed. F. Tóth. London: Earthscan.

2001. *The Collapse of the Kyoto Protocol and the Struggle to Slow Global Warming*. Princeton University Press.

2002. "Electric Power." In *Technological Innovation and Economic Performance*, eds. Ben Steil, David G. Victor, and Richard R. Nelson. Princeton University Press.

2007a. "Fragmented Carbon Markets and Reluctant Nations: Implications for the Design of Effective Architectures." In *Architectures for Agreement: Addressing Global Climate Change in the Post-Kyoto World*, eds. Joseph E. Aldy and Robert N. Stavins. New York, NY: Cambridge University Press.

2007b. "What Resource Wars?" *National Interest online* (November 12).

2008. "On the Regulation of Geoengineering." *Oxford Review of Economic Policy* 24(2) (June 1): 211–238.

2009a. "Climate Accession Deals: New Strategies for Taming Growth of Greenhouse Gases in Developing Countries." In *Post-Kyoto International Climate Policy: Summary for Policymakers*, eds. Joseph E. Aldy and Robert N. Stavins. New York, NY: Cambridge University Press.

2009b. "Global Warming: Why the 2°C Goal is a Political Delusion." *Nature* 459 (June 18): 909.

2009c. "Plan B for Copenhagen." *Nature* 461 (September 17): 342–4.

2009d. "The Politics of Fossil-Fuel Subsidies." *The Global Subsidies Initiative: Untold Billions: Fossil-Fuel Subsidies, Their Impacts and the Path to Reform*. Global Subsidies Initiative, International Institute for Sustainable Development, October.

2010a. "The Political Context for California's Climate Change Policy." *Giannini Foundation of Agricultural Economics* 14: 6–8.

2010b. "The Politics and Economics of International Carbon Offsets." National Research Council Workshop on carbon offsets, Washington DC.

Victor, David G. and Lesley A. Coben. 2005. "A Herd Mentality in the Design of International Environmental Agreements?" *Global Environmental Politics* 5(1): 24–57.

Victor, David G. and Danny Cullenward, 2007. "Making Carbon Markets Work." *Scientific American*, December, 70–7.

Victor, David G. and C. Ford Runge. 2002. "Farming the Genetic Frontier." *Foreign Affairs* (May/June): 107–21.

Victor, David G. and Thomas C. Heller, eds. 2007. *The Political Economy of Power Sector Reform: The Experiences of Five Major Developing Countries*. New York, NY: Cambridge University Press.

Victor, David G. and Gordon J. MacDonald. 1997. "How to Make Kyoto a Success." *Nature* 389 (October 23): 777.

Victor, David G. and Richard Morse. 2009. "Living with Coal: Climate Policy's Most Inconvenient Truth." *The Boston Review*, September, 7–14.

Victor, David G., Thomas C. Heller, and Nadejda M. Victor. 2003. "Political Economy and the Hydrogen Revolution." Working Paper 17. Program on Energy and Sustainable Development, Stanford University, September.

Victor, David G., Joshua C. House, and Sarah Joy. 2005. "A Madisonian Approach to Climate Policy." *Science* 309(5742): 1820–1.

Victor, David G., Kal Raustiala, and Eugene B. Skolnikoff, eds. 1998. *The Implementation and Effectiveness of International Environmental Commitments: Theory and Practice*. Cambridge, MA: MIT Press.

Victor, David G., Mark Thurber, and David Hults, eds. Forthcoming. *Oil and Governance: State-Owned Enterprises and the World Energy Supply*. Cambridge University Press.

Victor, David G., M. Morgan, J. Apt, J. Steinbruner, and K. Ricke. 2009. "The Geoengineering Option: A Last Resort Against Global Warming?" *Foreign Affairs* (March/April).

Vidal, John. 2008. "Billions Wasted on UN Climate Programme: Energy Firms Routinely Abusing Carbon Offset Fund, US Studies Claim." *Guardian.co.uk*, May 26. www.guardian.co.uk/environment/2008/may/26/climatechange.greenpolitics.

2009. "Copenhagen Talks Break Down as Developing Nations Split over 'Tuvalu' Protocol." *Guardian.co.uk*, December 9. www.guardian.co.uk/environment/2009/dec/09/copenhagen-tuvalu-protocol-split.

Violetti, Daniele. 2008. "Global GHG Market Update." Presented at the Carbon Forum America 2008, UNFCCC, San Francisco, CA, February 26–27, cdm.unfccc.int/workshops/cfa/presa/ghgmarket.ppt.

2010. "Clean Development Mechanism: Achievements and Developments." Presented at the 6th session of the high-level task force on the implementation of the right to development, UNFCCC, Geneva, Switzerland, January 14. www.ciel.org/Publications/Violetti_CDM_14Jan10.pdf

Vogel, David. 1995. *Trading Up: Consumer and Environmental Regulation in a Global Economy*. Cambridge, MA: Harvard University Press.

Wagner, Gernot, Nathaniel O. Keohane, Annie Petsonk, and James Wang. 2009. "Docking into a Global Carbon Market: Clean Investment Budgets to Finance Low-Carbon Economic Development." In *The Economics and Politics of Climate Change*, eds. Dieter Helm and Cameron Hepburn. New York, NY: Oxford University Press.

Wara, Michael W. 2007. "Is the Global Carbon Market Working?" *Nature* 445: 595–6.

2008. "Measuring the Clean Development Mechanism's Performance and Potential." *UCLA Law Review* 55(6): 1759–1803.

Wara, Michael W. and David G. Victor. 2008. *A Realistic Policy on International Carbon Offsets*. Working Paper 74. Program on Energy and Sustainable Development, Stanford University, April.

Weart, Spencer R. 2007. "Roger Revelle's Discovery." The Discovery of Global Warming. Spencer Wright and the American Institute of Physics website. www.aip.org/history/climate/Revelle.htm.

2008. *The Discovery of Global Warming: Revised and Expanded Edition*. Cambridge, MA: Harvard University Press.

Weber, Max. 1918/2004. *The Vocation Lectures*. Indianapolis: Hackett.

Webster, Mort *et al.* 2009. "Analysis of Climate Policy Targets under Uncertainty." Report No. 180. MIT Joint Program on the Science and Policy of Global Change, September.

Weitzman, Martin. 1974. "Prices vs. Quantities." *Review of Economic Studies* 41(4): 477–91.

Westerling, A. L. *et al.* 2009. *Climate Change, Growth, and California Wildfire*. California Climate Change Center, August. CEC-500–2009–046-F.

Wettestad, Jorgen. 1998. "Participation in NO_x Policy-Making and Implementation in the Netherlands, UK, and Norway: Different Approaches but Similar Results?" In *The Implementation and Effectiveness of International Environmental Commitments: Theory and Practice*, eds. D. Victor, K. Raustiala, and E. Skolnikoff. Cambridge, MA: MIT Press.

Wigley, T. M. L. 2005. "The Climate Change Commitment." *Science* 307(5716): 1766–9.

Wigley, T. M. L., R. Richels, and J. A. Edmonds. 1996. "Economic and Environmental Choices in the Stabilization of Atmospheric CO_2 Concentrations." *Nature* 379: 240–3.

Wigley, T. M. L. *et al.* 2009. "Uncertainties in Climate Stabilization." *Climatic Change* 97(1–2): 85–121.

Wildavsky, Aaron. 1980. "Richer is Safer." *The Public Interest* 60(Summer): 23–39.

Winchester, N, S. Paltsev, and J. Reilly. 2010. "Will Border Carbon Adjustments Work?" Report No. 184. MIT Joint Program on the Science and Policy of Global Change, February.

Witte, Jan Martin. 2009. *State and Trends of Public Energy and Electricity R&D: A Transatlantic Perspective*. Policy Paper Series No. 4. Global Public Policy Institute Energy.

WMO (World Meteorological Organization). 1988. *The Changing Atmosphere: Implications for Global Security, Toronto, Canada, 27–30 June 1988: Conference Statement*. World Conference on the Changing Atmosphere. Toronto: WMO.

  1990. *Scientific Assessment of Stratospheric Ozone: 1989*. Report No. 20. Geneva, Switzerland: WMO Global Ozone Research and Monitoring Project.

Wolfers, Arnold. 1962. *Discord and Collaboration: Essays on International Politics*. Baltimore: The Johns Hopkins Press.

World Bank. 2006. *An Investment Framework for Clean Energy and Development: A Progress Report*. Development Committee. Washington DC: The World Bank, September 5. DC2006–0012.

  2009. *Climate Change and the World Bank Group, Phase I: An Evaluation of World Bank Win-Win Energy Policy Reforms*. Independent Evaluation Group. Washington DC: IBRD/The World Bank.

Yergin, Dan, Bennett Johnston, and John Deutch. 2009. "Oil Lessons from the 1970s." *The International Economy* (Fall): 26–29, 58–64.

Zhang, Jiu-Tian, Ying Fan, and Yi-Ming Wei. 2006. "An Empirical Analysis for National Energy R&D Expenditures." *International Journal of Global Energy Issues* 25(1): 141–59.

Index